PROFESSIONAL OFFICE PROCEDURES

Fifth Edition

Susan H. Cooperman
Montgomery College

PEARSON

Prentice Hall

Upper Saddle River, New Jersey
Columbus, Ohio

Library of Congress Cataloging-in-Publication Data

Cooperman, Susan H.
    Professional office procedures / Susan H. Cooperman. — 5th ed.
        p. cm.
    ISBN-13: 978-0-13-515664-3
    ISBN-10: 0-13-515664-5
    1. Office practice—Vocational guidance. I. Title.
    HF5547.5.C66 2009
    651.023'73—dc22

2007031111

Vice President and Executive Publisher: Vernon Anthony
Acquisitions Editor: Gary Bauer
Editorial Assistant: Kathleen Rowland
Project Manager: Christina Taylor
Design Coordinator: Diane Ernsberger
Cover Designer: Kellyn Donnelly
Cover photos: Super Stock; Corbis; Getty
Operations Specialist: Pat Tonneman
Director of Marketing: David Gesell
Marketing Manager: Leigh Ann Sims
Marketing Coordinator: Alicia Dysert

Trademark Information

Microsoft Network, Microsoft Office, Microsoft Publisher, Microsoft Word, Microsoft Access, Microsoft Excel, Microsoft PowerPoint, Windows 2003, Windows XP, Windows Vista are registered trademarks of Microsoft Corporation. Best's Insurance Reports is a registered trademark of Best Insurance and Financial Service. Best Western is a registered trademark of Best Western International, Inc. DHL is a registered trademark of DHL Worldwide Express. FedEx and Federal Express are registered trademarks of Federal Express Corporation. Forbes is registered trademark of Forbes, Inc. Macintosh is a registered trademark of Apple Computer, Inc. The New York Times is a registered trademark of the New York Times Company. PageMaker and Adobe InDesign are registered trademarks of Adobe Systems, Inc. QuarkXPress is a registered trademark of Quark. United States Postal Service (USPS) trademarks include Certified Mail Service, Delivery Confirmation, Express Mail, and First-Class Mail. UPS and United Parcel are registered trademarks of United Parcel Service. The names of all other products mentioned in this book are used for identification purposes only and may be registered trademarks of their owners.

Photo Credits: Photos courtesy of William Cooperman: Figures 1-1, 1-2, 1-3, 2-1, 2-2, 2-3, 3-24-1, 4-2, 4-3, 4-5, 4-6, 4-12, 4-13, 4-14, 4-15, 5-1, 5-2, 5-5, 5-10, 5-12, 5-13, 6-1, 6-2, 6-3, 6-4, 6-5, 6-6, 6-7, 6-8, 7-1, 7-2, 7-3, 7-10, 7-11, 7-12, 7-13, 8-1, 8-3, 8-5, 8-6, 8-7, 8-8, 8-9, 9-1, 9-2, 9-3, 9-4, 9-5, 10-2, 10-3, 10-8, 11-1, 11-2, 11-3, 11-4, 11-5, 11-6, 11-7, 11-9, 11-10, 11-11, 11-12, 11-13, 12-7, 13-1, 13-2, 14-2, 14-3, 15-1, 15-2, 15-3, 17-1, 17-2, 17-3, 18-1, 18-2, 18-3, 18-6.

This book was set in Sabon by GGS Book Services. It was printed and bound by Edwards Brothers. The cover was printed by Phoenix Color Corp.

Pearson Prentice Hall™ is a trademark of Pearson Education, Inc.
Pearson® is a registered trademark of Pearson plc
Prentice Hall® is a registered trademark of Pearson Education, Inc.

Pearson Education Ltd.   Pearson Education Australia Pty. Limited
Pearson Education Singapore Pte. Ltd.   Pearson Education North Asia Ltd.
Pearson Education Canada, Ltd.   Pearson Educación de Mexico, S.A. de C.V.
Pearson Education—Japan   Pearson Education Malaysia Pte. Ltd.

8 9 10 11 12 13 14 15 16 17 18   V092   17 16 15 14 13
                                            ISBN-13: 978-0-13-515664-3
                                            ISBN-10:   0-13-515664-5

Professional Office Procedures is dedicated to
my husband, Bill.

His assistance, support, encouragement, dedication, and
perseverance have made this fifth edition possible.

Professional Office Procedures is also dedicated in
memory of my mother, Libby, who believed in
and encouraged this project.

Thank you for all of your help.

Brief Contents

Contents   vii

Preface   xxii

Contents

CHAPTER 4 **Oral Communications**   63

PREFACE TO THE FIFTH EDITION

OBJECTIVE

The goal of *Professional Office Procedures* is to challenge and inspire the student to become an exceptional and outstanding employee and to develop into a dynamic leader as he or she travels up the career ladder.

THE CHANGING OFFICE ENVIRONMENT

Professional Office Procedures will assist, inform, and train people for office careers. This new edition has been revised and updated to meet the needs of employees in a technology-oriented workplace. The main objective of this text is to prepare the student for a career in today's high-tech, multicultural workplace. The contemporary workplace is no longer only the conventional office setting with a suite of offices, where the employee works a typical 9 to 5 day sitting at a desk. Today's workplace may be a car, a hotel room while traveling, an airport, a corner coffee shop, a company off-site location, a shared office, a home office, a kitchen table, or a combination of any imaginable office settings. Mobile office workers use a notebook or handheld computer and a cell phone to conduct their business wherever they are.

This innovative and exciting multicultural and multigenerational workplace operates 24/7 because technology has created a working environment where clients and customers expect an immediate response to questions, telephone communications, and emails. Regardless of the size of the organization, type of business, or the location of the workplace, all employees, from entry-level to management, need to know office procedures so they can function effectively in today's workplace.

The information contained in this book will be useful to students entering the world of business for the first time as well as those workers currently employed in business-related vocations. This material will also be useful to individuals returning to work after a period of time at home attending to family responsibilities as well as to persons who have made career changes. To survive in the current employment market, workers must have the skills to perform a wide variety of job functions. Office employees will find many practical procedures in this book to enhance their skills and assist their career advancement.

THINK, WORK, AND PERFORM BY DOING

The purpose of the text is to train people to think, work under stressful and difficult situations, and perform office duties in a professional manner. The focus of the book is to prepare students for the *realistic* problems and situations they will encounter in a state-of-the-art office environment. Instead of only reading about a topic, students are directed to practice the skills and discuss the professional office procedures presented in this book. Each chapter contains a series of activities that allows the student to implement the material covered. For example, in the discussion of business travel, students are given projects requiring them to call or use the Internet to obtain information about airline schedules and prices; and in the discussion of meeting planning, students are directed to contact local restaurants and inquire about luncheon costs. Shown below are sample activities from Chapters 1 and 18.

- Write a job description for the position you hope to obtain when you leave school. You may use the Internet to research this activity.
- Visit two offices and prepare a written report describing the office layout, use of color, use of plants, the amount of sunlight, and placement of equipment. Be prepared to give an oral summary of your report to the class.

AN EMPHASIS ON HUMAN RELATIONS

A special focus is given to the development of positive human relations skills, or soft skills, as they are often called, because these skills are indispensable for career success. Being able to work as a cooperative member of a team, getting along well with coworkers and managers, and dealing with difficult clients are all vital to a successful career. If there is conflict in the workplace a good job may turn into an aggravating situation. Consequently, this text emphasizes human relations skills so the student will be better equipped to manage difficult situations. The workplace coping skills discussed can easily carry over to personal relationships, thus developing a happier and well-adjusted person *and* employee.

Each chapter contains a section on developing human relations skills. Students are encouraged to analyze problem situations that occur in the workplace and to develop their own solutions. The problems are typical situations that occur in an office and often do not have a single right answer. To reinforce the human relations skills, each chapter contains two Human Relations Skill Development and three Situations questions, all of which concentrate on developing human relations management techniques. The following is a sample Human Relations Skill Development activity:

FUNCTIONING AS A MEMBER OF A TEAM

Working as a member of a team requires that all members be able to work together, even though they have different viewpoints. Learning to respect the thoughts of others and to listen to the views of others encourages a good working relationship. Completing your part of a project by the due date is a team requirement. One member of the team who does not complete an assignment on time may hamper the progress of other members of the team.

- What would you do if a member of your team did not complete an assigned project on time?
- What would you do if a member of your team took credit for an idea that you developed?
- What would you do if two members of your team had an argument and refused to work on a project?
- What would you do if a member of your team always needed extra help to complete projects?

WORKPLACE SKILLS

The book provides a knowledge base of tools that includes workplace responsibilities, customer service relations, listening skills, time management and organization skills, scheduling appointments, written and oral communications, working as a member of a team, mail management, computers, information and records management, meetings and conferences, business travel, business terminology, office environment and design, office equipment, diversity in the workplace, stress management, and business etiquette. The text directs the student through a step-by step process of personally analyzing career goals and objectives, which prepares the student to work in the profession of his or her choice. In addition, the student is guided through the process of creating a résumé, finding a desirable job, and navigating the interview process.

The student will also learn the tools and competencies required to advance in his or her career and eventually climb to the ranks of management. Special emphasis is placed on the duties and responsibilities of a supervisor or manager. In addition, the text stresses job motivation techniques, working with a new supervisor, and proper procedures when leaving an employer.

The last chapter, "Tips of the Trade," concentrates on the employee and improving office efficiency. The chapter is filled with hints and techniques that usually come only after years of on-the-job experience. These techniques are applicable to the workplace environment and to the employee's personal life.

This eighteen-chapter text and supplementary package are designed for a postsecondary, college-level, or continuing education course. The book can be customized to fit the individual needs of each class. Since the chapters, exercises, and supplementary material are each self-contained, they may be studied in any order or they may be included or omitted as needed, based on the instructor's and student's objectives. Depending on the number of chapters and exercises selected, the book may be used for a one-semester or two-semester class.

AUTHOR

The text is written by Susan H. Cooperman, a college professor with many years of educational experience in behavior management, business, and computers. In addition to educational experience, she has worked in the business field and has practical hands-on experience that is incorporated into all facets of the book.

NEW TECHNOLOGY INNOVATIONS AND UPDATES IN THE FIFTH EDITION

This fifth edition of *Professional Office Procedures* has been updated to reflect the technology-driven innovations in today's office environment. All chapters have been completely revised. In addition, chapters have been reorganized, and several chapters in the prior edition have been expanded and then divided into smaller learning units; also three new chapters have been added to augment student learning.

The fifth edition integrates computers, the Internet, and other office technologies into every aspect of basic office procedures that are essential to success in the business world. Each chapter contains information, activities, and projects that direct the student to use the Internet for information and research. All chapters also contain:

- Revised marginal sidebars, which call out the most relevant tips, hints, and definitions to the students.

- A new feature, "My Success Story," which is a personal reflection from a new employee. Employees from all walks of life explain and share their stories.
- A new marginal note feature that prompts the student to analyze, think, and respond.

The fifth edition contains a new testing feature. Each chapter now has a true/false test format, which works well with distance-learning courses. The short answer test for each chapter that was available in previous editions is also available in the fifth edition.

New updates for each chapter include the following:

Chapter 1—Workplace Skills and Responsibilities   Chapter 1 of the prior edition, "The Successful Employee," has been reorganized into the first two chapters in this edition. "Workplace Skills and Responsibilities" expands on material from the prior Chapter 1 and now includes new sections on Customer- or Client-Service Skills and also on Managing Visitors. Additional bulleted lists have been added and organized for easy comprehension.

Chapter 2—Working Effectively: Time Management and Interaction with Colleagues   This new chapter begins with a section on Listening Skills, which explains why listening skills are important in the workplace, and contains suggestions for improvement. The chapter also emphasizes the importance of time management and provides suggestions for organizing an employee's office, conducting telephone conversations, dealing with coworkers, and managing meetings. The chapter also includes a section on Working with Colleagues in Teams, which offers suggestions for the team leader and the team member. In addition, the chapter includes a section on Working with Nontraditional Work Schedules and Locations.

Chapter 3—The Written Word   Chapter 3 is an update of Chapter 2, "The Written Word," of the prior edition, and reflects current workplace practices. The chapter provides guidelines on writing business letters, reports, memos, news releases, newsletters, and emails.

Chapter 4—Oral Communications   Chapter 3, "Workplace Communications," of the prior edition, has been revised and updated to be part of Chapter 4 in the fifth edition. Chapter 4 incorporates the use of current telecommunications technologies in an office environment, as well as telephone ethics and etiquette, teleconferencing, and speaking before a group.

Chapter 5 Processing the Mail   The current Chapter 5 revises and updates Chapter 4, "Processing the Mail," of the prior edition. The chapter provides current information on sending and processing all classes of mail, sending time-sensitive mail, sending and processing faxes, and working with postage equipment. A new chart clearly displays the classes of mail and special services available from the USPS.

Chapter 6—Computers in the Office   Changes in computer technology available since the prior edition are reflected in the revised chapter on "Computers in the Office." Sections on handheld computer and smart phones have been expanded. The list of computer terms has been moved to the Appendix to increase the student's and instructor's flexibility in using the chapter.

Chapter 7—Information and Records Management: Filing   The focus of Chapter 7, which was Chapter 6 in the prior edition, remains the importance of file management and provides a review of standard guidelines for alphabetic filing. The use of technology in records management has been updated to reflect current technologies and workplace usage.

Chapter 8—Meetings and Conferences   Chapter 8 has been revised and updated to reflect current industry practices and includes information on planning a meeting, tips for a successful meeting, international visitors, identification badges, meeting-related Web sites, meeting themes, and virtual meetings.

Chapter 9—Business Travel   Chapter 9 has been revised and updated to reflect the current changes in the travel industry. The use of the Internet is stressed in all aspects of travel planning. The chapter includes the fundamentals of travel, travel agencies, airline travel, airport security, travel safety and security precautions, lodging, automobile travel, rail travel, travel funds, itinerary, passports and visas, computerized travel maps, and the technology demands of business.

Chapter 10—Business Terminology   Chapter 10, "Business Terminology," is an updated version of Chapter 9, "Terminology of Business and Commerce," of the prior edition. To increase flexibility in using the chapter, bulleted lists of general business, financial, legal, real estate, and accounting terms have been moved to the Appendix.

Chapter 11—The Office Environment and Design   This chapter has been revised and updated to reflect the many changes in the office environment and office technology since the prior edition. These changes include office security and safety, workplace violence, physical office environment, file and computer security, office furniture and equipment, off-site copying centers, office purchases, and office payments.

Chapter 12—Seeking Employment   Chapter 11 in the prior edition, "Seeking Employment," has been expanded and divided into two separate chapters in this edition, with the new Chapter 12 emphasizing seeking employment. The chapter includes planning for your career, finding employers, Internet job searches, letters of application, résumés, and references.

Chapter 13—The Interview and Job Offer   Information about the interview and the job offer has been expanded and is now Chapter 13. The chapter includes planning for the interview, researching the company, making an interview appointment, personal appearance at the interview, types of interviews, what to do and say at the interview, the job offer, and a discussion of job benefits.

Chapter 14—Career Advancement to Management   The sections on career advancement and management have been updated and reorganized into a new chapter. The chapter includes demonstrating your excellence, certificates of competency, how to ask for a raise, looking for a job, procedures for leaving a job, becoming a manager, distance managing, employee motivational incentives, welcoming a new employee, working with a new supervisor, employee evaluation, conflict resolution, personal conflict-resolution style, and an explanation of the company mission statement.

Chapter 15—Diversity in the Workplace: Understanding Those You Work With   Chapter 15 is a new chapter and emphasizes cultural diversity, the mixed-generation workplace, business travel in a global society, and government employment antidiscrimination regulations.

Chapter 16—Stress Management   Chapter 16 is a new chapter and includes the causes of stress, symptoms of stress, techniques to reduce stress, and suggestions for avoiding job burnout. The chapter illustrates that coping with tension in the workplace is also important for the student's personal life. Therefore, the suggestions for managing workplace pressure are transferable from the workplace to the student's personal life.

Chapter 17—Business Etiquette   Chapter 17 is a new chapter and includes the importance of business etiquette, greeting business associates, involvement with charitable activities, dressing for business functions, correct table manners, tipping suggestions, international business etiquette, and social business communications.

Chapter 18—Tips of the Trade   This chapter has been updated and includes discussions on almost 100 short topics, including office attire, sharing ideas, mentoring, thank-you notes, accessing personal business information, dealing with the news media, chain of command, common business acronyms, and civility.

VARIETY OF ACTIVITIES PROVIDE REINFORCEMENT

The end of each chapter includes the following seven sections: Chapter Review, Activities, Projects, Human Relations Skill Development, Situations, Punctuation Review, and CD Assignments. In addition, a Software Applications Review unit follows Chapter 18.

- The **Chapter Review** reinforces the topics discussed in each chapter with questions from the chapter.

- The **Activities** reinforce the topics discussed. Many activities require personal analysis and research skills. The student is often instructed to talk with someone in his or her chosen field to learn about their experiences.

- Each chapter has two **Projects** that require the student to use word processing software to keyboard typical office projects such as memos, letters, flyers, etc. The student is encouraged to think about and revise the documents as needed.

- The **Human Relations Skill Development** section contains two activities that provide problems encountered in the workplace and asks the student to respond with an appropriate solution.

- The **Situations** provide several short workplace situations and ask the student to solve typical workplace problems. This activity strengthens the student's ability to function in a difficult workplace.

- The **Punctuation Review** contains fifteen sentences for the student to punctuate. This activity reviews punctuation skills. A review of punctuation rules is found in the Appendix.

- The **CD Assignments** section contains additional activities located on the accompanying CD where the student must think about, analyze, research, keyboard, and respond to typical office projects. Many of the assignments ask the student to use the Internet.

The **Software Application Review** provides tasks using word processing, spreadsheet, and database software, which are all frequently used in the workplace.

TEXT SUPPORT

Instructor's resource materials are available online at www.prenhall.com.

1. Answers are provided for all chapter activities including the Chapter Review, Projects, Human Relations Skill Development, Situations, Punctuation Review, CD Assignments, and Software Application Unit.
2. Eighteen Short-Answer Tests and eighteen True/False Tests are available, one True/False Test and one Short-Answer Test for each chapter.
3. A PowerPoint presentation is available for each chapter.
4. Additional Punctuation Reviews, Situations, and Projects are included for use as needed.

Online Instructor's Resources

To access supplementary materials online, instructors need to request an instructor access code. Go to **www.prenhall.com**, click the **Instructor Resource Center** link, and then click **Register Today** for an instructor access code. Within 48 hours after registering you will receive a confirming e-mail including an instructor access code. Once you have received your code, go to the site and log on for full instructions on downloading the materials you wish to use.

ACKNOWLEDGMENTS

Special thanks to the reviewers of this text: Jody Derry of Allan Hancock College, Candace K. Eritano of Glendale Community College, and Patricia Partyka of Schoolcraft College.

CHAPTER 1

···

Workplace Skills and Responsibilities

Objectives

After studying this chapter, you should be able to:

1. List the personal traits of an office employee.
2. List the duties of an office employee.
3. Explain and describe a job description.
4. Understand how to schedule appointments.
5. Recognize an organization chart.

THE MODERN OFFICE

Technology in the Office

Today's office employee works in an environment shaped by technology. The modern workplace is centered on the use of computers, the Internet, and a variety of electronic equipment that were unavailable only a few years ago. Technology has thus modified and redesigned the nature of most office work.

The widespread use of technology has created an upheaval in many employee duties and responsibilities and has transformed the worklife of the office staff. The basic office tasks of placing and answering telephone calls, keyboarding documents, greeting clients, arranging meetings, filing, and numerous other jobs are no longer solely the responsibility of the administrative assistant.

Today these office-sustaining duties are performed by all workers regardless of their degree of responsibility, from an individual in an entry-level position to an employee at the management level. Knowledge of essential office procedures, including Internet skills, therefore cannot be limited to a secretary, administrative assistant, or administrative aide. Employees at all levels must be technically skilled and socially competent. Knowing only the technical aspects of a job is insufficient; soft skills, such as how to work with others, are also important. In addition to being able to discuss and articulate office-related issues, employees must function as members of an office community that values cordial and effective social interaction.

As technology has changed, so has the appearance and structure of the office. Almost anywhere you, your notebook computer, land-line telephone, cordless

What do you need to know to be successful?

1

telephone, and cell phone go can turn into your office. Consequently, the office has evolved from the traditional desk to a "car office," a "kitchen table office," a "hotel room office," even a "notebook computer traveling office."

Furthermore, the workplace is now a global and technology-driven environment where you will work with a diverse team of professionals. Because people and companies are electronically connected via the Internet, you will work with professionals throughout the world to achieve your personal and business objectives. Therefore, regardless of your office location, your workplace is not a remote and isolated site.

In the fifth edition of *Professional Office Procedures*, you will learn more than just the basic office skills that are the foundation of all business-related jobs. You will learn the real-life business techniques and skills that are essential for all employees. Because you will work in a technology-driven workplace, office technology is stressed in every chapter and activity. In addition, *soft skills*, the ability to work well with coworkers, colleagues, supervisors, and clients, is emphasized throughout your learning experience. Your mastery of these three elements—office skills, office technology, and soft skills—will enable you to become a successful employee and advance in your profession.

Customer- or Client-Service Skills

One of the most important soft skills you must learn is to value your customers. If you do not provide good service to your customers and meet their needs, you will not have a job, regardless of your skills. Customer- or client-service skills are essential for a successful career in an organization. In today's competitive marketplace, clients demand and expect superior customer service.

In the retail field, when customers make purchasing decisions, the decision can be based on the degree of customer service received. Therefore, a competent company recognizes that its greatest selling point can be its customer service. In addition, if companies are competing for the same customers, high-quality customer service skills may be the deciding factor. In an office, a customer can be anyone with whom you interact and to whom you provide a service. Therefore, your supervisor and coworkers deserve the same consideration and respect you would extend to someone from outside the office.

As a staff member, all employees should understand the philosophy of customer service and show a commitment to customer service in all aspects of the client/customer–company relationship. In addition, employees should understand the expectations of the client or customer. Excellent customer service means paying attention to every detail when dealing with customers.

To achieve outstanding customer-service skills, you must have excellent communication skills, have a positive attitude when dealing with the public, act in an ethical manner, and realize the benefits that excellent customer service can bring to the company. Since office employees interact with customers on a daily basis, outstanding customer skills are crucial. Dealing with the public can be difficult and stressful so you must be trained in working and understanding how to solve the problems of working in challenging situations.

Customer service is evident in your professional personal appearance, your voice mail, your telephone greeting, your telephone conversation, your email voice tone and comments, your letter tone and comments, and the appearance of your office. A friendly and pleasant office staff creates a welcoming office environment that translates into company profits and employee success. We live in an age of instant communications, and customers expect speedy replies and prompt solutions to problems. Therefore, a quick response time for telephone communication, email, or letters improves customer service.

<aside>
HINT

Technology has revolutionized the traditional office, transforming it into a computer-based administrative center, home office, or traveling workplace.
</aside>

<aside>
HINT

Customer-service skills are powerful.
</aside>

Figure 1-1   Customer service skills are important.

Customer-Service Do's

- Appreciate the customer.
- Put yourself in the customer's shoes and think how you want to be treated.
- Do not blame the customer. Identify what went wrong in a situation and solve the problem.
- First impressions are very important, and you may not have a second chance to solve a customer problem and create goodwill for your company.

MY SUCCESS STORY

My Name Is Jenny

When I was asked to be interviewed, I thought, "Why me?" I am not a special person, but then I thought about it. Yes, I am special because I succeeded in my career objective. After graduating from high school, I really did not know what I wanted to do with my life, so I just drifted around for a few years. I even spent three months wandering around Europe. It was a great trip, but I knew the time was coming for me to get on with my life. When I came home, I decided to take classes at a community college. While at the college, I took a business course, and then I was hooked. From that business course grew my interest in working for a stock brokerage firm, where I am now employed. Because I am constantly on the telephone, I realize how important my professional telephone image is to my career.

- You want the customer to be a returning customer, not a one-time-only customer, so customer service is important.
- Respect and value the customer's or client's time.
- Appreciate the customer.
- Take time to talk with and listen to the customer or client.

Customer-Service Don'ts

- Do not look down on the customer.
- Do not think the customer is stupid.
- Do not be rude or disrespectful to the customer or client.
- Do not treat the customer in an argumentative manner.

Regardless of your title or level of responsibility, you must treat your supervisor, coworkers, customers, and clients with courtesy, behave toward them in an honest manner, support their requests, and appreciate them; and they in turn will help create the foundation for your successful career.

Titles and Responsibilities

Many titles can be used to describe persons who work in an office. Some of these titles are *administrative assistant*, *administrative aide*, *personal assistant*, *coordinator*, *office manager*, *office worker*, *executive assistant*, and *clerk*. In the past, the term *secretary* described the office support staff individual responsible for keyboarding letters and reports. As office jobs have become more complex, the responsibilities of the office support staff have also increased. Today's administrative assistant makes decisions, plans job tasks, and accepts responsibility in addition to performing many other job duties. For the purposes of this book, the above titles will be used interchangeably to refer to office employees with a variety of skill levels.

Figure 1-2   The office receptionist.

The person who supervises the office employee can be identified by any of the following titles: *director*, *manager*, *supervisor*, *executive*, *boss*, *principal*, or *office manager*. These titles will be used interchangeably in this book.

Working as an office employee offers a wide range of job opportunities. For a person with skills, there are entry-level and advanced positions in accounting, merchandising, education, government, medicine, social services, law, technology, real estate, research, journalism, insurance, and many other fields. An entry-level position may eventually evolve into a professional or management position or to a new career in a related profession. An office employee position can be an open door to the future with advancement to a higher level position. With good skills and a professional attitude, you will be able to find a rewarding career.

CHARACTERISTICS OF A SUCCESSFUL OFFICE EMPLOYEE

Your Abilities

As an office employee, you are hired for your ability to assist your supervisor. The greatest ability you have, and the one most often overlooked, is simply your ability to think. An employee who does not think, solve problems, or show initiative requires frequent supervision by the manager. Usually, the employee who does not assist in solving office problems becomes part of the problem.

As a competent office employee, you should use initiative and accept responsibility. You were hired to assist in solving problems and to develop new and better ways to complete your work. Be sure you always meet deadlines, and do not make excuses. Plan to complete projects early in case there are last-minute problems. In summary, your goal should be to develop a reputation for dependability and reliability.

> **HINT**
> Do not make excuses. Accept responsibility.

Working together with your supervisor is a major component of the office routine, so do not be afraid of your supervisor. It is difficult to work in an environment where fear is your constant companion. Fear is a psychological feeling that many employees will experience sometime during their career. Fear can inhibit your decision-making capability and can lessen your ability to show initiative. If you are fearful, you will not be able to produce the work you are capable of doing.

Employees fear being

- Foolish before their colleagues or supervisor.
- Rejected.
- Dominated by another employee.
- Overlooked by management.
- Surpassed by a younger employee.
- Fired.
- Criticized.

Do not allow fear to control your life and become a barrier to your success. A successful employee realizes that people have fears but learns to control them. Remember, you were hired because you had the necessary skills to do the job.

Importance of Self-Esteem

High self-esteem is extremely valuable. If you believe in yourself:

- You will be self-confident.
- You will have a greater opportunity to achieve success.

- You will be more enthusiastic about your career.
- Your colleagues will believe in you, too.
- You will have insights that will stimulate you into becoming a leader.
- You will be able to cope with the difficult situations you may in find in the workplace.

Integrity

Your personal integrity is one of the most important personal attributes that is most valued by an employer. Integrity combines honesty and reliability. Always be honest with your employer. Once you say you will do something, do everything in your power to meet the deadline. If you lie or even mislead your supervisor, he or she will no longer trust you. You will then be seen as a hindrance rather than a valuable employee.

Human Relations Skills

How would you diffuse a situation?

An essential skill for all employees, regardless of the level or type of position, is the ability to get along with others. These skills are often called *soft skills*. Handling difficult human relations problems is an everyday occurrence in an office. As an office employee, you must learn to handle these problems diplomatically. This does not mean agreeing with everything that others say to you and doing everything that others want you to do. Everyone should be treated with courtesy, respect, and dignity. Treat others as you want them to treat you. Listen to their views, express your views, and then, if necessary, work out a compromise. Mastery of human relations skills, which are also called *people skills* or *interpersonal relations skills*, is important to the success of any employee; but it is especially important for the office employee who interacts with management, colleagues, and clients. More employees are fired from their jobs because they cannot get along with members of the staff than because they lack job skills. Employers say they can train employees to do the job, but the technical skills are not the only skills employers demand. A workplace where employees do not get along destroys productivity and office cohesiveness. In many cases, mastery of soft skills is the key to being a success in the work environment. Chapters 2, 15, and 17 concentrate on human relations skills. Since human relations skills are essential to a successful career, you will find two human relations exercises at the end of each chapter in this book.

HINT

Good human relations skills are crucial in the workplace.

Analytical and Communications Skills

HINT

Employees must be able to articulate their thoughts clearly and precisely.

All employees, regardless of the type of job they have, should possess basic analytical and communication skills. Although these skills may not be included in a job description, they are essential for a successful career.

Successful office employees must be able to

- Think.
- Listen to and understand directions.
- Handle office situations efficiently.
- Handle a crisis in a logical manner.
- Express themselves in a clear and concise manner.

Think before you speak. To communicate so others understand you, organize and plan what you are going to say. Obviously, you cannot plan every comment, but learn not to blurt out irrelevant remarks.

Figure 1-3 Professional employee at work.

Throughout this book, you will be presented with suggestions and practices that will prepare you to handle the daily challenges you will encounter in the office. Mastering these skills will help you succeed in both business and personal situations.

Essential Workplace Behavior Traits

The following lists include some of the essential traits of a successful office employee. Some of these skills can easily be learned in a classroom, while other traits are related to your attitude and personality. If you do not possess the characteristics of a successful office employee, you should work to improve your skills, attitude, or personality. Ask yourself if you currently meet all of these qualifications. If you do not, decide on a specific plan to develop them.

How would you describe yourself?

Behavior traits—the successful employee

- Projects a pleasing personality.
- Is dependable.
- Is self-reliant.
- Is loyal.
- Is sincere.
- Is courteous.
- Is reliable.
- Is honest.
- Is tactful.

- Is confident about personal abilities.
- Is prepared mentally and physically for the job.
- Projects a positive attitude.
- Believes in and has a good work ethic.
- Possesses a professional demeanor.

HINT
Multitasking is an important workplace skill.

Workplace performance—the successful employee
- Is knowledgeable of office procedures.
- Displays initiative.
- Demonstrates organizational skills.
- Is neat in appearance.
- Is a team player.
- Is a decision maker.
- Is committed to work.
- Is interested in and curious about the office.
- Maintains confidences.
- Is punctual.
- Is flexible.
- Is responsible enough to notify the office when absent.
- Follows instructions.
- Asks for clarification of a project when necessary.
- Works independently.
- Has the ability to think and analyze.

Workplace skills—the successful employee has
- The ability to spell correctly.
- Good computer skills.
- Good Internet skills.
- Good business skills.
- Good keyboarding skills.
- Good language skills.

HINT
What are your qualifications?

Language arts skills, which include oral and written communications, are essential for all persons who wish to succeed in today's competitive workplace. Knowledge of grammar and punctuation is fundamental for written communications; therefore, a punctuation review is included at the end of each chapter. If you are uncertain about punctuation or grammar rules, read the rules found in the Appendix.

Regardless of the economic forecast, jobs are generally available because businesses need well-qualified workers. The successful employee remembers that, without clients, the employee would not have a job. Therefore, first-rate employees understand that clients do not interrupt the employee's daily tasks but rather provide the opportunity for a job.

Personal Traits to Avoid

Some people possess negative personal traits that interfere with job performance. The following list describes some negative behaviors that an employee should avoid in the office:

A poor employee
- Has a bossy manner.
- Is a gossip.

- Displays a quick temper.
- Chews gum.
- Has poor listening habits.
- Cracks his or her knuckles.
- Brags.
- Uses slang.
- Is too aggressive.
- Is lazy.
- Has a bad attitude.

Ask yourself if you posses any of these negative traits. If you do, change your behavior.

HINT
What are the roadblocks to your success?

THE JOB DESCRIPTION

A *job description* is a list of all of the duties and responsibilities of a particular job. A good job description should also contain the outcomes the company expects the employee to provide as well as how the outcomes will be measured. As a new employee, you should be given a copy of your job description. Study your job description carefully so you will be familiar with your assigned duties and responsibilities. You do not want to be guilty of neglecting a job duty because you were unaware that it was your responsibility.

HINT
A job description is a list of job duties.

A typical job description

> *The office employee will perform the following duties: greet clients, answer the telephone, prepare expense and travel reports, organize and supervise the daily operations of the office, order and maintain supplies, keyboard documents, write reports, research projects, serve as a member of a team, use the Internet as a resource, and perform additional duties as deemed appropriate by the supervisor. The employee will be evaluated twice a year on his/her ability to perform the above listed duties.*

Most job descriptions end with a phrase such as "additional duties as deemed appropriate by the supervisor." These additional duties can be new and exciting projects, but they may also include making coffee or running personal errands for your supervisor. Because the duties of an office employee have become more professional in the last several years, some office employees have become uncomfortable completing jobs that they feel are personal rather than professional. The decision to complete tasks of a personal nature will be your own. You should base that decision on your work environment. For example, in some offices, making coffee is shared by all employees. If your supervisor is flexible about how you perform your job duties, you should be flexible about taking on additional tasks that you consider a personal chore rather than a professional duty.

Listed below are typical administrative assistant duties often found in job descriptions. The type of job and company will determine your exact responsibilities.

Typical administrative duties
- Processing written communications.
- Keyboarding reports, letters, and memos.
- Writing letters, reports, and memos.
- Sorting and routing the mail.
- Sending and receiving email.

- Sending and receiving fax messages.
- Photocopying.
- Filing documents and records manually and/or electronically.

Responding to the telephone and visitors
- Answering the telephone.
- Screening telephone calls and visitors.
- Greeting visitors.

Administering an office
- Maintaining time logs for completion of jobs.
- Maintaining employee attendance records.
- Preparing expense reports.
- Ordering supplies and equipment.
- Calling vendors for equipment repairs.

Scheduling activities
- Prioritizing work assignments.
- Maintaining and scheduling appointments.
- Arranging meetings.
- Making travel arrangements.

Working with colleagues
- Working as a team player with other members of the staff.
- Solving office problems.
- Guiding coworkers.

Using computer technology
- Researching on the Internet.
- Using computer application packages to create and revise word processing, spreadsheet, desktop publishing, and database management documents.

Performing other tasks as assigned
- Completing other jobs that are necessary for the efficient running of the office.

SCHEDULING

Making Appointments

As an office employee, one of your responsibilities may be to schedule appointments for your supervisor. Know your manager's preferences concerning days and times for appointments because certain days or times may not be convenient. For example, the office may have a staff meeting every Monday morning and a top management meeting on Friday afternoon. Frequently compare your appointment calendar with your supervisor's calendar and add appointments that the supervisor may have scheduled without your knowledge. (Even if it is not your fault, it is embarrassing for you to schedule an appointment at a time the supervisor already has an appointment scheduled.)

Consider the following when making appointments:

1. The name of the visitor. (Always verify the spelling and pronunciation of the visitor's name. If the pronunciation is difficult or unusual, write a note to yourself with the phonetic spelling of the name so you can pronounce it correctly.)

2. The name of the company where the visitor is employed.

3. The reason for the appointment.

4. When the visitor wants the appointment and the amount of time that will be needed.

5. The visitor's office and cell phone numbers in case the appointment must be canceled.

6. The visitor's email address.

7. If the appointment is not going to be held in your employer's office, obtain specific information concerning the meeting location.

8. Know in advance your employer's policy about scheduling appointments. Know who will be seen and who will not be seen. Diplomacy will be required if you are not allowed to schedule an appointment. For example, your supervisor may not be interested in seeing a particular sales representative who is very persistent about making an appointment.

Monday, September 1

	Name	Telephone No.
9:00		
9:30		
10:00		
10:30		
11:00		
11:30		
12:00		
12:30		
1:00		
1:30		
2:00		
2:30		
3:00		
3:30		
4:00		
4:30		

Figure 1-4 Appointment calendar.

Using Computerized Calendars

A calendar is an item that all office workers should use to schedule, organize work, and remember meetings for both themselves and their supervisor. Prior to the introduction of computers, the traditional office desk calendar was the size of a book and usually was kept open on the top of the desk for quick access. Numerous styles of desk calendars are still available, many of which are designed to also aid in organizing work through the use of to-do lists and sections for notes. Today's technology-driven workforce uses computerized calendars to organize their personal and professional lives. In many offices, computer calendars have replaced desk calendars.

One advantage of using a computer calendar is its ability to track the schedules of many people. Staff members in an office sharing a computer network can share a calendar, thereby making meeting planning simpler. The assistant may have access to the supervisor's calendar to make appointments. Scheduling software can display the calendars of several employees so time conflicts and open times can easily be identified. Using a shared calendar can eliminate the need to call and recheck the time availability of each person; thus simplifying the process of scheduling a meeting. Computer calendars can easily be revised, printed, and set to give an audio reminder of an appointment. Some computer calendar programs can be stored on the Internet for use by workers in different cities who must have access to the same calendar, by employees who frequently travel, or by employees who regularly check their schedules using cell phones or portable computers. With an Internet-based calendar, they can schedule meetings or check their calendar from any location with access to the Internet.

Computer calendars may be located on the desktop computer or in handheld computers referred to as Personal Information Management (PIM) systems or Personal Digital Assistants (PDAs). Handheld computers are very small and can be carried in a pocket or purse so appointments and notes can be entered at any time. The handheld devices and desktop computer can share the same calendar file, which promotes efficiency. It is important to synchronize the schedule in the handheld with the desktop computer calendar. Some handhelds can be linked with the office computer for synchronizing a schedule by using wireless technology or via a telephone connection. It is often the administrative assistant's responsibility to verify that the supervisor's schedule is kept up-to-date and to coordinate appointments made by traditional phone, cell phone, computer, and handheld devices. Additional information on handheld calendars can be found in Chapter 5.

Regardless of the type of calendar system, use your calendar as an organization and planning device to manage your day. Enter information on the calendar regarding office meetings, vacations for yourself and other employees, deadlines for projects, and the location of a traveling employee on a specific date.

Using a Tickler System

A *tickler system* is a reminder system for routine due dates and can be set up using large wall-planning calendars; using paper-based systems such as a daily desk calendar or 3″ × 5″ cards; or using electronic calendar systems on computers, cell phones, smartphones, or handheld organizers. Electronic tickler systems bring up reminders automatically at the beginning of the day and can easily be modified as dates and events change. If you are using a computer calendar, a tickler system can be included in your calendar or a separate calendar can be created for the tickler system. If a card box system is used, the card box should contain a separate guide for each day of the month. A 3″ × 5″ card with a description of the project and the due date is placed behind the appropriate guide. For example, the payroll reminder card is placed each month behind the date the payroll is prepared, not the date the payroll is due. A card may be used once or many times.

Managing Visitors

Remembering names and faces is an important skill for office employees. Some people have the gift to easily remember faces and names. If you do not possess this skill, make notes to help yourself remember. Think of ways to associate a person's name and face with something you will remember. It may be helpful to set up a 3″ × 5″ card file or a computer notepad system with information about your clients. Clients like to feel they are important to the company, so it is good business policy to address them by name.

All visitors should be greeted in a pleasant and professional manner. Invite the visitor to be seated. If a visitor must wait for your employer, offer a soft drink or coffee if your company has these items available for guests. Be pleasant but continue with your work.

Learn your supervisor's preferences concerning visitors who arrive without an appointment. Will your employer see clients, coworkers, friends, or family members if they stop by the office?

Before a visitor is ushered into your employer's office, notify the employer that the visitor has arrived. This can be done by calling on the telephone, taking a note to the employer, or walking into the employer's office and announcing the visitor. Always close the employer's door when you go into the office to deliver your message so your conversation will be private.

Interrupting your supervisor during an appointment requires diplomacy. Sometimes you may be required to remind a supervisor that there is another appointment waiting or that the supervisor must leave for a meeting. You should be aware of your supervisor's policy regarding interruptions. The manager's personal preference will determine how you handle each situation. Interruptions can be handled by calling the employer on the telephone, delivering a note to the supervisor during the meeting, or walking in and speaking with the employer. Sometimes your employer will ask that you interrupt an appointment at a set time as a way of ending an appointment.

Offices often maintain a visitors log for security purposes or to confirm that a client visited on a specific date and time.

Figure 1-5 Confirming a visitors log.

Date	Visitor	Company	Reason for Visit
4/5/XX	Joe Silver	Cakes, Inc.	Discuss June picnic
4/7/XX	Bill O'Dell	S & R Limited	Review project
4/8/XX	Penelope Patterson	Gallery Print Shop	Discuss brochure

Figure 1-6   Visitors log.

CHARTS AND MANUALS

Organization Chart

An office *organization chart* shows the relationships among employees, offices, or departments. On your first day on a new job, request a copy of the company organization chart. Study it carefully so you can understand the chain of command within the company and the relationship among its departments. The organization chart allows you to quickly learn important names and titles and also helps you avoid mistakes and embarrassment.

In organization chart in Figure 1-7, the business manager, production manager, and sales manager report to the company president, Roberta Wilkins. Clifton Daniels reports to the business manager, and Patrick Anthony reports to the sales manager.

Desk Manuals; Policy and Procedures Manuals

When you begin your new job, you may be presented with a company policy and procedures manual or with a desk manual, which may be in printed form or online via the company's internal Web site. The policy and procedures manual should inform new employees of items such as company policies, annual goals, leave policies, health benefits, and grievance procedures. It may also contain company rules and standard company procedures. The examples and explanations found in a policy and procedures manual will help you understand your job and make your work much easier.

A *desk manual* usually contains information specific to your job or department. It may include examples of forms regularly used in your office with an explanation of

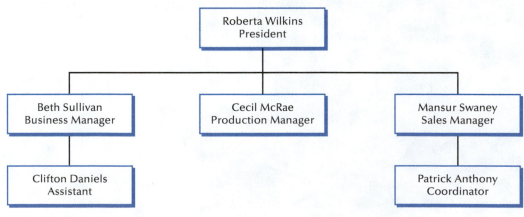

Figure 1-7   Organization chart.

how to complete them, an organization chart of the company, information about the work of your office, phone numbers often used by your office, and information regarding your business. You should consult the desk manual frequently so you will become familiar with the operation of the office. No person can be expected to remember every company policy or how to complete every item on every form. The desk manual should be your reference guide where you can find information on how to handle the many infrequent tasks you must complete.

If you are not presented with a desk manual, immediately begin to compile your own. If the person who previously held your position is available, ask him or her for information that would go into your desk manual. Ask your coworkers for information about the company and copies of forms used in the office, with instructions on how to fill them out. Keep your desk manual up-to-date as office policies and procedures change. Place copies of memos you receive regarding new office procedures, requirements, or forms in your manual.

Items that should be included in a desk manual

1. Location of company facilities.
2. Organization chart.
3. Procedures for operating the company telephone system.
4. Email and voice-mail instructions.
5. Letter and memorandum styles.
6. Samples of form letters.
7. Daily routines.
8. Due dates of routine matters.
9. Payroll procedures.
10. Vendor website addresses.
11. Important email addresses such, as those for clients, business associates, relevant government agencies, etc.
12. Procedures for handling the mail.
13. Additional information to efficiently run the office.

<aside>
Do you have the skills to meet the challenges of your future?
</aside>

CONCLUSION

An office employee is a well-rounded individual who possesses the skills and personal traits to succeed in today's chaotic office environment. As you progress through this book, you will develop and expand the skills and traits required for you to reach your goal of being the best office employee you can possibly be. You are embarking on a new journey that will provide you excitement and challenges.

<aside>
HINT
Set the stage for your future.
</aside>

CHAPTER REVIEW

1. List ten characteristics of a good office employee.
2. List five negative personal traits.
3. What is a job description?
4. What is a desk manual, and what should be included in it?
5. What is the purpose of an organization chart?
6. What are the advantages of a computerized calendar?

ACTIVITIES

1. Contact five businesses and ask what job titles are used for support staff in their companies.

2. Ask three assistants:
   a. To name the three most important points they have learned since they have been employed.
   b. To describe three positive aspects and three negative aspects of their particular jobs.
   c. How often they have changed jobs.
   d. How they handle difficult situations on the job.

   Ask any additional questions you feel important.

3. Write a one-page paper explaining why you want to become an office employee. You may use the Internet to research this activity.

4. Write a one-page paper explaining the duties of the job you expect to hold five years from now. You may use the Internet to research this activity.

5. Introduce yourself to two new people this week. Think of a way to remember their names and how to recognize them.

6. Invite an office employee to speak to your class.

7. Ask three companies for a job description for an entry-level support staff job. Review the job descriptions and determine whether you qualify for the positions.

8. Write a job description for the position you hope to obtain when you leave school. You may use the Internet to research this activity.

9. Request copies of policy and procedures manuals or desk manuals from three companies and review them. Make lists of the contents of each manual and compare them. When contacting a company for information, identify yourself as a student in an office procedures course. Of course, confidential information may be blocked out by the employer.

PROJECTS

Project 1

Key in the following document.

POLICY AND PROCEDURES MANUAL
L. Levy and Company
Revised June 1, XXXX
by Zev F. Carlton

Topics

- Company Locations
- Organization Chart
- Voice-mail and Email Procedures
- Letter Styles
- Memorandum Styles
- Fax Cover Letter Styles
- Payroll Procedures

- Project Due Dates
- Purchasing Procedures

Project 2

Create the following notice. If possible, include an appropriate graphic.

Time Management Seminar
Monday
December 9
Administration Center, Room 247
9–4
Learn Time-Management Techniques
Prepare for a New Job
To register, call Katie at 2477

HUMAN RELATIONS SKILL DEVELOPMENT

HR 1-1 My Coworkers Do Not Like Me

The first day of your new job, your supervisor introduced you to your coworkers. Everyone was friendly except Melissa and Mandy. When you see Melissa and Mandy in the hallway, they ignore you. When you enter a room, they walk away from you. You are mystified about what you did to create this problem. The day you were introduced to them, all you said was hello. You have now been employed for over a month and the cold shoulder continues. Casually you mentioned the problem to your supervisor, who said not to pay any attention to them. The situation makes you uncomfortable and you would like to solve the problem.

- Why do they not speak to you?
- What should you do to solve the problem?
- Is there someone you can turn to for help?

HR 1-2 A Colleague Who Asks for Advice

A colleague frequently asks you for advice about how to complete office tasks. In the beginning, you did not mind answering her questions, but now her questions are too numerous. Her questions are occupying more of your work time than you can devote to assisting her.

- Why are you asked for assistance?
- What should you do to solve the problem?
- Can your, supervisor help you solve the problem?

SITUATIONS

How would you handle each of the following situations?

- S 1-1 You are a receptionist in an office where Phil and Bill both work. When you transfer a telephone call to either one of them, you always seem to transfer the call to the wrong person.
- S 1-2 Last night your supervisor took a file home and forgot to return it today. You need the file today so that you can complete a report.

- S 1-3 Jennie is frequently late when returning from lunch. She tells you that she must run errands at lunch and asks you to cover for her.

ROLE PLAYING

Act out the following situations to demonstrate how you would handle each problem.

1. Assume the role of a receptionist. Greet the person sitting next to you and ask if the person has an appointment.

2. Give a firm businesslike handshake to the person sitting across from you.

3. Ms. Yee has just arrived for her 10:30 A.M. appointment. Your supervisor has been called out of the office on a personal emergency. You do not know when the supervisor will be back. Explain the situation to Ms. Yee.

4. Your supervisor told you that she does not want to talk to Mr. Bern, an important client. Mr. Bern called to talk to your supervisor at 10 A.M. At 1 P.M. he called again, and at 3 P.M. he called back a third time. What would you tell Mr. Bern each time?

5. Your manager had intended to return a telephone call from Mr. Morales, an important client, but neglected to do so and has left for a business trip. What do you say to Mr. Morales when he calls? Mr. Morales says it is urgent.

6. An irate person arrives at your office and insists upon seeing your employer, who is in a conference with an important client. What would you do?

7. You neglected to tell your supervisor that Mr. Colony called, and now he has called again and is upset.

8. Your supervisor has forgotten his lunch meeting with Ms. Stevens. Ms. Stevens has been waiting at the restaurant for an hour and now she is on the phone. Your supervisor went to lunch with another client. What would you tell Ms. Stevens?

PUNCTUATION REVIEW

Punctuate each of the following sentences. For a review of punctuation rules, see the Appendix.

1. Jerry who was hired last year has received a promotion

2. Because the machine was broken the report was late

3. Our stockholders have earned large dividends and our brokers have been helpful

4. Therefore a conscious decision was made to build up the reserves in the bond fund mutual fund and trust fund so future generations of the family would be financially secure

5. I cannot work late tonight however I can work late tomorrow

6. Zero-coupon bonds pay interest upon maturity but stocks pay dividends quarterly

7. On Friday July 12 the Commission intended to vote on the budget for the year but the attorney received a telephone call that called a halt to the vote

8. George Williams Jr an accountant teaches part time at the college

9. Industrial companies on the other hand benefit in the longer term from a dollar that has been stabilized

10. The mortgage rate has risen 1 percent a year but the selling price of most homes has risen 10 percent a year

11. The Dow Jones Industrial Average lost 25 points on Friday but gained 35 points today

12. Du Pont General Motors and IBM are blue chip stocks but Florida Power and Lights price earning ratio was better

13. Paul said Bertha wrote the last report

14. Anna said the process of changing the passwords is very complicated

15. Employees from the center met August 23 September 28 and October 15

CD ASSIGNMENT

CD Assignment 1-1

Open the file CD1-1_Appt on your Student CD and follow the instructions to complete the job. You will also need the file CD1-1_Cal, which is on your Student CD.

CHAPTER 2

Working Effectively: Time Management and Interaction with Colleagues

Objectives

After studying this chapter, you should be able to:

1. Improve your listening skills.
2. Know how to become an effective team player.
3. Improve your organization and time-management skills.
4. Recognize leadership skills.
5. Understand brainstorming.
6. Describe alternative work schedules.

LISTENING SKILLS

Working with people requires first-rate listening skills. In many jobs, you will spend more time listening, understanding, and reacting to directions and comments from your supervisor, colleagues, and customers than you will spend talking to others. Superior listening skills are essential for your career success.

Listening is a skill that most people think they possess, but many people do not listen, comprehend, and remember what they are told. The skill of listening can be strengthened and improved. Listening skills are vital in the office because most office instructions are given orally. Excellent listening skills also help you remember more of what you hear, understand more of what the speaker said, and respond more accurately to the speaker's words.

Once you hear something, you must interpret and understand it. When listening, concentrate on what is being said and do not allow your mind to wander. Summarize the important details to yourself so that you will remember them. You should, of course, feel free to request clarification of instructions if you do not understand them. Also recognize that people can become annoyed if they must continually repeat instructions because you were not paying attention, so stay focused.

Suggestions to help improve listening skills

- Be close enough to the person you are listening to so you can clearly hear what is being said.

- Concentrate on what is being said, and do not daydream. If your mind starts to wander, focus on what is being said.
- If music is played in the office, select relaxing background music. Do not play music that is distracting or that commands your attention.
- Pay attention to what is being said. Also be aware of gestures, facial expressions, body language, and voice tone—they add to the message.
- Direct your eyes on the person talking to you.
- Do not allow the speaker's personal mannerisms to interfere with your concentration.
- Ask questions to clarify and verify everything that you do not understand.
- Have paper and pen ready so you are prepared to take notes when someone approaches you with instructions.
- Do research and obtain background information about office projects so instructions will be clearer and more meaningful to you.
- Identify the main ideas in the instructions given.
- Be an active listener. Nod your head and use appropriate facial expressions to show the speaker that you understand the message.
- Repeat the important points to yourself.
- Listen to the speaker and allow him or her to finish speaking before you phrase your questions. You cannot listen if you are thinking about questions you want to ask.
- Avoid the pitfalls of biases that cloud the message when listening. Some people have difficulty listening to:

  Members of the opposite sex.

  Members of another ethnic group.

  Persons older or younger than themselves.

> Do you have good listening skills?

ORGANIZATION AND TIME MANAGEMENT

Organize Your Desk

An organized desk is essential to avoid paper clutter and lost materials. Organize your desk and supplies so you can quickly find files and materials. Design your desk so you have an in-basket, out-basket, pending file, bring-up file, and signature file. An *in-basket* is for incoming materials. Your manager and other employees can leave work for you in the in-basket. Depending on the workload, it may be helpful to have one in-basket for yourself, one in-basket for your supervisor's work, and a separate basket for other staff members' materials. The *out-basket* is for documents that you have completed and may contain materials to be delivered to other staff members. A *pending file* is for items that you are processing and for which you need additional information. It may be helpful to have several pending files in a horizontal file holder on your desk or a designated location in a file cabinet for in-process file storage. The *bring-up file* is used for items that you need to discuss with your manager. A *signature file* is where documents are placed until the supervisor has time to sign them. The use of a signature file eliminates interrupting the supervisor to sign a single document.

At the end of the day, clear your desk and place all working papers in a locked drawer that is designated for that purpose.

Figure 2-1　An organized office.

Peak Time

Do you have a particular time of day when you are more alert and are able to solve difficult problems? Are there times of day when you are more productive working individually or times when you are more productive working with others? Some people have more energy and do their best work early in the morning, while other people are most productive in the afternoon. Your peak time is when you are most productive; therefore, use your peak time to your best advantage. Whenever possible, plan your work so you do the difficult jobs that require problem-solving skills during your peak time and the routine jobs such as filing during your non-peak or low times.

MY SUCCESS STORY

My Name Is Nhu

For several years, I had a part-time position in my organization, but then I decided that I wanted a full-time position. To make myself indispensable to my company, I decided to use my expertise to become more visible to my supervisors. I took software training classes and offered to train my coworkers. My training sessions were cost effective for the company, and the participants learned to use the software packages. In addition, I became proficient at creating PowerPoint presentations. When anyone in the organization needed software or PowerPoint presentation help, I volunteered. My ideas and diligence paid off. A position became available, and the department supervisor suggested that I apply for the position. Yes, I got the job. Now I have a full-time position in a terrific organization.

Time Management

In an office, work never ends and employees are time starved. Most office jobs have a continuous flow of work—there will always be another project once the current activity is complete. Often, you will be working on several projects or activities at the same time. For that reason, it is important to manage your time carefully so you can work with maximum efficiency and productivity. Learn to juggle your regular job responsibilities while completing major projects. Be sure to schedule time for team projects and meetings. Set realistic timelines and build in additional time so you can respond to unexpected delays.

Do not think that your office life is going to be calm—everything will happen at once. It is important to always remain flexible to meet the unexpected tasks and crises that interrupt your daily routine.

Managing your time

1. The first step is to plan. Organize what needs to be done and estimate the time it will take to do those tasks. You should do your planning at least once or twice each day. Although last-minute changes may alter your plans, you should prepare daily and weekly work schedules. Also prepare a master one-month schedule, even if you do not always know in advance what all of the jobs will be. Start your schedule with the routine daily, weekly, or monthly tasks or meetings so they are not forgotten. Then plan your other projects around them.

2. Organize your desk. Place the most frequently used items in easily accessible locations.

3. Do not allow others to control your time with interruptions or unnecessary talk.

4. Include team projects in your schedule and make team projects a priority. Do not be the person who lets the team down.

5. Establish priorities for completing the most important work first. If you do not set priorities, you will have difficulty completing assignments and may disappoint your supervisor because important tasks are not completed on time.

Priorities

- Know your priorities.
- Do your priorities correspond with your supervisor's priorities?
- Create a to-do list based on priorities and follow it.
- Each day, review your priorities and reassign them if necessary.
- Focus your time and effort on each item on your priority list.

Avoid Wasting Valuable Office Time

It is very easy to waste time in an office. Your time is valuable to you and the company, so you must not allow your coworkers or clients to squander your time. Ten minutes wasted three times a day becomes a half hour of misused time each day. By the end of a week, you have wasted two and a half hours. Think of what you could have accomplished in those two and a half hours.

To avoid wasting time in the office, use the following suggestions.

Organize your office

- Have the back of your chair face the door. This will discourage people from stopping by your desk to chat.
- Have only one or two chairs in your office. This will discourage people from gathering in your office and wasting your time.

- Keep a clock in your office to remind yourself of the current time and the length of time you spend on a project.
- Process the daily mail efficiently and rapidly.
- Accept the fact that it is impossible to read every email, newspaper, magazine, advertisement, memo, letter, etc., that comes across your desk. Prioritize. Decide what you should read, skim, or throw away.

On the telephone
- Keep telephone conversations to a minimum.
- Do not let yourself get stuck on a long nonproductive telephone call.
- Use email to avoid playing telephone tag and to avoid lengthy telephone calls.

Dealing with coworkers
- Be concise and to the point when answering questions.
- Delegate work to others.
- If a colleague wants to chat too long, say, "I would love to continue our conversation, but I have to finish this project today."
- Socialize with your coworkers before or after your workday instead of during office hours.
- Be friendly with coworkers but socialize with them in places other than at your desk. Then you have the option of walking away when you want to get back to work.
- Stand when people are in your office because standing may discourage them from staying too long.

Meetings
- Make appointments for people to meet with you and stick to your time schedule.
- If you must attend meetings, diplomatically encourage leaders to adhere to the agenda.

WORKING WITH COLLEAGUES IN TEAMS

Team Players

Many projects are structured as group tasks where team members share ideas and work together to achieve a common goal. Collaborative teams are the core of many businesses. Teams are formed to complete projects, create new ideas, reengineer company policies, and perform many other functions. Do you have a team player mentality? Your career and job opportunities may depend on your ability to work as a member of a team.

Teams are successful because they bring together a variety of knowledge, experiences, cultural backgrounds, and insights. Team members may come from separate departments with members at many levels of job responsibilities. Therefore, an assistant in the purchasing department, a coordinator in the benefits department, and a director in the finance department may all work together as a team to complete a project. Thus, an effective team understands the importance of collaboration.

The team project launch meeting is important for the success of the project. It must be an upbeat and enthusiastic meeting where the project objectives are explained and discussed. In addition, the cohesiveness of the group is critical for the success of the project. Teammates who share common goals and interests are more successful, and regularly scheduled meetings improve the chances for success of the project.

The physical environment where a team works can contribute to the success of the project. Sunny and airy conference rooms equipped with pens; paper; computer access; email access; flipcharts; white boards; and snack areas with coffee, tea, fruit, sweet rolls, etc., all encourage employees to mingle and share ideas. Teams perform better when they have the resources to do their work.

Teams are not limited to working together in a room. A team with members in various locations may rely on technology to meet and reach its goals. The use of telephones, email, audio and video conferencing, and shared software make working as a team feasible regardless of location.

When teams are working on a project, they often share files. The software, referred to as *teamware*, *groupware*, or *collaborative software*, permits team interaction by allowing several members of the team to write alternative versions of paragraphs, worksheets, or project timelines, with each shown in a different font color or style. These files may be kept on a central computer server, which allows access for all team members. In addition, individual members may keep a copy on their personal computer. It is always important to verify dates when saving the shared files, thereby avoiding replacing the newer files with older versions.

Brainstorming is a technique teams often use to develop ideas to help solve a problem. In brainstorming, people try to think of any possible solution to a specific problem. All ideas are recorded; no idea is dismissed or belittled, no matter how silly or outlandish it seems. Because one person's idea will stimulate ideas in others, brainstorming is frequently used by a project team. As one idea prompts another idea, several possible solutions usually develop. Those ideas are then explored, and additional information may be gathered before a solution is reached.

Will brainstorming help you?

While teams are brainstorming ideas, they create multiple alternatives that are redefined into workable solutions. Unfortunately, not all ideas are feasible. Constructive criticism is encouraged, but destructive criticism is not allowed. Expect team members to disagree. Disagreement, when handled properly, can be a productive force because disagreements provide an opportunity for team members to examine contrasting ideas and thoughts. Disagreement, however, should not develop into hostility which divides team members. A divided team will not be successful, and failure of a team often reflects on each of the team members. Do not allow team meetings to turn into chat or argument sessions. Stay focused. Whatever is discussed in the team meeting is confidential and is discussed only among the team members unless members are asked to discuss the project with coworkers.

Do you want to be a team player?

Suggestions for team members

- The team should secure top management's agreement before beginning a project.
- Keep project team members focused.
- If possible, select your own team members. Select persons whose ideas are compatible with your ideas and who will work well with you.
- One advantage of working in a team is to showcase your talents to upper management and members of other departments.
- By contributing your ideas at team meetings, you increase your visibility, which can have positive or negative results. You could risk alienating a high-level executive who does not agree with you.
- Before you join a team, research the project and the team's members. Is one colleague the dominant member of the team? Prior to the first meeting, become an expert on the project's background and focus.

Figure 2-2 Team members working on a project.

- Be diplomatic when you express your opinions.
- When representing your team to other employees, always use *we*, not *I*.
- It is important for team members to have an understanding of the diversity of cultures among the teammates and the company's clients.

Team Leaders and Leadership Skills

Teams often have leaders or facilitators who transform a group of individuals into a unified team with the same goals and objectives. Outside the team's project, the team leader may or may not have supervisory responsibilities for members of the team.

Employees at all levels need to develop leadership skills so they will able to accept additional responsibilities as they advance in their careers. Depending on the circumstances, an employee may function as a member of the team or as the team leader.

What are the challenges of a team leader? While the team leader is a member of the group, the team leader also stands outside the group to lead, guide, direct, and initiate projects through new and innovative ventures. In addition, the team leader must interact and work with the team members as they progress through the projects. In order to achieve the objectives of the project, the leader must divide the project into manageable segments based on team size and project scope, identify resources, operate within a budget, keep the members focused and motivated, capitalize on each person's strengths and contributions, and solve team opinion and temperament conflicts.

A team leader must have good organization and communication skills because poor skills can doom any project. In addition, the leader must look to the future and analyze the current and long-term aspects of the project. Furthermore, the leader must also accept the responsibility for the success or failure of project.

Are you a born leader?

Working with Nontraditional Work Schedules and Locations

Opportunities

Today's office employee is no longer restricted to a work schedule with a fixed number of hours each day during a five-day week. Work schedules and places of employment have become flexible in response to the demands of modern businesses, employees, and society at large. Many employees have the opportunity to schedule their hours according to alternative work schedules, flextime, or job sharing. Some workers have the opportunity to change their workplace and work from home or alternative work sites via telecommuting. Employees working on these alternative schedules or from alternative work sites face challenges in interacting with their colleagues and remaining a member of the office team.

Alternative Work Schedules

Alternative work schedules permit the employee to work other than the traditional five days a week. With an alternative work schedule, an employee may work four ten-hour days a week to satisfy a job requirement. Another example of an alternative work schedule is a two-week schedule of longer days with alternate Fridays or Mondays off. For example, if an employee works eighty hours over a two-week period, an alternate work schedule may require an employee to work nine-hour days for eight days and one day of eight hours. The employee would then have the tenth day off. In some businesses, all the employees work the same alternative work schedule; in others, the schedules are staggered, for example, so only half the employees are off on any Friday. Alternative work schedules allow flexibility for the employee, save commuting costs, and reduce traffic and air pollution; but the alternative work schedule may cause scheduling problems for the employer. Furthermore, employees must be aware of colleagues' alternative work schedules when scheduling meetings or establishing deadlines.

Flextime

Flextime allows the employees to decide their own starting and ending times. Usually the company establishes a two- or three-hour time frame within which employees may select the start or end of their workday. With flextime, there are usually core hours when all employees must be present in the office, and all employees must work every day during the standard workweek. When flextime is an option, absenteeism and tardiness are usually reduced, production is increased, employee satisfaction is higher, and employee morale is improved. Flextime allows the employee greater flexibility in scheduling personal appointments and meeting personal needs such as medical appointments, childcare, and elder care. However, employees must be aware of their colleagues' flextime schedules when scheduling meetings. Employees on both alternative and flextime schedules may have to adjust their schedules in order to attend important meetings or to meet project deadlines.

Job Sharing

As business has become more amenable to the needs of the employee, *job sharing*, which is one job shared by two persons, has become more popular. A shared job often has one employee working in the morning and the other in the afternoon. Some companies require overlap time where both employees are at work at the same time to discuss shared projects. In job sharing, both workers may receive full or only partial job benefits. The major advantage to the employee is having time to pursue personal interests and fulfill personal responsibilities such as childcare or elder care. Companies also benefit from job sharing by hiring qualified employees who might not otherwise be available. A downside of job sharing for the employer is the increase in recordkeeping and related costs. The success of many job-sharing arrangements depends on the ability of the two employees to get along and to share both the work and the credit for its completion.

Telecommuting

Do you want to telecommute?

Telecommuting or *teleworking* allows the employee to work from outside the office with the assistance of communications equipment. Some companies allow employees to work from home a few days a week, a few days a month, or while working on a special project. Another telecommuting option is the use of a satellite office, which is an office where employees can work several days a week in their own region rather than commuting across large metropolitan areas.

Working from a home or satellite office has become easier with the widespread availability of the fax machine, computer, and access to the Internet. Telephone services using paging, voice mail, and conference calling allow more people to work from home. Computer group software allows employees at home to share email, calendars, and assignments. Also, companies now have computer systems that allow home workers to access company computer files in the same way they access information from the Internet. Voice communication is managed over the telephone, with a telephone at the employee's home office operating as an extension of the office telephone system.

However, not all workers are productive while working from home. There may be too many distractions for some employees, while others are unhappy without the social contact an office environment brings to the workday. Employees who work off site may miss being able to share ideas with colleagues and may feel out of the loop on ideas and discussions. In many organizations, telecommuting employees commute to the office for meetings and to maintain continuity on projects. In addition, it is important for telecommuters to establish frequent contact with the supervisor and coworkers by email or telephone to avoid the misconception that the telecommuter is relaxing at home. The nontelecommuter may be jealous of the telecommuter's apparent freedom.

A telecommuting employee who works at home should create a work environment with a closed door to secure privacy and quiet. If you are visited by business associates while at home, dress in a professional manner and design an office that is professional in appearance.

It is very easy to waste your business time while at home by allowing your personal life to interfere with your business life. If you work out of your home, establish regular office hours and adhere to them. Inform business associates and friends of your work hours. Since the telecommuting worker is close to the home refrigerator and television, snacking and watching television may become a problem. To remain focused on your business, you should designate a specific area of your home as your office and not allow your family life to interfere with your work activities.

Telecommuting parents have many child-related issues to consider. One of the most important issues is for the at-home child to understand that the parent is working and is unavailable during working hours. If possible, establish specific lunch and break times so the child can look forward to seeing the parent. The parent and child will both benefit from a designated work schedule and a work-at-home parent.

A varied work schedule, which includes flextime and telecommuting, is often important to employees at opposite ends of the age spectrum. Young employees, who have small children with many home responsibilities, and older workers, who value

HINT

It is especially important for telecommuters and job sharers to build a trusting relationship with their supervisors.

Figure 2-3 A home office.

their free time or who may be caring for elderly relatives, often desire a varied work schedule because of the flexibility it provides. Workers who are nearing retirement frequently use a varied work schedule as the first step toward retirement because of the possibility of additional leisure time.

Equipment

To establish an at-home office, you will usually need office equipment, which can include a fax machine, telephone answering machine, CD/DVD burner, flash drives, external backup drive, virus protection software, additional telephone lines (one for personal use and one for the office telephone), and high-speed Internet access. It is an advantage to configure the office email system to automatically forward email to your home computer. To maintain communications, it may help to have an instant-messaging system that allows you, your supervisor, and colleagues to chat via computer in real time.

Agreement

Employees who telecommute may sign an agreement with their company that describes the conditions under which the employee telecommutes and the responsibilities of the employer as well as the employee. The agreement may include information about the type of work to be done at home by the employee, the hours the employee must keep at the home office, whether the employer will provide a computer and other equipment, the extent of the employee's responsibility for maintaining the home office and equipment, whether the employee may care for children during work hours, and other conditions of the telecommuting arrangement. If you are considering a telecommuting arrangement, carefully review the telecommuting agreement with your employer so you can fulfill your obligations.

Suggestions for telecommuting workers

- Set a daily work schedule and follow it.
- Designate a work space.
- Communicate regularly with your supervisor.
- Communicate regularly with your colleagues.

- Organize yourself and decide in advance what materials you need to bring home.
- Make two copies of all computer files being transported.
- Email copies of all files to be used at home or to be returned to work.
- Do not allow personal activities to interfere with work time.

Benefits

Many employers and employees feel that the advantages of telecommuting surpass the disadvantages. Benefits of telecommuting for the employee include less commuting time and lower commuting costs, more flexible job hours, lower expenses for an office wardrobe, and being at home with young children or elderly parents. Telecommuting advantages for the employer including hiring employees who may not be able to work in a traditional office setting and a reduction in office-space costs associated with employees who work out of their homes. In addition, telecommuting provides environmental and quality-of-life benefits to the entire community. Generally telecommuting decreases the number of automobile trips in a community, which results in improved air quality and reduced traffic congestion.

Off-Site Locations

In some companies, an employee's usual work location may be off-site and the employee may not have a full-time company-provided office. To provide office support for these employees, some businesses provide temporary or flexible office space for a few hours or a full day on a call-ahead-and-reserve basis. Another option is *teaming space*, where employees share an office on a scheduled or nonscheduled basis.

Respect

Regardless of where employees actually do their work, they must be made to feel that they are part of the company community. The feeling of belonging is a shared responsibility that must be nurtured by the employee, the employer, and the employee's colleagues. Employees who telecommute or who are on an alternative work schedule deserve the same consideration and respect as those employees who work in a traditional office on a traditional work schedule. Employees who feel that they are valued by their employer will put the extra effort into a project and will be more productive.

CHAPTER REVIEW

1. Why is listening important?
2. List four suggestions to improve your listening skills.
3. Define peak time.
4. List three suggestions for team members as discussed in this chapter.
5. Describe brainstorming.
6. What are the advantages of telecommuting for the employee?
7. Explain the concept of alternative work schedules.

ACTIVITIES

1. Keep detailed records for one week showing how you spend your college-related time. Indicate assignments and deadlines for college projects. Did you meet the deadlines? How much time was spent on each project? Do you feel

you used your time efficiently? Did someone interfere with your ability to use your time efficiently? How should you have handled that situation? What changes would you make in your time-management techniques?

2. For three days, keep a list of the times when you are full of energy and the times when you are tired. Discover your peak time and learn how to plan important activities around that time.

3. Write a two-paragraph report with many important facts. Read the report to the class, and ask questions about the report to determine the listening skill level of the class. You may use the Internet to research this activity.

4. Read a detailed article to a partner. The partner should write a summary of the article. Compare the details in the article with those in the summary. (For additional listening practice, the partners can swap roles.)

5. To improve your listening skills, practice remembering telephone numbers and messages left on your voice mail.

6. To improve your listening skills, use the Internet to find directions from your home to a restaurant in your area. Read the directions to your partner and ask your partner to orally repeat the directions.

7. To improve your listening skills, ask your partner to describe his or her cultural background. Then orally repeat the description. Reverse roles.

8. To improve your listening skills, divide your class into teams with at least four people on a team. Each team member explains his or her career objectives. Write a summary explaining each team member's career objectives.

9. Describe a poor listener.

PROJECTS

Project 3

Key in the following document. Center the table and center the heading over the table. Make all other decisions and make any enhancements you desire.

Meeting Schedule

Team	Team Leader	Date	Time	Location
1	Gregory Benson	June 1	9 A.M.	Room 600
2	Tae Kim	June 4	10 A.M.	Room 804
3	Hawa Young	June 6	9 A.M.	Room 600
4	Mimi Forte	June 11	2 P.M.	Room 902
5	Brian Hawthorne	June 12	10 A.M.	Room 604
6	Kya Doubrava	June 13	11 A.M.	Room 600

Project 4

Create the following flyer and use clip art to capture the attention of your colleagues. Make all decisions and add any information you feel appropriate.

After-Work Get-Together
Let's Gather for a Fun Evening
Friday, September 21

Beginning at 6 P.M.

Ted's Tavern

1200 Executive Drive

Parking behind restaurant
Best burgers, chili, and wings in town

HUMAN RELATIONS SKILL DEVELOPMENT

HR 2-1 Functioning As a Member of a Team

Working as a member of a team requires that all members be able to work together, even though they have different viewpoints. Learning to respect the thoughts of others and listening to the views of others encourages a good working relationship. Completing your part of a project by the due date is a team requirement. One member of the team who does not complete an assignment on time may hamper the progress of other team members.

- What would you do if a member of your team did not complete an assigned project on time?
- What would you do if a member of your team took credit for an idea that you developed?
- What would you do if two members of your team had an argument and refused to work on a project?
- What would you do if a member of your team always needed extra help to complete projects?

HR 2-2 Complaints

When employees gather at lunch, during breaks, or at staff meetings, the conversation can quickly turn into a complaint session about the job. While complaint sessions may allow the airing of personal feelings, they are rarely productive in solving job-related problems. Sometimes people try to outdo each other with complaints, which results in additional employee aggravation and lower morale. If lunch or office breaks have routinely become gripe sessions, find another way to spend your time. If staff meetings frequently become gripe sessions, try to focus the group on the objective of the meeting.

- You are a member of the support staff and a question-and-answer session at the end of a staff meeting turns into a gripe session. What would you do?
- You are a supervisor and a question-and-answer session at the end of a staff meeting turns into a gripe session. What would you do?
- What would you do if your supervisor heard you make negative comments about him or her?
- What would you do if you are the supervisor and you heard negative comments about yourself?

SITUATIONS

How would you handle each of the following situations?

- S 2-1 You are the team leader, and during a meeting you heard Vanessa make a rude remark to Lester.

- **S 2-2** Joshua, your team member, said that the project was a waste of time and refused to complete a team assignment.
- **S 2-3** You are the team leader, and Victor, a team member, is frequently late for team meetings.

PUNCTUATION REVIEW

Punctuate each of the following sentences. For a review of punctuation rules, see the Appendix.

1. Ms. McNeil who is a twenty year employee is on track toward a rating of Commendable for this year
2. The ending date for this project is December 1 so the major activities in this project must be completed prior to that date
3. All forms and instructions as well as a link to our informational page may be found on our website
4. You are invited to a special party honoring Wilmer J Potts our founding director
5. Bring a colleague with you to our seminar on Monday September 17
6. See the enclosed card browse our website or call one of our friendly associates to help answer all of your questions
7. As an employee of Toots & Associates you are a lifelong member of our family
8. The state of the art auditorium opened on Sunday December 19 2006
9. The deadline to submit the proposal is Friday July 14
10. Next spring we will break ground on our new $50 million 200000 square-foot complex
11. We host many events in Albany Orlando Houston and Charlotte
12. As always feel free to contact us with any questions you have about our service plans
13. Your opinions feedback and ideas are important to us
14. This high-tech seminar offers a view of all of the new software that will soon be available
15. All events are announced via Events and You our free email service

CD ASSIGNMENTS

CD Assignment 2-1

Open the file **CD2-1_Pri** on your Student CD and follow the instructions to complete the job.

CD Assignment 2-2

Open the file **CD2-2_PA** on your Student CD and follow the instructions to complete the job.

CHAPTER 3

....

The Written Word

Objectives

After studying this chapter, you should be able to:

1. Compose email messages.
2. Prepare business letters.
3. Prepare reports.
4. Prepare memos.
5. Explain the purpose of a news release.
6. Explain the purpose of a newsletter.

THE BASICS

All businesses, nonprofit organizations, and government agencies rely on written communication when dealing with customers or other parts of their organization. Today, written business communications are prepared on a computer and may be printed on paper as a letter, memo, or report and sent through the mail, or they can be delivered electronically using email or text messaging. A written communication may be the only contact an individual or a company has with your office, and it will shape in a positive or negative way the reader's opinion of you and your company.

Depending on the situation, an office employee may be asked to keyboard, rewrite, or compose a variety of written communications, such as an email, a letter, a memorandum (memo), a report, or a news release. The assistant may also write or design a weekly, monthly, or quarterly newsletter describing the events, news, or announcements of the company. All written communications use the same writing techniques. The success of your writing will depend on your ability to make the reader understand your message. When you use verbal communications, you can use hand and facial gestures to help convey your thoughts. In addition, your vocal inflections and tone of voice can change the meaning of a sentence and can help the listener understand what you are saying. When you create a document, however, you must you use effective writing techniques because you do not have the benefits of verbal and visual cues to help express your message.

Your writing should be

- Clear.
- Concise.
- Correct.
- Complete.
- Courteous.
- Concrete.
- Conversational.

Writing suggestions

- Express thoughts clearly and concisely so they will not be misinterpreted.
- Come to the point quickly; use easy-to-understand language, and verify your facts.
- A completed document should contain all of the information necessary for the reader to respond to it. However, the document should not contain unnecessary information that would overwhelm, confuse, or mislead the reader.
- If you are asking the reader to take some specific action, clearly state the action you are requesting.
- Write in a courteous, friendly, and conversational tone as though you are talking to the reader.
- If you are angry, do not allow your anger to influence your writing style. Because angry people often write in a sarcastic manner, avoid writing when you are upset. If you feel compelled to write while in an angry mood, write the letter or email, but do not send it. After you have calmed down evaluate the document and decide if it should be sent.
- Since important business transactions are at stake, answer letters and memos within two days. Answer emails on the day of receipt or the next day.
- Ending a document with a "thank you" is determined by personal taste. Some people feel it is in bad taste to end a letter with a "thank you" for a future action, while others feel it is a positive reinforcement and encourages the requested action. Some writers end communication with "thank you in advance."

> **HINT**
> Is your writing clear and concise?

CORRECTING COMMON WRITING PROBLEMS

Clarity

The primary goal of all writing is to clearly convey a message to the reader. Incorrectly placed words and phrases are a common cause of misunderstandings. How would you rewrite these sentences to make them clear?

Driving a car, the office was only five minutes from the house.

Office desks are on sale in every store with printer stands.

Barry ate an ice cream cone walking down the street.

Misused pronouns are another source of misunderstandings. When using pronouns, make sure that the pronoun refers to the noun it is replacing—not another noun in the letter. The reference noun might have been obvious to the writer but confusing to the reader. The following are examples of confusing sentences:

June told Kathy that she was late. (Who was late?)

Linda and Peggy went shopping. She bought a computer. (Who bought the computer?)

Friendliness

In oral communication, the voice indicates the tone of the sentence. In written communication, the words alone must convey a friendly and helpful tone. Here are some examples of a friendly tone.

We are very happy to be of service to you.

We greatly appreciate the time you have devoted to our civic project.

We are truly sorry that we will not be able to be with you to share your joy on the occasion of your daughter's wedding.

Interesting Language

Inappropriate or Redundant Words

Many phrases that are commonly used in oral communications are inappropriate in letters. The following is a list of phrases that are inappropriate or redundant and should be avoided in written business communications.

awfully good	close up
each and every	good as gold
seldom ever	terribly good
upon receipt of	very complete

Slang

Do you use slang?

Do not use slang because it is inappropriate for professional communications, and it may not be understood by others. The following is a sample list of slang terms.

Awesome
Cool
Fat
Yea

Transitional Words

HINT
Transitional words carry the reader from one thought to the next.

Transitional words carry the reader from one thought to the next. If transitional words are not used, the sentences do not flow and the letter sounds choppy. Varying the length of the sentences helps a document read smoothly. The following is a list of transitional words that will help you improve your writing style.

accordingly	also	and
as	as a result	because
besides	briefly	consequently
finally	for example	furthermore
however	if	in addition
in essence	instead	meanwhile
moreover	next	obviously
on the contrary	since	so
therefore	thus	yet

Rewrite and improve the following paragraph by using transitional words:

We would like you to speak at the meeting. It will be January 17 at 8:00. The topic is "Foods in the Office." We hope you will come. Write me soon.

Vary Your Language

Repeating the same phrases or beginning every sentence with the same word is boring. People writing about themselves frequently begin sentences with the word *I*. However, constantly using *I* shows insensitivity to the reader, so avoid the *I* syndrome.

Use a variety of descriptive words to add interest to a letter, a memorandum, or an email. Furthermore, every sentence should not contain the same adjectives and adverbs. Computer word processing software packages contain a thesaurus that will help you select synonyms, which are words with similar meanings.

Gender Bias

Correspondence should be free of gender bias. If the gender of a person is not known, use nongender words instead of using *her* or *him* to express general concepts,

If the gender of a person is unknown:

Do not say:	Send the material to him.
Say:	Send the material to the manager.
	(Manager does not imply a gender.)
Do not use the salutation:	Gentlemen
Use the salutation:	Ladies and Gentlemen or Dear Sir or Madam

> **HINT**
> Do not be guilty of gender bias.

Moving the Reader to Action

Moving the reader to action requires tact so the reader is not alienated or offended. When people are told to do something, they often react in a negative way. Accordingly, people are more receptive to suggestions than to demands.

- Always write with the reader's point of view in mind, addressing the reader's concerns. A letter should be reader oriented—emphasizing what is important to the reader.
- If a negative message must be delivered, accent the positive aspects of the situation. If you must deny a request, place the denial after an encouraging comment, and always end the letter on a positive note.
- Never write "you are wrong" or "you made a mistake." This may anger the reader. Instead write that there is a problem or a mistake. If this approach is used, you are not placing blame for the error. Never imply that the reader is stupid.

Plain English

In the last several years, companies have adopted and the policy of creating documents written in *Plain English*, which is a writing style that is direct and informative with tight sentence construction. Plain English creates a document that is easy to read and understand and also does not use misleading jargon. In addition, it uses short sentences containing common everyday words. Plain English uses the active voice, where the subject of the sentence does the action, instead of the passive voice, where the subject receives the action. Readers understand the active voice more quickly than

Patrick Brothers Office Supplies
109 Spring Lane
Ft. Lauderdale, FL

June 30, XXXX

Dear Ms. Mendez:

We are very happy that you have enjoyed the service we have provided you. As you know, our customers are very important to us.

We received your letter of June 12 and have carefully considered your request. Unfortunately, we cannot extend the payment date on your account. Our credit policy is that a minimum payment of only $10 must be made within thirty days of the statement closing date. The remaining balance may then be carried over until the next month. Once the outstanding balance is below your credit limit, you will be able to make additional charges.

We hope that you will resume your visits to our store so we can continue to serve you as we have for the last twenty years.

Sincerely,

L. P. Lewis

skc

Figure 3-1 Letter with negative comments placed between positive comments.

the passive voice. Personal pronouns are used to address and inform the reader and to create a bond between the writer and the reader.

Example of a sentence in active voice:
The employee used the computer.

Example of a sentence in passive voice:
The computer was used by the employee.

There are several Internet sites that describe how to write documents in Plain English.

LETTERS

Before you start writing a letter, define the letter's objective and prepare an informal outline. This outline will help to organize your thoughts so the letter meets your objectives. An outline of the letter should consist of the following three main sections.

1. *Introduction:* This is a short paragraph explaining the purpose of the letter.
2. *Body:* The body includes all of the details necessary for the reader to understand the situation.

3. *Conclusion:* The conclusion is the closing paragraph of the letter. It should end the letter on a cordial note and may remind the reader to perform an action or contact the business for further information.

A letter should be:

- Clear and easily understood.
- Attractive and visually appealing.
- Error-free.
- Pleasant in tone.
- Truthful.
- Sincere.
- Concise but include sufficient information.
- Current and not contain any outdated or overused expressions.
- Well organized.

All mailed letters require a correctly addressed envelope using the two-letter state abbreviations and ZIP Code and must be properly folded. Addressing envelopes and folding letters are discussed in Chapter 5.

Format

Today, many new office employees are knowledgeable of their business but are unaware of techniques and formats used in creating written business communications. Employees may prepare letters, memoranda, and reports in their own personal styles because they are unfamiliar with standard document formatting. As an office employee, it may be your responsibility to tactfully correct the formatting of documents so they follow accepted business practices.

Letterhead

Business letters are usually printed on *letterhead stationery*, which includes the organization's name, address, city, state, ZIP Code, telephone number, facsimile (fax) machine number, email address, and Web address.

If plain paper is used, a return address must be keyboarded about 1.5 inches from the top of the letter. The return address includes the organization's name, address, city, state, and ZIP Code. Since the writer's name is in the complimentary close at the bottom of the letter, the writer's name is not repeated in the return address. Therefore, if

Figure 3-2 Confirming an address prior to mailing the letter.

you are printing a letter on plain paper, do not include your name in the return address, which is at the top of the letter.

Letter Margins

Standard paper is 8.5 inches wide by 11 inches long. Paper used for some legal documents is 8.5 inches wide by 14 inches long. Some firms have converted to paper sized in metric measurements, which is slightly different than the sizes mentioned here. For example, standard metric paper (A4) is 8.25 inches wide and 11.75 inches long.

A letter with equal margins on each side of the text creates an attractive presentation to a reader. The size of the margins you use in a letter will depend on the number of words in the letter. A person usually composes a letter starting with standard margins (1 or 1.25 inches on each side) and then adjusts the margins depending on the number of words in the letter. If the number of words does not fill the page, you can easily use the word processing software to change the margin. Most word processing packages have a fit-to-page feature that adjusts the text to the page. This feature is helpful if a document has only one line carried to another page. Word processing software also has a count feature, which counts the number of words in the document. By knowing the number of words in the letter, you can adjust the side margins to create an attractive letter.

The scale below shows appropriate margins based on words in the document.

Number of words	Left and right margins should each be
0–100	2 inches
101–200	1½ inches
201 and up	1 inch

Templates

Word processing packages have made document creation easier by offering a letter template feature. The letter template feature guides the writer through the creation of the letter and automatically formats the letter to a specific style. Several templates are available, providing styles intended to present a casual, formal, or professional appearance. After selecting a template, the user selects a letter part and keys in the letter-specific text. Word processing packages also include templates to assist the employee in preparing reports, memos, faxes, agendas, and other documents. Chapter 4 contains a discussion of faxes. While some offices use the templates that are standard in word processing software, other offices use templates specifically created for their company.

Letter and Punctuation Styles

If the writer does not use a computer template, a letter style must be selected. The letter style defines the letter placement on the page. There are two common letter styles, block style and modified block style. In the *block style* letter, all parts of a letter begin at the left margin. In the *modified block style*, you can place paragraphs at the left margin or indent the paragraph one-half inch. Also in the modified block style letter, the date and closing begin at the center of the paper. Since most stationary is 8.5 inches wide, the center of the page is 4.25 inches from the left margin. It may be necessary to reset a tab to properly begin the date and closing at the center point.

Letters written in either block style or modified block style may use open or mixed punctuation. The *open punctuation* style omits punctuation after the salutation and closing, while the *mixed punctuation style* includes a colon after the salutation and a comma after the closing. The use of open or mixed punctuation does not change the standard use of sentence punctuation.

Punctuation and language styles evolve in response to current usage. In written communications today, some writers use one space following a period at the end of a sentence, while other writers continue the traditional style of using two spaces following a period at the end of the sentence. People who use two spaces feel that two spaces separate the sentences visually and make the document easier to read.

Parts of a Letter

Most of the work in writing a letter concentrates on the text of the introduction, body, and conclusion. The entire letter, however, actually includes several additional parts. Some of these parts are required for all letters, while others are used only when there is a special need for them. An office employee must be familiar with the proper placement of each of these parts.

The chart below indicates the required and optional features of a letter. An explanation of each part follows the chart. Review the sample letter styles later in the chapter to see the placement of each part of the letter.

Parts of the Letter	Required	Optional
Return address		X
Date	X	
Special notation		X
Inside address	X	
Attention line		X
Salutation	X	
Subject line		X
Body	X	
Complimentary close	X	
Company name in closing		X
Writer's name	X	
Title of writer		X
Initials		X
Enclosure		X
Copy notation		X
Postscript		X

Return Address

If plain paper is used for the letter, a return address should be keyboarded as the first item on the page, approximately 1.5 inches from the top of the paper. For a short letter, the return address can be placed lower on the page to make the text appear almost centered from top to bottom. The *return address* includes the organization's name, street address, city, state, and ZIP Code. As previously explained, if letterhead stationery is used, the return address is not keyed in because the information is included in the letterhead.

Date

If plain paper is used for the letter, the date is placed on the line after the city, state, and ZIP Code of the return address. When using company preprinted letterhead stationery, place the date a couple of lines below the letterhead. Depending on the length of the letter, the date may be moved down a couple of lines on the paper to make the letter appear centered on the page and, therefore, more attractive.

Special Notations

Special notations regarding the mailing, such as "CERTIFIED MAIL," "REGISTERED MAIL," or special requests for the recipient, such as "HOLD FOR ARRIVAL" are placed a double-space below the date, at the left margin, and in all capital letters.

Inside Address

The *inside address* includes the name and full address of the person receiving the letter and is placed on the fourth line below the date. Further information about the two-letter state abbreviation and ZIP Code included in the full address can be found in Chapter 4.

Attention Line

An *attention line* is used when a letter is directed to a particular person at an organization. Keyboard the attention line as the second line of the inside address, and keyboard the envelope in the same style.

Professional Computer Services

Attention Ms. Valerie Biltmore

7800 West Fall Lane

Rochester, NY 46219

Ladies and Gentlemen:

Salutation

The salutation is the greeting to the letter. It usually includes the person's title and last name. It does not include the person's first name.
   Sample salutations

Dear Ms. Silver

Dear Dr. Patterson

Dear Rev. Harrison

If the letter recipient's name is unknown use the following:

Ladies and Gentlemen (Note that *Dear* is not included.)
Dear Sir or Madam

Subject Line

The *subject line*, which quickly explains the purpose of the letter, is keyboarded a double-space below the salutation. In a block style letter, it is keyboarded at the left margin. In a modified block style letter, the subject line may be placed at the left margin, indented, or centered. The subject line has increased in importance because people are busy and quickly glance at mail to determine whether they should read the entire document.

Body

The *body* of the letter is the main part of the letter and includes an introduction and conclusion. The lines of the body are single-spaced with a double-space between the paragraphs.

Complimentary Close, Company Name Writer's Name, and Title

The *complimentary close* includes a closing and the writer's name. It may also include the company name and writer's title. After keyboarding the complimentary close, press the Enter key four times (three blank lines) before keyboarding the writer's name. If the company name is used in the complimentary close, press the Enter key twice after the complimentary close, key in the company name in all capital letters, then press the Enter key four times, and key in the writer's name.

Sincerely,

Charles F. Wood

or

Very truly yours,

HARRIS & RUSSEL CORPORATION

Martha Wilson
Assistant Director

An employee may have the authority to sign a letter in the supervisor's absence. The two most frequently used methods of signing the supervisor's name are as follows:

Very truly yours,

Theodore L. Joseph/RS

Theodore L. Joseph
Assistant Director

The office employee signs the supervisor's name, Theodore L. Joseph, and then writes his or her initials. Another option is the following:

Very truly yours,

Rhonda B. Silver

Rhonda B. Silver
Assistant to Theodore L. Joseph

Initials

The *initials* of the person who keyed the document are placed at the left margin a double-space below the writer's name or title. If the writer's initials are used, they are keyboarded in all capital letters before the initials of the person who keyed the document. The initials are important because they identify who keyboarded the letter.

shc

LLR:shc   or   *LLR/shc*

Enclosure Notation

An *enclosure notation* is used if items are sent with a letter, and the enclosure notation is keyboarded at the left margin a double-space below the initials. There are several styles that may be used.

Enclosure

Enclosures (3)   (In this style, the number of items enclosed is shown)

Enclosures   (In this style, the specific items are listed)

   Report

   Check #3456

Copy Notation

A *copy notation* is used when a copy of the letter is sent to another person. The notation is keyboarded at the left margin a double-space below the initials. Copies are usually sent to keep everyone informed. If an enclosure is used, the copy notation is keyboarded a double-space below the enclosure. The following copy notations are used:

cc	Originally used to mean "carbon copy." Carbon paper is no longer used, but cc is still used by some people.
pc	Used for "photocopy."
c	Used for "copy."
bcc or bpc	Used for "blind carbon copy." or "blind photocopy," respectively; this notation is used when a copy of a letter is sent to someone without the knowledge of the addressee. To create a blind copy, print a separate version of the letter for the person receiving the blind copy and keyboard bcc at the bottom of the letter.

Examples of copy notations

- Copy sent to one person

  c   Katie J. Rosen

     or

  cc: Katie J. Rosen

- Photocopy sent to several persons

  pc   Mary D. Johnson

        Rodney H. Gibson

        Rhonda L. Hunter

If several copies are sent, a check mark may be placed beside the copy notation indicating to whom the copy is being sent.

  c   Kirk Kong ✓

  c   Deanna D. Liggett

  c   Jill R. Wood

If you are sending a copy of a document to a list of persons, alphabetize the names unless they are listed in order of importance to the company.

Postscript

A *postscript* is used to emphasize an idea. It is the last item keyboarded on the letter and is a double-space below the previous section. The postscript may be keyboarded at the left margin or indented to align with the paragraphs. Postscripts are normally used only in sales letters.

Postscript or P.S.	We hope to see you soon. We hope to see you soon

---

THE MARKETPLACE INC.
467 Meritor Drive
Cleveland, OH 45678-0923

May 19, XXXX

Ms. Valerie Jefferson
Linder & Peterson Limited
8009 Union Road
Suite 200
Joplin, MO 64801-1265

Dear Ms. Jefferson

Subject: Software Demonstration

Our sales representative, Joe Goldstein, will be in Joplin in the middle of June to demonstrate to you our new computer software. As we discussed at the Computer Expo in Kansas City, we have several new software application packages that will simplify your office management problems. The packages range from $1,250 to $5,000, and the updated versions will be available by the end of the summer. As part of each package, we provide reference materials and two days of training for your employees. In addition, our company is committed to working with each client to fulfill his or her individual needs, and our staff is available 24/7 to serve you. Mr. Goldstein will call you next week to arrange a convenient time to meet with you. We would like an opportunity to show you how our products can alleviate your office management concerns.

It was a pleasure meeting you and your staff in Kansas City, and I hope to see you at the Dallas Computer Expo in September.

Very truly yours

Ted J. Nicholas
Marketing Manager

skr

Figure 3-3 Block letter with open punctuation.

Two-Page Letter

The first page of a business letter is usually printed on letterhead stationery and is not numbered. Subsequent pages are printed on plain paper and use the same side and bottom margins as were used on the first page. The second page and all subsequent pages of all letters should include a heading. There are two styles that may be used for the heading, and they are created by using the header feature in a word processing package.

The following heading is keyboarded at the left margin.

Ms. Janie B. Gomez	(the person receiving the letter)
2	(page number)
September 1, XXXX	(date)

The second heading style begins at the left margin, the page number is centered, and the date is right justified.

Ms. Janie B. Gomez   2   September 1, 2008

INTEROFFICE MEMORANDA

An *interoffice memorandum (memo)* is correspondence to be delivered within the same company or organization, not mailed to a client or member of the public. An interoffice memorandum may be less formal than a letter, but the same writing rules of clarity, tone, and organization are applicable.

The tone of interoffice memos can vary from casual to very formal. Memos written to your coworkers can be written in an informal manner, while memos intended to be sent outside your immediate office or to company executives should use the same tone as a letter. When writing the memo, consider the recipient's personality, interests, likes, dislikes, and needs.

If bad news must be given, deliver it in person rather than in a memo. In addition, consider the implications of any memo that you write. A verbal comment may be forgotten, but the written word lasts forever.

Because memos are internal communications circulated within the office, they are often printed on non-letterhead blank stationery. Generally memos have one-inch side margins and may have a one-inch or two-inch top margin, depending on company preferences. In today's technology-driven office, an email with a memo attached is a quick and cost-effective method of distributing information.

While the specific format for a memo varies from office to office, the headings of interoffice memos include four basic items:

To:

From:

Date:

Subject:

When writing a memorandum, do not repeat the subject line in the first line of the memo because this information is already in the document. A memorandum should be concise, and many offices try to limit memos to one page if possible. After the body of the memo, the memo concludes with the same sections as letters regarding initials, enclosures, and copy notation. An alternative to keying in the memo format is to use a memorandum template from word processing software or a memo template created and customized by the business.

THE MARKETPLACE INC.
467 Meritor Drive
Cleveland, OH 45678-0923

May 19, XXXX

Ms. Valarie Jefferson
Linder & Peterson Limited
8009 Union Road
Suite 200
Joplin, MO 64801-1265

Dear Ms. Jefferson:

Subject: Software Demonstration

Our sales representative, Joe Goldstein, will be in Joplin in the middle of June to demonstrate to you our new computer software. As we discussed at the Computer Expo in Kansas City, we have several new software application packages that will simplify your office management problems. The packages range from $1,250 to $5,000, and the updated versions will be available by the end of the summer. As part of each package, we provide reference materials and two days of training for your employees. In addition, our company is committed to working with each client to fulfill his or her individual needs, and our staff is available 24/7 to serve you. Mr. Goldstein will call you next week to arrange a convenient time to meet with you. We would like an opportunity to show you how our products can alleviate your office management concerns.

It was a pleasure meeting you and your staff in Kansas City, and I hope to see you at the Dallas Computer Expo in September.

Very truly yours,

Ted J. Nicholas
Marketing Manager

skr

c Desi Perez

P.S. I know our software package can solve your application problem.

Figure 3-4 Modified block letter with mixed punctuation.

REPORTS

Writing a Report

Report writing is a common office activity. Reports may be directed to potential customers, stockholders, the general public, or senior management. Some reports are based on information generated by the business, such as describing a company project, presenting findings of a company research study, or reviewing the progress the business has made in meeting targeted goals. Information for reports about the company and its activities is usually found in the company's files. Other reports may be based on information from outside the company, such as preparation of background papers on an industry or information requested by a client. The process of researching and writing reports may be long and complex, and an office employee may be involved in this process at several stages. Today's office employee is often asked to write informal reports; briefing papers, which provide background information in a short summary format; and memo reports. These papers should have the same clarity, conciseness, and completeness as the writing techniques previously discussed.

Whatever your duties are in the preparation of reports, whether you are doing research or are keyboarding the report, you should be familiar with the process of writing a report. The process is the same if the information is gathered from within the company or from outside sources.

The first step in writing any report, after the subject is chosen, is to prepare an informal outline that helps organize your thoughts by listing the points you want to discuss. In the beginning of the project, you may not know what you want to discuss because you are not familiar enough with the topic. The outline should help identify those areas where additional information is required. Also, try to identify sources of information for the report. You should list people in your office whom you would contact in the search for information. If the report relates to company business activities, your supervisor should be able to help you identify the best sources for the information required.

The source of information for internal reports may be other employees or departments directly involved in the specific projects covered by the report. The larger the organization, the more difficult it may be to gather the relevant information required for a report. An office telephone directory and organization chart are useful when trying to locate the people who have the information required for a report. A good assistant is persistent in following leads from one office to another until the proper person is located. Do not be surprised if people are not eager to provide the information you require. Gathering information for your report may be seen as an interruption to another person's busy schedule. A polite but persistent approach may be needed—stressing how important the information requested will be to the report and to the ongoing business of the company.

Gathering information for internal reports based on the company's files can be easy if the files are available and other staff members are helpful. Researching information for reports from outside your company's files, however, may be a major task. The first thing you should do is try to identify people who already have some knowledge of the topic. They can be valuable resources in helping you identify other people you should contact or documents you should examine.

If you are unfamiliar with the subject, the Internet may be the first place you look for information. By typing in a keyword in an Internet search engine, you can find a vast amount of information. Because Web sites are frequently updated, it may be easier to obtain current information from them than from printed sources. While use of the Internet is quick, the question may be whether the information is relevant or even accurate. It is very important to use information only from reputable sources. Anyone can create a Web site and present inaccurate data. Always evaluate the credibility of the Web site you are using. Is the Web site sponsored by a reputable organization, or is it the work of a single individual? Is the Web site endorsed by credible rating organizations, or does it have links from other reputable Web sites? If you find a Web site

TO: Sid Bartow

FROM: Rose Henderson
           Director of Employee Relations

DATE: September 30, XXXX

SUBJECT: Physical Fitness Center Opening

Mr. Charlton will be out of town on October 15, and he has requested that we postpone the grand opening of our Employee Physical Fitness Center from October 15 to October 17. He also suggested that we include a demonstration of physical fitness techniques by the Senior Fitness group that meets at the Grace Community Center. Information about this group is enclosed.

I indicated to Mr. Charlton that we would review the plans for the grand opening by the close of business tomorrow and get back to him with our recommendation.

Please prepare a status report on the plans for the grand opening. We will meet in the conference room tomorrow at 2 P.M. to review what adjustments must be made to reschedule the grand opening to October 17.

jpg

Enclosure

c   Arnold Hardy
    Sally Moore

Figure 3-5   An interoffice memorandum.

that is helpful, mark it for future reference by using a Web browser's bookmark feature. The Internet and bookmarks are discussed in greater detail in Chapter 5.

There are many Internet search engines that will help you find information on a specific topic. Because search engines and information change rapidly, try several search engines when you are looking for information and bookmark those you find most useful. Shown below are sample Internet search engines, which you may find helpful. In addition, libraries have online book, newspaper, and magazine locator services that may help with the research.

www.askeeves.com
www.AltaVista.com
www.Google.com
www.HotBot.com
www.Northernlight.com
www.WebCrawler.com
www.Yahoo.com

If you are using information you found on the Internet, print out a copy of the Web page and keep it in your files for reference. It may be difficult to return to the same

Web page if you need to verify the information. Also, information on Web pages is often updated frequently and if you return to the Web site the next week, the information may have changed. By printing out the Web page, you document the source and accuracy of your research.

Do not rely solely on the Internet for research. There are many documents and reports that are not on the Internet, and there is so much on the Internet that it is often difficult to find relevant and accurate information. Do not overlook using books, magazines, newspapers, periodicals, pamphlets, statistical reports, research dictionaries, and other research materials in preparing a report. Information may be available from references located in your company's research library, or information may have to be sought from outside sources, including public libraries, governmental agencies, or other businesses.

After you have developed the outline and identified several information resources, you are ready to begin researching the topic. As you do the research, you should review your outline and revise it to reflect the new information you have found. You should develop your own method of organizing your research. Keep good records that include the name of the book or magazine, date of publication, author, publishing company, and pages used.

Instead of handwriting research information while away from the office, a notebook computer can be used to save time. Then the data can be transferred from the notebook to the office computer system.

Write the report from your notes using your outline as the guide. Where appropriate, use *footnotes*, which are references printed on the bottom of the same page as the quoted material. Footnotes cite sources of information or give credit for quotations or ideas gathered from documents researched. Word processing packages have removed the drudgery of keyboarding footnotes because software packages automatically place the footnote at the correct location on the page. Another way to simplify the keyboarding of footnotes is to place the references on a separate page at the end of the report and call them *endnotes*. When footnotes or endnotes are added or deleted, they are automatically renumbered by the word processing package. The completed report may be edited and revised several times to refine the copy and delete errors before it is finalized. As a precaution, create several backup copies of your files and store them at several locations. When the report is completed, it should be printed and distributed.

Reference Materials

You should have basic reference materials at your desk so you can quickly answer questions or look up information that may be needed in your office. Having these references will not only help you in your research, but will allow you to help others in the office and also demonstrate that you are a professional who anticipates the need for common reference materials. In your office, you should have books and/or Web site bookmarks for the following types of reference materials:

- Almanac.
- Atlas, North American, and World Atlas.
- Book of quotations (this is helpful when writing speeches, reports, newsletters, etc.).
- Computer reference books for the software packages you use.
- Computer software packages for ZIP Codes, addresses, telephone numbers, encyclopedias, and maps.
- Dictionary.
- Dictionary of misspelled words (this book lists words the way you think they should be spelled, not how they are spelled).
- Office reference manual with letter and memo formatting styles, grammar rules, and punctuation rules.
- National Five-Digit ZIP Code and Post Office Directory (USPS Publication 65).
- Specific references for your industry.
- Thesaurus.

Report Organization

The following format is often used in reports:

Summary	Most reports begin with a summary. The summary includes the recommendations or conclusions of the report and is helpful to a busy person who does not have the time to read the entire report.
Table of contents	The table of contents indicates where particular information is found in the report.
Introduction	The introduction explains what the report is about.
Body	The body develops the important topics in the report.
Conclusion	The conclusion reviews the important points and the recommendations of the report.
Bibliography	The bibliography lists references used in preparing the report.
Endnotes	The endnotes are references for direct quotes or the ideas of others and are placed at the back of the report. If these references are placed at the bottom of each page, they are referred to as footnotes.

HINT

Report organization: Summary, Table of Contents, Introduction, Body, Conclusion, Bibliography, Endnotes

Keyboarding Reports

The margins of the report will depend on whether the pages are to be loose (unbound), leftbound (as in a book), or topbound with a single staple. Guidelines for keyboarding reports follow.

Margins:
Unbound Manuscript Margins

Top margin	
Page 1	2 inch
Subsequent pages	1 inch
Side margins	1 inch
Bottom margins	1 inch

Leftbound Manuscript Margins

Top margin	
Page 1	2 inch
Subsequent pages	1 inch
Side margins	1.5 inch left and 1 inch right
Bottom margins	1 inch

If the pages are to be printed on both sides in a book, the side margins should alternate so that a 1½-inch margin is on the left side for odd-numbered pages and on the right side for even-numbered pages.

Topbound Manuscript Margins

Top margin	
Page 1	2.5 inch
Subsequent pages	1.5 inch
Side margins	1 inch
Bottom margins	1 inch

Begin all page numbering on page 2 of a report.

NEWS RELEASE

A *news release* is a written announcement that is given to the news media. News releases are often used to announce the promotion of an employee, election of officers, introduction of a new product, or the hiring of a new employee. Standard new release format is used to assist news editors in preparing a story for publication in a newspaper or for broadcast on the radio or television.

Requirements of a news release

1. Double-space the text.
2. Use two-inch side margins.
3. Include a suggested headline.
4. At the top of the page, indicate the date of the press release.
5. Place a notation at the top regarding whether the information is for immediate release or whether it must be held until a specific date and time for release. (If a press release is distributed before the date the information is to be made public, the words "embargoed until {date}" should be placed at the top.)
6. Include the name and telephone number of a person to contact for further information.
7. Keyboard the word *More* at the bottom of the page to indicate that the news release is continued on another page.
8. Keyboard "###" at the end of the news release.

Serobus Incorporated
3500 Executive Drive
Kingston, GA 31548
Telephone 912-555-8900
FAX 912-555-8901
Email Sero.ego.com

May 16, XXXX

Hold for Release: 10 A.M. May 21

Director of Marketing for Serobus Incorporated

Patricia Sanez has accepted the position of Director of Marketing for Serobus Incorporated. Her duties begin on June 1. Prior to her move, Ms. Sanez was Assistant Director of Marketing for Taylor Markets in Tacoma, Washington. Serobus Incorporated, which is located in suburban Mayfield, manufacturers door locks and hardware. Serobus Incorporated projects sales of $10 million for next year.

For further information, contact: Greg H. Castleman
Public Affairs Office
617-555-6666

Figure 3-6 A news release.

NEWSLETTERS

Many organizations prepare newsletters to distribute information to their employees, clients, or members of the public. There is no standard format for a newsletter, and newsletters can vary widely in their size, content, and frequency of publication. *Newsletters* are intended to be part of a series of publications that are presented in a similar format and distributed on a periodic basis, such as a weekly, monthly, or quarterly. A simple newsletter can be printed on one sheet of 8.5-inch by 11-inch paper and include information regarding a single topic. More complex newsletters may be printed on 11-inch by 17-inch paper, which is folded in half to result in four pages, each of which measures 8.5 inches by 11 inches. These newsletters usually contain several articles and may include photos, artwork, and other graphics. Simple newsletters may be prepared using word processing software and consist primarily of text, with perhaps the insertion of computer files of clip art or pictures. In addition, newsletters can be prepared using specialized publication software such as Microsoft Publisher, Adobe InDesign, or Quark XPress, where the emphasis is on graphic layout and formatting as well as text. Word processing and publication software contain many templates that can be modified by an office so the newsletter reflects the style and specific interests of the organization. Many newsletters are now being sent via email. These email newsletters may contain photos and graphics and resemble Web pages, or they may just be plain text.

EMAIL

Electronic mail (email) is an electronic system for sending and receiving messages. Using email, a business can send a short electronic message as well as large documents such as reports, graphics, pictures, spreadsheets, etc. Delivery is practically instantaneous and the cost does not depend on either the size of the documents sent or the distance between the sender and the recipient. Because email is quick and easy to use, it is now essential in today's business environment.

Email works between computers in the same office or between computers connected to the Internet that may be located anywhere in the world. With an electronic mail system, the receiving computer receives and automatically stores a message. To send an email, the sender directs a message to the email address of the recipient. Each employee or computer has an assigned email address. (A typical email address is in the form yourname@businessname.com.). The message is sent over the Internet and stored in the receiving computer. When the recipient returns to the office, the computer's email software must be checked for messages. Typical email software packages used by many businesses include Outlook and GroupWise. The messages can be read on the computer screen, printed, saved, or forwarded to another email address. A major advantage of electronic mail is that recipients can quickly respond to a message and return an answer to the sender. Email can also be used with mobile devices, including portable computers, cell phones, and Personal Digital Assistants.

The use of email can speed up business decisions because the turnaround time for electronic mail messages can be a matter of minutes, while the same message sent by traditional mail could take weeks. Because of its convenience, speed, and low cost, email has dramatically decreased the number of letters prepared by many businesses and the number of faxes sent over telephone lines. Faxes are discussed further in Chapter 5.

Since it is an easy and efficient method of communications, email is often used in offices to send short, informal messages. Email allows you to send a message to a person you do not know well, and would be uncomfortable approaching, as easily as sending a message to someone you do know well. Furthermore, email provides a comfort level that may not be felt in a person-to-person telephone call.

To ensure that the email message remains confidential, each user can be assigned an individual password that must be entered before the user can open his or her mailbox. When you use email, it is wise to change your password periodically to maintain security. Select a password that you can remember, but not a password that is easy for someone to guess. You should avoid using your name, birthday, address, etc., as passwords because they are easy to guess.

Email programs show a list of incoming messages. To read a message, select it. After reading the message, there are usually several options for further action—reply, forward, save, print, or delete. The recipient may select one or more of the options. Email programs have a Reply command that automatically addresses a return email to the person who sent it. Replies can be sent to one person or, by using the Reply All option, replies can be sent to an entire distribution list of all recipients of the original email. By using the email program's Forward feature, you can send the email you received to additional persons who would be interested in the message.

Although there are Web sites that provide email addresses, there are few printed email directories. Consequently, you should make your email address readily available. Email addresses can be included on letterheads, placed on business cards, included in the body of a letter, and given verbally. You should create your own directory of business associates' email addresses, which can be kept in a calendar software contact list, organization software, 3″ × 5″ card file, etc.

Using notebook computers, wireless handheld organizers, or cell phones, employees often retrieve email messages while out of the office. Some computer software programs can convert email into spoken words so users can dial into their office computers and listen to audio versions of their email by telephone. When sending emails that will be received by wireless handheld organizers, cell phones, or voice systems, the messages must be kept short because these technologies are not designed to handle long documents.

One of the problems with email is the large number of messages received each day. Much of this email is often referred to as spam, or junk email. *Spam* is email that is sent to thousands, even millions, of computers containing messages regarding get-rich-quick schemes, so-called wonderful opportunities, and other junk. An email user has to carefully manage the receipt of many emails, both legitimate business messages and spam. It is helpful to create email folders for saved emails. Some people like to create folders named for each month. Other people like to create folders with client or project names. In addition, there should be a *Pending* or *To Do* email folder. To manage the number of emails, it is important to quickly act on each email. There are three basic choices: respond, delete, or additional information required. If the email requires more time or information to respond to, move it to a Pending or To Do folder. Set specific times each day to respond to emails. Many people like to read emails as soon as they arrive at work, after lunch, and at the end of the day. In addition set a time to respond each day to emails in the Pending or To Do folder. If you do not set a time for the Pending or To Do emails, you may never respond to them. Spam emails should be moved to a separate folder that should be cleared or cleaned each day.

Because email is very time consuming, many executives do not read their own email. In some cases, the email is first screened by an assistant who may even respond to general emails. Emails that require the attention of the executive are printed or moved to a separate email account for later review by the executive.

The advent of email has promoted the electronic sharing of jokes, which can become overwhelming and time devouring. Save time by deleting jokes without reading them, but verify that you are actually deleting jokes, not important office communications.

Email messages may contain links to Web pages where additional information on a special subject may be available. Links are created in an email message by keying in an Internet address. The recipient can click on the Internet address and immediately view the Web page.

Older workers often like a more respectful workplace and expect email messages to follow the same conventions of grammar and punctuation skills that are used in letters. Emails sent without capitalized letters or punctuation, or those containing informal email abbreviations such as BTW for "by the way" do not reflect your professionalism and also reflect poorly on your business. Be aware of your office environment and use appropriate grammar and punctuation skills in all your emails.

Although employees think their email is private, it may not be. Companies have a legal right to monitor employee email to ensure that employees are using their time and company equipment appropriately. Learn your company's policy regarding use of company email and its policy on monitoring email. A supervisor who is reading the employee's email should be looking for violations of company policy, but some supervisors may be eager to satisfy their curiosity about the employee's personal business.

Do you know everything about email?

Email Guidelines

Composing and sending

- Always verify that you have correctly keyed the email address—even one incorrect letter could send the message to another person. If the message is received by the wrong person, it could be very embarrassing. Some companies use the first letter of a first name with the last name as the individual's email address; therefore, J. Rosen and L. Rosen could easily receive the other person's email if the address is incorrectly keyed.

- Use an appropriate subject line because the decision to read or delete email is often based on the subject line.
- Do not use all capital letters when composing a message. The message reads as though you are shouting.
- Begin your email with a friendly comment. This sets a courteous tone for the email.
- Email may take less time to create than a mailed letter or memo because email does not contain all of the parts of a letter or memo, but basic writing skills still apply.
- To save time with email, create a template with frequently used responses that can be quickly pasted into the email.
- Compose complex email messages using your word processing software to take advantage of the Save, Edit, etc., features. After the message is written, it can be copied into the email message or it can be included as an attachment to the email.

Replying

- Never send a nasty email because it may come back to haunt you. Remember that emails can be saved, printed, and forwarded to other people. Decide if your message should actually be sent.
- Respond quickly to email, generally within 24 hours.
- Some people spend a lot of time replying to emails to confirm their receipt of the original email. In order to save time, some individuals end the original email with "No reply needed."
- Do not use the Reply All or Copy features unless the recipients actually benefit from the email. Workers frequently complain about the amount of unnecessary and redundant email received.

Checking and receiving

- To avoid missing an important email message, check your email often.
- Use automatic replies when you are out-of-town. Most email software has an automatic reply feature that you can use to notify the sender that you will be away for a period of time.
- Email can be sent to one person or to a distribution list, which is an efficient method of sending the same email message to several persons simultaneously.
- Email can be sent at all hours. It does not interrupt like a telephone. Therefore, sending communications to a person in a foreign country or in another time zone is not restricted by your local time.
- When sending email internationally or to individuals from other nations who live in this country, be aware of cultural differences. Do not use slang because it may be misconstrued or may be considered a breach of etiquette. Be careful about emails that may be misunderstood and offend persons of other cultures.
- Instead of sending a printed memo to office employers, an email message with a memo attachment has become common.
- Email allows the sender to attach a file containing a letter, memo, report, graphic, or picture.
- If the computer is on, most email systems can be set to display a message or sound a beep so the user will know that a message has been received. The user can be working with any software package, not only email, when a message is displayed or a beep is heard.

Email safety

- Do not open questionable emails. If you do not know the sender or if the subject line is strange, it could contain a virus.
- Software developers have created email tools that automatically respond to customer questions by selecting an appropriate response and then sending a return email. If desired, the response can be routed automatically to an employee for verification prior to sending the email.
- Software is available that will generate email based on Web-transaction information. Companies use this type of email to market products and services to current or prospective clients. By personalizing email to target audiences, the customer response rate is increased.
- Under U.S. law (the Controlling the Assault of Non-Solicited Pornography and Marketing Act of 2003, also known as the CAN-SPAM Act of 2003), it is illegal to send commercial email that (1) uses a false address, header, or subject line to mislead the recipient regarding the subject of the email; (2) does not provide the recipient with the opportunity to request not to receive future emails from the sender; or (3) the recipient has indicated an objection to receiving.
- For security purposes, some offices use encryption software to protect its email. If your office computer offers encrypted email, use it when appropriate.

Symbols

- Because words cannot convey hand or facial gestures, symbols called *emoticons* are used to convey emotions. Emoticons are cute but should be used only sparingly in business communications.

Examples of emoticons

:)	smile
;)	wink
:-o	surprise
:-(	frown
<Grin>	grin
:-\	thinking

Situations That Should Not Be Communicated by Email

There are many times when it is better to talk with a person rather than send an email because some messages are too personal or too sensitive for email. There are often situations, such as during negotiations of contracts and discussion of personal issues, when the direct give-and-take of a voice conversation is vital. A conversation permits listening to the other person's tone of voice, which can help express his or her feelings. If it would be better not to have a written record of a communication, place a telephone call instead of sending an email.

Text Messaging

Many smartphones, cell phones, and handheld organizers have the ability to read email and send short text messages. With these devices, a person may be able to read a full email or view a Web page. However, these devices do not have full keyboards for composing long messages. They may have a virtual keyboard on a small touch-sensitive screen, a keyboard on which a person can type with his or her thumbs, or telephone keypad that can be used to compose text. Because of the slowness in keying messages on these devices, text messages sent by these devices usually are very short, often use abbreviations, and contain a minimum of punctuation. Despite this limitation, these devices are becoming increasingly popular for business communications. Because the devices are so small, many people always carry one of them in their pocket or purse.

CHAPTER REVIEW

1. What is meant by a conversational tone?
2. List six transitional words.
3. Explain how gender bias is avoided in writing.
4. Show one example of how an assistant would sign a letter for an executive.
5. When is an office memorandum used?
6. What are the requirements of a news release?
7. List two Internet search engines.
8. Explain why information obtained from a Web site should be carefully evaluated.

ACTIVITIES

1. Save twenty business letters. Analyze each letter and on a separate sheet of paper, indicate the good points and the bad points of each letter. Select the five worst letters and prepare a revision to correct or improve them. To maintain confidentiality, block out all names, addresses, and personal information.
2. Use a word processing template to create a letter. You supply the specific letter information.

WRITING ASSIGNMENTS

Supply any information needed to complete the letter assignments and write your response to each of the following situations.

1. Write an email congratulating a colleague on receiving a promotion.
2. Write a letter explaining that there is an incorrect charge of $50 to your account.
3. Write a letter to a well-known member of your community inviting the person to speak at a luncheon. Include all necessary information about the event.
4. Assume that you are the invited speaker in Writing Assignment 3. Write a letter and accept the invitation.
5. Assume that you are the invited speaker in Writing Assignment 3. Write an email and graciously decline the invitation.
6. You received a book order for *Working Keeps Me Happy*. The letter indicates that a check was enclosed, but it was not enclosed. Write a courteous letter stating that company policy will not permit shipping a book without receiving payment in advance.

7. Write a letter requesting the completion of a survey your company is sending to 300 businesses in your area to obtain information about the training opportunities offered to employees.

8. Order a subscription to *Working in the Modern Office* for yourself and three of your friends. Enclose a check for each subscription. (Include each person's name and address in your letter.)

9. Your employer stayed at the Miami Hotel the nights of December 6, 7, and 8. While reviewing the travel records, you noticed the following: your employer checked out on December 9 at 9 A.M., but the bill showed a room charge for December 9. Write a letter requesting a credit to the American Express card for the room charge of December 9.

10. Answer the following letters after reading the comments in the margins.

Dear Peter,

Write a letter indicating that I will attend

Our annual stockholders' meeting is scheduled for January 15 at 9 A.M. in the Mirror Room of the Charleston Hotel. The hotel is located at 8900 Cosmo Drive, so take the Cosmo Drive exit from Interstate 170.

I will need a reservation for Jan 14 & 15

After the meeting, the officers of the company will get together for lunch and a discussion of our next project.

We hope you can attend. Let me know what time you expect to arrive and if you plan to stay overnight. I will be glad to make a hotel reservation for you.

Dear Ms. Lighter:

Write a letter

I plan to be in Washington November 7, 8, 9, and 10 for the annual Broadcasters Convention. I will be staying a few additional days to meet with some colleagues. While I am in Washington, I would like to talk with you about the agenda for the next association meeting.

Ok meet in my office

Will you be available to meet with me on November 11 at 9 A.M.? We could meet either at your office or at the Association Building on 7th Street. Either location is fine with me.

Please let me know soon if this date and time are convenient for you.

PROJECTS

Project 5

Send this letter to Ms. Mary Carmel, Star Real Estate Services, 2207 Lee Lane, Roanoke, VA 22804. Use a block letter style. Make a file copy. Use an appropriate closing and sign the letter from yourself as Associate Director.

I have accepted a new and exciting position with Colony Industries, which has several branch offices in your area. By accepting the position, I have made the commitment to move to your region. Penny Carlton in the human resources department at Colony Industries suggested I contact you to begin the process of finding a new home in the Falls Heights area. She indicated that you have a terrific relocation service.

My wife and I have two children, ages nine and twelve, who will be attending schools in the area, so a home in a good school district is important to us.

We are interested in a house with at least four bedrooms, three baths, and a first-floor family room. We have a deck on our current home and would enjoy having either a screened porch or a deck on our new home.

Since I have already accepted my new position and am extremely busy, my wife, Patricia, will be managing the move. Please contact her at 415-555-1266 to arrange a time when we can view homes in the area.

We look forward to working with you.

Project 6

Send this memo to the staff and supply all necessary information. The memo is from Alice Garrison, Public Relations Director.

We need your help on a project to honor the 100th birthday of our company. Your help, creativity, and ideas are needed to make our birthday a wonderful celebration.

Put on your thinking caps and decide on a plan for our celebration. Send your suggestions to Walter Mason. Four checks of $25 each will be given to the employees with the best suggestions.

The deadline for suggestions is February 14, so start thinking.

HUMAN RELATIONS SKILL DEVELOPMENT

HR 3-1 Working with People of All Ages

While you may be most comfortable working with people your own age, in the typical office your coworkers will probably range in age from those who have just graduated to those reaching retirement. Your supervisor may be older or younger than you. If the supervisor is older than you, you may be reminded of your parents, or if the supervisor is younger than you, you may be reminded of your children. Some people have difficulty following the directives of a younger person. When you are in the office, disregard the age factor; remind yourself that the company is paying for the supervisor's expertise in the field, not for the supervisor's age. Above all, you must remember that as an employee you must adhere to the guidelines established by your supervisor.

- How are you going to handle the situation if your supervisor reminds you of your father or mother, and you do not get along with your parents?
- How are you going to create a good working relationship with a supervisor who is fifteen years younger than you are?
- How would you develop a good working relationship if you and your supervisor are the same age?
- How would you develop a good working relationship if your supervisor reminds you of your younger sister, and you think your sister is a brat?

HR 3-2 Money in the Office

Plan your budget so you always have money with you at the office. You may be asked to attend a last-minute luncheon with a client or another employee, or you may be asked to contribute to a collection for going-away party, a condolence gift, birthday gift, or wedding gift. The more employees in an office, the more frequently you may be asked to contribute to an office collection. You should control decisions about how you spend your money but be aware that office collections are a common occurrence. It is not prudent to have a reputation as a person who never gives to anything, but you may have to learn the knack of saying no without offending others in your office.

- How are you going to handle the situation if you are approached to contribute to the going-away gift for a member of another department?
- How are you going to handle the situation if you are approached to contribute to the baby gift for your supervisor's daughter?

- Recently you have encountered many business expenses for lunches, dinners, and gifts. You are now invited to another luncheon. What are your options and how are you going to handle the situation?

SITUATIONS

How would you handle each of the following situations?

- **S 3-1** You sent an envelope to Mrs. Rose and just discovered that your assistant did not include the letter. What action would you take?
- **S 3-2** A sales representative, who will be working with your office for a few weeks, annoys you by making snide remarks.
- **S 3-3** Your supervisor has asked you to talk to Joyce about her clothing. The supervisor feels that Joyce's skirts are too short and tight for an office. Plan your conversation with Joyce. Also, indicate the tone you would use in the conversation.

PUNCTUATION REVIEW

Punctuate each of the following sentences. For a review of punctuation rules, see the Appendix.

1. Ellen was the elevator working when you arrived today
2. After a closed door meeting the company announced that Ms Sheldon the president had resigned
3. The attorney entered a guilty plea and everyone went home to celebrate
4. The trade deficit fuel economy and bank failures were all discussed at the convention
5. The Dow Jones Average rose 5.8 percent therefore the stockholders were pleased
6. The Daniels Center which has its international headquarters in Denver was established on February 20 1974 to promote better public relations among worldwide companies understanding among cultures and cooperation among workers
7. Yes the report was hand delivered
8. The dues which all members pay allow us to fund our scholarship programs
9. As you mentioned the report was late
10. Our manager Mr Lander was sick yesterday
11. Is the photocopier broken again Ted asked
12. Julie said I always attend the department meetings
13. Under a Chapter 13 filing International Footwear will reorganize and reschedule debt payments to its creditors
14. The #5345 womens dress will be available in the following colors peach avocado mauve and lemon
15. Yes the meeting was held at the Coral Marina Resort on 9th Street

CD Assignments

CD Assignment 3-1

Open the file CD3-1_NR on your Student CD and follow the instructions to complete the job.

CD Assignment 3-2

Open the file CD3-2_NRJ on your Student CD and follow the instructions to complete the job.

CD Assignment 3-3

Open the file CD3-3_MG on your Student CD and follow the instructions to complete the job.

CD Assignment 3-4

Open the file CD3-4_EM on your Student CD and follow the instructions to complete the job.

CD Assignment 3-5

Open the file CD3-5_SH on your Student CD and follow the instructions to complete the job.

CD Assignment 3-6

Open the file CD3-6_PR1 on your Student CD and follow the instructions to complete the job.

CD Assignment 3-7

Open the file CD3-7_PR2 on your Student CD and follow the instructions to complete the job.

CHAPTER 4

....

Oral Communications

Objectives

After studying this chapter, you should be able to:

1. Use voice mail.
2. Speak on the telephone in a professional manner.
3. Make long-distance domestic and foreign telephone calls.
4. Understand the use of specialized telephone services.
5. Understand audio and video teleconferencing.
6. Understand techniques for delivering speeches.

BACKGROUND

All employees, regardless of the type or level of their position, need excellent oral communication skills. Each day you will speak with people whose knowledge of your company and projects vary greatly. Therefore, it is a mistake to assume that each listener always understands everything you say about your company and its projects. To improve communications, plan what you are going to say and speak distinctly. Good oral communications demand exactness and clarity. If the spoken word is not understood, there is no written reference to consult.

You may need to practice expressing yourself so others understand what you are saying. Before you speak, organize your thoughts so they flow in a logical sequence. When speaking, pronounce each word correctly, talk loudly enough to be heard, and pause to indicate the end of sentences or a transition to a new thought. While speaking, you must look for feedback from the listener in the form of facial expressions and body gestures. By observing the listener, you will learn how well your message is being received. You can then rephrase thoughts that were not clearly expressed or cite examples to clarify your ideas.

Semantics and perception are barriers to effective communications. Misunderstandings often occur because two people may hear the same words but interpret them differently. For example, a supervisor may ask you if you are going to return a telephone call soon. If you answer yes, the supervisor may interpret your statement to mean that the phone call will be returned within a few minutes, whereas you may have meant the next day.

> **HINT**
> Your communication style can influence your success.

HINT

Barriers to communications include semantics, perception, and withholding communications.

Another barrier to effective communications is the withholding of communications. One staff member may not tell other employees important information, thereby causing problems in the office. Information may not be communicated because of busy schedules, forgetfulness, or even a desire to withhold the information from others. Learn to recognize a breakdown in communications before it causes misunderstandings that will be difficult to resolve.

During the past decade, there have been major innovations in communications technology, and the future will bring additional communication changes to the office. This chapter will explain many communications technologies present in the workplace.

RECEIVING AND MAKING TELEPHONE CALLS

Answering the Telephone

Are you courteous on the telephone?

When you answer the telephone in your office, you are giving the caller an image of yourself and your company. If you speak with a pleasant voice, you create a courteous image of yourself and create goodwill for the company. However, if you are abrupt or rude, you present a poor impression of yourself and your company. We have all experienced rude people and are aware that impolite people often make us irritated, annoyed, and aggravated. Consequently, most people are reluctant to patronize a company if the employees are discourteous.

To portray the image of a helpful person:

- Speak clearly.
- Vary the tone of your voice.
- Speak directly into the telephone.
- Use a friendly, pleasant, and helpful voice.
- Use professional words, not slang.
- Speak slowly.
- Project a pleasant manner.
- Be courteous.
- Use the caller's name.
- Be alert; give the caller your full attention.
- Listen and respond to what the caller is saying.
- Talk naturally; use your own words.
- Project an enthusiastic personality.

Do you have excellent telephone skills?

MY SUCCESS STORY

My Name Is Penny

I am a typical recent high school graduate who went to college because her parents told her it was the next step in my life. After the first few weeks, I realized that I really wanted to go to college because I want a good-paying job. I know that at some point, I will have to support myself, and a good job is the answer. While attending college, I decided to get a part-time job to help pay my car expenses. That part-time job, combined with my education, gave me the knowledge and experience I needed to get an entry-level position with the government. I am now working in an interesting department that will be the launching pad for my career.

Figure 4-1   Employee having a telephone conversation with a client.

When you talk on the telephone, speak loudly enough so you can be heard, particularly if you normally speak softly. It is difficult to talk into the telephone mouthpiece and be heard if you have the telephone receiver wedged between your shoulder and your chin. People who frequently speak on the telephone use headsets, which free their hands for keyboarding or writing the information they are hearing. Never talk on the phone if you have food or gum in your mouth.

When answering the telephone, pronounce the name of the company and the name of the person whose phone you are answering so they can be understood. The way you answer the phone may depend on whether your office usually receives calls directly from the public or whether the calls are transferred from a central company operator. To provide better service to customers and avoid transferring of calls, many organizations distribute the phone numbers of individual departments and even of individual employees. An example of one common way to answer a phone received from the outside is to say the company name and individual office, for example, "Clifton and Lewis Corporation, Ms. Wood's office."

Many phones have displays that indicate whether a call is coming from an outside phone line or has been transferred from within the company. If you know that the call was transferred from another office in your company, you may say "Ms. Wood's office" or "Libby Wood's office." In some instances, you may wish to include your name, for example—"Ms. Wood's office, Penelope Rosen speaking." However, do not overwhelm the caller with a long speech such as "Good morning. This is the Clifton and Lewis Corporation, Ms. Libby Wood's office. I am Penelope Rosen. May I help you?"

If you must ask the caller to wait, speak so the caller hears you. Often people answer the phone, and slur "Please wait." If additional information is necessary or another telephone rings, say, "May I place this call on hold for a moment?" or "Please hold." As soon as possible, return to the caller and say, "I am sorry to have kept you waiting." Then talk with the caller. Do not keep the caller on hold for a long time. If you cannot quickly get back to a caller, ask for his or her phone number so you may return the call.

If you do not have voice mail and you must leave your desk (even for only a couple of minutes), you should ask someone to answer your telephone. An unanswered telephone does not promote goodwill for the company.

Figure 4-2   An employee taking a message.

You may screen telephone calls for your employer because the employer may be too busy to talk or may not wish to speak with a specific person. You must be very clever and skillful when screening calls. Some callers are offended when they know that their call is being screened. When screening a call, do not say, "Who is this?" Instead say, "May I ask who is calling?" or "May I tell Ms. Wood who is calling?"

Taking Messages

Taking messages is a very important aspect of office work. If the person being called is not available, ask if you can take a message or if the caller would like to have the person's voice mail. Unfortunately, many people do not know how to take messages. First, always have a pencil and paper available when the telephone rings. Do not say, "Wait—I have to get pencil and paper." Taking a message is a standard task when answering the phone so be prepared. Begin writing notes as the caller speaks. It is easier to write information as it is given rather than trying to remember a comment a few minutes later.

Immediately write the required information on a message pad. Some companies use a message pad that automatically prepares a copy of the message. If it is difficult to read your handwriting, write your notes on scrap paper and immediately rewrite the message on the message pad. As soon as the call is completed, deliver the message or place the message where the recipient will pick it up.

Today, messages may be recorded and distributed via computer systems, and many office email systems have templates designed to record telephone messages. These templates are electronic message forms and will help you record information regarding an incoming phone call. If you have primary responsibility for answering the phone and taking phone messages, you should have a phone messages form always open on your computer so you can enter the information directly in the computer. Distributing phone messages by email is quick and easy and provides a computerized record of the call.

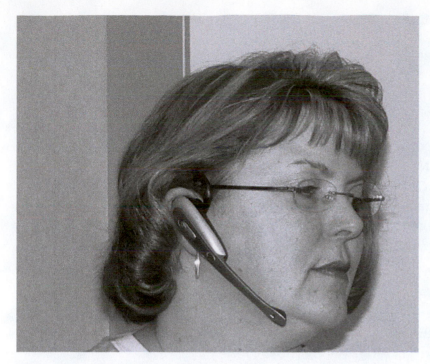

Figure 4-3   Employee using a telephone headset.

Telephone messages should include the following:

- Caller's name. Verify the spelling of the caller's name with the caller; you may also need to make a note about how to pronounce unusual names.
- Telephone number, including an area code and extension if applicable.
- Reason for the call.
- Indicate if the person receiving the call should return the call.
- Message, if any.
- Date of the call.
- Time of the call. The exact date and time can be very important.
- Name or initials of the person who took the call. This is needed if a question arises concerning the call. This information will be automatically entered if you are using a computer system.

Before ending the conversation, verify the telephone number and caller's name. For example, you might say, "Thank you, Mr. Bouquet, for calling. I would like to verify that your telephone number is 202-555-5555. I will ask Ms. Paddington to return your call as soon as possible." It is impossible to return a telephone call if the telephone number on the message form is incorrect. Not returning a telephone call creates a bad image of your office.

Each person who answers the telephone should have a copy of the corporate directory with employee names and telephone numbers. This eliminates the need to ask important officials of the company to spell their names and give you their telephone numbers.

In today's technology-driven world, companies save paper and printing costs by not providing printed company telephone directories. If your company's telephone contact list is available only via the computer, you may want to print telephone numbers for commonly call departments and place the information in your desk manual.

Messages

To   _____

Date   _____

Time   _____

Caller   _____

Company   _____

Telephone No.   _____

Return the Call   _____

Will Call Again   _____

Message Taken By   _____

Message

_____

_____

_____

Figure 4-4 Telephone message form.

Internal Telephone Calls

In some businesses, calls can be placed to company offices in the same building, an on-site building complex, or a company facility across town by dialing only the last four or five digits of the telephone number. Often a company needs quick communications between offices in distant cities. The company may use a dedicated private line service that links the offices. The employee accesses the private line by dialing a simple code, perhaps the number "8," and then dials the office in another city. Large companies with many offices can install their own internal phone system that connects with their local phone company. Some companies have established their own private telephone systems to connect offices in different cities by using satellite communications or leasing long-distance phone lines from commercial providers. In these situations, the company can call offices in different cities without using the regular public telephone system.

Personal Telephone Directory

Maintaining a personal telephone directory of your supervisor's and your frequently called numbers increases your efficiency and reduces the number of searches for unknown telephone numbers. There are several personal telephone directory options. Many office employees record phone numbers on a small card kept in a loose card file holder, often called a rotary card file holder. Business cards that you receive can be kept in a similar type of holder. Furthermore, computer calendar and organization software programs create address books or contact lists; some software automatically dials a number after clicking the name. In addition, cell phones and office telephones often have a memory capability for twenty to eighty frequently called numbers. If you do not have a telephone number for a person you need to call, there are many Internet sites that may be helpful.

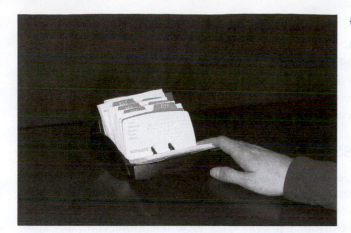
Figure 4-5   Card file holder.

Placing Telephone Calls

When you place a telephone call, first identify yourself by saying, "I am Katie Scott from American Systems." Then state with whom you would like to speak.

Before making a telephone call

- Verify the telephone number you are going to call.
- Plan what you are going to say. If necessary, prepare a short outline of the points to cover.

Figure 4-6   An employee assisting a customer.

Oral Communications   69

- Have reports and letters available for quick reference.
- If the call is long distance, determine the time at the location you are calling and decide if it is a reasonable time to place the call.
- Plan what action you would suggest if the caller is not available. Do you want to leave a message with an assistant, leave a voice-mail message, have the call returned, or speak with someone else?

Long-Distance Services

Long-distance telephone charges can be a major expense for a business. Businesses can select from several alternate long-distance phone companies and calling plans to reduce their long-distance phone charges.

After a business selects a long-distance provider, the local telephone company automatically sends long-distance calls to the appropriate long-distance company. Many local phone companies now also provide long-distance service. Each company providing long-distance service can call any telephone in the world using standard telephone numbers; people commonly make long-distance calls without ever thinking of the particular long-distance company being used.

Most of the major long-distance companies offer the same basic services, including long-distance telephone calls to foreign nations. However, if you use a long-distance company that is not your regular long-distance provider, it is important to know the special prefix code required to access the long-distance carrier.

Businesses that are heavy users of long-distance telephone service can seek specialized services tailored to their needs. WATS (Wide Area Telephone Service) service provides a business with dedicated lines for outgoing long-distance service at a flat hourly rate. Also, many businesses provide their customers with a toll-free incoming telephone service using an 800 area code. As the 800 area code has filled with more users, the phone system added 888, 877, and 866 as other toll-free area codes. As these area codes fill, the phone system will add additional area codes, such as 855, for toll-free incoming calling.

Some businesses have phone numbers that start with the 900 area code. Phone calls to the 900 area code are not free. Businesses with a 900 area code are selling information or providing a service. The caller usually must pay a charge that can range from a dollar to several dollars per minute. The per-minute charge is supposed to be disclosed at the beginning of the phone call, and typical charges for a call are sometimes disclosed in written material about the phone service. Use of 900 phone services should be done with care because the per-minute cost is charged even if the caller is on hold; therefore, the calls can quickly become expensive.

Calling Long Distance

Most long-distance calls are made by dialing the phone number directly. To make a long-distance call within the United States and Canada, a caller simply dials 1, the area code, and the telephone number. This is a total of eleven digits (e.g., 1-605-555-1212). In the United States if you do not know the number, you can obtain phone numbers by dialing 1, the area code, and 555-1212. You will be asked for the city and name of the party you are calling. Many telephone companies now charge a fee for locating a telephone number for you. Telephone numbers may be found at no charge by searching the Web.

If you would like the party you are calling to pay for your long-distance call, place a *collect call*. This type of call can be made by dialing 0, the area code, and the telephone number. After dialing the phone number, a telephone company operator will ask for your name. Then the operator will ask the party called if he or she will accept the charges from the caller.

Another type of call made through the operator is a person-to-person call. This type of call allows you to speak only with the specific person requested. If that person is not available, there will be no charge for the call. This type of call is very expensive, so many offices do not use it.

Changes in Area Codes

While most local telephone directories contain a list of selected cities and their area codes, they often are not complete and can quickly become out of date. As more people and offices add phone lines for computers, fax machines, and cell phones, area codes are running out of available phone numbers. As a result, many new area codes are being added each year. Sometimes a city will get a new area code or be split between two area codes. Occasionally, there will be two area codes serving the same city or region. New numbers for telephones, faxes, and cell phones in a region may be assigned to the new area code, which means that two people on the same street could have phone numbers with different area codes.

You should be aware that the phone number of an organization can have a new area code, even if the organization has not moved and still has the same street address. Sometimes, the first information you receive about an area code change is when you try to complete a phone call and receive a message that the area code has changed or the phone is not in service. If this happens, call telephone information at the old area code by dialing the old area code plus 555-1212, and verify the area code and phone number. If you find that an area code has changed, change all phone lists and any programmed fax machines, computer dialers, or phone dialers. Area codes can be found on the Internet.

Time Zones

Before making any long-distance calls, determine the time of the place you are calling. The mainland United States is divided into four time zones: Eastern, Central, Mountain, and Pacific. Most of the state of Alaska is in the Alaska time zone, which is 1 hour earlier than the Pacific time zone, while Hawaii and the Aleutian Islands of Alaska are in a time zone two hours earlier than the Pacific time zone. Therefore, when it is 9 A.M. in New York City (in the Eastern time zone), it is 6 A.M. in Los Angeles (Pacific time zone) and 4 A.M. in Honolulu (Hawaii-Aleutian time zone). Canada includes the same four time zones as the mainland United States, plus the Atlantic time zone for the Maritime Provinces, which is an hour later than the Eastern time zone. The United States territories in the Caribbean, Puerto Rico, and the Virgin Islands are also in the Atlantic time zone. The time zone of the Canadian provinces of Newfoundland and Labrador are a half-hour later than the Atlantic time zone. Most telephone books include a map of the time zones in the United States and Canada.

> **HINT**
> U.S. time zones: Eastern, Central, Mountain, and Pacific.

The section of your local telephone book dealing with foreign telephone calls often includes information about the time difference between a foreign country and standard time. Standard time is usually the time zone for the area represented by the telephone book. In a New York City telephone book, for example, France is indicated as "+6 hours" from Eastern Standard Time (9 A.M. in New York City is 3 P.M. in Paris). Japan is "+14 hours," so when it is 9 A.M. in New York City, it is 11 P.M. in Tokyo. Many countries move their clocks an hour forward in the summer for Daylight Saving Time. Most of the United States observes Daylight Saving Time from the second Sunday in March to the first Sunday in November. In Europe, summer time changes are from the last Sunday in March to the last Sunday in October.

Many communities located at the edge of a time zone may actually follow the time of the neighboring time zone, or they may not follow Daylight Savings Time with the rest of their time zone. If an hour or two time difference is critical for reaching your

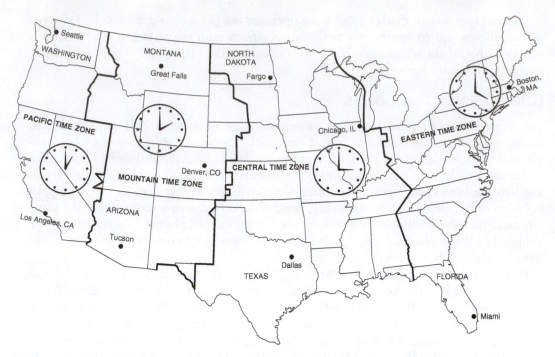

Figure 4-7   United States time zone map (not including Alaska and Hawaii).

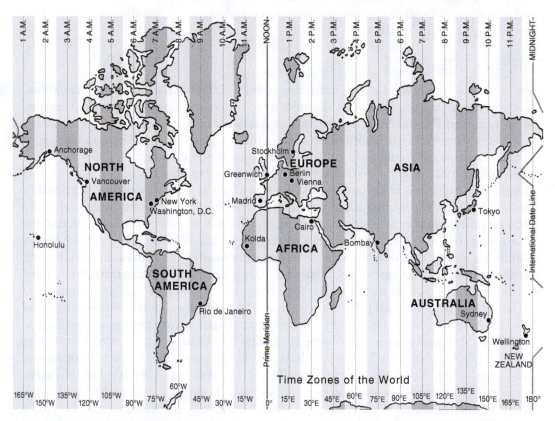

Figure 4-8   Worldwide time zone map.

party and you are unsure of the time of the area you are calling, dial the telephone operator and ask for the time in the city you are calling. Also, you can check the current time in hundreds of cities throughout the world on the Internet. Start by typing "time in [name of city]" in a search engine.

San Francisco   Chicago   New York   London   Tokyo

6 A.M.   8 A.M.   9 A.M.   2 P.M.   11 P.M.

Figure 4-9   If it is 9 A.M in New York, what time is it in Chicago, San Francisco, London, and Tokyo?

Calling International Long Distance

Making a call to some foreign countries can be as easy as making a domestic long-distance call. Long-distance calls among the United States (including Hawaii and Alaska), Canada, and many islands of the Caribbean are dialed the same as domestic long-distance calls; "1" + area code + phone number.

Many foreign countries can be dialed directly. Foreign long distance is usually accessed by first dialing "011" (instead of "1" for domestic long distance). Then a two- or three-digit International Access Code, called a country code, must be dialed. Some countries then use a city code or long-distance code (one, two, or three digits) before the local phone number. For example, calls to Mexico City must use a country code of "52" and a long-distance code of "55" before the eight-digit local telephone number is dialed. Local phone numbers vary in different countries. In the United States and Canada, all phone numbers are in the format 555-1212.

Lists of country and city codes of foreign nations that can be directly dialed are often included in the front sections of telephone books. Most foreign countries can be dialed directly. If an International Access Code for a country is not listed in the front of your city's telephone directory, contact the telephone operator and ask if the nation can be dialed directly. Also check the Internet for lists of countries that can be dialed directly; type "country code [name of country]" in one of the Internet search engines. If the country cannot be dialed directly, then the operator must place the call. A long-distance operator-assisted foreign call may involve your local operator contacting several international operators to establish a circuit to the country you are calling. Completing an operator-assisted foreign call to a country without direct dialing access can be time-consuming so you should plan extra time to complete a telephone call of this type.

Long-distance calls to each foreign country are a little different because the local phone systems are so different. It will be helpful for you to keep a file of foreign long-distance calls made, which includes the local telephone number, a complete set of the access codes required, the time difference from your city, and any special problems

Date of Call   _____

Telephone Number Called   _____

Person Called   _____

Name of Company   _____

Reason for Call   _____

Name of Caller   _____

Telephone Number of Caller   _____

Figure 4-10   Long-distance record.

encountered in making the call. If your foreign long-distance call does not go through, check the Internet to see if the country has changed its international calling system. Because of the time zone differences or the amount of time required to make some international calls, international messages are often sent via fax and email if real-time two-way voice conversation is not required.

Some offices request that a record be made of all long-distance calls. This record is used to verify phone charges that appear on the company phone bill.

Calling Card and Phone Card Calls

When you are out of the office, you can make long-distance telephone calls using either a calling card or a prepaid phone card. A calling card works like a credit card for telephone calls. If your office has established a credit plan with its long-distance company, you will receive a calling card and a Personal Identification Number (PIN). You can then make a long-distance call by calling the long-distance company on a toll-free number, entering the PIN, and then dialing the number you want to call. The phone charge will be included on the office's regular monthly phone bill. Calling card plans can also be established with your home long-distance provider so you can easily make personal long-distance calls while traveling.

Many companies sell prepaid phone cards that allow a person to purchase a fixed number of long-distance minutes. With a prepaid phone card, you purchase a card for a fixed cost such as $5, $10, or $20. Each phone card has a unique authorization number. Using a phone card, you make a long-distance call the same way that you do with a calling card. You can make a long-distance call from any telephone by calling a toll-free number, entering the authorization number, and then dialing the number you want to call. The cost of the call is then subtracted from your account balance. Phone cards can be purchased at many grocery stores, gas stations, and other convenience stores, as well as through the Internet. Calling cards and phone cards are available for international as well as domestic long-distance calls. Calling cards used to call the United States from foreign counties require additional access codes. If your supervisor is traveling outside North America, confirm that arrangements have been made for both business and personal calls back to the United States.

USING VOICE MAIL

One of the difficulties of using the telephone is the difficulty of reaching people at the exact moment they are in their office. Voice mail is a telecommunications technology used to overcome this limitation by storing a caller's voice on a sophisticated telephone answering system for later playback. Most offices have a central voice-mail answering system that serves an entire office instead of having an answering machine for each telephone. A voice-mail system does not require the caller to use any special equipment because the caller is simply dialing a phone extension. If the person being called does not answer, the caller is asked to leave a message, which is recorded on the voice-mail system. The receiving party uses a regular touch-tone telephone to open a private voice mailbox assigned to that person. The mailbox is opened by keying in an individual access code to ensure privacy and then the recorded message is played. After listening to a voice-mail message, the message can be deleted, forwarded to another office extension, stored in an archive for future replay, or replied to by dialing an office extension if the message was sent from within the office phone system. Voice-mail messages can also be retrieved from a home or cell phone. To check messages while outside the office, the employee calls the office's central voice-mail phone number and enters his or her access code. The user then has the ability to use the features of the voice-mail system.

When you call someone, always be prepared to leave a voice-mail message if he or she is not there.

When leaving a voice-mail message:
- Never chew food or gum.
- Speak slowly and distinctly.
- Organize your thoughts before you leave the message.
- Leave your name and telephone number. Your voice may not be recognizable to the recipient, and your call cannot be returned if your telephone number is unclear.
- Leave a short concise message; do not ramble.
- Indicate why you are calling.
- Indicate when you will be in the office to receive the return telephone call.
- If you leave a long message, repeat your telephone number again at the end of the message.

> Did you leave an understandable voice-mail message?

Setting up your voice mail
- Your office will instruct you how to set up your voice mailbox and record your greeting, which is the message a caller will hear if you are out of the office or on another line. Some voice-mail systems identify the mailbox for the caller by using a standard greeting and insert the name and voice of the person being called.
- When recording your voice-mail greeting, sound professional and enthusiastic. Do not make a cute or humorous voice-mail greeting.
- Keep your voice-mail greeting brief. People do not want to listen to a long greeting before leaving their own message.
- If you are going to be out of the office for more than a day, change your voice-mail greeting so the caller will be able to contact another employee for assistance in your absence.
- Select a personal access code that is easy to remember and easy to enter on a telephone keypad. Do not use an access code that is simple for others to guess, such as your birthday.

Listening to Your Voice Mail

Most voice-mail systems alert you that a message is waiting either by displaying a lighted button on the phone or by generating a distinctive sound when you pick up the telephone rather than the usual steady dial tone. You should check your voice mail early each morning in case you received messages after you left the office the previous evening, and check your voice mail throughout the day. It is possible to receive a voice-mail message while you are talking on the phone with another caller. When you return to your office after a short absence, check your voice-mail for messages and frequently check for messages left while you were on the telephone.

Since most offices have voice-mail systems, listening to your voice-mail messages will be a habitual task. It is common to receive fifteen or more voice-mail messages each day, so it may be helpful to develop a form to record the voice-mail messages you receive. The form should include the name and phone number of the caller, the date and time of the message, and information about the call or expected action. At a later date, your records will be available to document that the call was received, that you have taken the requested action, or to retrieve a telephone number.

Date	Time	Caller	Company	Telephone No.	Message	Returned Call

Figure 4-11   Voice-mail form.

Telephone Ethics

Personal telephone calls should not be made from an office telephone. However, it is difficult to avoid all personal telephone calls during office hours. Personal calls should be kept short and limited to those that are essential. Some offices have stated policies regarding making and receiving personal telephone calls on business phones or personal cell phones. Ask what the company policy is and adhere to it without exception.

Office telephones should not be used for personal long-distance calls. Occasionally companies will make their long-distance service available to employees for personal use. Be sure of company policy before using the company's long-distance service. Do not simply assume that the company allows employees to use the long-distance service because other coworkers make personal long-distance calls from the office.

SPECIALIZED AUDIO SERVICES AND EQUIPMENT

Specialized Telephone Services

In addition to the standard telephone service, many specialized services now provide efficient voice communications for the office. The list on the next page is not exhaustive and phone companies continually design new services to offer to their customers.

Figure 4-12   Office telephone, telephone headset, and speakerphone.

Be sure you understand which specialized phone services are available on your office phone system and how to access them.

- *Automatic Callback* can be used when a call is made to a phone that is in use. When the phone is free, the system automatically redials the number and notifies the caller.

- *Call Block* sends incoming telephone calls to a recorded message indicating that the call will not be accepted.

- *Call Forwarding* allows calls to be forwarded from one telephone to another. All calls from an unattended telephone can be forwarded to a telephone that is attended.

- *Call Return* automatically dials the number of the last incoming call.

- *Call Waiting* allows a single-line telephone to handle two telephone calls when the phone is in use. A beep signals that an incoming call is waiting. This feature allows the first call to be interrupted while the second call is answered. It is then possible to return to the first call.

- *Caller ID* displays the caller's telephone number.

- *Different Rings*. Internal calls (calls from within the same company) and external calls (calls from outside the company) can be distinguished by the type of ring heard when a phone call is received.

- *Holding*. To place a call on hold, depress the hold button. Calls may be placed on hold while another call is being answered or while information is being found. Telephone receivers should not simply be left open and placed on the desk because the caller can hear office background noises and conversations.

- *Multiline Telephone* has more than one telephone line. If a line is being used, the telephone displays a steady light. A flashing light indicates that a line is ringing.

- *Preferred Call Forwarding* permits calls from specific telephone numbers to be forwarded.

- *Repeat Number*. Repeating the last number dialed can be done by depressing one key on the telephone.

- *Speed Dialing*. Numbers that are frequently called can be coded so that they can be dialed quickly using one or two digits.

- *Transferring*. It is often possible to transfer a call from one to extension another within the same company by dialing the last four digits of the extension.

Most large offices have established internal telephone systems that provide direct telephone numbers for each extension and include many of the specialized services noted above.

Voice over Internet Protocol (VoIP) Telephones

The integration of digital technology and the Internet with voice communications has expanded the services available on the office telephone. Phone service using VoIP technology is available for the modern office. VoIP phones operate very much like standard telephones, but the voice message is converted into a computerized sound file and processed using Internet protocol procedures.

Because VoIP telephones are digital, they can store and display information about a phone call. VoIP phones usually have a display screen that can display the length of time of a phone call, a list of all calls made, a list of calls received, and a list of calls

> **HINT**
>
> With VoIP, the voice message is converted into a computerized sound file and processed using Internet protocol procedures.

missed. The phone can store a personal telephone directory, and selecting an entry can automatically dial the phone call. The VoIP phone makes and receives calls the same way a standard phone operates, and can include features such as voice-mail and call forwarding. An office can have VoIP telephones that use the digital features internally but are still connected to the usual public switched telephone system to complete the calls. The use of VoIP technology is transparent to both the caller and the person called.

If a business implements a full VoIP system, long-distance calls using the Internet are almost free because the Internet does not charge for the amount of voice or data sent or the distance between sender and receiver. There are even VoIP systems that support phone calls by plugging a special telephone directly into a computer and then using the Internet to carry the long-distance call. The cost to call foreign countries can be much cheaper than conventional long-distance telephoning.

Cell Phones

Are you aware of cell phone etiquette?

Cell phones are small, wireless phones that permit a person to call and receive telephone calls while away from the office. For the busy office worker, cell phones have become a standard means of communication. People commonly use cell phones while in the car, on the street, in homes, and in offices. Cell phones weigh less than a pound and can fit into a pocket or purse. Most metropolitan areas and many rural areas of North America are served by cell phone services. Cell phone service is also available in many areas of Europe, Asia, and South America. A cell phone operates like a traditional telephone with its own telephone number and can receive calls like any other telephone.

Modern cell phones use digital technologies, which permit the storing of personal phone directories in the cell phone, review of phone calls sent, and review of calls received or missed. Cell phones come with many features including caller ID and voice mail. Cell phone technology has rapidly changed, and many cell phones can send and receive emails. Cell phones can be used to connect to the Internet and read Web pages or connect to a fax machine to send written messages. Cell phones can also be used to send or receive music, pictures, and even short video clips. Cell phones are being built into many small handheld organizers and Personal Digital Assistants (PDAs) which are discussed in Chapter 6. These enhanced cell phones are sometimes called *smartphones* because of the many features they contain.

As the technology has advanced, cell phones, smartphones, and even handheld organizers now come with the ability to view the Web and receive email, which increases their usefulness for businesses and their employees. In addition to taking pictures with built-in cameras, many cell phones can play music and video. These small cameras have become a security concern and businesses, manufacturing facilities, and government offices may prohibit bringing cell phones and handheld organizers with cameras into restricted areas. Additionally, people are also concerned about the presence of cell phones with cameras in areas of personal privacy, such as bathrooms and health club showers.

HINT

Carry in your brief case or car a cell phone charger with a car outlet adaptor.

One of the reasons that cell phone service has expanded so widely is the lowering of prices through the use of flat-rate pricing. For a single monthly fee, the cell phone user receives a set amount of cell phone minutes with an extra charge for additional minutes.

Many cell phone plans include free night and weekend service or a family service plan that offers several phones for a specific price. Most cell phone services provide long-distance calling at no extra charge if the phone number called is within the service area of the cell phone company.

The cell telephones that are used in the United States usually do not work overseas, which can be a problem for international business travelers who are accustomed to

Figure 4-13 Using a cell phone.

using cell phone technology. There are literally dozens of different cellular telephone standards used around the world, and a cell phone that works in Athens, Georgia, may not work in Athens, Greece, or the country of Georgia in Eastern Europe. Companies now sell and rent cell phone systems that allow the international business traveler to communicate overseas. In addition, many airports contain shops where arriving travelers can rent local cell phone service.

If you speak on a cell phone, respect others by keeping your voice low enough not to disturb others. A low voice also enhances the privacy of the conversation.

Satellite Phones

There are several limitations to traditional cell phones. While cell phone service is very convenient and is available in most areas of the United States, there are still regions of the country where cell phone service is not available. There are vast areas of the world, such as the oceans, that have no cell phone service at all. Persons traveling outside North America or even within the United States and Canada may find that the local cell phone service, when available, does not work with their cell phone because of incompatible technology. In the event of natural disasters, such as hurricanes, cell phones may not work because the electricity that powers cell phone switching equipment may be disrupted. During times or in places where people have the greatest need for telephone communications, such as in remote areas or during emergency situations, cell phone service may not be available.

Satellite telephones have been developed to provide a single, reliable telephone service from anywhere in the world to anywhere else in the world. A satellite telephone is very similar to a cell phone, except that it uses communications satellites orbiting hundreds of miles above the earth as a relay in the phone system. A satellite phone is portable and can be the size of a cordless phone, so it can be placed in a briefcase or carried in a pocket. Placing or receiving a call on a satellite phone is the same as using a cell phone. Some satellite phones also work as cell phones and will try to use the local cell phone service before accessing the satellite service. Satellite phone service is more expensive than cell phone service but is a way for a busy executive to stay in touch when regular phone or cell phone service does not exist or is unreliable. Satellite phones can be purchased or rented.

Airline Telephones

While normal cell phones cannot be used on airplanes for safety reasons, airline telephone service is available while flying in commercial airplanes over the United States and on international flights to Europe or Asia. In some airplanes, the telephones are located at the individual seat, while other airlines have several phones located in the passenger cabins. The service is operated by the use of a major credit card. To operate the phone, insert the credit card, remove the handset, and place a call. When the handset is returned, the call is charged to the credit card and the credit card is then released. Use of airline telephones is expensive and should be used only when the cost is justified. The Federal Communications Commission has recently approved rules that will allow airlines to offer high-speed Internet service over the radio frequencies currently used by these seatback phones.

Paging Equipment

A *beeper*, a paging device, is a small receiver that can be carried on the person and beeps to alert the individual that a message has been received. Beepers or pagers can also notify the recipient of a message by lighting up or by vibrating. A telephone number or short message is displayed, and then the person paged makes contact with the caller by using a regular telephone. Some paging equipment can record a voice message. Paging services cost much less than cell phone services and are usually used where people have relatively easy access to a telephone to contact the person sending the message. Some pagers have the ability to provide two-way communications. These pagers have small keyboards and allow users to send and receive text messages and faxes as well as access email and the Internet. While the use of paging equipment has decreased as the use of cell phones has grown, paging equipment can often be received inside buildings that block cell phone calls. Paging equipment remains an important communications device for many people.

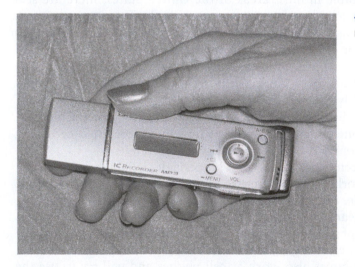

Figure 4-14   Digital voice recorder.

Digital Voice Recorders

A digital voice recorder is another telecommunications tool to assist the busy employee both in and out of the office. Most digital voice recorders are small, lightweight, and easy to use; have reasonable sound quality; and include software for transfer from the recorder to the computer and folder organization systems. Despite the small size of digital voice recorders, they can hold over fifty hours of voice recordings. Messages are dictated into the digital voice recorder and are stored digitally. The voice can be transcribed later or transferred to a computer file. Messages can be saved, edited, or emailed, thus increasing office productivity.

TELECONFERENCING

A teleconference is a meeting where one or more of the participants attends through the use of audio or video equipment, rather than physically being in the same room with the other participants. A teleconference can be conducted quickly and inexpensively using a speakerphone or more elaborately using complex multisite video teleconference equipment. A participant who teleconferences to a meeting saves the time and money of travel to the meeting site. Teleconferences can be successful or can fail depending on premeeting planning and the willingness of the participants to include the distant attendees in the group.

HINT

Teleconference: A meeting where the participants are not in the same room but use audio or video equipment to communicate.

Audio Conferencing
Speakerphones

A *speakerphone* is a piece of equipment—a telephone that has a loudspeaker and a microphone so several people can participate in a phone conversation. A speakerphone can also be used without the speakerphone feature activated for regular private telephone conversations.

A person may also use a speakerphone during a normal phone call when it would be inconvenient or tiring to hold a telephone handset. Speakerphones are often used when a person is on a lengthy audio conference call, which may last an hour or more. Speakerphones are also useful if you need to get out of your chair or use both hands for other activities during the call.

If you do not have a private office, you should be considerate of other people in your office area when using a speakerphone. When the loudspeaker is turned on, other people in the office will be able to hear both ends of the conversation. You should not interfere with the privacy of others in your office by using a speakerphone, and you should also recognize that your phone conversation will not be private. Therefore, it is common courtesy to ask your caller if you may put him or her on a speakerphone so he or she is aware that the call is not private. Because the other caller is being heard over a loudspeaker, it is wise to close your door, even if you have a private office, so people in the halls or the next office do not overhear your conversation.

Speakerphone features are included in many desktop phones and cell phones, and separate speakerphone attachments are available so the loudspeaker and microphone can be placed in the middle of a table during a group meeting. A call from a speakerphone is placed as a regular phone call, and then the speakerphone feature is turned on. Using a speakerphone is a simple method of bringing people at two locations together for a telephone meeting.

HINT

Speakerphone is a telephone that has a loudspeaker.

Conference Calls

A conference call is a telephone meeting that usually involves participants in more than two locations. Regular phones are used in conference calls, and some desktop telephones have the ability to set up a conference call among several participants. Conference calls with a large number of participants may need to be set up with a telephone company operator in advance of making the call. At the time the arrangements are made, the employee notifies the operator of the time of the call, as well as names, locations, and telephone numbers of people participating in the call. The meeting participants are provided a telephone number with an access code. Internal telephone systems in many businesses are equipped with conference call capabilities that allow employees to place their own conference calls. Directions for using these systems are usually found in an office telephone manual. There are also private companies that provide conference calling without the need for a telephone operator to set up the conference.

Tips for using speaker phones and participating in conference calls

- Identify yourself the first few times you speak so other participants know who is talking.
- When you speak, face the microphone.
- Remember that the people listening cannot see you. Your words should convey your message because you cannot use verbal cues or gestures to support your statements.
- Do not interrupt another speaker.
- Do not make a private comment to another person in your room; it could be overheard.
- Use your telephone mute button when you are not talking to reduce background noise during the conference call.
- Do not use your telephone hold button during the conference call if your phone system plays music for calls on hold.
- Prepare for the conference call as you would for any other meeting. Prior to the conference call, distribute a list of participants and an agenda.
- When the telephone conference is over, thank the person who arranged the call.

Video Teleconferencing

Video teleconferencing is usually more expensive than audio teleconferencing but allows the participants to see as well as speak with each other. Often one-way video teleconferencing is used where the main speaker is seen by the participants, and the participants can respond to the speaker via voice-only telephone. Most video conferencing does not have the look or video quality of a regular television broadcast because broadcast quality video requires expensive equipment and staff. Some companies have established their own full-time high-end video teleconferencing facilities; in many large cities, businesses that provide video conferencing services have been established for the occasional user of this service. High-end video conferencing systems may include several cameras and the ability to add other audio and graphics to a presentation.

Video conferencing signals can also be sent using fiber-optic lines or telephone lines, either on the Internet or using dedicated video lines. Midlevel video conferencing equipment usually integrates cameras and a television monitor. The camera is often fixed to view the entire room; sometimes it can be controlled by remote control from the other video conference site. In some systems, both ends of the video conference must have similar equipment that operates on the same software. Using this equipment, video conferencing can be used by businesses on a routine basis. Business with remote offices may place midlevel video conferencing equipment in a designated conference room and then hold all of their video conferences from those rooms. Starting a video conference can be as easy as making a telephone call. In addition to business meetings, video conferencing is now being used for staff training, answering customer questions, and solving technical problems.

With advances in computer technology and the increasing availability of broadband, video conferencing is also available on a desktop computer connected to the Internet. Using a small camera clipped to a computer monitor and inexpensive software, the costs of establishing a video conference among several sites is now within reach of many offices. However, a desktop system may have only a fixed camera that will show only the face of a person sitting in front of a computer.

The quality of the video conference picture can vary with the sophistication of the equipment/software used and the speed of the video line or Internet access. The quality of video conferencing can range from a series of still pictures (*called freeze frame*) occupying part of the computer screen, to *slow scan video* (a slow-motion picture), to a *full motion video* picture that fills the computer monitor screen. If several sites are involved in the video conference, they may each be seen in a box occupying a portion of the screen. By using video conferencing over the Internet, small businesses can conduct meetings across the country while saving the time and cost of staff travel.

How you dress for a video conference is very important. Avoid wearing bold patterns—they look busy on the screen. Also, a solid white or black dress or jacket is not a good choice. Blue and gray are reasonable color choices because they do not blend into the background but also do not stand out and attract too much attention. It is also important to remember that your personal habits will be transmitted for everyone to see. Therefore, do not twirl your hair, stick your finger in your ear, continually scratch your nose, or so on. Eye contact with the audience makes you appear credible and friendly. If you continually look at the computer screen, you will appear like a stiff head. If you are making a formal presentation on a video conference, you may want to have a dress rehearsal to practice your presentation. If you do not have equipment to practice with, rehearse in front of friends or a mirror. Remember, you do not want to embarrass yourself or your employer.

SPEAKING BEFORE A GROUP

As you advance up the career ladder, you may be asked to speak in front of a group. Oral presentations are often given to members of the department, supervisors, or members of the board of directors at the conclusion of a project. In addition, community groups may request that you address their organizations. Being comfortable speaking in front of a group is an asset to your career advancement. Each speech should be designed to meet the specific needs of the audience. The research techniques used when collecting data for a written report are also used when preparing an oral report or speech. When developing the speech, ask yourself what are the goals and interests of the audience. Then prepare your thoughts to meet the needs of the audience.

Speech preparation
- Determine your objectives and know your topic well.
- Organize your thoughts with an outline.
- Remember that members of the audience have their own interests. Explain how your ideas will benefit them.

- Include the fundamental points in your speech but do not overwhelm the audience with too many facts. If you desire, you can distribute a handout with additional information.
- Do not memorize your speech. Prepare notes on index cards or prepare a sheet of keyboarded notes. List specific words or phrases you want to use. If you know your topic well, your notes should be a guide to keep your thoughts organized.
- Do not express your biases or prejudices.
- Do not use ethnic jokes that may offend someone.
- Under some circumstances, the complete speech may be written. It is easier to read a keyboarded double- or triple-spaced speech printed in larger than normal type than reading a handwritten speech. Do not appear to read the speech. Look at your audience and occasionally glance at the printed page.
- Regardless of the type of notes you use—PowerPoint slides, notes created in a word processing package, handwritten hints, or index cards—always number them. It can be very embarrassing to drop the notes and lose your place in your presentation.
- Practice delivering the speech to your family or in front of a mirror.

Personal suggestions
- Bring breath mints so your breath will be fresh when you talk with the attendees before and after your presentation.
- Bring a notepad so you will be able to make notes when you talk with the attendees.
- Bring your business cards to distribute after the speech. Always bring plenty of business cards because it is embarrassing to run out of cards.
- To avoid a rush to the bathroom during or right after your speech, do not eat or drink too much prior to the speech.
- Have a bottle of water in case your throat becomes dry and throat mints in case you start coughing. Sometimes water is provided, but it is better to bring your own in case it is not provided. Keep the top on the water bottle to avoid spills.
- Bring a wristwatch with a large face that glows in limited light so you can easily see the time. Seeing the time will allow you to speed up or slow down your presentation when necessary.
- Being a little nervous before you speak is good because it engages you in the project, raises your involvement level, and gives you extra energy to help you give a great performance.
- Because you do not want people to look at your clothing instead of listening to you, wear conservative clothing. Wear clothes you are comfortable in because a tight skirt or slacks may become more uncomfortable as you speak. Also consider the room temperature when selecting an outfit. A jacket or sweater that may be easily removed may solve the room temperature problem. Since you are going to be standing before, during, and after your speech, comfortable shoes are essential. If a woman is seated on a platform, a short skirt can cause awkwardness and embarrassment.
- Women need to consider where to put a purse with its valuables during the presentation and afterward when many people may come to the podium with questions or personal comments. Options include hiding it under the podium, asking a trusted person to watch it, or leaving the purse in the car and putting your car keys and personal identification in a pocket.

During the speech

- When the occasion requires your thanking the organization for inviting you, begin your speech by expressing your pleasure at receiving the invitation.
- Remember that the first words that come out of your mouth set the stage for your entire presentation. Make the opening comments attention-getting and important. A good icebreaker will help your audience respond favorably to you. Begin each speech with an attention-getter, which can be a joke, anecdote, question, or quotation.
- Do not talk to your audience in a condescending manner. The audience members may tune you out if they feel you are patronizing them.
- Stand so you can be seen and heard. Do not slouch. Do not rock back and forth.
- Be enthusiastic.
- Smile.
- Appear interested in your audience and in the topic of your speech.
- Pause between major divisions of the speech. This will allow the audience to better understand your topic.
- Speak clearly and distinctly.
- Move your head so that you view the entire audience.
- Appear to look people in the eye. If gazing directly at people disturbs you, appear to look at them but look slightly over their heads.
- Use props to explain your ideas. An image can save a thousand words. For example, if you are making a speech selling sound-reduction panels, bring music and raise and lower the volume to demonstrate the sound reduction.
- If you are speaking with a partner, coordinate your speech in advance. Confirm that both of you are in agreement on the topic and politics involved in the topic. It is counterproductive to have one partner disagree or argue with the other. Also, decide in advance the roles of each presenter. Who will speak first? Who will distribute materials? Who will make the introductions? Who will summarize? Speaking with a partner can be a fun and rewarding experience or it can be a nightmare.

Handouts and equipment

- If you will distribute a handout, decide whether you will distribute the handout before or after the speech. If handouts are distributed prior to the speech, the audience will be able to write notes on them. However, if they are distributed before the speech, people may read them during your speech and not listen to you, or they may leave before the speech is completed.
- If you are going to use handouts, make them easy to read and attractive. Use an appropriate font. If you have a professional presentation, a casual, cutesy font may not be appropriate. Do not decrease the margin size so you "stuff" more text on the page. If the text is too crowded, no one will read it. Leave blank space for the eye to rest. If you have funds in your budget, print the handout in color or use colored paper as an attention getter.
- Use charts, large transparencies, flipcharts, white boards, or computer presentation software to illustrate the speech.
- If you are using computer or projection equipment that is provided by the organization, arrive early and verify that it works. If you are bringing your own computer equipment, confirm that you know how to hook it up so it works. Speakers often become nervous and forget how to plug everything into the correct outlets. Also have available an extra electrical strip plug.

- Do not turn off all the lights in the room. People need some light to take notes. A dark room encourages people to daydream or doze—especially after eating.

Questions, summary, and evaluation

- Always ask for questions (Q&A session) at the end of the speech. If no one has questions and you still have time, you should have a list of additional thoughts to discuss or questions you can ask the audience.
- Some speakers like to provide a fun incentive to persons asking questions by giving a small gift such as a candy bar or a T-shirt.
- If you do not understand a question, say, "I would like to answer your question, but I am a little confused. Please ask your question again." Notice you did not say, "You did not ask a good question." You said, "I did not understand the question."
- Sometimes it is easier for the speaker not to be interrupted by questions that can move the presentation in another direction. If you take questions during the speech, you may not have sufficient time to deliver the entire speech. If you do not want to be interrupted during the presentation, distribute question sheets so the audience can jot down their questions during the presentation and not forget the question. At the end of the presentation, ask for questions or collect the question sheets. The question sheets can be created attractively using a word processing or desktop publishing software package, can include a border and clip art, and can be printed in color or on colored paper. The question sheet can include your email address or Web page so participants can contact you after the presentation.
- Always use a summary sheet, which is distributed at the end of the presentation. In addition, use preprepared flipcharts to summarize points that you have made.
- If you are going to ask your audience to complete a presentation evaluation sheet, create a short and easy-to-complete form. If you want a truthful response, do not ask for the person's name or identifying information. Indicate that you are seeking constructive feedback. Remember that at the end of a presentation, participants are anxious to leave, so keep the evaluation short and allow time to complete it. If you take presentation time to have your audience complete an evaluation, read the evaluations and make appropriate modifications to your next presentation.

Figure 4-15   A flipchart.

Visual Aids for a Presentation

Visual aids enhance a presentation in several ways. People remember more from a picture than they do when they listen to a speech. Visual aids reinforce the oral message, create a mental image that is easy to remember, and create additional interest in the oral presentation. Pictures, displays, and charts add variety and therefore simulate the listener's involvement in the presentation. To enhance the effectiveness of your speech, use some of the visual aids discussed below.

Boards

Many conference rooms have a large whiteboard or other colored board mounted on the wall that can be written on during the presentation using a special marker. Writing can be erased with a special eraser so only a few words or thoughts can be shown at any one time.

Easels and Flipcharts

Easels and flipcharts hold pads of large sheets of paper. Visuals on the pages can be prepared before the meeting or they can be written on the pages during the presentation. The pieces of paper can be flipped over or torn off the pad and placed on the wall so several can be viewed during the presentation.

Transparencies

Transparencies are sheets of clear plastic that can be prepared prior to a presentation or written on during it. Transparencies must be used with an overhead projector. A speaker can use colored transparency sheets to add visual variety to the presentation. Transparencies can be mounted in hinged Vugraph frames to permit the overlay of several transparencies in a sequence to create a complex visual. Transparency markers are available in a range of colors and allow the speaker to write directly on the transparency plastic. It is difficult for the audience to read transparencies that are exact copies of keyboarded pages because the print is too small. However, many photocopiers have the ability to enlarge text. In addition, word processing software packages easily enlarge the font size of keyboarded text to improve legibility when used to print text on a plastic transparency.

Computer Presentations

To enhance presentations, many speakers use computer software packages. Computer software packages permit the creation of a presentation that includes graphics, charts, sound, clip art, and animation to capture the attention of the audience members and retain their interest. Presentation software must be used with a computer and video projector to project visual material onto a screen for audience viewing. Additionally, the use of miniature computers and PDAs that are equipped with presentation software offer presentations capabilities for the on-the-go business executive. While the audience views the presentation, the speaker explains and reinforces the important discussion points. Computer software presentation packages have become an indispensable business tool used by many speakers. One of the most popular computer presentation software packages is Microsoft PowerPoint. Because of their flexibility and ease of preparation, computer presentations have generally replaced the use of plastic transparencies in presentations.

Slides

Slides can include photographs or other graphic material and must be prepared well before the meeting. Slides must be shown in a predetermined sequence using a slide projector, and slides cannot be altered during the presentation. Because most photographic material is now taken with digital cameras and can be adjusted with computer software, the use of slides in presentations has decreased.

CHAPTER REVIEW

1. Explain how internal telephone systems operate.
2. Explain VoIP.
3. Describe the appropriate voice techniques to be used when answering the telephone.
4. What information should be included in telephone messages?
5. Explain how a speakerphone is used.
6. List two hints for a teleconference.
7. List three hints for a successful speech.
8. Describe visual aids that can be used when speaking to a group.

ACTIVITIES

1. Find a telephone partner for role playing. One person will be the caller and the other will be the administrative assistant answering the telephone. In the first role-playing activity, the administrative assistant will be pleasant when the caller requests an appointment. In the second role-playing activity, the administrative assistant will be rude and bored. Notice how the rude administrative assistant causes the caller to become angry and upset. After the two role-playing activities, reverse the caller and administrative assistant roles and role play the calls again.
2. Using a computer software package, prepare a personal telephone directory listing all friends and businesses that you call frequently.
3. Visit an office supply store and look at the types of message pads available. Write a paragraph describing each pad and noting the differences. Be sure to note the prices of pads available. You may use the Internet to research this activity.
4. Keep a record for two days of all of the telephone calls that are received in your home. Indicate which calls are personal business and which are business.
5. Create a message form for home telephone calls. Record all telephone calls received during a twenty-four-hour period.
6. Ask an administrative assistant to describe three difficult types of telephone calls that are often received. Explain how the calls are handled.
7. Using a tape recorder, prepare a recording of your voice. Speak in a conversational tone. Listen to the tape and analyze your voice. Is it too high-pitched? Does it sound whiny? Is it difficult to understand? Do you speak in an enthusiastic and friendly manner? What changes should you make in your voice?
8. Using the Internet, find business telephone numbers for two businesses in your area.
9. Using the Internet, find telephone numbers of two relatives or friends who live in other states.

PROJECTS

Project 7

Key in the letter to Ms. Mollie C. Hayes, 818 Oakmont Drive, Seattle, WA 98028. Use a modified block letter style and provide any additional information needed to complete the letter. The letter is from J. C. Murray.

Dear Mollie:

I do not know if you have heard the news. At last month's Board of Directors meeting, I announced my intention to retire in about a year. The Board appeared surprised about my announcement, but I have been thinking of retiring for a long time. As you know, I would like to spend more time with my family.

You have several potential candidates for my position in your department, and I hope that you will encourage them to apply for the job. When we met at the Houston convention, we discussed possible employment opportunities with my company. As you know, the company is on the high-tech track and is in a good position to develop and launch a new program. The Director of Personnel is anxious to receive your applications.

I hope you and your family are well. Please give them my regards.

Project 8

Send this memo to the staff. It is from Nicole J. Nelson.

Please join me in welcoming Ms. Laura Berkeley as our new Communications Director. Ms. Berkeley will be arriving next week, and she is very excited about the opportunities and challenges facing her at our company.

Ms. Berkeley, who received both her undergraduate and graduate degrees in Communications from Michigan State University, comes to us from Northeast Communications, Inc. Ms. Berkeley is highly respected in the communications field and will be a fine addition to our company.

A reception will be held in her honor on Friday from 2 to 4 P.M. in the Board of Directors Conference Room.

I look forward to seeing you at the reception. Ms. Berkeley is anxious to begin her work here, so take this opportunity to welcome her and offer her your support.

HUMAN RELATIONS SKILL DEVELOPMENT

HR 4-1 Praise

Most people enjoy receiving praise for a job completed satisfactorily. Unfortunately, some managers do not give praise often enough, and some do not give praise at all. Praise increases job satisfaction and demonstrates that the company knows how valuable the employee is.

- What do you say to an employer who praises you for a job well done?
- How can you encourage your employer to reward the staff with positive comments when a job has been completed?
- In your role as supervisor, what would you say to an employee who stayed late to complete an important last-minute report?
- What would you say to praise your employer?

HR 4-2 Prejudice

Do not allow your personal prejudice to influence your work in the office. Here are some examples of unfounded prejudices: Have you always thought that people with certain hair color are rude? Do you think that people who wear unusual or flashy clothing are not professional? Do you think that people who are heavy (or slender) are not as smart as others? Do you have a dislike for people who have unusual accents? Do you dislike persons who have a particular personality trait? Everyone with whom you work should receive your respect and courtesy. Treat every colleague as a professional, and expect to receive the same treatment in return.

- What are your personal biases?
- How are you going to control or overcome your biases?
- Have you demonstrated a negative reaction to a person because of a personality trait? What was the trait?

SITUATIONS

How would you handle the following situations?

- **S 4-1** Your supervisor asked you to arrange a conference call for tomorrow morning. You set the call for 8 A.M. because your supervisor, who works in Washington, D.C., always arrives at work at 7:30. The participants are in New York, Chicago, Dallas, and San Diego. What did you do wrong?
- **S 4-2** This is the third time that you have not received a telephone message. What are you going to say to your assistant?
- **S 4-3** You have difficulty obtaining your supervisor's attention. The last time you approached your supervisor with a question, she continued to work and told you to make your comments quickly.

PUNCTUATION REVIEW

Punctuate each of the following sentences. For a review of punctuation rules, see the Appendix.

1. Due to a recent increase in the cost of materials we must adjust our prices by 3 percent for each unit
2. Mollie who is the manager frequently took the train because it was more convenient
3. Katie also registered for the lecture
4. I need the following items audiotapes videotapes and transparency markers
5. Through a new computerized reservation system that was shown yesterday by Travelers Incorporated business travelers will be able to get information from their travel agents about hotel chains such as Hyatt Marriott and Sheraton
6. For office managers this certificate can serve as a valuable tool for performance evaluations which are the keys to advancement
7. Janie the computer was moved to the new building
8. However Nelson Wagner Jr noted that the action signaled new confidence in the industry

9. Jack asked did interest rates rise

10. Under the new legislation a tax credit was given to students under the age of twenty five and those earning less than the minimum poverty level wage

11. The stock market had a net gain of 29.34 points but my stock price declined

12. The planned merger of ATEX and METRA which should occur in January is the brainstorm of three individuals Janice Helfstein Olga Rocher and Phillip Francis

13. Since office rents are high in the East they moved the company headquarters to the Midwest

14. Most people prefer to be close to their offices but housing downtown is very expensive

15. Alicia changed the filing system therefore the efficiency of the office was increased

CD ASSIGNMENTS

CD Assignment 4-1

Open the file **CD4-1_ISP** on your Student CD and follow the instructions to complete the job.

CD Assignment 4-2

Open the file **CD4-2_ID** on your Student CD and follow the instructions to complete the job.

CHAPTER 5

Processing the Mail

Objectives

After studying this chapter, you should be able to:

1. Process and sort incoming mail.
2. Prepare a mail register of incoming mail.
3. Prepare a chronological register of incoming mail for a traveling executive.
4. List the services offered by the United States Postal Service (USPS).
5. Explain the classes of mail offered by the United States Postal Service.
6. Explain franked and penalty mail.
7. Evaluate express mail services.
8. Recognize the two-letter abbreviations for the United States and the Canadian provinces.
9. Explain the use of ZIP Codes.
10. Explain the use of postage machines.

PROCESSING INCOMING MAIL

Mail Delivery

While the use of email and facsimile (faxes) has increased dramatically in recent years, one of the most important responsibilities of an administrative assistant continues to be the processing of incoming mail. In a small company, the mail is delivered to the office once a day by a United States Postal Service (USPS) carrier. In a large business, the mail may first be delivered to a company's central mailroom, where it will be sorted by building, department, or floor before it is distributed to individual offices. Depending on the volume of mail and the size of the company, deliveries may be made more than once a day. While the central mailroom relieves the administrative assistant of some of the routine duties of processing the mail, the presence of a central mailroom also means that an additional step has been added to the mail-sorting process. This extra step may mean delays of half a day or more in both sending and receiving the mail. In response to current world tension concerns, government agencies and some business scan mail for explosives or dangerous substances. This scanning process further delays the timely delivery of mail to each office. Since traditional mail delivered is slower than mail transmitted electronically, traditional mail is sometimes referred to by its slang term: *snail mail*.

When the mail is received, it should be opened and the letter or document inside stamped with the date of receipt. The stamping, which may indicate the time and date of receipt, can be done by hand with a rubber stamp or by a machine. Documenting the date of receipt is critical for many businesses. While most mail is opened by the administrative assistant, company policy may permit mail addressed to specific individuals or mail designated "personal" to be distributed unopened.

Sorting and Distributing the Mail

After the mail is opened and stamped for receipt, it should be prepared for distribution to the proper recipient. Often, action is taken on the mail by the administrative assistant before the mail is forwarded to other employees. Receipt of the item might be entered into a computer log, a tracking number may be assigned, or data entry may be made of the action requested or to whom the mail is directed.

Depending on the size and layout of the office, the mail should first be sorted according to department, floor, section, office, or similar division. The mail should then be sorted for each person within an office. It is usually the administrative assistant's responsibility to sort general mail addressed to the office so that it is forwarded to the proper employees. In many offices, mail is often addressed to the office head, while actually intended for other office staff. The administrative assistant must know how to distribute the mail efficiently so that the proper person quickly receives it. For example, all payments may be forwarded to one person, all invoices to another, and correspondence regarding a specific project may be directed to the person responsible for that project. You should keep a list at your desk of how office projects are assigned to aid in the sorting of mail.

Regular mail and interoffice mail are usually placed in individual mailboxes, often stacked trays, which are in a central location. Express mail and mail for top

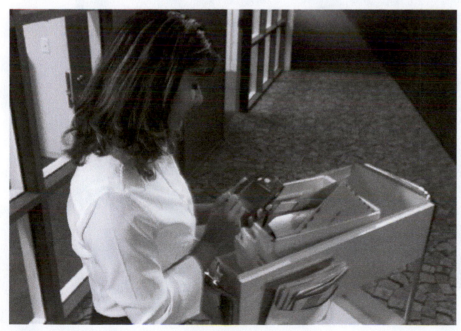

Figure 5-1   Mail delivery. Courtesy of Pitney Bowes.

executives may be taken directly to their offices. Depending on the volume of mail and the procedures of the office, individual mail may also be sorted according to urgency of the item.

Individual mail may be sorted into the following categories:

- Certified and Registered mail
- Overnight deliveries (USPS Express Mail, FedEx, DHL, UPS)
- First-class and personal mail
- Newspapers, magazines, advertising materials, and catalogs
- Packages

In some offices if the supervisor is out of town, a *mail register*, which is a chronological list of all mail received, may be prepared. This list enables the returning executive to quickly review all mail received.

Coding the Mail

After receiving the mail, some people code or write notes in the margins indicating what is to be done with the letter. Examples of these notes are, "file," "find file folder," "answer this letter," "talk with (another person) about the letter," "what do you think of this suggestion?" etc. Color coding can be used to indicate the processing procedure. For example, a blue check mark may mean "file," a red check mark may mean "hold for response," and a yellow check mark may mean "handle for me."

Rubber stamps can also be used to speed the coding process. A small form containing the codes used most often can be stamped on the mail, permitting the recipient to check the code appropriate for the item. To speed the processing of the mail even more, a single rubber or machine stamp with the date of receipt and coding may be used. Many people code mail by writing on sticky notes and attaching the notes to the letters.

Figure 5-2 Manager coding the mail.

May 17, XXXX

Ms. Susan Churchill
8934 Jefferson Blvd.
Indianapolis, IN 46260

Dear Ms. Churchill:

I have carefully read the report of your last trip on the South Pacific, and I am impressed with your findings.

I do need clarification of a few points.

1. What is the projected cost to refurbish the lobby of the Island Hotel?

Check the file 2. How long do you anticipate the renovation will take? *3 months*

3. Would you recommend (Polynesian Construction, Inc.,) or R. N. Woo Construction Company?

4. Do you recommend refurbishing the (entire) hotel at one time or refurbishing over a period of years?

As we discussed at our last teleconference, I am eager to begin this project. I would appreciate receiving your responses as soon as possible.

Sincerely,

B. W. Biltman   *write a response for my signature*

B. W. Biltman

rty

Figure 5-3 A coded letter.

After a manager codes the mail, an administrative assistant completes the action required. In some offices, an administrative assistant opens the letter, reads it, and prepares the necessary response. The letter is then filed in the appropriate file. A copy of the letter with a note indicating the action taken is given to the manager so the manager can monitor the action or make revisions before the letter is mailed.

MY SUCCESS STORY

My Name Is Felicia

To pay my college expenses, I worked at a local department store. There were days I hated the job, but it paid for books and tuition. As time went on, I met the store manager, who took an interest in me. I guess you could call him my mentor. He watched out for me, answered my questions, and really guided me. When an opening for an entry-level management position opened, he encouraged me to apply. I was nervous, but I applied for the job. I am happy to tell you that today, I have a terrific job as a manager in the corporate office. I am thankful that someone took an interest in me and helped me. When I have more experience in a few years, I plan to return the favor and mentor another young student.

FAXES

A facsimile machine (usually called a *fax machine*) is a standard piece of equipment in most offices, and it is used to send photo images of reports, letters, graphics, etc., over a telephone line. A photocell or laser scans a page and converts an image, text, or graphic into an electronic signal. Information in the document does not need to be keyed again into a computer, so time is saved and the accuracy of the transmission is assured. Graphics, hand written materials, and copies of original signatures can be transmitted as easily as typed or printed material. A document, converted into electronic signals, is sent to a receiving fax machine. When the document is received, a copy is printed. Some machines send the signals to a computer instead of a fax machine, and the document is stored on a disk. Unless the receiving machine has a computer attached, only the hard copy is available when received—nothing is saved on tape or disk.

Most fax machines conform to international standards and can send a document to a foreign country at the cost of a telephone call. Fax machines connected to their own telephone line can answer the telephone automatically and receive the information transmitted. Using fax machines can, therefore, be very useful in sending information during normal business hours in North America to a foreign country where the local time could be the middle of the night.

The advantages of using fax machines, therefore, are similar to that of email. Fax machines are especially useful when you need to send an exact copy of a document including signatures, handwritten notes, letterheads, date stamps, etc. Faxes are also used when you do not have an electronic version of the document. If you have a document in hand, it is often easier to fax it than to search for the electronic file and email it. You may also want to fax documents with many graphics, which may be slow to send via email.

Sending Faxes

Fax machines contain their own telephone keypad, so sending a fax is the same as making a telephone call. When sending a fax, carefully key in the telephone number of the receiving fax machine. If the fax is sent to an incorrect phone number, it will probably be thrown in the trash, and the sender will be unaware that it was not received. Many fax machines print a transmission log that contains the phone number to which the fax was sent. Check the number on the transmission log to be sure that the fax was sent to the right number. It is also a good idea to keep a copy of the transmission log to document that the fax was sent and that the transmission was completed. Some fax machines even print the first page of the fax on the transmission log as additional documentation that the correct fax was sent, along with the date, time, and receiving phone number. In addition, various fax machines automatically print monthly reports of faxes sent and received, and companies keep these fax records as part of their office documents.

When using a fax machine, remember that anyone at the receiving end can read the document. Obviously, confidential material should be faxed with care. Some fax machines have mailboxes that store documents until a personal code access code is entered. If the document you are faxing is urgent or contains sensitive information, it is wise to notify the receiver that a fax is coming.

Frequently a cover sheet is used when a document is faxed. The cover sheet helps in the delivery of the fax at the receiving end and may also give the recipient background information about the document faxed. Review the sample fax cover sheet shown in Figure 5-4. Companies often create their own cover sheet or use the cover sheet templates which are included with word processing software packages.

HINT
Fax sends exact copies of reports, letters, graphics, etc., over a telephone line.

Figure 5-4 Fax cover sheet.

L & J Corporation
14 Lee Street
Washington, DC 20023
Fax 202-488-9000
Phone 202-488-9001

FAX

To: _____

Company: _____

Fax No. _____

Telephone No. _____

Date: _____

Pages: _____

Subject: _____

From: _____

You can fax a document directly from many word processing programs without having to print the document first on paper. If your computer or network is connected to a fax modem and has the proper software, it is easy to fax a message to one person or to 100 people. You can set up a series of address lists and then fax a document to all people attending an upcoming meeting or to all salespersons in a particular region. This method of faxing is referred to as *broadcast fax* and is a time-saving way of sending faxes to many people. A broadcast fax is an efficient method of distribution, and it can be scheduled for sending overnight or during weekends when the fax machine is not otherwise in use.

To obtain a fax number, use a fax directory, which is similar to a telephone directory, and lists company names and fax numbers. Fax phone numbers are also available as part of online Internet services. Try typing "fax phone directory" into an Internet search engine.

Fax-back capability permits a person calling an organization to automatically receive a fax without human intervention. A phone call is answered by a computer that responds with recorded messages. The caller may have a prepared list of publications available or the computer may use a synthesized voice to recite a listing of information available through the service. Using the telephone keypad, the caller enters the number of the item requested as well as the phone number of the fax machine that will receive the document. The computer then automatically faxes the information to the caller's fax machine or computer. Fax-back capability is a service for the distribution of information on demand and is available any hour of the day without the need for live staffing.

If you have a large list of clients to contact, there are companies that offer blast fax and blast email or combined blast fax and blast email services. If you provide the company with a computer file or paper document, the service will send mass faxes or blast emails to many recipients. This relatively low-cost medium is a powerful method of reaching many clients efficiently and quickly. The fax and emails can even be personalized for each recipient. These techniques, however, should be used with care and should be used only to send information to people who request it. Under

Figure 5-5 Employee sending a fax.

federal law, it is illegal to send unsolicited faxes (spam faxes), a crime punishable by a $500 fine for every fax sent.

Sorting Incoming Faxes

In some offices, the administrative assistant is also responsible for sorting and delivering faxed material. Many offices place their fax machine near the administrative assistant's desk so incoming faxes can be quickly processed. Check the fax machine after each incoming fax is received to determine if it is urgent. If the material is routine, the document can be processed as part of the incoming mail.

Often, incoming faxes are sent in response to a telephone call from a staff member who needs the material immediately. You may get a call from a staff member asking

Routing Slip

Sent To   _____
Sent By   _____
Date   _____
Procedures
    Read   _____
    File   _____
    Forward To   _____
    Discuss With   _____
    Handle   _____
    Other   _____

Figure 5-6 Routing slip.

For Your Information

Sent By _____

Date _____

	Date	Comments
Woo Chang	_____	_____
Rhonda Chapel	_____	_____
Brad Cosmo	_____	_____
Leroy Silver	_____	_____
Charlie West	_____	_____
Rodney Healy	_____	_____
Connie Johnson	_____	_____

Figure 5-7   Routing slip with staff names.

that you look for an expected incoming fax. If the incoming fax is not routine, contact the appropriate staff members and ask if they need the fax delivered immediately. Do not be surprised if staff members sometimes linger around the fax machine waiting for an incoming document.

INTERNAL DISTRIBUTION OF MAIL AND FAXES

Mail and faxes can be forwarded to individuals within an office through the use of a routing slip. This procedure allows the same mail to be sent to one or more employees and indicates what employees should do after receiving the mail. An

INTERDEPARTMENTAL MAIL

Name _____	Name _____
Dept. _____	Dept. _____
Name _____	Name _____
Dept. _____	Dept. _____
Name _____	Name _____
Dept. _____	Dept. _____
Name _____	Name _____
Dept. _____	Dept. _____
Name _____	Name _____
Dept. _____	Dept. _____
Name _____	Name _____
Dept. _____	Dept. _____

Figure 5-8   Interoffice envelope.

administrative assistant should develop and reproduce a routing slip that is appropriate for the office.

Interoffice envelopes, which usually are not sealed, are used to send items within the same company. Interoffice envelopes are usually about 9.5 × 12.5 inches in size so they can hold several documents. The envelopes can be used several times. Each user crosses out the name of the previous user and writes the name of the new addressee on the next available line. A supply of interoffice envelopes should be made available to employees who send interoffice mail.

PREPARING FIRST-CLASS MAIL TO LEAVE THE OFFICE

For an administrative assistant, processing outgoing mail is a much more complex task than processing incoming mail. You will have to prepare the mail for delivery across your city or across the world. Mail must comply with regulations or standards established by the United States Postal Service (USPS) or other private carriers.

The standard way to send letters, business correspondence, checks, personal letters, and cards is to use USPS First-Class Mail. First-Class Mail is used to send standard-size letters, and you should expect delivery within one to three days, depending on the distance the mail has to travel.

Mail that is sent first-class mail must meet the following size requirements:

Shape:	Rectangular			
Height:	Minimum:	3½ inches	Maximum:	6⅛ inches
Length:	Minimum:	5 inches	Maximum:	11½ inches
Thickness:	Minimum:	.007 inches	Maximum:	¼ inch
Weight:	Less than 13 oz.			

Most business mail is sent in a standard business-size envelope, which is often referred to as a No. 10 envelope. This envelope measures 4⅛ inches by 9½; inches and is well within the size requirement for First-class mail.

There are many circumstances when you cannot use First-Class Mail. If the mail does not meet the sizing requirements of First-Class Mail, or if delivery must be quicker than the standard delivery time for First-Class Mail, you will need to consider other ways to send mail. The USPS provides several other classes of mail service that can deliver mail or packages larger than the sizes permitted for First Class, faster than First Class, or less expensive than First-Class Mail. There are also several private companies that provide next-day mail delivery or that transport packages. The use of next-day delivery or package delivery services is very important to many businesses. Information about these services is contained later in this chapter.

For an additional charge, First-Class Mail can be enhanced with the following services: Certified Mail, Certificate of Mailing, Insured Mail, Registered Mail, Delivery Confirmation, Signature Confirmation, and Collect on Delivery.

Whether you use USPS First Class, another service from the USPS, or a private delivery company, you must follow the same basic requirements in preparing the outgoing mail.

Folding the Letter

Most letters are prepared on regular size stationery, which is 8.5 inches by 11 inches. A letter on this size paper can be folded in thirds and mailed in a standard business-size No. 10 envelope. To fold a letter so it is placed in the envelope properly, start with the letter facing you as you would read it. Pick up the bottom of the letter and make a fold about one-third of the way up. Then fold the top of the letter down so that it is about ¼ inch short of the first fold. This ¼-inch gap will assist the reader in unfolding the letter. Place the letter in the envelope with the ¼-inch gap facing you and toward the top of the envelope. Documents of more than about five pages are usually too thick to place in a No. 10 envelope. These thicker documents should be mailed in large manila envelopes.

Addressing Envelopes

The USPS uses computer scanners called optical character readers (OCRs) to read the addresses on envelopes so the mail can be efficiently processed. To enable the computer to read the envelope, follow the USPS suggestions listed below.

- Use a block style for the address.
- Use at least 10-point type with a simple font.
- Use black ink on white or light paper.
- A mailing notation—"REGISTERED MAIL" or "CERTIFIED MAIL"—is keyboarded to the left of the stamp or postage meter imprint.
- Use approved abbreviations for street suffixes. The approved abbreviations consist of two, three, or four letters such as ST (street), ALY (alley), and BLVD (boulevard).
- Approved USPS abbreviations can be found on the Internet.
- Use the two-letter state abbreviation. (If the state name is spelled in full, it is too long for the computer to read.) A list of the two-letter abbreviations for states, the U.S. territories, and Canadian provinces appears later in the chapter.
- Leave two spaces between the two-letter state abbreviation and the ZIP Code.
- Capitalize all letters and do not use commas or periods in the address. (For example, the last line of the address would be WASHINGTON DC 20001)
- If the mail is being sent to a foreign country, the bottom line of the address (a line below the city and postal code) should show only the name of the country in capital letters.
- A notation—"PERSONAL," "CONFIDENTIAL," or "HOLD FOR ARRIVAL"—is keyboarded in all-capital letters two lines below the return address and ¼-inch from the left edge of the envelope.

The following is an example of an address prepared according to the United States Postal Service guidelines.

COOPER AND SONS
ATTENTION MR THEODORE COOPER
1902 BRANCH DRIVE
DAVENPORT IA 67992

The United States Postal Service suggests that addresses placed on letter-size mail should be located within an imaginary rectangle (the OCR read area) on the front of the letter formed by the boundaries as shown in Figure 5-9.

If you send mail by a private mail carrier or use USPS Express Mail, you must prepare special mailing labels that are provided for that service. All companies use the two-letter state abbreviations and ZIP Code developed by the USPS.

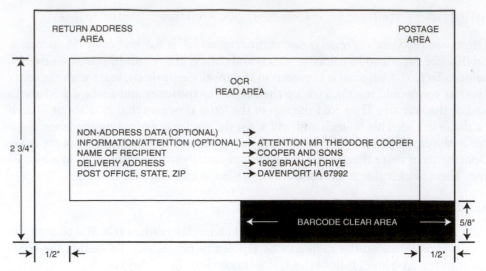

Figure 5-9 How to address envelopes. Courtesy of United States Postal Service.

Two-Letter State Abbreviations

When the United States Postal Service (USPS) began using scanning equipment to sort the mail, it requested that two-letter state abbreviations be used to expedite the mail. The following two-letter abbreviations for the United States and for Canadian provinces are always capitalized.

State Abbreviations

Alabama	AL	Montana	MT
Alaska	AK	Nebraska	NE
Arizona	AZ	Nevada	NV
Arkansas	AR	New Hampshire	NH
California	CA	New Jersey	NJ
Colorado	CO	New Mexico	NM
Connecticut	CT	New York	NY
Delaware	DE	North Carolina	NC
Florida	FL	North Dakota	ND
Georgia	GA	Ohio	OH
Hawaii	HI	Oklahoma	OK
Idaho	ID	Oregon	OR
Illinois	IL	Pennsylvania	PA
Indiana	IN	Rhode Island	RI
Iowa	IA	South Carolina	SC
Kansas	KS	South Dakota	SD
Kentucky	KY	Tennessee	TN
Louisiana	LA	Texas	TX
Maine	ME	Utah	UT
Maryland	MD	Vermont	VT
Massachusetts	MA	Virginia	VA
Michigan	MI	Washington	WA
Minnesota	MN	West Virginia	WV
Mississippi	MS	Wisconsin	WI
Missouri	MO	Wyoming	WY

Abbreviations for the District of Columbia and United States Territories

American Samoa	AS	Marshall Islands	MH
District of Columbia	C	Northern Marianas Islands	MP
Federated States of Micronesia	FM	Palau	PW
		Puerto Rico	PR
Guam	GU	Virgin Islands	VI

Military Abbreviations

Armed Forces Africa	AE	Armed Forces Europe	AE
Armed Forces America (except Canada)	AA	Armed Forces Middle East	AE
		Armed Forces Pacific	AP
Armed Forces Canada	AE		

Canadian Province Abbreviations

Alberta	AB	Nova Scotia	NS
British Columbia	BC	Nunavut	NU
Manitoba	MB	Ontario	ON
New Brunswick	NB	Prince Edward Island	PE
Newfoundland and Labrador	NL	Quebec	QC
		Saskatchewan	SK
Northwest Territories	NT	Yukon	YT

ZIP Code, ZIP+4, and Bar Codes

The ZIP Code is used to expedite mail delivery by assigning a number to each post office and mail carrier route in the country. You must use at least the five digit ZIP Code; using the nine-digit ZIP+4 Code results in faster delivery because it can identify specific floors in a building or departments in a large firm. The nine-digit ZIP+4 includes five digits, a hyphen and four additional digits (for example, 28050-4327). To find the ZIP Code of a United States address, visit www.usps.com or call 1-800-275-8777.

Bar codes can be placed on envelopes to assist in the sorting of mail because they can be quickly read by scanning computers. Mailers may use a ZIP Code plus a bar code. The information content of the bar code is indicated by the height of the bars. The bars represent the nine digits of the ZIP+4 Code and an extra digit for error correction. Word processing software can be used to automatically print the proper bar codes on envelopes.

Canadian and International Postal Codes

The Canadian government and other governments have their own postal codes used to speed mail delivery. The forms of these codes differ from those used in the United States and may combine letters and numbers in varying combinations. For example, the postal code for a location in Canada is in the following form: letter, number, letter, space, number, letter, number; L8E 4Y2 is one example.

USING OTHER MAIL CLASSES AND SERVICES

In preparing outgoing mail, you should select the most economical service that safely delivers the mail within the time span required by the document contained in the envelope or package. To make this selection, you should understand the services provided both by the United States Postal Service, which handles most of the mail delivered in the United States, and other carriers that provide specialized services that supplement the services of the USPS.

USPS Special Services

USPS provides several additional services that can be added to First-Class Mail for an extra fee. These additional services can provide proof of mailing, protection during transit, and confirmation of delivery. These additional services can also be added to other classes of USPS mail and are discussed later in this section.

The following is a summary of some of the extra services provided by USPS. Many of these services are available for mail classes other than First Class. For current information about the requirements and fees for these services, visit the USPS Internet site at: www. usps.com/send/waystosendmail/extraservices/optionalserviceandfeaturefees.htm#top.

Certificate of Mailing

A Certificate of Mailing indicates that the mail was received at the post office. It must be purchased from a clerk at a post office or from a rural carrier. It can be purchased only at the time of mailing. It is an inexpensive method of obtaining proof that the mail was received by a USPS employee. The Certificate of Mailing does not provide proof that the mail was delivered to the addressee nor does it provide insurance coverage for loss or damage to the item.

Certified Mail

Certified Mail provides a receipt stamped with the date of mailing, and a tracking number that allows you to go online and verify delivery. For an additional fee, you can order a return receipt that is signed by the addressee and returned to the sender.

Figure 5-10   Compact postage machine. Courtesy of Pitney Bowes.

Certified Mail does not provide additional security, and it does not travel faster than First-Class Mail.

COD

COD means "collect on delivery." This service is used to deliver merchandise ordered by the addressee. When the item is delivered, the addressee pays the cost of the item plus postage and a COD fee. This service is not available for international mail or for mail addressed to APO and FPO addresses. This service must be purchased from a clerk at a post office or from a rural carrier.

Delivery Confirmation and Signature Confirmation

These two services provide information about the delivery of your mail. Delivery Confirmation provides you with the date, ZIP Code, and time the letter was delivered. Signature Confirmation adds the name of the person who accepted the mail. Both Delivery Confirmation and Signature Confirmations information can be viewed over the Internet or received through the toll-free telephone number 800-822-1811. You can also receive a copy of Signature Confirmation information from the USPS by fax or mail.

Insured Mail

Mail sent by First-Class Mail, Priority Mail, and Parcel Post can be insured for the actual value of the contents, up to $5,000. For items valued over $5,000, you should use Registered Mail. This service must be purchased from a clerk at a post office or from a rural carrier.

Registered Mail

This is the safest way to send valuables through the mail. Movement of the mail is recorded by a series of signed receipts at each stage of delivery, from the sender to the addressee. When the item is mailed, its full value must be declared. Insurance protection for the item up to a total value of $25,000 can be purchased for domestic delivery. Registered Mail to Canada is subject to a $1,000 indemnity limit. For all other foreign countries, the indemnity limit is currently $40.45. A receipt of delivery is available at an additional cost. The return receipt shows to whom, when, and where the item was delivered. The delivery date, time of delivery, and number of delivery attempts may be viewed online. This service must be purchased from a clerk at a post office or from a rural carrier.

Restricted Delivery

By using Restricted Delivery, the sender specifies that the mail can be delivered only to a specific addressee or to someone authorized in writing to receive mail for the addressee.

Return Receipt

A Return Receipt documents proof of delivery and can be purchased for mail sent First Class, sent Express Mail, combined with COD, insured for more than $50, sent registered, or sent certified. A return receipt provides a postcard with the signature of the person who signed for the item and the date it was delivered.

Return Receipt for Merchandise

By using the Return Receipt for Merchandise, you receive both a mailing receipt and a Return Receipt postcard. It is used when sending merchandise to customers.

Special Handling

Special Handling service is required for parcels whose unusual contents, such as live poultry or bees, require special care from postal employees. Special Handling service is not necessary for sending ordinary parcels that contain fragile items when the items are packed with cushioning and the package is clearly marked "Fragile."

Other USPS Services and Postal Classes

In addition to First-Class Mail, the USPS provides a wide variety of services to deliver mail anywhere in the world. Fees are charged depending on the class of mail and any of the special mailing services listed in Figure 5-11 that are added to the letter or package. Current information about USPS requirements and fees for any of the following services can be viewed on the Internet at www.usps.com/consumers/domestic.htm#first.

Priority Mail

Priority Mail consists of packages up to 70 pounds with a maximum size of 108 inches—which is the combined distance around the largest part of the package and its length. Delivery is usually within two to three days to addresses within the United States. Letters over 13 ounces can also be sent via Priority Mail for preferential treatment at a lower cost than Express Mail. You can obtain free Priority Mail envelopes, tubes, and boxes from the post office. You can send any amount of material that will fit into a Priority Mail envelope for a flat rate. Delivery Confirmation is a feature of Priority Mail at no additional cost.

Parcel Post

Parcel Post consists of packages up to 70 pounds with a maximum size of 130 inches—which is the combined distance around the largest part of the package and its length. Delivery of Parcel Post packages is slower than that of Priority Mail packages but also significantly cheaper.

Periodicals

The USPS has a special postage rate for publishers and registered news agents to mail periodicals such as magazines.

Standard Mail

Standard Mail is used to send printed matter, flyers, circulars, advertising, newsletters, bulletins, catalogs, and small parcels. Standard mail is used only for bulk mail with minimum of 200 pieces or weighing 50 pounds. The USPS has several other specialized classes of mail for printed material, including bound printed matter, media mail, library mail, and periodical mail. You can find out more about these special classes of mail at the USPS Internet site at www.usps.com/send/waystosendmail/senditwithintheus/domesticdeliveryoptions.htm.

Government Mail (Penalty Mail/Franked Mail)

The federal government sends business letters and checks by penalty mail. Special envelopes for penalty mail sent by the federal government are usually imprinted "Official Business, Penalty for Private Use" and the name of the federal agency. Members of Congress and other government officials are permitted to send mail by franked mail. Franked mail uses the original signature or a facsimile signature of the sender instead of a stamp. Envelopes using penalty or franked mail are available only in offices authorized to use that type of mail.

Service	Can Be Combined with the Following Services	Service Is Available when Using Postal Class			
		First Class	Express	Priority	Parcel Post
Certificate of Mailing	Special Handling	Yes		Yes	Yes
Certified Mail	Restricted Delivery Return Receipt	Yes		Yes	
Collect on Delivery	Delivery Confirmation Registered Mail Restricted Delivery Return Receipt Signature Confirmation Special Handling	Yes	Yes	Yes	Yes
Delivery Confirmation	Collect on Delivery Insured Mail Registered Mail Restricted Delivery Return Receipt Special Handling	Yes		Yes	Yes
Insured Mail	Delivery Confirmation Restricted Delivery Return Receipt Signature Confirmation Special Handling	Yes	Yes	Yes	Yes
Registered Mail	Collect on Delivery Delivery Confirmation Restricted Delivery Return Receipt Signature Confirmation	Yes		Yes	
Restricted Delivery	Delivery Confirmation Return Receipt Signature Confirmation Special Handling	Yes		Yes	Yes
Return Receipt	Delivery Confirmation Restricted Delivery Signature Confirmation Special Handling	Yes	Yes	Yes	Yes
Return Receipt for Merchandise	Delivery Confirmation Insured Mail Special Handling			Yes	Yes
Signature Confirmation	Collect on Delivery Insured Mail Registered Mail Restricted Delivery Special Handling	Yes		Yes	Yes
Special Handling	Collect on Delivery Delivery Confirmation Insured Delivery Return Receipt Signature Confirmation	Yes		Yes	Yes

Figure 5-11 Summary of extra services available with postal classes.

International Mail

The postal rates for international mail vary with the weight of the envelope and the specific destination. Most international mail is now sent using air mail service. However, packages may be sent by surface mail, which may take several weeks or even months to arrive at its destination. Information about international mail rates is included in a postage chart available from the U.S. Postal Service and is available on the USPS Web site at ircalc.usps.gov.

Calculating Postage and Fees from the USPS Internet Site

The USPS provides many different classes of service, many of which can be used at the same time. Estimating the final postage can be a complex matter. The USPS Internet site will help you calculate postage and fees for sending either domestic or international mail. The Web site asks for information about your office ZIP Code, the destination to which the letter or package is to be sent, the weight and size of the package and then asks about any additional services that you would like to add. Using the calculator, you can change the class of service and compare postage rates. You may find that it is less expensive to send a package by Express Mail rather than by Priority Mail. Other aids in calculating postage are postal charts and scales, which are discussed later in this chapter. The USPS calculator can be found on the Internet at www.usps.com/tools/calculatepostage/welcome.htm.

Post Office Boxes

Post office boxes and drawers may be rented from many post offices. Boxes and drawers are located in the post office lobby, and mail is placed directly in them after it is sorted by postal clerks. The box holder has a key and can retrieve mail whenever the lobby of the post office is open. A business may use a post office box to receive mail for a specific project or for privacy reasons.

NEXT-DAY MAIL AND PACKAGE DELIVERY SERVICES

The United States and Canada, like most countries of the world, give government agencies such as the USPS and Canadian Post the exclusive right to deliver First-Class Mail. Delivery of other mail or packages, however, may be left open to competition from private companies. Both the USPS and private companies deliver next-day mail and packages.

Next-day mail is a specialized service that provides quick delivery of packages and documents and is used when time-sensitive materials must be sent to another party. The United States Postal Service (USPS) and several private companies such as DHL, FedEx (Federal Express), and UPS (United Parcel Service) provide next-day mail and package delivery services. The services offered are all very similar but one company may meet your rush or critical delivery needs better than others. Price, convenience of drop-off location, and delivery time may help you make a decision about which company to use. If the delivery time is not critical, some carriers offer reduced rates for an afternoon delivery instead of a morning delivery, or for second-day delivery rather than next-day delivery.

Several private companies, including DHL, FedEx, and UPS, offer same-day and overnight package and document delivery services. These companies offer a wide variety of both domestic and international delivery services. The Internet sites of these companies include information on drop-off locations; assistance in calculating rates; tracking shipments; and ordering the company's special envelopes, boxes, and waybills. Since the services each company offers are often updated in response to customers' needs and competitors' offerings, only a few of the services of each company are listed here as examples of the range of services available. For current information, you should check with each company's Web site, which is listed in their respective sections. The following outlines some of the services available.

USPS

USPS offers Express Mail delivery service 365 days a year with no extra charge for Sunday or holiday delivery. This is a guaranteed delivery service that includes tracking information; signature on delivery (upon request); and automatic insurance of up to $100 with the option of purchasing of additional insurance up to $5,000. You can track the progress of the Express Mail and view confirmation of its delivery on the Internet at the USPS Web site. Mail and packages sent using Express Mail Next-Day Service can be taken to any of over 40,000 designated Express Mail post offices, deposited in one of 26,000 Express Mail collection boxes across the country, or given to a postal carrier. In addition, Express Mail offers a flat-rate-per-stop pickup service by calling 1-800-222-1811. USPS Express Mail International Service is also available to 200 countries around the world, and Express Mail military service is available to select U.S. military addresses (APO and FPO addresses) in Europe, Asia, and Panama with two- to three-day delivery. To quickly identify Express Mail, specifically designed envelopes and boxes are available from local post offices with no charge for the envelope or box. In addition, Express Mail labels can be printed from the USPS Internet site, and business customized preprinted labels are available by contacting the local post office. The fees for Express Mail are based on weight (with a maximum weight of 70 pounds) and type of service. However, a ½-pound flat rate option is available regardless of weight for mail that will fit into the Express Mail flat rate envelope. More information about Express Mail can be found on the USPS Internet site at www.usps.com/shipping/expressmail.htm.

DHL

DHL provides same-day service for all types of packages with delivery on the next flight to the required destination. DHL also provides overnight next-day delivery services that are guaranteed for delivery by 10:30 A.M., noon, or 3 P.M., depending on the service and charge selected. USA 2nd Day service provides delivery by 3 P.M. the second business day. Pickup service can be arranged via the Web. DHL also provides ground delivery of package within one to five business days for items up to 150 pounds and 108 inches in length. DHL provides a variety of services for international package delivery to 228 countries. These include Worldwide Priority Express, which ships packages subject to duty worldwide; and International Document Service, which provides for international door-to-door delivery of non-dutiable items such as reports and letters. Through its partner Deutsche Post Global Mail, DHL can provide mail delivery anywhere in the world. For additional information about DHL, visit www.DHL.com.

FedEx

FedEx's quickest service provides for same-day delivery within the United States for packages not exceeding 70 pounds and not larger than 48 inches. Next-day delivery is available with early morning, midmorning, or midafternoon delivery options at differing costs. Also, FedEx offers second-day and third-day deliveries. International delivery service is available to more than 200 countries for packages up to 150 pounds, with delivery choices from one to five days. In addition, FedEx provides a ground delivery service and delivers packages to the home. FedEx offers a large variety of freight shipping options, including same-day service and even truckload shipments. For additional information about FedEx services, visit www.FedEx.com.

UPS (United Parcel Service)

UPS's same day service is called SonicAir and provides pickup at the customer's location and delivery to more than 180 countries around the world. UPS provides three levels of next-day service, delivery by 8 A.M., by 10:30 A.M. or by 3:00 P.M. Second-day air is available with a choice of noon delivery or afternoon delivery, and a third-day delivery is also available. UPS provides worldwide express delivery service with next-day delivery guaranteed to many cities in Europe and Canada. For many years, UPS has delivered packages throughout the United States through its network of brown vans. Additional information about UPS is available at www.ups.com.

Using Next-Day Services

If you need to quickly send a document or package, first determine if your company has an account with a particular next-day mail delivery company. An account enables the company to bill your office directly for the delivery. If your office does not have an account or if you wish to evaluate the cost and efficiency of your present delivery service, you should obtain information from the Internet sites listed and consider the following:

- Pickup charges.
- Location of mail drop-off boxes.
- Whether the customer must deliver the package to the carrier.
- Delivery to the community of the addressee.
- Delivery by a specific time.
- Weekend pickup and delivery.
- Delivery cost.
- Insurance availability and cost.
- Availability of extra services.

Courier and Air Courier Services

Many large metropolitan areas are served by courier services that will pick up and deliver a package or document within the area in a matter of hours. A phone call is placed to a courier service, and a messenger picks up the package for immediate delivery. In downtown areas, couriers often use bicycles to speed documents through congested city streets.

Documents or packages must sometimes be sent to another city and even a next-day delivery would miss the deadline. As you saw in the previous section, several of the package delivery services offer same-day delivery service. Same-day service is also available from several airlines and specialized delivery services that can place a letter or small package on the next flight to the destination city. Airline services may deliver the item only to the airport and require pickup of the item at the airport by the receiving party. Specialized delivery services may complete the delivery to the recipient's address. An example of a same-day service provided by an airline can be found on the Internet site of Delta Airlines, at www.delta.com/prog_serv/cargo/dash/index.jsp.

POSTAL SCALE AND INFORMATION CHART

A business sending mail by USPS has the responsibility of calculating the correct postage required on each piece of mail. Most businesses use a postal scale that can accurately weigh envelopes to the half ounce. Use of a postal scale can save up to 20 percent of postage costs because the correct postal charge can easily be determined, rather than simply placing an extra stamp on an envelope "just in case" the envelope is too heavy. A scale is especially useful for businesses that mail large envelopes (reports, catalogs, etc.) that vary in weight. Many postal scales automatically display the postage required for an item, while older scales may have built-in charts that must be consulted to determine the amount of postage required for each class and weight of mail. In addition to calculating the item for USPS rates, many digital scales also determine charges for FedEx or UPS. Postage charts list the postage required for all USPS classes and services of mail that are available from the U.S. Postal Service. These charts also list postage required for foreign countries. The information on the postal charts is revised when postage rates change. The Internet sites of the USPS and the next-day delivery services include sections to help calculate the cost of sending an item. The user enters the weight or size of the item, the ZIP Codes of the sending and receiving sites, and the type of delivery or service requested. The Internet sites often provide the user with delivery alternatives that can reduce the mailing cost.

Many post offices have self-service postal scales connected to computers that you can use to calculate the rate for an envelope. Using a touch screen, you can enter the class of service and ZIP Code. The system calculates the postage and prints the postage on an adhesive label that you can place on the package or envelope. Payment can be made by using a credit card

POSTAGE MACHINES

Instead of placing individual stamps on letters, most businesses use a postage meter to print the postage on an envelope. The postage machine operator can set the proper amount of postage to be printed for each letter or package according to weight,

Figure 5-12 Office-size postage machine. Courtesy of Pitney Bowes.

Figure 5-13 Office mail slot.

class of mail, and special services ordered. A postage meter prints directly onto the envelope or onto a tape that is placed on a large envelope or parcel. A postage machine consists of a base, which is an envelope handler used to transport the envelope; a feeder, which guides the envelope through the meter; a meter, which prints the postage; a sealer, which moistens and seals the envelope; and a stacker, which holds the metered mail. Since postage is based on weight, many meters automatically weigh the item. Under Federal regulations, meters cannot be purchased but must be rented from a USPS-approved vendor. As postage is used, additional funds can be transferred to the postage meter electronically over the telephone or over the Internet at the site postagebyphone.com. Postage meter vendors charge extra for last-minute and emergency refills, so plan your postage needs in advance.

COLLECTING OUTGOING MAIL

Office buildings often have mail-drop boxes or mail slots on each floor, in the lobby of the building, or in close proximity to the building. If this is not the case, outgoing mail must be deposited in a blue USPS collection box for pickup. It is often the administrative assistant's responsibility to deposit the outgoing mail in the collection box. If you are depositing mail, check the collection time posted on the box to determine if the mail will be picked up later that day. Collection times vary from box to box. Locate a box where the pickup is after 5:30 P.M. so last-minute mail can be deposited for pickup that same day.

In a large office, outgoing mail may be collected for processing by mailroom employees before the mail is sent to the post office. Outgoing mail is often collected by the mailroom staff when incoming mail is being delivered. Outgoing mail can also be taken directly to the mailroom for processing. The office may require that outgoing mail be sorted by the first three ZIP Code digits in order to qualify for discounts on postage. Some offices require that each piece of mail be coded with an office number so postage can be charged to the department originating the mail. It is important to learn the requirements for sending outgoing mail so the mail can be processed quickly and postal costs charged to the correct office.

CHAPTER REVIEW

1. Explain how an incoming letter is coded.
2. Explain the use of a routing slip.
3. What is the purpose of a mail register?
4. Explain the purposes of registered and certified mail.
5. Explain priority mail.
6. Define franked and penalty mail.
7. What criteria should be considered when using express mail?
8. Explain how postage meters are used.

ACTIVITIES

1. How would you send each of the following?
   a. A letter to Paris, France.
   b. A gift package to a client in Albany, NY.

c. A letter that must be received by tomorrow.

d. A package that must be received by tomorrow.

e. A stock certificate.

f. A letter to someone in Guam.

g. A package from Boston to Seattle that must be received tomorrow.

2. Go to the post office and locate the private boxes available for rent. Check the lobby hours and price to rent a box.

3. Verify the current rates for first-class letters and postcards. You may use the Internet to research this activity.

4. Contact three express mail carriers and compare their rates for mailing a five-page letter. Is the location for mail drop-off convenient for you? Do they have an office pickup service? By what time do they guarantee delivery? What is the cost for the service? You may use the Internet to research this activity.

5. What is the cost to mail letters to Mexico, Italy, and England? You may use the Internet to research this activity.

6. Describe the proper materials used when mailing a package. Where in your area would you purchase the materials and which company would you use to send the package?

7. Ask an assistant how much time is devoted daily to sorting and processing office mail.

8. For one week, keep a mail register of the all of the mail received in your home.

9. Prepare a routing slip to send a newspaper or magazine article to four members of your class.

10. What is the closest post office to your school? What is the last time mail is picked up there? If you miss the last pickup there, what is the next closest location, and what is the time of the last pickup there?

11. Where is the main post office in your area? During what hours are the lobby windows open?

12. Address an envelope to each of the following people.

- Marilyn Horan, Acting Director, Watkins Industries, 3409 Research Lane, Detroit, Michigan 48875

- Shu Tau, Administrative Assistant, Brandywine Inc., 4877 Garden Avenue, Chicago, Illinois 60067

- Reynolds Manufacturing, 19 Wood Drive, Columbus, Ohio 43227, Attention of Lucy Wagner

- Personal letter to Stanley R. Wells, Boyer and Sons, 404 Vine Street, Columbia, Maryland 21045

- Certified letter to Paula T. Huffman, Managing Director, Birch Systems, Ft. Wayne, Indiana 46815

PROJECTS

Project 9

Create the form below, and write a memo to Peter Bahrami, Ralph Harris, Sarah Rothman, and Pepe Gomez asking them to complete this form ASAP. The memo is from you and your title is Director.

Activity	Percentage of Daily Time Spent
Using email	
Faxing	
Sorting mail	
Filing	
Answering telephone	
Writing reports	
Writing letters	
Making travel arrangements	

Project 10

Create the following table and calculate mailing costs for each month.

Mailing Costs in Dollars

DEPT	JAN	FEB	MARCH	APRIL	MAY	JUNE
101	2,500	1,875	900	800	2,500	2,500
102	1,600	2,200	800	900	2,300	1,500
103	1,800	2,500	750	700	2,600	2,200
104	2,250	1,300	500	600	1,800	2,700
105	3,600	1,500	900	750	1,700	2,000
106	1,500	2,400	500	900	2,000	2,500

HUMAN RELATIONS SKILL DEVELOPMENT

HR 5-1 Office Friendships

Remember that the office is the place where you work, not the place where you play. Do not tell office friends all the details of your personal life. These individuals may later supervise you, and the details of your personal life may have a negative impact on their evaluation of your work. It is also possible that an office friend, with whom you later have a disagreement, might tell others the details of your personal problems. Be friendly with everyone in your office, but do not divulge all the secrets of your life.

- Have you told someone about an event in your life and later wished you had never mentioned it?
- What would you do if your supervisor began telling you personal information you did not want to know?
- Describe the types of information about yourself that you would like to share with your coworkers.

HR 5-2 Working with Disorganized People

It can be discouraging to work with disorganized people, particularly when their behavior affects you. Postponing the beginning of meetings because a person is always late, waiting for materials to be found, and delaying projects because a person has not completed a portion of the project can be very frustrating. Depending on the individual, there may be little you can do to remedy the situation. You can diplomatically encourage the person to become organized, discuss the importance of being prompt, and tactfully express your frustration about the situation.

- Are you a disorganized person?
- What can you do to become more organized?
- What can you do if your supervisor is disorganized?
- How would you encourage a coworker who is disorganized to become more organized?
- Do you arrive on time for events?
- Do you have friends who are habitually late for events?
- How can you encourage a person to be prompt?

SITUATIONS

How would you handle the following situations?

- **S 5-1** You arrive on time at your office, but you cannot find your office keys.
- **S 5-2** Your supervisor would like you to do personal errands when the supervisor is too busy to do them. You are told that the errands can been done on company time.
- **S 5-3** Your coworker loudly chews gum and pops it frequently, which annoys you.

PUNCTUATION REVIEW

Punctuate each of the following sentences. For a review of punctuation rules, see the Appendix.

1. Edward K Bowman our president has meetings in Virginia Pennsylvania and New Jersey
2. Bill the executive director joined the company in June of this year
3. The most effective manager Ms Engle is well organized
4. Yesterdays price report while representing only a single month gave no indication that inflation is a growing concern to the economic future of the nation
5. Of course we missed the train and were late for the meeting
6. Since fall is here we must reevaluate the project
7. Food prices after increasing 3.6 percent in January declined 2.4 percent last month which is further evidence that the effects of the drought may be less than originally feared by economists
8. The west coast office assistant I understand is the employee of the month
9. No the salary was not the issue
10. Her next interview is in Chicago Illinois on Friday April 17 at 10 AM
11. The presentation was a success and we received the contract
12. You will I think benefit from the Friday seminar
13. Several economists cautioned against expecting such price increases to continue said Ms Woo
14. Wendy who will be on a business trip the month of October is the new director
15. The bank was closed yesterday and I wanted to cash a check so I would have sufficient cash for my next business trip

CD Assignments

CD Assignment 5-1

Open the file **CD5-1_IPM** on your Student CD and follow the instructions to complete the job.

CD Assignment 5-2

Open the file **CD5-2_IPS** on your Student CD and follow the instructions to complete the job.

CD Assignment 5-3

Open the file **CD5-3_Hunt** on your Student CD and follow the instructions to complete the job.

CD Assignment 5-4

Open the file **CD5-4_FCP** on your Student CD and follow the instructions to complete the job.

CD Assignment 5-5

Open the file **CD5-5_FML** on your Student CD and follow the instructions to complete the job.

CHAPTER 6

Computers in the Office

Objectives

After studying this chapter, you should be able to:

1. Understand the terms associated with computers.
2. Understand the use of a variety of computer software programs for the office—including word processing, databases, and spreadsheets.

INTRODUCTION TO COMPUTERS

Computers have become an integral part of the everyday life of most office employees. In the modern office, computers are used for many activities in addition to word processing. Computers are used for recordkeeping, budgeting, retrieval and analysis of data, daily calendars, messages, and many other tasks.

It is almost impossible to function in today's modern offices without the ability to operate computer equipment. Proficiency in computers requires hands-on experience with specific equipment, and many schools offer courses in specific computer programs where students gain skills in using computer programs.

While many people use computers, they may have only a passing familiarity with computer concepts and terms. This chapter provides an overview of computers and presents background information on general computer terminology and concepts so you can understand the computer equipment used in the office. In addition, the chapter introduces some computer programs that you are likely to use in an up-to-date office environment.

HARDWARE

The terms *hardware* and *software* are often used when discussing computers. Hardware is the physical part of a computer system and consists of several parts. Computer hardware, however, will not operate unless the equipment is used with software, the instructions that tell the computer equipment what to do. Different software programs permit the same hardware to perform numerous functions such as word processing, database management, and accounting.

While each computer system is different, a typical computer system may include a central processing unit (CPU), keyboard, monitor, external storage (such as a disk drive, CD, or DVD drive), modem, and printer. The CPU, disk drives, CD, or DVD are usually contained within a single computer case. Additional computer hardware, such as a monitor, keyboard, and printer are usually separate items connected to the computer by cables. Many computers are also connected to peripheral devices such as scanners or audio speakers. Each of these computer hardware items is described in the following sections.

Central Processing Unit (CPU)

The central processing unit (CPU) is a small silicon computer chip (called a *microprocessor*) that is the brains of the computer. The CPU interprets the software, performs calculations, and sends instructions to the other hardware in the system. Next to the CPU in the computer case are other computer chips that serve as the computer's memory; these computer ships are called *random access memory (RAM)*. The microprocessor works only with information available on the computer's RAM chips. The microprocessor first transfers information to the RAM chips from a computer's mass storage devices, such as a hard drive, CD, or DVD, all of which are discussed later in this chapter. Once the information is in the RAM chips, it is used by the microprocessor to complete a word processing, spreadsheet, graphic, or other task.

The larger the amount of RAM, the quicker the computer can process information and the more programs can be run at the same time. A typical computer has from 512 MB of memory to several gigabytes of memory. The abbreviation MB stands for megabyte, which is the unit of measure for computer memory. The computer can store 1 million characters (such as letters or digits) in each MB of memory. A gigabyte can store approximately 1 billion characters and is equal to 1,024 megabytes.

Because of the importance of the CPU (microprocessor) in the computer system, the term *CPU* is often used to describe the entire computer case that contains the microprocessor, the RAM chips, the hard drive, and DVD. This computer case is connected with a cable to other computer hardware such as a keyboard and monitor.

Keyboard

A keyboard is a primary input device of the computer system, where a person manually enters or keyboards information into the computer. Unfortunately, computer keyboards are not fully standardized and may contain from 84 to 103 keys. People who use computers for long periods each day sometimes complain of pain in their arms or wrists. One style of keyboard, called an *ergonomic keyboard*, has been designed to reduce the stress caused by long-term computer use. An ergonomic keyboard divides the standard keyboard into several parts and angles some of the keys to reduce arm motion and stretching. There are many designs of ergonomic keyboards. While an ergonomic keyboard may look strange and have a different feel than a standard keyboard, many people find these keyboards very useful in reducing stress.

Monitors and Displays

The video screen on the computer is called a monitor or flat-panel display. The minimum useful size for a monitor is about 12 inches, though most people now use monitors of 15 inches, 17 inches, or 19 inches in size. (All screen sizes are measured diagonally.) The larger monitors are useful when viewing detailed graphics.

Mass Storage Devices

In order to run the many computer programs used in the office, computers need more information than can be stored on RAM chips. Computer programs and information are saved on mass storage devices usually using either magnetic or optical technologies.

The most common way to store computer programs or information is on magnetic disks such as hard disk drives. Other technologies used for mass storage include optical mass storage devices, such as CDs and DVDs; flash memory computer chips; and small diskettes, which are often called disks or floppy disks.

Magnetic Memory: Hard Drives and Disks

The main memory storage device on a computer is the hard disk drive, also referred to as a *hard drive*. A hard disk drive is a magnetic storage device made up of many circular metal disks. Because the information on a disk is read by tiny heads in the disk drive, the computer can quickly retrieve information from any part of the hard disk. Every computer has at least one hard drive built into the computer case. Additional hard drives can be connected to a computer with a cable. Small, portable hard drives are available, so large amounts of information can be carried or stored at another location for safety. A hard disk can store many programs and thousands of pages of text and other information, including graphics, pictures, and video. As the size of computer programs have expanded, the amount of hard disk storage found on computers has also greatly increased. A typical hard drive in a modern computer may have a storage capacity of anywhere between 80 GB to 500 GB.

Magnetic tapes and *cartridges* are used to store data from a hard disk as a backup in case the hard disk is damaged. Offices may also use a tape to back up all the data on a computer network. These tape backups take several hours and are often completed overnight when the office staff is not using the computer.

Diskettes are thin, portable disks which are 3.5 inches in size that are inserted into *disk drives*, which may be built into a computer case. Inside the diskette plastic cover is a small magnetic disk that can store up to 1.44 MB of information. The storage capacity of any diskette is limited and modern computer programs and data such as graphics or video are too large to fit on a single diskette. Because of their small storage capacity, diskettes are rapidly disappearing from use in favor of CDs, DVDs, and flash memory devices. Many new computers do not come with disk drives installed. Since disk drives are vanishing from the workplace, offices need to transfer information stored on diskettes to other technology while they still have the equipment to transfer the data.

Optical Storage Devices: DVDs and CDs

DVDs and CDs are storage systems that save information optically and are very similar to music CDs and movie DVDs. The storage capacity of the most common DVDs, 4.7 GB, is much greater than that of a CD, which can hold up to 700 MB of

---

MY SUCCESS STORY

My Name Is Yuri

College classes were always hard for me. I am not dumb; I just did not have a lot of time to study. I worked two jobs so I could go to school. When I finished my education, I got a great job using all of the business skills I learned. My only regret is that I did not spend more time learning. To increase my knowledge of business, now I spend my time reading business publication and surfing the Web about current business developments.

HINT

DVDs are designed to store large amounts of data or video information.

information. A *DVD drive*, or *CD drive*, is now built into most computers. Because a DVD drive can also read information from a computer CD or audio CD, DVDs are replacing CDs for computer storage

Because of their vast storage capacity, the DVD provides the immense storage space necessary for picture, audio, and video files that may be used for creating computer presentations or other uses You can create your own DVD disk or CD disk if your computer has a DVD-writable or CD-writable drive. Unfortunately, there are several DVD writable formats available in the marketplace, so you may see references to a DVD+R and DVD−R. Each DVD format (+R and −R) is supported by a group of DVD manufacturers, but some manufacturers make DVD-writable drives that can produce both.

There are two important points to remember about being able to create DVDs on a computer. First, there are several kinds of blank DVDs and the one you use must match the type of writable DVD drive in your computer. A DVD+R writable drive can write only to a +R blank DVD, and a DVD−R writable drive can only write only to a −R blank DVD. There are some DVD+R/−R writable drives that can use either type of blank DVD.

Second, to further complicate the creating of DVDs, blank DVDs that end in +R or −R can be written only once, while those that end in +RW or −RW can be written many times. If you want to create a DVD that someone else can only read, use the R type of blank DVD. If you want to create a DVD where you can continually update your information, use the RW type.

Flash Memory Storage

HINT

Flash memory consists of a recordable computer chip that can store information in a very small physical space.

Flash memory consists of a recordable computer chip that can store from 16 MB to over several gigabytes of information in a very small physical space. There are several formats of flash memory. One type of flash memory is available on cards smaller than a matchbox. Several examples of these flash memory cards are Compact Flash, MultiMediaCard, SD Card, and SmartMedia. These flash memory cards are of different sizes and can be inserted into an appropriate slot in a desk or notebook computer, digital camera, printer, handheld computer, or other digital device. Adaptors are available so you can use several types of flash memory with your computer and some computers contain several different size slots so a variety of flash memory cards can be used. Flash memory cards are reusable; therefore, they can be used for permanent or temporary storage.

A second type of flash memory is the size of a pack of gum. These units are called thumb drives, key-chain drives, memory sticks, or *universal serial bus* (*USB*) flash drives

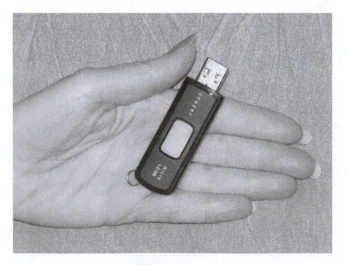

Figure 6-1 A USB flash memory stick.

because they all have a standard connector that fits into the USB ports on a computer. USB is now the standard connector (port) used to link computers to other devices, such as printers, scanners, external hard drives, and small flash drives. Accordingly, all new computers come with USB ports. Flash drives store up to about 16 GB of information, so they are very convenient to transport files and presentations. Flash drives are rapidly becoming the most convenient way to carry computer files.

Internet Connections

An office can use several technologies to connect computers to the Internet. Regardless of the method used in your office, technology has developed so your connection to the Internet will probably be done automatically with a single mouse click to open an Internet browser. Most offices use high-speed connections, such as cable modems, ISDN or DSL telephone lines, or optical fiber, all of which permit a full-time connection so the Internet is always available. Companies with many employees using the Internet often have an optical fiber connection within their office because it can serve many users at the same time.

Network Cards

If your computer is connected to a computer network within your office, your computer has a network card inside the computer case so it can exchange information with other computers on the network. An office network allows each computer to connect to the Internet through a *gateway*. The office network is also referred to as an *Intranet*. It is used for internal communications and also allows employees to work collectively on documents.

Wireless Technology

In today's high-tech world, immediate information is desired and often critical. Business has moved outside the traditional office to the car, golf course, kitchen table, vacation home, client's office, coffee bar, and other nontraditional locations. On-the-go employees require access to voice mail, email, news, and the Internet. There are several wireless communications technologies that are widely used by businesses. Wireless technology is used in portable computers, cell phones, personal digital assistants (PDAs). The latter are sometimes referred to as handheld organizers. Portable computers and handheld organizers are discussed in the next section of this chapter. Advances in technology encourage the concept of the virtual office, where the employee is available 24/7.

> **HINT**
> To use wireless technology, the computer must have a wireless communication card or must be within the range of a compatible wireless transmitter.

Many portable computers and handheld organizers have *wireless cards* that can transmit and receive signals so a computer user can access the Internet or receive email while out of the office. Wireless technology can also be used within an office or home to connect a portable computer to a network or to the Internet. Security is an issue when using wireless technology. Because the computer's information is being sent through the air, other computers can receive it. The computer data must be encrypted so other users in the area cannot pick up the transmission and read the data.

Perhaps the most popular wireless technology is called *Wi-Fi* (short for *Wireless Fidelity*). Wi-Fi cards are available for a wide variety of computer, cell phone, and other electronic equipment. Many airports, hotels, coffee shops, bookstores, and other businesses and public places have established Wi-Fi connections where people with portable computers can connect to the Internet for free or for a modest fee. These locations are often referred to as Wi-Fi "hot spots". Wi-Fi equipment can be purchased for homes and businesses so portable computing equipment can connect to the Internet and to local area networks.

Another wireless technology used in computers is called *Bluetooth*. Bluetooth technology is best used for connecting devices within 30 feet of each other, although sometimes it can be used for longer distance interconnections. Bluetooth technology is used in computers, printers, cameras, cell phones, and other devices. More information about Bluetooth technology can be found on the Internet at www.bluetooth.org and www.bluetooth.com.

Audio Speakers

Small audio speakers are usually built into portable computers but external speakers must be added to most desktop computers. External speakers can range from small inexpensive speaker boxes to full stereo systems that provide the volume and sound quality required where audio and video is an important part of the computer experience.

Scanners

A scanner is an input device that reads printed or graphic material, including photographs, prepared art, and business logos, and converts the scanned material into a computer file. Using a scanner, a photograph can be scanned into a computer and then inserted into a document or report. A page of text can be scanned into a computer rather than having to be entered by the keyboard. If the computer has Optical Character Recognition (OCR) software, the text can then be inserted into a word processing package for editing. Scanners can be separate units or can be built into photocopy machines. Some electronic scanners are so small that they can be held in one hand.

Figure 6-2   Printer in the office.

Printers

A printer is a primary output device of the computer and provides the hard copy—a single-page letter or a multi page report—that can be distributed throughout an office or around the world. These printed copies can be in English or in many foreign languages. Printers can also create transparencies for overhead projectors or print detailed graphs and complex engineering drawings. Printers with various capabilities are available in many price ranges to serve a variety of needs. Large printers can store several different papers, which can be of different sizes, in different colors, or on different letterheads. Often these different papers can be selected directly from the computer.

Offices usually use a *laser printer*, which uses a beam of light to form images on paper. Laser printers are high-quality printers, but they can be expensive. Laser printers can reproduce high-quality graphics and letter-quality documents and can easily print a variety of fonts and font sizes. Furthermore, a laser printer can print letters sideways on paper, called landscape printing, in addition to regular printing, called portrait printing. Laser printers can print detailed graphics and are therefore used to print documents created with desktop publishing programs. Some laser printers can print in color as well as black and white. Laser printers use large cartridges of dry ink called *toner,* which must be replaced when empty.

Ink-jet printers spray ink onto paper to form letters and characters. Ink-jet printers have many of the same capabilities as laser printers and are often used in homes and small businesses because of their lower cost, though the quality of the printing is not as exact as that of laser printers.

Printers do not need to be directly connected to a computer but can be connected to an office network or the Internet. In this way, several employees or offices may share the use of an expensive printer. Many office printers have internal memory to store many pages of text or graphics until the printer is ready to print. Printers can also have adaptor slots where flash memory cards or digital cameras can be connected to print without the printer being connected to a computer or computer network.

Digital Cameras

Digital cameras have become popular because they can quickly save a picture in digital format. Digital cameras do not use film but replace the traditional roll of film with a reusable memory card that stores pictures. Most modern digital cameras store pictures using flash memory cards such as CompactFlash, SmartMedia, MMC, SD, xD, or a Memory Stick. Digital cameras may have an optical or digital zoom and a movie mode, which allows a person to record a short video. After the pictures are taken,

Figure 6-3 Digital camera.

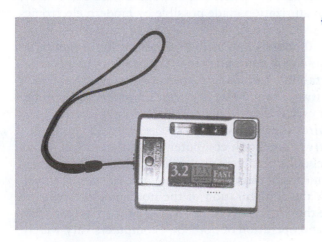

they may be stored or printed. If you use an expensive digital camera to obtain quality photos but use an inexpensive printer, you may not produce quality prints. Purchasing an expensive high-quality printer is one option, but another option is to send the picture file to a photo-finishing site to print the photo. Photos can be uploaded to a photo-finishing Web site or sent by email. Photos taken with a digital camera can easily be inserted into email, word processing, spreadsheet, desktop publishing, and presentation software packages.

Hardware Operating Systems

The parts of the computer—the CPU, the monitor, and disk drives—require an operating system that connects them together and allows them to work. The operating system is a specialized type of software that directs information between each of the pieces of hardware and the CPU. When the computer is turned on, the operating system on a hard disk drive is usually automatically run (booted). The three most commonly used operating systems are the Windows family of software from Microsoft Corp.; MAC OS from Apple Corp.; and Linux, which is an open operating system that is available free or at little cost.

TYPES OF COMPUTERS

As electronic devices become smaller and cheaper, a wide variety of specialized computer and computer-like devices have been developed to serve the needs and wants of businesses and the public. A computer no longer needs to sit on a desktop with a monitor, CPU, and hard disk. There are now a whole range of computers, many designed to perform a specific function or to attract the user by being smaller than comparable units.

In addition to the standard desktop computer, several categories are commonly used to distinguish the varieties of computers available. The terminology used to categorize computers is often confusing because different manufacturers may refer to the same type of computer with different terms, in part to try to distinguish their product from their competitors. For example, the terms *handheld organizer*, *handheld computer*, *personal digital assistant (PDA)*, and *personal information manager (PIM)* all refer to the same type of product. What many people call a laptop computer is now usually referred to as a notebook computer.

Notebook Computers

Notebook computers combine the CPU, a flat-panel display, and a hard drive into a single, small, portable unit. The miniaturization made possible by modern electronics provides a full computer system in a single package the size of a briefcase. Notebook computers usually weigh less than 10 pounds and include a battery so the computer can be operated anywhere. While notebook computers may cost more than a comparable full-size computer, their portability has made them very popular. Notebook computers can operate the same software as full-size desktop computers. The configuration of notebook computers can vary widely. Many notebook computers include a writable CD or DVD drive and a wireless card to connect to the Internet.

Today many businesspersons carry a notebook computer when they travel. Some employees may have the use of notebook computers on a full-time basis, while others have to borrow a notebook computer from a stock that is available for use by travelers. Prior to the trip, always check the configuration of the notebook computer to verify that the computer can handle the software needed. Review how to use the computer because the keyboard layout and operation of notebook computers vary widely.

Figure 6-4 Working at a café using a notebook computer.

You should always charge the computer's battery before a trip. In addition, it is always wise to take the following extras when traveling: extra battery and battery charger, electrical extension cord, electrical adapter to convert a three-hole to a two-hole plug, and emergency startup disk. To protect the computer, use a good-quality carrying case. Unfortunately, these extra items add considerable weight, which can become a problem for a traveler.

Many hotels frequented by business travelers have updated their wiring systems by adding additional electrical and phone outlets to accommodate computers, and many provide high-speed broadband connections to the Internet. These modifications allow travelers to check email and complete projects. In addition, many business hotels provide access for their guests to send and receive faxes. Hotels frequently charge for these services.

Handheld and Portable Electronic Devices

As electronics become smaller each year, computers have shrunk and are now small enough to fit in your hand. These computers may be referred to as handheld organizers, handheld computers, personal information management systems, electronic organizers, or personal digital assistants. Sometimes they are called Palm computers, after the name of one of the most successful brands of this type of computer (Palm Pilot). All of these handheld computers are so small and light they often fit into a coat pocket or purse and can be carried throughout the day. These computers can be as small as 6 by 4¼ inches in size. Handheld computers have no hard drives but store their information in built-in memory. Flash memory cards can be inserted into some handheld computers to increase the memory or load additional programs.

Handheld computers were originally designed to keep information previously stored in a pocket calendar, address book, memo pad, or scheduler. While the screens on these handheld computers display only a few lines of text, the information can be

Figure 6-5 A PDA with a touch-sensitive screen.

organized, searched alphabetically, searched by date, and so on, because the information is kept in digital format. Handheld computers have become very popular, and there are now thousands of computer programs that can be used on handheld computers. Many of these programs allow a user to download information from a regular computer. You may be asked to keep your executive's schedule on a desktop computer and transfer the information to a handheld computer so the executive can have an updated schedule when going to a meeting or on a trip. Word processing documents, spreadsheets, presentation software, and other programs can also be downloaded from a desktop computer and used on handheld computers.

There are several types of handheld computers. One type includes a small keyboard to input data. The keyboards on these computers are so small it is difficult to touch type as one does on a regular computer keyboard. The keyboards of some handheld computers are actually designed so a person can type using his or her thumbs. Another type of handheld computer does not include a keyboard but instead uses software that understands letters handwritten on a touch-sensitive screen.

As technology has developed, the capability of handheld computers has dramatically increased. Some handheld computers have wireless capability and can access the Internet. If the handheld has wireless access, the user can view the Internet and send and receive email. Other handhelds have telephone capability and can send and receive phone calls like a cell phone. In response, many cell phones now also include calendar, scheduling, address, and memo programs. A device that combines a cell phone, email, Internet access, and an organizer is sometimes called a *smartphone*.

Several handhelds take pictures with built-in small cameras. These pictures can be saved on flash memory cards or, if the handheld is wireless, can be immediately sent over a phone line or over the Internet. Some handheld computers have a *Global Position System* (*GPS*), which can locate and display exactly (to within 20 yards) the user's location. A handheld with a GPS and a mapping program can be very useful for a traveler. In addition to telephone or Internet capabilities, some handheld computers are designed to perform specific functions such as taking orders or managing data.

SOFTWARE

Computer Programs for the Office

A large variety of programs are available to organize and run an office efficiently. Commercial programs can be purchased from a computer store, and programs can be written by a computer programmer to meet the unique needs of a particular office. The needs of an office determine the computer programs used. For example, a travel

Figure 6-6 Smart phone.

office will use a reservation program to book airline flights, an auto parts store will use an inventory program to aid in the reorder of sold parts, and a doctor's office will use a scheduling program to schedule patient appointments.

Several types of computer programs are commonly used to support the basic functions of the office. Several of them are reviewed in the following sections. Many of the software programs increase office efficiency by transferring information created in one program into another program. Often this can be done by using the Copy and Paste features. For example, text created in a word processing document can be copied into a desktop publishing or presentation document. Likewise, graphics created in a desktop publishing or presentation document can be copied into a word processing or spreadsheet file. The integration of various software packages increases productivity and saves time for employees. As you learn to use computer software, be alert for the ability to exchange information from one computer package with another.

In the past, most software was installed on the individual computer or network computer system. Today we see a trend toward using software hosted over the Web. This software is often free or available by a subscription, but it may have fewer features that some of the traditional software packages. Using online software allows a user to access the software and his or her data files from any computer that has Internet access.

Which software can you use?

Word Processing

The major activity of most offices is the processing of information: ideas, data, and policies expressed in words or numbers. Word processing software, therefore, is the most common computer program used in offices. Today's word processing software does more than just assist the office worker in preparing reports and letters. Word

Figure 6-7 Employee using word processing software.

processing includes many features that increase the productivity of the office worker and enhance the quality of the finished product. These features include spell checks, thesauruses, and clip art. Word processing packages also create Internet Web pages.

Word processing software packages contain *templates*, which are a set of predefined styles for word processing projects. Most packages have templates for letters, reports, memos, newsletters, calendars, faxes, envelopes, and many additional documents. Microsoft Word is a commonly used word processing software package.

Word processing programs also provide the office with the ability to design and produce its own newsletters, brochures, forms, and manuals. Word processing software can be used by people who possess little artistic ability or design background but who wish to produce a professional-quality product. Many word processing software programs permit the operator to perform basic desktop publishing without the need for specialized software. Word processing programs provide numerous font styles and sizes, and include draw features and art that are used to enhance the document. In addition, text can be printed in columns or around illustrations for a professional appearance.

Desktop Publishing

Desktop publishing programs are available with advanced or specialized features that provide capabilities beyond those found in standard word processing packages. Programs are available for designing office forms, banners, and cards. More complex software programs are used for designing newsletters and brochures. Microsoft Publisher, a desktop publishing package, is part of the Microsoft Suite. Adobe InDesign and QuarkXPress are sophisticated publishing packages.

Database Management

Before computers arrived in the office, offices manually kept records for each customer, employee, project, or item inventoried. In today's office, a computerized file using a database management program would be used instead of manually maintaining records. Databases are commonly used where consistent information is required for a large number of items, such as personnel records, inventory records, and sales records.

Figure 6-8 Employee performing data entry.

The value of a database management program is its ability to store and organize large amounts of data. A handwritten file folder can be organized in only one way. The data in a database management system, however, can be organized, sorted, and reported in many ways.

The data in a database program is organized into *fields*, with each field containing one piece of information. For example, a college student database could contain information such as the student's last name, first name, college identification number, number of credit hours earned, date of enrollment in the school, and so on. The collection of fields for each student would be called a *record* (student record), and all of the student records would be considered a *file*.

Entering information into a file can be done at any time using a data-entry screen. Data-entry screens are written to ask for the specific information required for the file, and they can be designed to minimize operator errors. For example, the attempted entry of the date of February 20 would not be accepted if the data-entry screen were programmed to accept only valid calendar dates in the format 02/20/2009.

After data entry, the information in the file can then be sorted by several fields, selected, analyzed, summarized, and printed into reports. A variety of reports can be programmed in advance and printed whenever required. A college, for example, can use the database to review the progress of all students who entered school in a specific year by retrieving such information as: which department students are enrolled in, how many are still enrolled, and how many credit hours they have earned toward graduation. A report of this nature can be prepared in a matter of minutes using a computer, while the same report prepared from handwritten records could take days to prepare.

One of the most powerful aspects of database management systems is the ability to link the data from more than one file. If two database files have a field with identical information, such as a student identification number, they can be linked. Reports can be created from the new database file without having to reenter information into the computer.

Furthermore, database programs have the ability to create custom menus, screens, and reports. Many employees who use a company system or an inventory system are actually using a database management system in which the screens have been customized for use by that specific office. Microsoft Access is a commonly used database program.

Spreadsheets

Computer spreadsheet programs are useful to persons working with figures or money. Spreadsheets are constructed of grids consisting of *horizontal rows* and *vertical columns*. A single spreadsheet can consist of hundreds of rows and columns. Each blank space on the spreadsheet is called a *cell* and can be identified as the intersection of a row and column. Numbers in any cell can be added, subtracted, multiplied, or divided by any other number, or cell, on the spreadsheet. Each cell can also represent a complex mathematical formula.

Companies use spreadsheets to analyze financial data. The main advantage of a spreadsheet is the ability to change the number in any cell and have that change reflected automatically in all of the other numbers or formulas on the spreadsheet that are linked to that cell. This spreadsheet feature is used to consider "what if," and it is very useful in making projections. In seconds, an operator can see the effect of changing a single number or of changing a series of numbers. Then a decision can be made to accept the "what if" or not to accept it. Spreadsheets are very useful, therefore, in preparing budgets and sales projections.

Because cells and rows can be changed easily within a spreadsheet, spreadsheets are also often used to create tables just consisting of normal text. The editing features of spreadsheets are usually more powerful and flexible than the table features of word processing software, and the resulting table can be inserted into word processing and other software.

Spreadsheets are usually printed with columns of text and numbers, but spreadsheets can display the data in the form of graphs as well. Spreadsheets can exchange information with word processing software so the information can be incorporated in the text of another document such as an annual report or a presentation. Spreadsheets can also be formatted to accept changes in fonts, point sizes, row heights, and column widths. Clip art may be inserted, and borders and shading may be added to enhance the appearance of a presentation. Two commonly used spreadsheet software programs are MS Excel and Quattro Pro.

Presentation Software

Speakers at conferences or meetings often use presentation software to prepare visuals to highlight the main points of their speech. An effective presentation can quickly inform an audience, persuade listeners to accept a new idea, or entice an audience to purchase a product. With presentation software, graphics, text, and artwork can be combined into a display that is quicker to prepare and more flexible than using slides or overhead transparencies. By linking a desktop or notebook computer to a projection system, a presentation can be displayed to the audience directly from the computer. Sound and moving video can be added to text and graphic material to enhance the presentation. Using computer software, an employee can easily create a powerful presentation that an audience will remember. Microsoft PowerPoint is one of the most commonly used presentation software packages.

Clip Art and Drawing Software

The expanding graphics capabilities of computers can be used to create artistically attractive documents. Clip art can be inserted into word processing, desktop publishing, spreadsheet, and other software programs. With the appropriate software, anyone can draw perfect circles, squares, shapes, and straight lines, thereby creating professional looking art. The imaginative use of graphics can make reports and other printed materials more interesting.

Computer-Aided Design (CAD)

Computer-aided design software uses the computer to assist in the creation of technical drawings. CAD software is often used for the creation of engineering and architectural drawings and can create views showing two dimensions (2D) or three dimensions (3D). The computer can rotate a 3D CAD design to it can be viewed from all perspectives. CAD software is a quick way to fully visualize a design.

Scanning Software

Scanning software allows documents to be scanned using scanning equipment and saved to a computer file. Scanning software permits each scanned image to be given a name so it may be filed and easily retrieved. A page scanned into a computer is usually stored as a single image.

Project Management

Project management software is used to develop timetables for completing projects. With project management software, a project is broken down into many steps, and each step is assigned the amount of time needed to complete it. Using project management software, timelines can be created for a project. When project management software is used, it is easy for the user to determine the effect a delay in any step of the project can have on the overall completion of the project. Project management software is often used to plan complex projects that are completed by several team members.

Internet Browsers

Most people use part of the Internet referred to as the World Wide Web (or more simply, the Web). The Web uses a special computer language called *HyperText Markup Language* (*HTML*) or Extensible HyperText Markup Language (XHTML) for display of graphics and text. Internet browser software is used to connect to the Internet, search for information in HTML on the network, and download the results to the individual user's computer. Commonly used Internet browsers are Microsoft Internet Explorer, Firefox, Mozilla, Opera, and Netscape.

Web Development Software

Web pages can be created using a variety of software and codes. While special development software is available, word processing, spreadsheet, presentation programs, etc., can save a file for posting on the Web. Using Web software, literally everyone can become a worldwide publisher by posting their own information on the Web.

Antivirus Programs

A *virus* is an extremely dangerous computer program designed to interrupt or damage your computer or files. Viruses can destroy computer data or even erase all data on a hard disk. Viruses can be received from an email message or a shared diskette, or they can be downloaded from an Internet site. It is important to use an antivirus program to safeguard your computer. An antivirus program should be used to check a flash drive and hard drive to determine if it contains a virus. Updates to antivirus programs should be downloaded from the Internet frequently so your computer is protected against new viruses. If a virus is detected, the antivirus program will remove the virus from the computer before it causes damage.

> **HINT**
> Protect your computer with virus protection software.

Firewall

A firewall is a security software program or computer hardware that protects a computer from access by unauthorized users. Firewalls are used to protect the integrity of computers and networks from people who wish to steal information from the computer, change information in the computer system, or harm the computer system.

Email

One of the most common types of software used in business today is a program that exchanges electronic mail (email). Email programs handle the composing, sending, receiving, and storing of email messages and their attachments. Email programs include an address book where you can store the email addresses of people with whom you normally exchange messages. Furthermore, addresses can be organized into group lists so a single email message can be sent to all the people on the list.

Instant Messaging

Instant Messaging (IM) is an almost instant text messaging feature that appears via pop-up windows on computers. For example, if a company uses IM software, customers can click on icons on emails or Web pages and immediately connect with a sales representative. The instant chat option increases communication between the customers and the company, provides immediate answers to the customer, and demonstrates that the company cares about its customers. Instant Messaging is also available on cell phones.

CHAPTER REVIEW

1. Define hardware and software.
2. Explain flash memory.
3. Describe printers.
4. Explain the advantages of desktop publishing.
5. Explain the "what if" feature of a spreadsheet.
6. List six types of computer software used in an office.
7. What is an antivirus program?

ACTIVITIES

1. Read an article about the features of the newest version of a popular word processing program. Prepare an oral and written summary of the article. You may use the Internet to research this activity.
2. Survey several computer magazines and list the names of database management, word processing, and spreadsheets programs that are advertised or discussed.
3. Read the advertisements in computer magazines and compare the prices of three computer software packages.
4. Ask an office employee to describe two software application packages. Write a report describing the features they like and the features they dislike.
5. Go to a computer store and see what electronic calendar programs it carries. Write a short report about the features of the different programs. You may use the Internet to research this activity.

PROJECTS

Project 11

Keyboard the following letter and make all decisions concerning the letter style. Supply any additional information necessary. The letter is from Van Quieret, President of Russell Corporation.

Send this letter to Phyllis Maller and a copy to Daniel Kinsley, Meeting Coordinator. Ms. Maller's address is 324 Dixie Street, Moscow, ID 83843; and Mr. Kinsley's address is 8912 Columbia Blvd., Tucson, AZ 85701.

> There will be a stockholder's meeting on Monday, June 4, in my office, which is in the Dalton Building, 2004 K Street, NW, Washington, DC.
>
> We would like all stockholders to be present because there will be a discussion of changes in the bylaws. After the discussion, a vote will be taken on the proposed new bylaws. If you cannot be present, please send your proxy to me prior to the meeting.
>
> In addition to the discussion of the bylaws, we will review the Meadman Report and make a final decision on it. I am enclosing a summary of that report.
>
> I hope to see you on June 4.

Project 12

Keyboard the following letter and make all decisions concerning the letter style. Supply any additional information necessary.

Send this letter to the attention of Raymond A. Barron, Truax Corporation, 3859 Plains Drive, Chicago, IL 60627-1057. Include a subject line. The letter is from Denise D. Berlin, Purchasing Manager.

> Thank you for the demonstration of your communications software package. Also, I appreciated the specification sheets and computer documents you left with us. They have been helpful in reviewing your product. The operational procedures and documents have already been sent to our regional offices for their analysis and input. As you can imagine, we are eager to begin the project.
>
> If you have any additional information to add to your proposal, please fax it to me immediately.
>
> As I mentioned, we are evaluating several packages, and we have a committee already studying the proposals. As soon as a decision is made, I will call you.

HUMAN RELATIONS SKILL DEVELOPMENT

HR 6-1 The Employee in the Middle

It is possible to have two supervisors with conflicting ideas supervising one person. Receiving conflicting directions, projects, and assignments can put you in a difficult situation. If possible, arrange a meeting with both supervisors and yourself to discuss the project. Continue to meet as a group during the project. If you find yourself meeting individually with one supervisor in a decision-making session, write a for-your-information memo for the other supervisor or talk with the other supervisor before proceeding with the project.

- What would you say to two supervisors who continually give you conflicting directions on a project?
- Describe personal reasons that may cause two supervisors to have opposing views on all projects.

HR 6-2 Dealing with an Angry Client

You may need to calm an angry client on the telephone or in person: managing anger is a reoccurring problem in the workplace. Identify why the client is angry but do not react to the anger personally. When you become angry, you lose your ability to handle the situation objectively. Once you have determined the reason for the client's anger, encourage the client to discuss the problem even if the client needs to shout to do it. The anger should dissipate as the client discusses the problem. Once the client calms down, a solution to the problem can be discussed.

- Discuss the last instance when you were an irate client or customer.
- What types of business situations make you angry? Why?
- How would you handle an agitated client who had spoken to you several times in an angry voice?
- What tone of voice would you use with an irate client?

SITUATIONS

How would you handle the following situations?

- S 6-1 You made a mistake and scheduled two appointments at the same time on the same day. Both clients are now waiting to see your supervisor.
- S 6-2 As a supervisor, you must deal with the problem of personal use of the company copy machine. Company regulations prohibit personal use of the photocopier, but employees have been using the machine. While walking past the copy room, you notice Jennifer copying a cookbook. What would you do?
- S 6-3 The refrigerator and coffee pot in the lunch room are dirty, and no one wants to clean them. As a supervisor, what should you do?

PUNCTUATION REVIEW

Punctuate each of the following sentences. For a review of punctuation rules, see the Appendix.

1. Sue asked when is the annual meeting
2. Yes I have an account at that bank
3. Ralph asked if we joined the Wellness Program
4. Marcie Ross who prepared the communications has been with the company since March 17 1996
5. I transcribed the affidavit replied Martin
6. Based on our projections income should rise at least 25 percent for each of the next three years
7. Whether you are expanding your computer network system creating new databases or developing new application packages you most continually update your skills
8. We service the geographic areas of the U S Virgin Islands Puerto Rico and Hawaii
9. After working in the health services field for over twenty years she was ready for a career change

10. In managing this project Ms Wingate demonstrated considerable skill and professionalism
11. As you mentioned the duties were not explained
12. Our director Mr Wood attended the University of Rochester
13. Max said I cannot locate the executive director
14. Charlton Corporation is located at 289 West Field Drive Sarasota Florida
15. We offer a flexible reporting service which allows the customer many options

CD ASSIGNMENTS

CD Assignment 6-1

Open the file **CD6-1_ITM** on your Student CD and follow the instructions to complete the job.

CD Assignment 6-2

Open the file **CD6-2_IHC** on your Student CD and follow the instructions to complete the job.

CD Assignment 6-3

Open the file **CD6-3_Scan** on your Student CD and follow the instructions to complete the job.

CHAPTER 7

....

Information and Records Management: Filing

Objectives

After studying this chapter, you should be able to:

1. Set up a file drawer and prepare file folders.
2. Understand the concepts of subject and geographic filing.
3. Understand the concepts of electronic filing.
4. Apply alphabetic filing rules to a filing system.

TECHNOLOGY IN RECORDS MANAGEMENT

One of the ways that the Internet is revolutionizing office procedures is in the receipt of data and processing of records. As you saw in the previous chapter, many offices use database management software to maintain information and to organize and retrieve data. In a database system, data can easily be stored, added to, deleted, sorted in many different ways (such as alphabetically, by number, by amount), and reorganized. As use of the Internet continues to grow, people and business are completing more transactions electronically. When people use the Internet to purchase items, register a software purchase, view a credit card bill, or apply for a government benefit, they are entering information into a computer database. These computer databases handle the filing and retrieval of information quickly and accurately without human intervention. As more transactions are performed over the Internet, records management will increasingly be done using the computer. As long as people and businesses continue to use paper documents, however, there is a need to record, store, and retrieve documents in the office.

WHY FILE?

Every office receives information, letters, reports, applications, or orders that relate to the business. After these documents are processed, they must be stored in an organized way so they can be quickly and easily retrieved when they are needed. The ability to

Figure 7-1   Moveable file shelves.

locate these documents is vital to the efficiency and success of an office. Documents or files that cannot be found when required cause many problems:

- Valuable office time is wasted looking for lost files.
- It is embarrassing to tell clients that their files cannot be found.
- A file that cannot be located may contain valuable information that will require considerable time and expense to reassemble.

Can you find the file?

FILE CABINETS

HINT

Standard file cabinets are vertical or lateral.

The most common way to store paper documents in an office is to use either a vertical or lateral file cabinet.

- *Vertical file cabinets* are available in two-, three-, four-, and five-drawer models, with one drawer stacked on top of the other. Each drawer is approximately 28 inches deep and can be pulled forward to its entire length. Therefore, vertical cabinets must be placed where room is available for a person to work when a drawer is fully extended. Vertical files may be

MY SUCCESS STORY

My Name Is Katie

I have been administrative assistant for almost fifteen years. Although my career choice is often stressful, I love my job. Each day is another adventure filled with new challenges. Yes, I feel that I am up to a new challenge every day. I am high-energy person and thrive on keeping busy. I work for a large company with many opportunities for advancement. I enjoy the variety of job I perform and am eager to learn new jobs. My personality style is a good match for my company and job responsibilities. This is the perfect career choice for me.

Figure 7-2   Employee using a lateral file cabinet.

purchased in legal-size widths, for papers 8.5 inches × 14 inches, or in letter-size widths, for papers 8.5 inches × 11 inches.

- *Lateral file cabinets* are approximately 15 inches deep and from 36 to 42 inches wide. Opening a drawer exposes all files in the drawer at once. Lateral cabinets take up more wall space than vertical files, but they can be used along walkways because of their design. Lateral files are available in models that contain two, three, four, five, or six drawers, and they are available for storage of legal- or letter-size papers. Lateral file cabinets can contain a shelf located at a comfortable working height so papers can be processed while standing at the file cabinet.

File storage units have changed to meet the requirements of a variety of users and the need to store new technologies. There are many other styles of file storage units that meet specific needs, such as special media cabinets for storing microfiche, microfilm, computer disks and tapes, CDs, or DVDs. There are cabinets built for each of these media where drawers are the correct height to reflect the size of the microfilm, DVD, or other medium. Using these media cabinets, an office can store the maximum amount of items with no wasted space.

In addition, file storage units can be built into a wall, such as small pigeonhole units used to store working files. Specially sized cabinets are available to store papers, cards, brochures, etc., that are 3 × 5 inches, 4 × 6 inches, 8.5 × 11 inches, and 11 × 14 inches. Open shelves can be built into a wall to store files, or shelves can be placed on rollers to expose many files at once. Large, wall-size electronic filing systems can utilize all the space from floor to ceiling, and files are retrieved electronically with the touch of a button.

STORAGE OF DOCUMENT IMAGES

While most offices store original paper documents in large filing cabinets, technology can assist in the storing of documents as images in electronic or photographic form. Storing documents electronically or photographically saves significant space, and a copy of a document can be printed easily when a paper copy is required.

Figure 7-3 Pigeonhole filing cabinets.

Microfilm

Microfilm photographs documents on high-resolution film and stores the information in miniature form. Thousands of pages of documents can easily be photographed and stored on a single piece of microfilm. This process greatly reduces the requirements for storage space, and a room full of paper documents can be contained in a single microfilm drawer. Microfilm is available in several forms:

- *Microfiche* is a 4- × 6-inch sheet of film on which the pages are photographed in columns and rows. Each page can easily be located without having to go through all the previous pages.

- Cassettes, cartridges, or reels of microfilm contain as many as five thousand pages of copy that are photographed consecutively. Microfilm comes in two sizes—16 millimeter and 35 millimeter—and is loaded on long rolls or spools of film.

- *Aperture cards* have an opening in which a frame of microfilm is mounted. Aperture cards are often used for engineering drawings. Because the cards are keypunched (they have small holes punched in them, which represent letters and numbers), they can be easily sorted to find a single image.

- *Microfilm jackets* contain clear material sealed together on at least two sides. Inside the jacket are channels where the microfilm can be placed. Individual frames can be inserted easily, and updating of files is a simple task.

- Microfilm must be placed in a microfilm reader that enlarges the image so it can be read. Many microfilm readers can also print a page from the microfilm.

Today existing microfilm, microfiche, and aperture cards are being digitized so the information can be stored on CD-ROMs, DVDs, or PCs, and then filed, faxed, and networked. By digitizing this information, the information can easily be updated and shared with many users through standard computer technologies. Microfilm is still used because the information can be archived for 500 or more years and the life of digitized information is unknown. The Library of Congress and the Smithsonian continue to microfilm data to ensure the ability for their long-term retrieval.

Computer Storage

Computers are used to store files electronically. As discussed in Chapter 6, documents can be entered into a computer using a scanner, and each page of the document is stored as an image. Computer software treats the documents as though they are stored in a filing cabinet. Documents can be organized in folders, drawers, and cabinets. Pages can be automatically indexed, or indexing can be done manually so the user can find a document. Electronic notes can be attached to the documents, just as handwritten notes are attached to paper documents.

Electronic storage of document images requires considerable memory and could overwhelm the hard drives of most computers. Copies of documents generated by computers are stored in several ways.

- *CD*—either a CD-ROM (used only once) or writable CDRW (can be rewritten and used again). Documents can be stored on a CD, read on the computer, and printed on paper.
- *Digital video disk (DVD)* is the same physical size as a CD but holds more information. The storage of many documents or images requires large computer files, and the use of DVDs is now replacing the use of CDs for large storage needs.
- *Computer Output Microfilm (COM)* allows the computer to transfer data in computer files to a laser, which then creates a microfilm or microfiche.

SETTING UP FILES

File Folders

Before you place a document in a file cabinet or other storage unit, you should prepare a file folder and label. A large selection of file folders, labels, and accessories is available, each designed for a specific purpose and all intended to simplify the filing process. The most common file folder is made of heavy manila (beige) paper and has a tab on the top on which to place a label. The tab may extend across the entire top of the folder (*full cut*), across one-third of the folder (*third cut*), or across one-fifth of the folder (*fifth cut*). The use of third-cut or fifth-cut folders allows filing personnel to stagger the labels for easy reading or to designate subdivisions of a project. File folders are creased on the bottom so the folder can expand to hold more paper without blocking the folder label. Folders are available in a multitude of colors other than the standard manila. The use of colored folders can reduce errors and save time when filing or retrieving documents by using folders of the same color for a particular project, type of activity, or year.

Some offices use *hanging folders*, which are suspended from tracks along the sides of the file drawer. Documents can be filed directly in a hanging folder, or they can be placed first in a file folder and then related file folders can be grouped by placing them together in a hanging folder. Color coding of the file folder or hanging folder improves organization and quickly locates a specific file. Other types of folders include plastic file folders, which are good for heavy files, and expanding folders,

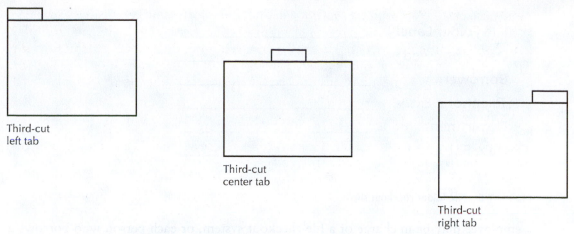

Third-cut
left tab

Third-cut
center tab

Third-cut
right tab

Figure 7-4 Third-cut file folders.

which are designed with expansion folds at the bottom to accommodate several inches of documents. Also, file folders may contain fasteners to secure papers. Some folders have a fastener in the front for a limited number of pages, while others fasten all of the papers in the folder. File folders with internal panels are available so papers can be grouped together for easy reference.

Folder Labels

File folder labels are small slips of paper attached by adhesive to a backing sheet and are available in an assortment of colors, sizes, and shapes. While many offices use standard white labels, color-coded labels are often used as a method of organizing a filing system. If a label has a line of color, the label should be prepared so the color is at the top of the label.

Prepare the label by writing or keyboarding the file name while the label is still attached to the backing sheet. Labels can also be generated by computer software packages and printed on file folder label sheets purchased from an office supply store. After the label is prepared, it is removed from the backing sheet and quickly placed on the file folder. Information about the various types of labels available can be obtained on the Internet.

When keyboarding a folder label for the name of an individual, key the last name, a comma, space, the first name, space, and then the middle name or initial. Labels for company names are keyed according to the indexing units discussed later in this chapter.

Organizing the Filing System

An efficient filing system should contain *guides* that organize and subdivide the contents of the file drawers. The guides are made of heavy cardboard or other substantial material and direct the eye to the desired file. The guides divide a cabinet drawer into smaller sections based on the filing system used; typical guides are included in the discussions of filing systems in the next section. In a geographical filing system, guides may be organized by state with city subguides. The labeled file folders are then placed in the drawer using the guides and divisions.

A well-organized filing system goes beyond the preparation of file folders and takes into account how the files are used in the office. In many offices, files will be borrowed from the cabinets by employees. When files are borrowed, there is always the question of when and if the files will be returned. To ensure the return of file folders, a checkout system should be established. When files are borrowed, only complete folders should be taken. Individual items should not be removed from file folders. A designated

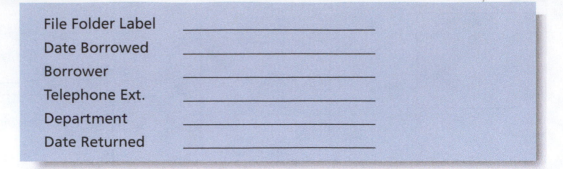

File Folder Label	_____
Date Borrowed	_____
Borrower	_____
Telephone Ext.	_____
Department	_____
Date Returned	_____

Figure 7-5 File folder checkout slip.

employee may be in charge of a file checkout system, or each person who borrows a file may be responsible for completing a checkout slip. A sample checkout slip is shown in Figure 7-5. The checkout slip may be a 3- × 5-inch card kept in a box, a large cardboard sheet placed in the drawer where the folder is kept, or a computer-designed checkout form. Regardless of the system used, an established procedure should be followed to encourage prompt return of file folders.

Because filing space is usually limited and expensive, inactive or old files should be moved to an inactive storage area so active files are easily accessible. Files can be moved at a specific time or whenever the file drawers are full. The beginning of the calendar or fiscal year is a common time when offices move older files created before a specific date to inactive storage so there is ample room for the new files. Inactive files can be placed in corrugated or plastic storage boxes purchased from office supply stores. These boxes are available in legal and letter size.

Rules for consistent filing have been developed by many organizations, but some offices use their own filing procedures instead of following standardized procedures. Therefore, when you are working with a new filing system, review the system carefully before filing or retrieving documents.

If a file could be placed in several locations or you are uncertain about how to file it, cross-reference it. A cross-reference indicates alternate methods of filing a document. For example, if you are unsure of how to file a document with a company name, you can file the document where you think it should be placed, then place a sheet of paper, the cross-reference, at the location of your second filing option to inform the user where the folder is located. A list of all cross-references can be kept in the file drawer directing the user to look at alternate filing locations.

FILING SYSTEMS

HINT

Filing systems:
Chronological
Subject
Geographic
Numeric
Alphabetic

Five types of filing systems are commonly used to organize documents for easy retrieval: the chronological, subject, geographic, numeric, and alphabetic filing systems.

Cross-Reference List

4007	McHale, Laura
4008	Livingston, Mary J.
4009	Kanawha Industries
4010	Fernando Maxwell
4011	Amos Industries

Cross-Reference List

Amos Industries	4011
Fernando, Maxwell	4010
Kanawha Industries	4009
Livingston, Mary J.	4008
McHale, Laura	4007

Figure 7-6 Cross-reference for numeric filing.

Chronological Filing

Some offices maintain a chronological file, often called a *chron file*, which is a date order filing system that contains a copy of everything that has been mailed or prepared for Internet use. This document file is kept in date order, with the most recent date on top. The chronological files is used as a quick reference or review of a project and can be helpful if you do not remember how something was filed but know the approximate creation date. A drawer in a typical chron filing system has guides to separate files by year, then by month (January, February, March, etc.).

Subject Filing

Subject filing is a filing system where files are arranged by the topic of the document rather than the name of a person or company. With subject filing, a letter concerning the purchase of the Webster Building is filed under the topic, Webster Building.

Budgets
Year 2010
Year 2009
Year 2008
Year 2007
Year 2006
Year 2005

Company Forms
Employee Assistance Programs
Employment
Evaluations
Leave
Local Travel
Long-Distance Travel

Personnel Files
Baldwin, Jenny
James, Tammy
Lewis, Sally
Peterson, Julie
Potter, Laura
Tran, An
Zhou, Dave

Seminars
Budget Forecasting
Computer Software
Environmental Safety
Human Relations Skills
Management Techniques

Vendors
Brooks & Sons
Lee Industries
Robertson Supplies

Figure 7-7 Sample subject filing.

Figure 7-8   Sample geographic filing.

Florida
Ft. Lauderdale
Ft. Myers
Miami
Sarasota

Maryland
Baltimore
Frederick
Rockville

New York
Buffalo
Rochester
Syracuse

Within the topic, the files are arranged alphabetically or chronologically. A drawer in a typical subject filing system has guides to separate files by subject in alphabetic order or perhaps by topic (for example, Contracts, Personnel, Complaints, Bigelow Project). To facilitate locating files, a cross-referencing system using an index of subjects is often established.

Geographical Filing

Geographical filing is a filing system where files are arranged according to geographic location. Businesses that are organized by geographical locations, such as sales districts, often use geographic filing. Files are arranged alphabetically within the geographic divisions. A drawer in a typical geographic filing system has guides to separate files by year, then by main geographic unit (such as a state), then smaller units (such as counties or cities).

File drawers are usually established with the main geographical categories as the primary guides. Secondary guides are used for subdivisions. For example, the system in Figure 7-8 uses the state as the primary guide and the city as the secondary guide. The file folder first lists the state, and then the city, and then a specific client in that city.

Numerical Filing

Numerical filing assigns a number to each company, person, or project. The numeric code is placed on each document to be filed. Numeric files are often used in banking, credit card accounts, and accounts receivable where each client has a separate account number. The account numbers are a quick way to identify persons who may have similar names. A drawer in a typical numerical filing system has guides to separate files by number, perhaps a guide for every 100 files. To assist in locating files, the office must have a cross-referencing system using a card-file index or computer list of clients and their numeric codes.

Figure 7-9   Sample numeric filing.

4076
4077
4078
4079
4080

Alphabetical Filing

Although alphabetical filing is the most commonly used filing system, there is no single set of alphabetic rules used by all offices. Some offices use filing rules developed by the Association of Records Managers and Administrators (ARMA), but alphabetical rules vary from office to office. As an employee, you should study the filing system used in your office prior to filing documents.

An understanding of the alphabetical filing system is also required to establish and use subject and geographic filing systems. This chapter will contain common alphabetical filing rules used in many offices, examples of the filing rules, practice exercises for each rule, and a continuous review of previously learned rules.

The first step when filing is to index the name. Indexing means dividing the name of an individual, company, or title into separate units. Each word is considered an *indexing unit*.

Filing rules follow alphabetic order. Because "a" comes before "b," "apple" would be filed before "banana." When filing two names, look at the first letter of each name to determine which would be filed first. If the two first letters of each name are the same, look at the second letters and follow the alphabetic order of the second letters. If the second letters are the same, look at the third letters, and so on. This procedure determines which name should be filed first.

Figure 7-10   Managing a large filing system.

ALPHABETIC FILING RULES

Rule 1: Simple Personal Names

- When filing personal names, divide the name into the following indexing units.

Unit 1	Last name
Unit 2	First name
Unit 3	Middle name or initial

Names	Unit 1	Unit 2	Unit 3
Lillian Kay Martin	Martin	Lillian	Kay
Edward Fairfax	Fairfax	Edward	
Stacy Ann Moore	Moore	Stacy	Ann
Kenneth Ted Hardy	Hardy	Kenneth	Ted

- After determining the indexing units, alphabetize the names according to unit 1. The above group of names is filed in the following order:

Unit 1	Unit 2	Unit 3
Fairfax	Edward	
Hardy	Kenneth	Ted
Martin	Lillian	Kay
Moore	Stacy	Ann

- If you have two unit 1s that are exactly alike, unit 2 determines which name is filed first. If units 1 and 2 are exactly alike, alphabetize according to unit 3.

Names	Unit 1	Unit 2
Patricia Dunlap	Dunlap	Patricia
Roger Dunlap	Dunlap	Roger

  Patricia Dunlap is filed before Roger Dunlap.

- Individual letters are considered as indexing units. The period following the initial is ignored.

Names	Unit 1	Unit 2	Unit 3
Emma B. Ball	Ball	Emma	B
Doyle R. Beyer	Beyer	Doyle	R

- If a name is abbreviated, index it using the abbreviation.

Names	Unit 1	Unit 2	Unit 3
Bill O. Levy	Levy	Bill	O
Joe C. Rose	Rose	Joe	C

Rule 2: File Nothing Before Something

- Consider the following names. Since Orlans is the last name for both persons, look at the first name—L and Libby. The initial L has nothing following it so L is filed before Libby.

Names	Unit 1	Unit 2	Unit 3
L. Orlans	Orlans	L	
Libby Orlans	Orlans	Libby	

- Consider the following two similar names.

Names	Unit 1	Unit 2	Unit 3
Robert France	France	Robert	
F. Frances	Frances	F	

France is filed before Frances

France_   File the blank space (nothing) before the s.
Frances

Practice 7-1

Use one 3- × 5-inch card for each folder to be filed. Divide each name in the following list into its indexing units, and write the names on the 3 × 5 cards. Move the cards around so that the first card in alphabetical order is on top, the second card is next, etc. After all the cards are alphabetized, open the Practice Filing Form **CH7_FF** on your student CD. On your Filing Form file, key in the information from your 3 × 5 cards. Key the information from the first card in alphabetical order onto line one, key the second card in alphabetical order onto line two, key the third card in alphabetical order onto line three, etc. Use Save As to save the file with the name **Practice 7-1**. Print the file.

Folders to be filed

1. Holly Arnold
2. Amos J. Homer
3. Norma Joan Pendell
4. Anne Elizabeth Anderson
5. Donna Emily Parker
6. Louis K. Yeager
7. Donna Emilyann Parker
8. Louis Kenneth Yeager
9. Greg Snyder
10. Randy Ray Tuckwillar
11. Martha R. Norris
12. Norma Jean Pendell
13. Lillian Phyllis Martin
14. Henry R. Feliciano
15. Cyrus Martine
16. Argelio F. Fellows

Figure 7-11   Card filing cabinets.

Rule 3: Identical Names

- If people have identical last, first, and middle names, then the city, state, street name, and street address are used to determine the filing order. Consider the following two similar names.

Suzy Gomez
890 Butler Road
Ft. Wayne, Indiana

Suzy Gomez
712 Grazing Drive
Chicago, Illinois

Ms. Gomez of Chicago would be filed before Ms. Gomez of Ft. Wayne.

Unit 1	Unit 2	City
Gomez	Suzy	Chicago
Gomez	Suzy	Ft. Wayne

Rule 4: Seniority Titles

- Seniority titles are used as the last indexing unit in a name. Seniority titles include Junior, Senior, Jr., Sr., II, and III. Companies differ on spelling in full or abbreviating Jr. and Sr. Always cross-reference if necessary.

Names	Unit 1	Unit 2	Unit 3	Unit 4
Richard B. Davis	Davis	Richard	B	
Richard Davis, Jr.	Davis	Richard	Junior	
Richard Davis, Sr.	Davis	Richard	Senior	
Donald R. Miller, Jr.	Miller	Donald	R	Junior

Rule 5: Business Names

- Index names of businesses according to how the names are written on the letterhead.
- However, if the company name contains a person's first and last name, some organizations use the person's last name as the first indexing unit and the first name as the second indexing unit.
- If a company name contains single letters, index each letter as a separate indexing unit.
- If a business name contains an acronym (a word formed from the first letters of several words) or an abbreviation that is printed in capital letters on letterhead, index the unit as one word. For example, in the name MGM Grand Hotel, the first indexing unit is MGM.
- The rules in your office may vary when indexing company names containing a person's first and last names. Review your company's procedures before filing materials.

Names	Unit 1	Unit 2	Unit 3
Broad Equipment	Broad	Equipment	
Shady Road Hospital	Shady	Road	Hospital
Coastal Resorts	Coastal	Resorts	
Sunny Day Deli	Sunny	Day	Deli
L J Enterprises	L	J	Enterprises
LAJ Enterprises	LAJ	Enterprises	
MGM Grand Hotel	MGM	Grand	Hotel
Ronald Watson Jewelers	Ronald	Watson	Jewelers
(alternate method)	Watson	Ronald	Jewelers

Rule 6: Abbreviations

- Abbreviations in business names should be spelled in full. Examples of abbreviations in business names include Inc. (Incorporated), Co. (Company), Ltd. (Limited), and Mfg. (Manufacturing).
- The terms *Mr., Mrs.,* and *Ms.* preceding personal names are not considered abbreviations and are not used as an indexing unit. They may, however, be placed in parentheses at the end if necessary for clarification.

Names	Unit 1	Unit 2	Unit 3
Champagne Interiors Inc.	Champagne	Interiors	Incorporated
Mrs. Sally Rogers	Rogers	Sally (Mrs.)	
Mr. William Rogers	Rogers	William	

Rule 7: Possessives

- If a name is possessive, ignore the apostrophe.

Names	Unit 1	Unit 2	Unit 3
Chuck's Garage	Chucks	Garage	
Frances' Gift Shop	Frances	Gift	Shop
Royce's Fruit Market	Royces	Fruit	Market

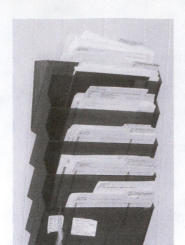

Figure 7-12 Wall-mounted filing system.

Practice 7-2

Use one 3- × 5-inch card for each folder to be filed. (You may reuse the cards from the previous practice by drawing a line through the names.) Divide each name in the following list into its indexing units, and write the names on the 3 × 5 cards. Move the cards around so that the first card in alphabetical order is on top, the second card is next, etc. After all of the cards are alphabetized, open the Practice Filing Form **CH7_FF** on your student CD. On your Filing Form file, key in the information from your 3 × 5 cards. Key the information from the first card in alphabetical order onto line one, key the second card in alphabetical order onto line two, key the third card in alphabetical order onto line three, etc. Use Save As to save the file with the name **Practice 7-2**. Print the file.

Folders to be filed

1. Martin J. Davis III
2. Elmer I. Elliott, 900 Pear Drive, Austin, TX
3. Dennis K. Watson, Senior
4. Paul R. Bates, Senior
5. Lottie Russell, 8934 Crown Avenue, Tacoma, WA
6. Phil W. Morgan, 5810 Earlston Drive, Seattle, WA
7. Floyd Haque
8. Phil W. Morgan, 3478 Albia Road, Portland, ME
9. Cecil's Department Store
10. Horn's Antiques, Ltd.
11. C. Jay Istar, Junior
12. Kelly's Leather Shop
13. Jerry's Garage
14. Elmer I. Elliott, 1723 Eagle Court, Atlanta, GA
15. Martin J. Davis II
16. Lottie Russell, 700 Fordham Drive, Salem, OR
17. Paul R. Bates, Junior
18. Ronald Freeman, Jr.
19. Eugene Frederick, Jr.

20. J. Elmer Elliott, 3078 Veirs Road, Bethesda, MD

21. Dennis K. Watson, Jr.

22. S. Hanson

23. Shamsul Hanst

24. Floyd D. Haque

25. Phil S. Morgan, 2309 Diamond Avenue, Portland, OR

26. M. Shamsul Hanst

27. Samuel Hanson

28. C. Jay Istar, Senior

29. Krammar's Grocery

30. Randy's Bakery

Rule 8: Personal Titles

- If a name contains a title, disregard the title if it is used with a complete name. Place the title in parentheses at the end.

Names	Unit 1	Unit 2	Unit 3
Dr. George Quade	Quade	George	(Dr.)
President Harold Roselli	Roselli	Harold	(President)
Sylvia Walters, Ph.D.	Walters	Sylvia	(Ph.D.)

- If a title is used with an incomplete name, the title is the first indexing unit. An incomplete name does not have a first and last name.

Names	Unit 1	Unit 2
Father Malone	Father	Malone
Rabbi Wise	Rabbi	Wise

Rule 9: Married Woman's Name

- When indexing a married woman's name, include her first name as an indexing unit, if it is known.

Names	Unit 1	Unit 2	Unit 3
Joyce M. Davis	Davis	Joyce	M
Brenda Sue Morell	Morell	Brenda	Sue
Mrs. Fred Sikes (Linda)	Sikes	Linda	

- Some companies place the husband's name in parentheses.

Name	Unit 1	Unit 2
Kate Mullens (Mrs. Harry Mullens)	Mullens	Kate (Mrs. Harry)

- Ms. or Mrs. may be placed in parentheses at the end.

Name	Unit 1	Unit 2	Unit 3
Ms. Helen C. Harvey	Harvey	Helen	C (Ms.)

- If only the husband's name is known, index using the husband's name and place the personal title at the end.

Name	Unit 1	Unit 2	Unit 3
Mrs. Harry Mullens	Mullens	Harry (Mrs.)	

Rule 10: Hyphenated Names

- A hyphenated name is considered one indexing unit, and the hyphen is ignored.

Names	Unit 1	Unit 2	Unit 3
After-School Plaza	AfterSchool	Plaza	
Jane Bailey-Starr	BaileyStarr	Jane	
Mason-Todd Garage	MasonTodd	Garage	
Peck-Boyd Shop	PeckBoyd	Shop	
Kay Stone-Albert	StoneAlbert	Kay	

Rule 11: Directions

- If a business name contains a directional word, index it as written.

Name	Unit 1	Unit 2	Unit 3
Northwest Business	Northwest	Business	
North West Foods	North	West	Foods
Southwest Service Center	Southwest	Service	Center

Practice 7-3

Use one 3- × 5-inch card for each folder to be filed. (You may reuse the cards from the previous practice by drawing a line through the names.) Divide each name in the following list into its indexing units, and write the names on the 3 × 5 cards. Move the cards around so that the first card in alphabetical order is on top, the second card is next, etc. After all the cards are alphabetized, open the Practice Filing Form **CH7_FF** on your student CD. On your Filing Form file, key in the information from your 3 × 5 cards. Key the information from the first card in alphabetical order onto line one, key the second card in alphabetical order onto line two, key the third card in alphabetical order onto line three, etc. Use Save As to save the file with the name **Practice 7-3**. Print the file.

Folders to be filed

1. Judge Richards
2. Adkins-Anderson Clothiers
3. Leslie Pratt-Wallace
4. Senator Robert C. Byrd
5. Mrs. Sharon Salamon (Mrs. John)
6. Sister Melissa
7. Judge Raymond Rebuck
8. Mini-Mart Stores
9. Louise Abbott-Lawford

10. Mary-Rose Foods
11. Congresswoman Barbara Jordan
12. W. Richard-Hardkins
13. Ms. Hanna Haye
14. South East Movies
15. Dr. Mary Salcetti
16. Reverend Iverson
17. Edward Recht, Senior
18. North West Cleaners
19. Judge S. Rebuck
20. Reverend Daniel P. Villegas

Rule 12: Minor Words and Symbols

- Minor words and symbols are indexed as separate units. The following are
  examples of minor words: *the, and, for*. The following are examples of
  symbols: &, #, $, *, and @. If *The* is the first word in a name, place it as the
  last indexing unit.

Names	Unit 1	Unit 2	Unit 3	Unit 4
The Clays	Clays	The		
Kids on the Move	Kids	on	the	Move
Young & Bates	Young	&	Bates	

Rule 13: Prefixes

- If a name begins with a prefix, consider the prefix and the word that follows
  as one unit. Examples of prefixes are *l', el, la, las, mac, mc,* and *o'*.

Names	Unit 1	Unit 2	Unit 3
Jose DeSardo	DeSardo	Jose	
El Grande Hotel	ElGrande	Hotel	
Pierre La Piana	LaPiana	Pierre	
Belle LaPlante	LaPlante	Belle	
Richard N. LeVan	LeVan	Richard	N

Figure 7-13 Pamphlet filing system.

Rule 14: Numbers

- Business names with numbers are divided into indexing units as written. If the number is spelled out, index it spelled out in alphabetical order. Numbers in digit form are considered one unit and written in digit form. Business names in digit form are filed in numerical order before alphabetical names are filed.

Names	Unit 1	Unit 2	Unit 3
24 Hour Shop	24	Hour	Shop
500 Lounge	500	Lounge	
Big Ten Shop	Big	Ten	Shop
Biglerville 2000 Club	Biglerville	2000	Club
One Market Place	One	Market	Place

Practice 7-4

Use one 3- × 5-inch card for each folder to be filed. (You may reuse the cards from the previous practice by drawing a line through the names.) Divide each name in the following list into its indexing units, and write the names on the 3 × 5 cards. Move the cards around so that the first card in alphabetical order is on top, the second card is next, etc. After all the cards are alphabetized, open the Practice Filing Form **CH7_FF** on your student CD. On your Filing Form file, key in the information from your 3 × 5 cards. Key the information from the first card in alphabetical order onto line one, key the second card in alphabetical order onto line two, key the third card in alphabetical order onto line three, etc. Use Save As to save the file with the name **Practice 7-4**. Print the file.

Folders to be filed

1. The Ladder Store
2. Peter W. LeBrun
3. P & R Incorporated
4. 52 Week Travel
5. The Big Men
6. Nancy McDonald
7. Hartz & Porter
8. T. M. LeBlanc
9. Martha Sue O'Connor
10. Luigi Ira LeBow
11. Amy McCabe, D.D.S.
12. U. S. Construction
13. Atkins and Jackson Associates
14. Women for Success Inc.
15. Rollins Shoes
16. Young at Heart Golf
17. Clay's Bed and Bedding
18. 300 Sovern

19. Come and Go Cleaners
20. Jose's Books
21. J. W. Rollins Shoes
22. Romeo Design Interiors
23. Cooking 24 Hours
24. Dr. Amy Sanford
25. Books on Travel

Rule 15: Banks

- Index banks according to the most important word.

Names	Unit 1	Unit 2	Unit 3	Unit 4
Maine Federal Bank	Maine	Federal	Bank	
Reid Thrift Bank	Reid	Thrift	Bank	
Savings Bank of Roanoke	Roanoke	Savings	Bank	of

- If the bank names are exactly alike, use the city, state, street, and building number—in that order—to determine the filing order. Consider the following three branches of the Chain Savings Bank:

Chain Savings Bank
200 Williams Drive
Boston, MA

Chain Savings Bank
500 Colonial Drive
Boston, MA

Chain Savings Bank
3200 Hampton Lane
Braintree, MA

Unit 1	Unit 2	Unit 3	Address
Chain	Savings	Bank	Boston, MA Colonial Drive
Chain	Savings	Bank	Boston, MA Williams Drive
Chain	Savings	Bank	Braintree, MA

Rule 16: Radio and Television Stations

- Radio and television stations are indexed as though the call letters were a word. When AM, FM, or TV are included with the call letters, they are Unit 2.

Names	Unit 1	Unit 2
KANG	KANG	
KONG-FM	KONG	FM
KONG-TV	KONG	TV
WZTF(FM)	WZTF	FM

- Some companies use the words *Radio Station* or *Television Station* as the first two units.

Name	Unit 1	Unit 2	Unit 3
KANG	Radio	Station	KANG

Rule 17: School Names

- A school name is indexed in the order written unless it contains a person's first name and last name. In that case, the last name is the first indexing unit. Some companies use *University* as the first indexing unit, and others place the most important word in the title as the first unit. For example, University of Washington may be filed as *University of Washington* or as *Washington University of*. Always cross-reference the file when there is a question about how to file it.

Names	Unit 1	Unit 2	Unit 3	Unit 4
Arnold Junior High School	Arnold	Junior	High	School
The John Dewey School	Dewey	John	School	The
Maine Academy	Maine	Academy		
University of Washington	University	of	Washington	
(alternate)	Washington	University	of	

- Schools with identical names are first indexed by the school name. After the school name, index by city first and then by state, if necessary.

  Green Elementary School, Dayton, Ohio

  Green Elementary School, Fairmont, West Virginia

Unit 1	Unit 2	Unit 3	Unit 4
Green	Elementary	School	Dayton
Green	Elementary	School	Fairmont

Practice 7-5

Use one 3- × 5-inch card for each folder to be filed. (You may reuse the cards from the previous practice by drawing a line through the names.) Divide each name in the following list into its indexing units, and write the names on the 3 × 5 cards. Move the cards around so that the first card in alphabetical order is on top, the second card is next, etc. After all the cards are alphabetized, open the Practice Filing Form **CH7_FF** located on your student CD. On your Filing Form file, key in the information from your 3 × 5 cards. Key the information from the first card in alphabetical order onto line one, key the second card in alphabetical order onto line two, key the third card in alphabetical order onto line three, etc. Use Save As to save the file with the name **Practice 7-5**. Print the file.

Folders to be filed

1. McArthur Federal Savings, 2200 Lake Street, Dayton, OH
2. Berkeley Springs Country Inn
3. Williams Resort and Inn
4. Washington Federal, 702 Russell Avenue, Seattle, WA
5. Valley Bank, 307 Jefferson St., Rockville, MD

5 6. McArthur Federal Savings, 300 Wilkins Blvd., Cincinnati, OH

16 7. WETA-FM

9 8. Oaklands High School, 3789 Spring Drive, Norfolk, VA

19 9. WKZA-TV

3 10. Captain Standish Motor Lodge

4 11. Kensington Elementary School

10 12. Rochester High School

11 13. San Diego High School

8 14. Oaklands High School, 3200 Luck Road, Houston, TX

13 15. Valley Bank, 3000 River Rd., Bethesda, MD

7 16. Oahu High School

17 17. William Howard Taft Elementary

15 18. WCHS

2 19. The Bank of Cincinnati, 1775 Hughes Drive, Cincinnati, OH *The*

20 20. WWVA-TV

Rule 18: Churches and Synagogues

- When indexing churches and synagogues, the first unit is the word that identifies the organization. Do not use *church* or *temple* as the first word. When in doubt about how to file a church or synagogue, cross-reference the file.

Names	Unit 1	Unit 2	Unit 3
B'nai Israel Temple	Bnai	Israel	Temple
Church of Hope	Hope	Church	of
St. John's Church	Saint	Johns	Church

- Some companies do not spell out *Saint* and file the name as written. When in doubt, cross-reference the file.

Rule 19: Organizations

- When indexing organizations, use the most distinctive word as the first unit.

Names	Unit 1	Unit 2	Unit 3	Unit 4
United Guild of Barbers	Barbers	United	Guild	of
Networking Associates	Networking	Associates		
Retired Teacher's Club	Teachers	Retired	Club	

- Most telephone directories do not index using this rule. Telephone directories usually list organizations in the order the names are written. For example, Association of American Planters would be listed in the telephone directory under *Association*. Also, common abbreviations and acronyms are usually listed in the telephone directory without spelling out the words. When in doubt, cross-reference the file.

Rule 20: Newspapers and Magazines

- In most instances, magazines are indexed in the order in which the names appear. Newspapers should be filed with the name of the city as the first indexing unit. If the name of the newspaper does not begin with the city name, place the city name first, followed by the name of the newspaper. When in doubt, cross-reference the file.

Names	Unit 1	Unit 2	Unit 3
Journal of Accountancy	Journal	of	Accountancy
Kirby Post Dispatch	Kirby	Post	Dispatch
Newport City Journal	Newport	City	Journal
Daily News (Tilden, UT)	Tilden	Daily	News
Time Magazine	Time	Magazine	

Rule 21: United States Government Agencies

- United States government agencies are indexed as

Unit 1 United

Unit 2 States

Unit 3 Government

Unit 4 Main word in the name of the division

Note: Cabinet departments are not indexed.

United State Government will be units 1, 2, and 3, respectively, in both of the following examples.

United States Government, Department of Labor, Bureau of Labor Statistics

Unit 4	Unit 5	Unit 6	Unit 7
Labor	Statistics	Bureau	of

Note: Department of Labor is the cabinet department and is not indexed.

United States Government, Department of Commerce, Patent & Trademark Office

Unit 4	Unit 5	Unit 6	Unit 7
Patent	&	Trademark	Office

Note: Department of Commerce is the cabinet department and is not indexed.

Rule 22: Political Subdivisions

- Index political divisions by name of the state, county, or city. Then index by the name of the department or division, using the most important word first. Some companies may use *Department of*, *Bureau of*, etc., only when needed for clarification.

Name	Unit 1	Unit 2	Unit 3	Unit 4
Board of Education, Houston	Houston	Education	Board	of
Idaho Department of Parks	Idaho	Parks	Department	of

Practice 7-6

Use one 3- × 5-inch card for each folder to be filed. (You may reuse the cards from the previous practice by drawing a line through the names.) Divide each name in the following list into its indexing units, and write the names on the 3 × 5 cards. Move the cards around so that the first card in alphabetical order is on top, the second card is next, etc. After all the cards are alphabetized, open the Practice Filing Form **CH7_FF** on your student CD. On your Filing Form file, key in the information from your 3 × 5 cards. Key the information from the first card in alphabetical order onto line one, key the second card in alphabetical order onto line two, key the third card in alphabetical order onto line three, etc. Use Save As to save the file with the name **Practice 7-6**. Print the file.

Folders to be filed

1. First Baptist Church
2. Association of Engineers
3. Department of Water and Sewer, Knoxville, TN
4. St. Mark's Church
5. Mapping Agency, U.S. Department of Defense
6. American Association for Counseling
7. U.S. Department of Commerce, Bureau of Economic Analysis
8. *Anaheim Examiner*
9. First Montrose Church
10. Institute of Cardiology
11. Department of Recreation, Nashville, TN
12. Church of Christ of Danville
13. *Dallas Daily Reporter*
14. American Psychology Association
15. Department of Travel, Chattanooga, TN
16. Housing and Community Development, KY
17. *The New York Times*
18. Temple Shalom
19. Maryland Boating Association
20. The Pasta Depot

FILING HINTS

HINT

Create a master index. Make it accessible to everyone.

1. Develop a master index of the filing system and make it easily accessible to everyone who uses the files. The master index should include the divisions of the filing system. It is also useful to have a list of all folders in subject and geographic files. Update the master index frequently.

2. Repair torn pages before filing them.

3. Remove all paper clips before filing and staple the pages of multipage documents. (Paper clips can attach pages that should be placed in different files.)

4. To simplify the filing process, code documents before filing. As the code, use the name or number of the folder where the document should be filed. Use

Burgess	Gerald	S	
Cincinnati	Enquirer		
Cleveland	High	School	
Glassblowers	Guild		
Herandex	Gloria	R	
Heritage	Associates		
Kearney	Donald	M	
Libby's	Restaurant		
Lore	Ronald	Thomas	
Maxwell	Lana	Maria	
Miami	County	Animal	Research
Ottenberg	Rhonda	Connie	
Rose	Accounting	Incorporated	
Saint	Marks	Church	
Schwartz	Jewelers		
Simons	Pharmacy		

Figure 7-14   Master index.

the master index to assign the code and write the code in the top right corner of the first page of the document. On an incoming letter, you might simply underline the name of the company in the letterhead with a red pen. On a copy of an outgoing letter, you might underline the name of the company in the inside address. If you prefer not to write directly on a document, use a sticky note with your coding remarks.

5. Prior to filing, arrange all papers in the order in which they will be placed in the file cabinet. This prior planning eliminates the constant opening and closing of alternate file drawers.

6. Establish a specific time each day to file because a large stack of unfiled documents may become so large that it becomes a major project. In addition, a seemingly lost document may actually be in the to-be-filed pile.

7. If a file folder is too full, divide the contents into two folders.

8. Use a miscellaneous folder for each file subdivision until there are sufficient documents to establish a separate folder. The minimum number of documents to start a new folder is usually five.

9. Allow about 4 inches of free space in each file drawer for working room.

10. Stagger the heading tabs on file folders to make it easier to find materials.

11. To locate missing papers:
    - Carefully check the folder where the paper is supposed to be.
    - Check the folders in front of and behind where the lost item should be.
    - Consider alternate ways the item could have been filed and look in those folders. For example, it could have been filed under a person's first name instead of the last name.
    - Ask other employees if they have the folder.

12. Create a color-coded Important Information Folder and place copies of documents in this folder. Select a specific color and use it only for this type of folder. This is an easy method of quickly locating important documents.

13. As part of your personal filing system, keep a file of people you meet. Put information about everyone you meet in your file. These contacts can be very helpful if you have a problem, and a last-minute crisis may be solved by a person on your contact list. This file list can be kept in your business card file, 3 × 5 card index system, word processing file, computer database file, calendar software file, organizer file, or computer software contact list file.

HINT
To locate missing papers:
1. Look again in the folder.
2. Check folders in front of and behind the folder where the papers belong.
3. Check alternate filing locations.
4. Ask if anyone has seen it.

CHAPTER REVIEW

1. Explain subject filing.
2. Explain geographic filing.
3. Explain numeric filing.
4. Explain the nothing-before-something rule.
5. Explain the filing of a hyphenated name rule.
6. Explain the filing of a United States government agency rule.

ACTIVITIES

1. Visit an office supply store and look at the variety of file folders, labels, and filing storage units available. Prepare a written report describing your findings. Be prepared to give an oral summary of your report in class.

2. Ask three businesspeople:

   a. What type of filing systems they use.

   b. What type of filing storage units they use.

   c. If they use a cross-reference system.

   Prepare both an oral and a written report describing the comments you receive.

PROJECTS

Project 11

Create the following memo from Michelle Kaplan, Managing Director, to Theodore Nash, Executive Director, concerning file cabinets.

This memorandum is being prepared in response to your request for reorganization of the filing system.

As we discussed, the reasons to reorganize are:

1. The need to archive files that are crowding the office environment.

2. The need for additional filing cabinets.

The staff appreciates the opportunity to provide input in meeting this challenge. We are well aware of the unsightly conditions in the file cabinet space adjacent to the offices. The current conditions are not only very inefficient in locating files, but also reflect poorly on the staff in the eyes of those in the industry who visit us. The following recommendations, if adopted, will increase the efficiency of the files, reflect a proper image of the department, and provide a more pleasant office environment for the staff.

The current files are retained in the individual offices. All other files are kept in the outer offices entered through the reception area. Currently, this room has twenty-six file cabinets, varying in type, size, and color. These cabinets are used to store the following:

- Files for approximately 1,000 projects.
- Approximately 300 new proposals.
- Approximately 200 projects that are not reactivated from the previous year.
- Records of the twenty years of the department.
- Stock of forms.
- Stock of miscellaneous publications distributed to other departments.

There is an increasing need for space to contain the files for these projects.

1. More projects are entering the department than are leaving.

2. The size of the files has increased dramatically from the original projects.

With the increased requirements of recent years, the folder size of current projects is twice the size of those projects processed in the 1990s. Therefore, removing the inactive folders does not provide sufficient file space for all active folders.

As a result of these factors, there is not enough room in the existing twenty-six file cabinets for files, storage of forms, and historical or processing information on the most recent projects. Files of every nature are placed on the top of cabinets and in boxes or in stacks on the floor.

Information in these files must be readily accessible to the staff. These files are used to monitor the current projects. During the processing of projects, the files are consulted to review prior support of the applicant and provide background material useful to the staff in their evaluation of proposals.

Recommendations for Reception Room

The following recommendation provides for more efficient use of the space in the reception room to ensure that sufficient file space is available for the files, forms, and information.

- Obtain twenty uniform lateral files, five drawers high, for placement in the outer offices. To accommodate the available space, eleven of these lateral files should be the 42-inch size, while the nine remaining should be the 36-inch size.
- Relocate three cabinets that do not have pull out drawers and are six shelves high to Building 800. These cabinets will be used as storage of forms and will not interfere with the use of this area as a mini-conference room and office for visiting associates.
- Relocate the five lateral files in this room to employee offices to create additional storage in those locations.

The twenty lateral file cabinets will be a much more efficient use of space and will actually provide 46 percent more shelf space then currently occupied by the twenty-six file cabinets in this room. Additional storage space will be created in the staff offices and in the reception room.

As a result, file space will be available for both the current folders and those files that are projected to enter the system in the next several years. Also, the appearance of the room would be greatly improved.

Room 1810

Since there are no chairs for visitors, a chair should be provided in the redesign of this area. One file cabinet can be removed and replaced by a small chair for a visitor.

Project 12

Send this memo to the staff. It is from Mary C. Putnam, Director.

We are happy to announce the opening of our employee day-care center.

On January 6, our new $2 million child day-care center will open. Children three months and older will be accepted into the all-day program. In addition, there will also be a program to meet the needs of children in school. Bus service from the elementary schools in the community will be provided, thus eliminating a transportation problem for parents.

Registration will begin October 1, and forms may be obtained from the benefits department in Suite 205.

Costs for the program will be shared by the employee and our company. Therefore, the employee cost will be very reasonable.

At 9 A.M. on September 1, there will be a meeting in the auditorium to explain the details of this service. We hope all employees who have children will be able to attend this discussion.

HUMAN RELATIONS SKILL DEVELOPMENT

HR 7-1 Standing up for Your Rights

Being agreeable in the office is important, but being agreeable should not interfere with your principles. You should not allow a colleague to take advantage of you. Assertive behavior (standing up for your rights) is acceptable; aggressive behavior (influencing others by physical or emotional force) is not acceptable.

- When was the last time someone took advantage of you?
- Describe the personality traits of the last person who took advantage of you.
- When was the last time you asserted yourself?
- How did you feel when you asserted yourself?
- Describe the last time you used aggressive behavior.

HR 7-2 Accepting and Rejecting Advice from Coworkers

During your business career, it is possible that you may work with someone who freely gives advice about all situations. Unsolicited suggestions can be annoying. Dealing with this advice in a diplomatic manner can be the difference between a comfortable working relationship and an antagonistic one. It is not essential for you to accept the advice, but it may be wise for you to listen to it. First, the suggestion may be beneficial to you. If you choose not to follow the recommendation, that is your decision. Consider the reason the counsel is given. Perhaps, the giver's objective is to get attention and recognition. If that is the case, just listening should solve the problem.

- Describe the personality traits of the people from whom you accept advice.
- Describe the last time you were wise to accept someone's advice.
- Describe the last time you advised someone. Were your recommendations followed?
- Describe how you would handle an overbearing person who is attempting to counsel you, although you did not seek the guidance.

SITUATIONS

How would you handle the following situations?

- **S 7-1** Your boss, Ms. Canton, is with Ms. Taylor and has asked you to bring Ms. Taylor's file to her office. Although you saw the file yesterday, you cannot find the file now.

- **S 7-2** Although you left your office in plenty of time to pick up your supervisor at the airport, an accident on the interstate caused a backup in traffic. When you finally arrived at the airport, your supervisor was furious at you for being late.

- **S 7-3** You were invited to your supervisor's house for dinner, and you spilled coffee on the beautiful Oriental rug in the living room.

PUNCTUATION REVIEW

Punctuate each of the following sentences. For a review of punctuation rules, see the Appendix.

1. Economic expansion is often accompanied by rising costs but the consumer continues to purchase goods and services.
2. Jack asked did interest rates rise
3. Have you planned the convention Sara asked.
4. My attorney Laura Reston is well known in the community.
5. Web City for example is a large retail discount store located near Interstate 15.
6. The director Phil Joseph moved from Houston to San Diego.
7. The new employee Patricia Wilson was late for work.
8. We are sorry that you did not receive your supply order by your due date therefore we will credit your account for $100.
9. The office supply store which is on Route 28 is open after work.
10. Doug said the computer paper arrived damaged.
11. No the package was not delivered.
12. The meeting is scheduled for Monday August 6 XXXX.
13. Her office was in an old dingy building.
14. Jane Kipper Ph.D. will address the next session at the conference.
15. John Tasky II was my roommate in college.

CD ASSIGNMENTS

CD Assignment 7-1

Open the file **CD7-1_IFS** on your Student CD and follow the instructions to complete the job.

CD Assignment 7-2

Open the file **CD7-2_ME** on your Student CD and follow the instructions to complete the job.

CHAPTER 8

Meetings and Conferences

Objectives

After studying this chapter, you should be able to:

1. Plan on short notice a meeting that is to be held in the office.
2. Plan a meeting using a conference room.
3. Plan a meeting at a facility outside your office.
4. Plan food for a meeting.
5. Evaluate sites for a meeting.
6. Prepare minutes of the meeting.
7. Understand the use of audio and video conferencing.

THE MEETING

While meetings are a fact of modern business life, many people look upon meetings as a waste of their time. Unfortunately, this is often true because some meetings are unproductive or the limited results of the meeting do not justify the time invested by all of the participants. Meetings are often unproductive because the meeting was poorly planned or the persons attending the meeting were poorly prepared. This chapter will help you create successful meetings. When discussing meetings, it is important that you understand the following terms related to meetings:

Attendee:	A person who attends a meeting.
Participant:	This is another term used for a person who attends a meeting.
Organizer:	The person who plans a meeting.
Presider:	The person who speaks or introduces other speakers at a meeting.
Facilitator:	The person who eases the transition from one session or speaker to another. The facilitator manages the meeting atmosphere and sets the tone for the meeting. The facilitator encourages everyone to participate and does not allow one individual to control the meeting.

Figure 8-1 Meeting area in a private office.

Meetings with coworkers or customers/clients are very common in today's workplace, and a suitable facility enhances the success of the meeting. The format of a meeting and the place where a meeting is held are often determined by the number of people attending and the meeting's purpose. There are three general types of meetings that can be distinguished by the meeting's location. Each of these meetings is discussed further in this chapter.

- **Private offices.** Most face-to-face business meetings have a small number of participants and can usually be held in a private office.

- **Conference rooms.** When more than six people attend a meeting, they are generally more comfortable sitting around a table in a conference room than sitting in a private office. Most private offices do not have a sitting area for more than six people. In addition, sitting around a table in a conference room aids note taking and encourages conversation because all participants can see everyone easily.

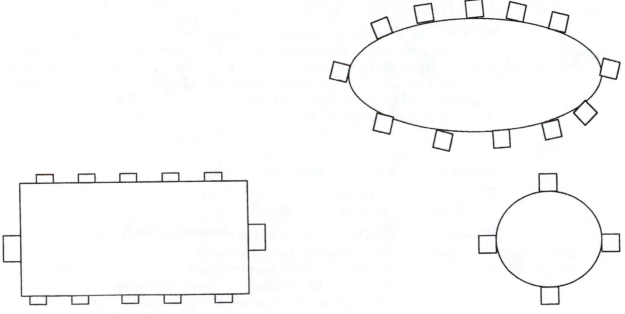

Figure 8-2 Conference room tables.

- **Meeting rooms.** A meeting with more than twenty participants may have special requirements in regard to the type and number of rooms required for the meeting. Meetings with more than twenty participants are usually held in special meeting rooms, often in a conference center or hotel. Larger meetings with many attendees may require a large meeting room, where all attendees may gather to listen to opening remarks or to a keynote speaker, and several smaller rooms for breakaway or concurrent sessions, where participants can focus on a specific task or topic.

In addition to a meeting with clients or an informational meeting, many businesses send their staff members to meetings and retreats away from the office to strengthen team building while addressing the meeting objectives. Furthermore, businesses often feel that off-site meetings improve communication and camaraderie among the participants. Frequently there is a greater sense of accomplishment with an off-site meeting than from weekly staff meetings.

Meetings and conventions are big businesses, and most communities have a local Convention and Visitors Bureau that can provide meeting planning assistance and information about community facilities.

Agenda

All successful meetings, a small informal gathering in an office or a large formal day-long conference, require careful preparation. When planning a meeting, estimate the length of time required to complete the meeting objectives, but keep the meeting as short as possible because people are busy with their own projects and responsibilities. Most people feel an obligation to attend meetings but would prefer not to attend. If the meeting lasts more than one and a half hours, people become restless and may need a break. Meetings that run an entire morning or afternoon should have a fifteen-minute restroom/coffee break.

Every meeting, regardless of the number of participants, has an agenda, which is a list of items to be discussed at the meeting. Sometimes the agenda is known only to the person who called the meeting; this often happens in small office meetings. A written agenda, distributed to meeting participants, helps focus the meeting's discussion and contributes to its success. If it is possible to have a written agenda, send a copy of it to all participants prior to the meeting so that they will have an opportunity to prepare for the items to be discussed. If the agenda is not sent in advance, it should be distributed at the beginning of the meeting. Even if it is sent in advance, additional copies of the agenda should be available at the meeting for those who did not bring one. The agenda should include a start and ending time for the meeting so participants can plan their schedule. Be realistic when determining how long a discussion will last. It is important to remember that most people like to share their views, so

<table>
<tr><td>**HINT**</td></tr>
<tr><td>Agenda: Topics to be discussed at a meeting</td></tr>
</table>

MY SUCCESS STORY

My Name Is Patrick

Some people may think I do not have a career in business, but they are wrong. I manage a high-end jewelry store, and human relations skills are vital to my job. I must be able to get along with my clients and manage my employees. Organizations skills are absolutely essential because time is in short supply. During the hectic holiday season, I supervise a staff of over fifty employees. I must prioritize and keep up with everything. I have a busy and exciting career, and I think it is terrific.

**Patrick Research and Management
324 Research Drive
Suite 600
Charleston, WV 25311**

**2 P.M. on May 19, XXXX
Room 620, Central Building**

Agenda

1. Minutes of the last meeting.
2. Review of Ms. Harris's proposal.
3. Review of computer purchase.
4. Review of marketing plan.
5. Discussion of annual charity ball.
6. Discussion of proposed health benefits package.
7. Set date of next meeting.
8. Adjournment.

Figure 8-3 Agenda.

allow a sufficient amount of time for each participant to talk. The agenda is determined by the supervisor, but the administrative assistant is responsible for keyboarding, duplication, and distribution of the agenda.

The Informal Office Meeting

Informal office meetings are usually scheduled by telephone or email. A supervisor asks an assistant to contact several people and arrange a short meeting for a specific date and time. Prior to contacting other participants, you should review the supervisor's calendar to determine several alternate times when the supervisor is available. You should discuss with the supervisor which of the alternate times would be preferable and which participants are essential to the meeting. A shared calendar, which is discussed in Chapter 1, can make meeting planning easier. If all the meeting participants are from your office and your office uses computer calendar software, you may be able to schedule the meeting by comparing the calendars of the participants and selecting a time when everyone is available. You should send emails or call the participants and ask that they confirm their availability. It may take several emails or phone calls and rescheduling of the meeting to ensure that your supervisor and the essential participants can attend. Some email software includes templates asking people if they will accept or decline a meeting invitation. You should also consider where to have the meeting. If the number of participants is too large for the supervisor's office, a conference room should be scheduled.

For a successful meeting to occur, it is also important for key participants to be in attendance. Therefore, you must know who the key participants are when attempting to schedule the meeting. If a decision maker cannot attend, then the meeting must be rescheduled. A meeting without the key players is wasteful. For the meeting objectives to be successful, it is important to know who must buy into the agenda items, so arrange the meeting time to accommodate the schedules of key people.

The time of a meeting can influence the discussion and meeting results, so knowing when to schedule a meeting can influence the outcome. Sometimes meetings drag on

Figure 8-4   Meeting room with a long table.

and on, so to keep a meeting short and focused, schedule it before lunch or near the close of the business day. People are usually eager to leave for lunch or to go home.

The day before the meeting, remind your supervisor of the meeting schedule and verify that sufficient copies of meeting materials have been prepared.

Because cell phones have become entrenched in today's business and personal world, cell phone etiquette is a significant issue. At the beginning of meetings, it is a good idea to remind everyone to turn off their cell phones or set them on vibrating. A ringing cell phone is an annoying interruption to everyone at a meeting. Do not allow your telephone call to interrupt the meeting, and do not talk on the telephone in the presence of others. Courtesy also requires that a participant avoid text messaging or checking emails during a meeting.

Meetings in Conference Rooms

While it may be obvious that the number of attendees determines the size of the room, conference rooms and meeting rooms vary in purpose and design. Rooms can often be rearranged to meet the specific requirements of a particular meeting. A room with a large central table is often called a *conference room*, and it may have a marker board on a wall and a built-in screen for use with slide, film, and overhead projectors for computer displays or transparencies. Rooms can be equipped for audio and video teleconferencing. Flipcharts can be brought in if they are required. An electronic whiteboard is very similar in concept to the traditional board in classrooms where notes and information are recorded, but an electronic whiteboard also allows the recording and storage of notes written on it during a meeting. In addition, the electronic whiteboard may be attached to a computer and projector so the notes are projected on a screen for greater viewing by all meeting participants. Notes made on an electronic whiteboard can also be printed after the meeting.

Conference rooms may have built-in microphones to record a meeting or for audio conferencing. Some conference rooms have television equipment and/or equipment for two-way video conferencing. If a wireless microphone and cordless mouse are available, the speaker will have greater freedom of movement when making computer presentations.

Figure 8-5 Theater-style meeting room.

If the meeting is held in a conference room or office that is frequented by many staff members, it is helpful to let the other employees know that a meeting is in session. Some conference rooms have a "Meeting in Session" sign that can be placed on the door during a meeting. If your meeting room does not have such a sign, create one to avoid interruptions and embarrassment to the intruder. The sign can be created using a word processing, publishing, or greeting card software package. A decorated sign can also be created by purchasing card stock or colored foam tags from a craft store.

Meetings in Meeting Rooms

A larger room with chairs set in rows is frequently called a *meeting room*. Meeting rooms usually are designed for flexibility and often contain podiums with microphones so all participants can see and hear the speakers. Some meeting rooms have film and slide equipment located in a small projection booth at the rear of the room. Rooms can be equipped for audio and video teleconferencing, and additional equipment can be brought in if required.

Some meeting rooms have fixed chairs on a sloping floor like those in a theater. Other meeting rooms, especially those located in hotels, may have movable walls and portable chairs that can be rearranged to serve a variety of needs. Meeting rooms in hotels are often arranged in rows of chairs set at a long table, which facilitates note taking. In addition, large conventions may use rooms with an audience response system, which allows participants to use a keyboard to respond to questions by keying a specific number or to signal the chairperson that they wish to speak.

Information about planning a large meeting or conference is discussed later in this chapter.

Arranging for Food

Often it is assistant's responsibility to order or purchase food for a meeting in a private office or conference room. If your company has a cafeteria or restaurant, you may make food arrangements with employees there. For a small early morning meeting, you may be required to stop on the way to work and pick up donuts, pastries, bagels, fruit, yogurt, and so on. Even if your office will pay for coffee and snacks, you may be required to make coffee.

A meeting that continues longer than anticipated may require a last-minute food arrangement. You may need to call a restaurant close to the office and make a reservation for lunch, or you may go to the cafeteria or local delicatessen (deli) and purchase sandwiches. You should be familiar with your manager's preferences regarding carry-out delicatessens or restaurants in case last-minute lunch arrangements are required.

In addition, you should be aware of the company's policy regarding payment of breakfast, lunch, or snacks for meeting attendees. Will the company pay the entire bill? Will a company credit card be used to pay the entire bill? Will each participant pay? Will separate checks be provided at a restaurant? Procedures for paying for any meals or food should be worked out between you and your supervisor before the meeting to avoid embarrassing discussions while clients are present.

TIPS FOR A SUCCESSFUL MEETING

Suggestions for the presider/organizer

- Do not schedule meetings the day before a holiday or Friday afternoons when people are anxious to leave for the weekend.
- Distribute the agenda well in advance so your associates can read and think about the agenda.
- Decide in advance how long to wait for late participants.
- Begin the meeting by stating the meeting's objective and the desired outcome.
- Be aware of the nonverbal communications from participants.
- Be aware of any tension between participants, and do not allow the tension to alter the meeting's purpose.
- Do not allow verbal attacks on other attendees. If necessary, remind attendees that verbal attacks are unprofessional and will not be tolerated.
- Do not allow a discussion to ramble on. Always stay focused.
- Do not allow the meeting to divert from the agenda.
- Use flipcharts to organize the discussion, and use one piece of paper for each topic. This procedure also helps keep the group focused on one topic because the topic under discussion can be seen by all participants.
- If one person monopolizes the conversation, encourage others to speak. The presider can say, "Let's hear what others have to say. What are your thoughts, Libby?"
- Always summarize each agenda item prior to moving to the next item.
- Avoid belittling an individual's comments.
- If someone makes a suggestion that is off the wall, say, "Thank you for your idea." Then quickly move on to the next comment.
- If a problem occurs, respond with diplomacy and move on to the next topic.
- If someone frequently tries to sabotage the meetings, talk with him or her privately about his or her attitude, behavior, and job responsibilities.

Suggestions for the attendee

- Prepare for the meeting by reading background material about the agenda items.
- Always arrive on time. Your colleagues may feel that your arriving late is inconsiderate, disrespectful, and a waste of their time.

Figure 8-6   Conference room with flipcharts and whiteboards.

- Bring key documents such as the agenda and pertinent reports to the meeting, but do not overburden yourself with background material.
- Always be courteous to all attendees.
- Because you will not remember everything, take notes during the meeting.
- Meet new business associates at the meeting. Do not talk only with coworkers you know. This is your opportunity to expand your network of business associates.
- Do not talk privately to the person sitting beside you. Always talk to the group.
- New employees attending meetings should follow a wait-and-see attitude. Do not jump into the conversation immediately; you may not know all of the facts or background of the items under discussion. Listen and watch first. Also, observe the meeting tone, gestures, and climate before venturing into the discussion.
- At the meeting conclusion, thank the meeting organizer.

Why meetings are not successful
- The meeting chairperson and the attendees differ on the topics to be discussed.
- The timing of the meeting is poor because attendees have other projects that must be completed.
- The participants are not interested in the meeting topics.
- The attendees feel that there is no reason to have the meeting other than the custom of having a meeting at that time. Weekly staff meetings often fail because there is no real reason to have a meeting.

PLANNING A LARGE MEETING

Several terms are used to describe meetings. A *conference* can be any meeting for discussion or fact finding, and therefore the term is used for a meeting in a small conference room. Often the term *conference* is used, however, for a large meeting with many participants. Conferences may be held on a one-time basis and may have several hundred or more participants. The term *convention* usually means a meeting that is held on a periodic basis, usually annually, and includes an exhibit. Other terms used to describe large meetings include *show, congress,* and *assembly.* Although the terms have different meanings, they are frequently used interchangeably.

The Meeting Plan

Large meetings require careful preparation but having sufficient time to plan a small or large meeting is usually a luxury. Before you make any definite decisions about a meeting, review your company's meeting policy and bring any questions you have to your supervisor's attention.

You should establish a basic plan for large meetings and keep it in your computer files. When you are asked to arrange a meeting, your plan will be available. In addition, whenever you visit potential meeting facilities in your area, always request brochures and information about the facility. If you need to plan a meeting at the last minute, that information will be in your files. Also, keep all of your planning lists and information about completed meetings because they could be useful in planning the next meeting.

In addition to maintaining meeting files on your computer system, put a copy of the computer file (on CD, DVD, diskette, or flash drive) containing all information about the meeting in the meeting file folder so it will be found easily the next time you plan a meeting. At a future date, your office computer may have been replaced, and your computer meeting file may not have been transferred to the new disk drive.

Your basic meeting plan should include a checklist so you are sure that every detail is covered. You should not assume any aspect of the meeting will be taken care of by someone else. Do not leave any question unanswered. If you omit important details, any resulting mistakes will reflect upon you and your supervisor.

Anticipate what could go wrong with your meeting arrangements, and then create a plan to solve it. If something does go wrong, keep calm. Consider the following factors when planning a meeting.

Basic meeting decisions

1. What is the purpose of the meeting? What is the anticipated outcome of the meeting?
2. When will the meeting be held? Before a final date and time are selected for the meeting, contact important individuals who will attend the meeting to verify that they are available.
3. Where will the meeting be held? The location for the meeting will be determined by the number of participants, the facilities available, the length of the meeting, and your office budget.
4. How many participants will attend and who are they? If a similar meeting has been held in the past, how many people have attended? What does the follow-up report for that meeting indicate?
5. What is the planned length of the meeting? Will the meeting be scheduled for an hour, several hours, one day, or several days?
6. When will the meeting begin and when will it end?
7. What is the budget for the meeting?
8. Will there be a theme?
9. How will the meeting be evaluated?

Meeting requirements

1. How many meeting sessions will be planned? If this is a large meeting with concurrent sessions, how many meeting rooms will be required?

Figure 8-7   Hotel business center manager.

2. Will food be served? If food is served, money must be included in the budget to cover its cost. You will also need to determine whether the food will include a full meal or just a snack. An early morning meeting often begins with coffee, donuts, pastries, bagels, fruit, and so on.

3. Will water pitchers and glasses be provided for the speakers? Will they be provided for the attendees?

4. Is presentation equipment required for the meetings? If so, what equipment is necessary—a computer and projector, an overhead projector, or a slide projector? Are any other items needed? How will the equipment be obtained? Who will operate the equipment? During what sessions will the equipment be needed?

5. Will there be an audio or video recording of the meeting's sessions?

6. Will there be exhibits or displays?

7. Will there be out-of-town guests for the meeting? If so, will your office be responsible for making hotel accommodations? Will transportation costs need to be included in the budget?

8. Will RSVP notes be sent out to invited guests? Will email reminders be sent?

After all the preceding factors have been considered, you are ready to begin implementing the meeting plan. If the meeting will be held at a location other than your office, arrange to visit the facility. The visit will provide information regarding the site as well as a sense of the site management's responsiveness to your needs.

Today the Web sites of many hotels and conference centers provide virtual tours of their facilities. While these online tours may be helpful in eliminating possible sites, the final decision on a site should be made after an in-person tour, not a virtual one.

Computer software and the Internet have made meeting planning easier by creating Web sites that provide assistance in planning meetings. In addition, software is available to

Figure 8-8   Hotel business center.

organize and maintain the paperwork of meeting planning. As the number of large meetings has grown, event planning has become a common activity. Many hotels and restaurants have Web sites that include maps, basic information about the facility, specific information about the meeting rooms, sample menus, and other helpful information.

Where to Hold the Meeting

Meetings can be held at hotels, motels, restaurants, private clubs, resorts, state parks, conference or convention centers, and similar locations. Many large companies have their own attractive meeting facilities. Past experience and recommendations from friends and business associates can help you select a facility for your meeting. If your company has held a similar meeting in the past, pay particular attention to the meeting facility evaluations and feedback from meeting participants. Consider the following factors when selecting a location for your meeting.

The facility

1. Availability is the first consideration. Is the facility available when you need it?

2. Price is the second factor to be considered. Is the facility in your price range?

3. Is the location convenient for those attending? Is it close to main roads or interstate highways? If attendees are flying in, is the facility conveniently close to an airport? Is airport transportation available or must special transportation be provided?

4. Are the facilities fully accessible to people with disabilities, as required by the Americans with Disabilities Act?

5. If the meeting will be held in a hotel, does the hotel have a block of rooms available at a reasonable price for participants staying overnight?

6. Is parking available? Is it adequate for the size of the meeting? Is there a parking fee?

7. Are the employees pleasant? Do they seem to be efficient and interested in servicing your meeting?

8. Is the site clean and attractive?

9. Is there a lobby or registration area available? Is the area large enough, and is it convenient to the meeting rooms?

10. If you plan to have displays or exhibits, is there an area for them?

Meeting rooms

1. Are there a sufficient number of meeting rooms?

2. Will the meeting room accommodate the anticipated number of participants?

3. Are the chairs in the room comfortable? Are tables available if necessary?

4. Are meeting rooms comfortably climate controlled? Rooms that are too hot or too cold can detract from the success of a meeting.

5. Is there sufficient lighting?

6. Are there shades or drapes to block the sun?

7. Is the meeting room near distractions such as an elevator with a constantly ringing bell?

8. Is the meeting room near the kitchen so the clatter of dishes is heard?

9. Is the meeting room near a window with street noise and distractions?

10. For longer meetings, will the meeting room be available for twenty-four hours or will someone else use it a portion of the day? What security is available to protect equipment and other important items?

Audio-visual and other support

1. If equipment (such as computer projection units, overhead projectors, or slide projectors) is needed, will the facility supply them? What is the cost of supplying this equipment?

2. If a broadband connection is required to connect to the Internet, is it available?

3. If a satellite hookup is required, is it available?

4. Is a sound system available? Are microphones handheld, lapel style, wireless, or on a podium?

5. Are there sufficient electrical outlets for the equipment?

6. Is there a technician available if there is a problem with the equipment?

7. What is the quality of the food? Is the food served quickly? What is the cost for food service?

8. If a loading dock is necessary to bring in large items or exhibits, is it available and convenient?

Not all of these questions may be relevant to your meeting, and a negative response on any one item should not necessarily disqualify a facility from consideration. Remember that there is no perfect meeting site; therefore, the meeting's organizers will have to determine which of these criteria are most important in selecting a meeting site. A sample evaluation form is shown in Figure 8-9.

Food Service

An important consideration when planning many meetings is whether food will be served. The time of day and length of the meeting will often determine whether food will be served, and your food budget affects the choice of menu. In addition to providing food at normal mealtime (breakfast, lunch, or dinner), food can be served as snacks during meeting breaks or before and after the meetings.

Site Evaluation Form

Date of Visit _____

Facility _____

Address _____

City _____   State _____   ZIP _____

Telephone Number _____

Email _____   Fax _____

Contact Person _____   Title _____

Date(s) Facilities are Available _____

Overall Appearance of Facility _____

Atmosphere of Facility _____

Desirable Features _____

Description of Meeting Rooms _____

Number of Meeting Rooms _____   Cost per Day _____

Number of Sleeping Rooms _____   Cost per Night _____

Food Quality _____   Food Cost _____

Special Equipment and Services Are Available (lectern, audiovisual etc.) _____

Handicapped Accessible? _____

Additional Comments _____

_____

_____

_____

_____

_____

_____

Figure 8-9   Site evaluation form.

If food will be served, the availability and cost of food should be considered before making a decision on the location of the meeting. If a meal is served, the charge for the meeting room may be reduced or even free. A free meeting room usually requires that a specific number of meals be served. Since many convention or meeting facilities do not allow you to bring in any food, confirm their policy regarding outside food if you intend to provide your own. Outside food may include a special cake, candy, nuts, or mints, so it is important to be aware of the facility's food policy.

The cost of the food is usually based on a per-person charge. Sometimes the more meals that are served, the lower the cost per person. Before you select the food to be served, review with the proposed facility the sample menus and the prices for each menu item. When selecting menus, do not limit your choices to only your favorite foods; select foods that appeal to everyone. Today many people are on special diets, for example, low-sodium, low-fat, low-carbohydrate, or vegetarian. Be sure to ask if it is possible to prepare a vegetarian meal or if the facility can accommodate people on special diets. It is important to consider alternative diets when selecting food for a meeting.

Hotel/Motel Rooms

Meeting participants who plan to stay overnight require hotel reservations. If only a few participants need hotel reservations, your only role may be to recommend hotels that are convenient to the meeting site. Therefore, you should be familiar with hotels that are convenient to the meeting site, their quality and cost, and the facilities they have available for guests. If the meeting will be held in a hotel, most participants staying overnight will want the convenience of staying in the conference hotel.

If a large number of participants are staying overnight, you may need to reserve a block of rooms at a hotel. One of the advantages of reserving a block of rooms is that hotels usually reduce the room rates when they are reserved in quantity.

Companies can use several different arrangements regarding the making of hotel reservations and payment of hotel bills. If meeting participants pay for their own hotel rooms, you need to decide whether the participant or the company will make hotel reservations. Meeting participants are usually encouraged to make their own hotel reservation. If you have reserved a block of rooms, the participant should tell the hotel that he or she is attending your meeting to receive any special room rates you have arranged. Often the hotel assigns a special promotional code that the participants use to receive their reduced rate.

If the company makes the reservations, but the guests will be responsible for paying room charges, you may need to get credit card numbers (with expiration dates) from the participants so you can guarantee the reservations when you make them. In this instance, the participant pays for the hotel room and then may seek reimbursement for the hotel bill using their expense account.

It is also possible for the company to contract with the hotel for rooms and pay the base room rate directly. In such cases, the participant may still be required to pay the hotel for personal expenses such as room service or phone calls.

More information about hotels and motels can be found in Chapter 9.

Contracts for Meeting Rooms

After a selection is made concerning a meeting location, a contract is usually signed with the facility. Although you may not be the person who signs the contract, read it carefully to verify that the contract includes everything you discussed about the meeting's arrangements. Nothing should be omitted. For example, if a reception table is promised, it should be written into the contract. Your contact person at the hotel or restaurant may have changed jobs by the time you have the meeting, and the new employee may be unaware of an oral promise.

HINT
Read the contract before signing. Verify that all details are included in the contract.

Very Important People

If very important people (VIPs) will be attending your meeting, they may be given special treatment. These VIPs may include company officials, honored guests, or invited speakers. Discuss with your supervisor whether any individuals should be given VIP treatment.

Dealing with VIPs

- Who are the VIPs?
- Will the VIPs be met at the airport or train station? Who will meet them?
- Will there be baskets of candy, fruit, nuts, or flowers in their hotel rooms?
- Will you need a car and/or driver for the VIPs?
- Tell the bell captain and meeting services manager who the VIPs are.
- As an extra gesture, you might want to gather information about the likes and dislikes of the VIPs.

Meeting the Needs of All Participants

If your meeting will include hearing-impaired, wheelchair bound, or visually-impaired participants, ask what accommodations you should provide for their assistance. Be sure the meeting facility is fully accessible, as required by the Americans with Disability Act. You may need a sign-language interpreter, materials translated into Braille, or someone to provide personal assistance to wheelchair bound or visually-impaired participants. You should be able to locate a sign-language interpreter by contacting your local sign-language interpreter association, contacting your local convention bureau, or conducting a Web search for local interpreters. For additional information, search the Web for the following sites: Americans with Disabilities Act, Registry of Interpreters for the Deaf, National Association for the Deaf, and National Association for the Blind.

> Does your meeting site accommodate all participants?

International Visitors

Because most large corporations, educational institutions, nonprofit agencies, and governments operate in a global environment, there is a good possibility that foreign visitors may attend meetings. An international population may require interpreters or additional assistance to meet the needs of those not familiar with the area or customs. When meeting with business associates from foreign countries, gifts are often exchanged. Also, foreign visitors may appreciate receiving a list of embassies with addresses and telephone numbers. Under security procedures implemented after the 9/11 attack on the World Trade Center and the Pentagon, there are new procedures regarding the entry of foreign visitors into the United States. You may need to become familiar with visa and entry requirements for foreign visitors to assist them in attending your meeting. Additional information about working with foreign visitors is included in Chapter 15.

For information about visitor visas for entry into the United States, go to the following Web site: www.travel.state.gov.

> **HINT**
> Plan for foreign visitors.

Identification Badges (Name Tags and Name Badges)

To help remember names and meet new business associates, people attending meetings often wear name or identification badges. Name tags can be prepared in advance for those participants who are preregistered for the meeting, but pens and extra name tags should be available for persons who register at the meeting. To make it easy to read the name tag, it should be printed in a large font size; often the first name is printed larger

Figure 8-10   Name badge.

than the last name. Some badges include the name of the company where the person is employed, in addition to the person's name. There are two basic types of labels used for name badges. An adhesive label can be placed directly on clothing, while a nonadhesive label is placed in a plastic holder and clipped to clothing. Name tags can be placed on a jacket, shirt, or blouse by removing an adhesive from the backing label. They can also be pinned on, clipped on, or worn around the neck with a cord called a lanyard. Adjust the length of the lanyard so the name can be read easily. Wearing the name tag on the right side allows another person to see your name easily while shaking your hand. Men often clip a name tag to the top left pocket on a suit coat.

The use of a name tag is not limited to a large meeting or conference. Identification badges can be helpful for small groups where participants are not acquainted. At large conferences name tags often contain an electronic strip with the participants contact information. Exhibitors often scan name tags into database management software so additional product information can be sent to interested conference participants.

> **HINT**
>
> Name badges are important.

Meeting-Related Web Site

To assist your meeting attendees, create a Web site or add additional pages to your current Web site with information about the meeting. This allows attendees to obtain information at their convenience without additional staff time and costs for your organization. The Web site should contain details about the hotel accommodations and location, meeting agenda, background papers, airfare, and auto rental, and it should contain an online meeting registration option. The meeting Web site should also have city and hotel maps and links to the Web sites of appropriate organizations.

Adding Special Interest to the Meeting

A large meeting may have a theme or slogan that can be used on decorations, printed materials, the Web site, and banners. The theme may also include the company logo or have its own graphic identifier. A theme can create interest and can improve the productivity of what otherwise might be a monotonous meeting. If a meeting does

Figure 8-11   Name badge with company name.

not have a company-related theme, you can create a theme for the meeting by using local attractions or a holiday if a meeting occurs near a holiday. A meeting that occurs during the fall or spring, on Valentine's Day, near the Fourth of July, etc., would use appropriately colored napkins, plates, and table decorations.

Meeting Evaluation

Many large meetings conclude by having the attendees evaluate the meeting. Evaluation forms are often distributed at the beginning of the meeting for participants to return before they leave. Evaluation forms must be designed, keyboarded, printed, and distributed prior to the meeting.

Hints for Improving Your Meeting

- Inform the facility of all changes in the meeting plans as they occur. If the number of participants changes, notify the facility immediately. It may be impossible for the facility to include additional attendees or to remove empty rows of chairs or unoccupied luncheon tables at the last minute. A room with many empty rows or chairs or unoccupied tables looks uninviting.
- Plan for meeting materials. Will a packet of meeting materials be given to each participant? What will be included? Who will prepare and distribute the packet? Will paper and pens or pencils be provided for note taking?
- Decide in advance who will pay the bill for the meeting and decide how it will be paid—cash, check, credit card, or direct billing.
- Consider transportation needs. Must someone be picked up at the airport? If the guest and the driver do not know each other, identification will be necessary. Prepare a sign for the driver with the name of your organization or a sign with the guest's name.
- Send a map and information about ground transportation to out-of-town participants.

MEETING DAY AND FOLLOW-UP

The Day of the Meeting

Arrive early and verify that everything is completed to your satisfaction. Have available extra copies of the agenda, pens, meeting packets, maps of the area, and anything else that would be helpful to the attendees. If flowers, candy, nuts, or similar items have been ordered, verify that they have been delivered and that they are placed where you want them.

When the meeting begins, try to adhere to the time schedule you have set. Deviating from the schedule could cause problems for the service staff. If lunch is scheduled for noon and the meeting runs late, the food service may have difficulty serving the lunch at 1 P.M. However, if the meeting runs late, check with the service manager and see what adjustments can be made in the food service. Also, take breaks when they are scheduled because the service staff may straighten the meeting room or deliver refreshments during breaks.

Meeting Conclusion

At the end of any meeting or conference, it is useful to summarize the meeting discussion; review findings, conclusions, and recommendations; remind participants of assignments; solicit involvement for other projects; and announce the date of the next meeting, if appropriate. Sometimes these items are discussed verbally at the end of a meeting; other times there is a concluding session at a conference to summarize the meeting's conclusions and expected outcomes.

Meeting Follow-Up

A working meeting where the participants are asked to complete specific projects or research particular ideas needs a follow-up. If the work assignments or decisions arrived at during the meeting are not implemented, the meeting has not accomplished its objectives. It may be the administrative assistant's responsibility to follow up and contact the participants to determine if they have completed the materials they agreed to prepare, if they have talked with the people they were to communicate with, or if they have reached the goals that were established.

After the meeting, the person who sponsored the meeting should have a summary prepared. Notes may have been taken by the assistant or by one of the meeting's participants. It is often the administrative assistant's duty to prepare the minutes of the meeting, which is a written report of the meeting, and then to send a copy to all of the participants. In addition, the assistant may be responsible for organizing and reviewing the meeting evaluation forms.

Minutes of Meetings

A written summary of a meeting is called the minutes of the meeting. Each organization uses its own preferred format for minutes of a meeting, so you should review past minutes to determine the standard format used by your organization. Usually the minutes include the date, time, place of the meeting, and names of those attending. If the meeting is a formal gathering, such as a meeting of the board of directors of a corporation, it is also important to include the names of absent members. The minutes are routinely written in the past tense, and they include a summary of the discussions and actions taken.

Minutes may be taken at informal staff meetings and business gatherings or at formal board of directors meeting. Minutes are usually prepared immediately after the meeting. Prior to the next formal meeting, each member should receive a review copy of the minutes of the previous meeting. At the next meeting, members vote to either approve the minutes as written or to make corrections. The approved version of the meeting minutes are usually signed by the secretary of the board or the president of the organization.

The preparation of the minutes of a meeting requires the combination of highly developed listening skills, concentration, and note-taking ability. During the meeting, an assistant must be able to listen, take notes, and summarize the points being discussed while the discussion continues.

The minutes should be accurate, so the person taking the minutes must be alert and must concentrate on the subjects discussed. The note taker should be familiar with the participants because the minutes of a meeting indicate the names of the individuals who attended the meeting, participated in the discussions, made motions, and seconded motions. If the note taker is unfamiliar with the attendees, name plates may be helpful. You can make a name plate by folding an 8.5- $\times$ by 11-inch sheet of card stock paper in half and writing or printing a person's name on it. Office supply stores carry name plate paper with a perforated folding line for easy writing and printing. When taking minutes, quickly record all important comments, discussions, motions, and resolutions. To eliminate uncertainty concerning what was said at a meeting, tape recorders are often used to record the entire meeting. When the minutes of the meeting are prepared, information not essential to the minutes can be omitted. If the meeting is recorded, it is customary to inform attendees of the fact.

> **Minutes of the Orlando Business Association**
> **March 1, XXXX**
>
> The monthly Board of Directors meeting was held at Mike's Seafood House. The Board of Directors meeting was called to order at 7 P.M. by Vice President Sue Phong.
>
> Present: Stephanie Coffman, Eli Stone, Najar Pooser, Marcia Pearce, Sue Phong, and Earl Button
>
> Absent: Stella Meyer, Anita Bradford, Mike Beller, and Libby Wayne
>
> Minutes of the February meeting were read and approved.
>
> Treasurer's report showed that $1,500 was raised by the calendar sale.
>
> Eli Stone moved, seconded by Marcia Pearce, that an honorarium of $200 be approved for guest speakers. The motion unanimously passed.
>
> Stephanie Coffman moved, seconded by Earl Button, that July 25 be selected as the date of the art auction. The motion passed unanimously.
>
> Stephanie Coffman moved, seconded by Najar Pooser, that the president appoint a committee to plan the fall fundraiser. The motion passed: 4 yes, 2 no.
>
> Meeting was adjourned at 9 P.M.

Figure 8-12 Minutes of a meeting.

After the Meeting

As you plan the meeting, keep notes of the names of people who were helpful. After the meeting, write thank-you letters or emails to everyone who helped you. In some instances, a gift or tip should be given to those who assisted you.

VIRTUAL MEETINGS

Audio and Video Conferencing

As discussed in Chapter 4, audio and video conferencing are often less expensive alternatives than bringing participants together at a face-to-face meeting. These technologies are also used within a traditional meeting setting to bring in participants who could otherwise not be present. An expert or high-level government or business official may be able to participate in your meeting for an hour via audio or video conferencing when he or she would otherwise be unavailable. Many meetings are held for the purpose of being able to hear from people via teleconferences when it would be impossible to schedule a personal visit from that individual. If audio or video teleconferences are included on the agenda of your meeting, a major requirement in the selection of a meeting site is the availability of equipment required to support these teleconferences.

Web Meetings

Another technology-based meeting option is Web conferencing. With Web conferencing, participants are directed to your Web site to view a presentation. The participants can communicate via instant messaging or via a telephone conference call. As with a traditional meeting, thought should be given to the scheduled length of a Web meeting. Because participants often have short attention spans, they may easily become bored and allow their minds to wander. Therefore, Web meetings should not exceed two hours. Looking at a computer screen can become boring, so keep participants active and focused by initiating questions and actions that require responses. Preplanning is very essential for a participant-active meeting.

Although Web conferencing may be slow or stiff, it is often used because it is relatively inexpensive to set up. Be aware of the technology limitations of your system. For example, some systems experience a transmission delay in communications. It is important to stay close to the camera for a full-face camera view instead of a small face against a large background. Use the technology to your advantage by displaying photos to illustrate points and include computer-based presentations, demonstrations, flipcharts, equipment, etc. If participants in a Web conference are connected by an audio conference call, they should use the mute feature on their telephone to avoid noise clutter. Also, never place your phone on hold if your phone system plays music when callers are on hold. To avoid embarrassment, do not say anything during a Web conference with audio talkback that you would not want overheard.

Whiteboards can also be used as part of Web conferences to focus the attendees' attention. There are two basic types of whiteboards: (1) wall-size whiteboards with Internet connection where pictures or graphics can be viewed, and (2) wall-size or personal-drawing-tablet-size where presenters can draw or write during the meeting. Virtual whiteboards allow the use of shared files, where attendees can modify the drawing during the actual meeting.

CHAPTER REVIEW

1. Define attendee, organizer, participant, facilitator, and presider.
2. Describe the desirable features of a meeting room.
3. Define an agenda.
4. List five suggestions for the presider.
5. List five suggestions for the attendee.
6. List five points that should be considered when planning a meeting.
7. List six points that should be considered when selecting a location for a meeting.
8. List three points that should be considered when planning for VIPs.
9. List two suggestions for accommodating visually- or physically-impaired participants.
10. What information should be included on an identification badge?
11. What information should be included in a meeting Web site?
12. Define minutes of the meeting and list what should be included.

ACTIVITIES

1. Call or visit the Web site of three hotels/motels and investigate charges for:
   a. A meeting room.
   b. Sleeping accommodations.

c. A lunch meeting for fifty people.

d. A dinner meeting for 100 people.

2. Call or visit the Web site of three restaurants and ask about:

a. Lunch costs for twenty people.

b. A sample lunch menu.

c. The charge for a meeting room.

3. Call or visit a bakery and request prices for donuts, croissants, and pastries to serve twenty-five people.

4. List ten facilities in your area where you could hold a one-day meeting. You may use the Internet to research this activity.

5. Plan a retreat a couple of hours from your home. Where would you hold the retreat? Submit a detailed list of your plans.

6. Ask two administrative assistants how often they plan meetings. Also, ask them to comment about planning large and small meetings. Write a summary of their comments.

7. Make all of the plans for an informal one-day meeting at a facility other than your office. There will be fifteen participants, but none of them will be from out of town. Submit a detailed list of your plans.

8. Make all of the plans for a four-day meeting. There will be twelve out-of-town guests, one out-of-town VIP, and four in-town participants. Submit a detailed list of your plans.

9. Use the Internet to find information about three restaurants in your city where you could hold a meeting. Write a summary of your findings.

10. Attend a meeting of a local organization (college, social, garden, political, etc.) and take minutes of the meeting. Prepare a copy of the minutes using correct format.

PROJECTS

Project 15

Create the following table. Add a column for the cost of exhibition space. O'Brien, Community, and Power each will pay $1,200. Blackstone will pay $1,500, Chamber and Fairdale will pay $2,475, American Donations will pay $1,300, and McFarlin will pay $1,250. Calculate a total cost for the column.

Convention Exhibitors
Chicago
Spring xxxx

Company	Contact	Phone
American Donations, Inc.	Eugene Hartzell	703-439-8613
O'Brien Engineering	Barbara Wilmore	703-946-8153
Chamber Designs	Treva Semanick	703-270-7765
Power Technology	Jody Peerke	202-593-7514
Blackstone, Inc.	Colleen Storch	202-963-2493
Community Appliances	Andrew Knowles	703-854-4487
Fairdale Atlantic	Saba Tollie	202-449-1014
McFarlin Agency	Victoria Gannon	202-686-2556
Total		

Project 16

Send this memo to the staff. It is from you, and your title is Training Director. Send a copy to Sharon Barber, Marcia Morton, and Sang Seegars.

Computer training classes will be offered as follows. If you have questions, please call Clifton at extension 6177.

All classes are held from 9 to 4, with a lunch break of one hour. The classes will be held in room 809.

I encourage you to register as soon as possible as classes fill quickly.

Date	Class	Instructor
January 15	Introduction to Access	Hainer
January 28	Intermediate Access	Hainer
February 10	Intermediate Word	Leroy
February 20	Introduction to PowerPoint	Perez
March 4	Introduction to Excel	Zang
March 8	HTML Fundamentals	Anderson
March 15	Advanced HTML	Anderson
March 22	Introduction to Digital Imaging	Powers

HUMAN RELATIONS SKILL DEVELOPMENT

HR 8-1 Working with Pessimistic People

In your working environment, you may encounter a person who sees the negative side of everything. When dealing with this person, do not permit yourself to become pessimistic also. If possible, keep your contact to a minimum and encourage other workers to be present when the two of you are together. After being with this type of person, make a list of positive thoughts.

- Who among your acquaintances has a pessimistic outlook?
- Describe your feelings when you are around pessimistic people.

HR 8-2 Problems with Your Supervisor

Never take a problem to someone above your supervisor without first discussing the problem with your supervisor. If the situation persists after several unsatisfactory attempts to solve the problem with your supervisor, it can be taken to a higher level. Depending on the circumstances, it may be wise to tell your supervisor that you are seeking a response from another person. Whenever you discuss a problem, respect the other person's opinions and be tactful with your comments.

Before taking your problem to a higher level, decide if the situation is important enough for you to pursue it. Taking a problem to a higher level could alter the relationship between you and your supervisor—no matter how the problem is resolved.

- What tone of voice would you use when discussing a problem with your supervisor?
- Describe your approach when taking a problem to your supervisor's manager.
- Describe three types of problems that are too petty to take to a higher level.
- What are you going to do if the supervisor's manager does not agree with you? What will be your reaction to this situation?
- Describe a problem that your supervisor cannot resolve and explain how you would handle it.

SITUATIONS

How would you handle the following situations?

- **S 8-1** A meeting is continuing longer than you anticipated and everyone is hungry.
- **S 8-2** Your supervisor asked you to attend a meeting on the same day as your sister's college graduation. You planned to attend the graduation.
- **S 8-3** Last weekend at a party you heard confidential information about a project you are completing.

PUNCTUATION REVIEW

Punctuate each of the following sentences. For a review of punctuation rules, see the Appendix.

1. The community needs affordable housing and a balanced budget
2. Patrick of course understands the importance of completing projects by the due dates
3. I received the Outstanding Employee of the Year award and I was very surprised
4. Cincinnati my hometown is the site of the next annual meeting
5. While Max was in Paris his mail was forwarded to him
6. As you mentioned the minutes of the meeting were incorrect
7. Hedys mother Mrs Hoffman was the director responsible for the revised budget
8. Opal Marshall Executive Manager for Personnel has a large office
9. While the Marketing Department remains on the third floor the Administration Department has been moved from the first floor to the second floor
10. Ed who is active in community affairs is an excellent speaker
11. Rachel who exercises daily has lost 20 pounds as a result of her involvement in the Employee Wellness Program
12. When it comes to management skills demonstration is more important than paperwork
13. In her struggle to combine a career and a personal life she developed health problems
14. This notion of course runs counter to all you have learned in the seminars you have attended
15. Every department has a desk manual and it is your job to locate it and to become familiar with it

CD ASSIGNMENTS

CD Assignment 8-1

Open the file **CD8-1_AG** on your Student CD and follow the instructions to complete the job.

CD Assignment 8-2

Open the file **CD8-2_ICE** on your Student CD and follow the instructions to complete the job.

CHAPTER 9

....

Business Travel

Objectives

After studying this chapter, you should be able to:

1. Make airline reservations.
2. Make hotel and motel reservations.
3. Use the Internet to plan a business trip.
4. Determine the rental car that best meets your needs.
5. Apply for a passport.
6. Prepare an itinerary.
7. Prepare an expense report.

FUNDAMENTALS OF BUSINESS TRAVEL

Travel is an integral part of today's business world. Business trips planned at the last minute are often the norm, not the exception. If your company has a travel department, your only responsibility may be to notify that department of the impending trip, including location, date, and travel preferences.

However, as an office employee, it may be your responsibility to make travel arrangements. The first requirement is to be aware of your company's travel policies. These policies might cover items such as: limitations on the combination of business travel and personal vacations; preference for the use of specified airlines, hotels, or auto-rental agencies; restrictions on the use of first-class airfare; and the use of company credit cards for travel. The second requirement is to know the preferences of the traveler. Personal preferences might include the method of transportation, particular airline, preferred auto-rental company or chain of hotels or motels, desired room location, time of day of travel, airline food preferences, and so on. If you do not know your supervisor's travel preferences, you should ask. Usually you will be given the information regarding the destination and time for a trip, and you will have to arrange the itinerary yourself.

If it is your responsibility to prepare the travel arrangements, first organize your thoughts. Knowing the specifics of the trip is important before proceeding. Decide

Figure 9-1   A hotel receptionist.

what additional information you need before making the travel arrangements. For example, will the person be traveling by air, rail, or personal car? Your company may have a contract with an airline, auto-rental company, or hotel chain that provides discounts from the standard rates. If so, check with the airline, auto-rental company, or hotel chain to see if they serve the city to be visited. In some organizations, the use of a company airplane may also be an option.

If the traveler does not have a preference about the travel arrangements and your company does not have contracts with an airline, auto-rental company, or hotel chain, you must decide how you are going to make the travel arrangements. The following sections of this chapter discuss several methods you can use to gather information and make travel arrangements, including using the Internet, travel agents, toll-free phone numbers, and other sources. Each of these sources has its own advantages.

When using any travel resource, you should always be aware that the first prices quoted will probably not represent the final cost that a traveler must pay. Increasingly, airlines, hotels, and auto-rental companies add additional service fees, surcharges, and taxes to their advertised rate. For example, an airline ticket advertised at $392 might actually cost $430 after adding taxes, governmental fees, and other charges, such as an airport passenger facility charge, a federal segment fee, and the September 11 security fee. International flights will include additional foreign and U.S. government-imposed charges. Some Internet sites show all the fees and charges when you first view a flight schedule; others place them at the end just prior to purchase. Before you make any reservation, be sure that you receive and understand what the final cost will be and all the fees and charges that will be added to the basic rate.

TRAVEL ASSISTANCE

The Internet

Most people now use the Internet as their main source of travel information. The Internet can be very helpful for obtaining information on travel and destinations both in the United States and around the world. In the interest of reducing travel costs, many companies encourage their employees to use the Internet for travel arrangements.

Travel information from the Internet can be accessed from office and home computers, as well as many mobile devices such as cell phones and notebook computers. Retrieving information and making reservations is quick and inexpensive. The information is usually up-to-date and can change several times a day. You can use the Internet to find information and to make reservations for airline, auto, rail travel, and dinner at your destination.

Finding travel reservation information on the Internet is usually very easy. Many of the common Internet browsers have sections devoted to travel. Selecting a travel link brings you to a world of travel information. If your Internet browser does not have a travel link, entering the name of a destination in a search engine will usually bring up many relevant Web sites. You will be able to find city maps, lists of hotels, city services, restaurants, and special events in an area. Frequently you will be able to link to Web sites sponsored by hotels or events in the area you are researching.

Most airlines, auto-rental companies, and hotel chains have an Internet site where you make a reservation online. There are also several Web sites that will provide information from numerous airlines, auto-rental companies, and hotels so you do not have to check the Web site of each company individually. Several of these general travel sites are www.expedia.com, www.orbitz.com, and www.travelocitycom. Several sites search many other sites to find the cheapest fares. These sites include www.kayak.com, www.sidestep.com, and www.cheapfares.com.

Airline tickets, automobile rentals, hotel reservations, and train tickets all can be reserved on the Internet. For some reservations, you have to connect directly to a specific company's Web site. When you deal directly with an airline's Internet site and with many of the general reservation sites, you can enter the passenger's frequent-flyer membership number, make seat selection, or request a special meal. Making travel arrangements on the Web has proved to be a major use of the Internet. The Web-based services provided by airlines, auto-rental agencies, hotels, and general travel sites are continually being expanded and upgraded. Each travel site is unique and presents its information in a different manner. You may find some sites easy to use and other sites cumbersome. You may need to use a site several times before it truly becomes useful. If one site does not meet your needs, there are many alternatives on the Internet.

Internet travel and airline Web sites send weekly emails to subscribers announcing last-minute bargain opportunities. Since travel can be a costly business expense, receiving these travel announcements may be helpful when planning last-minute trips. However, you should limit the number of travel sites you sign up for or you will have to deal with many travel messages in your email.

You should maintain a file of useful travel Web sites. These sites can change often so always be on the lookout for new and interesting Web sites. To get started, ask coworkers or your supervisor for sites they have found useful. New sites are recommended in newspapers, magazines, or in a company's advertisements. You will find new useful sites as links from older sites. When you find a useful Internet site, you should bookmark the site on your Internet browser so it is easily available. You should use word processing or spreadsheet software, create a list of Web sites, and back up your list. You do not want to lose Web addresses to a computer crash or as the result of an upgrade to your Internet browser software.

Shown below are sample Web sites with travel information.

Center for Disease Control and Prevention	www.cdc.gov/travel
Currency conversion chart	www.oanda.com/converter/travel
Passport Information	www.travel.state.gov/passport
Travel books	www.fodors.com
Travel health risks	www.travel.state.gov
Travel opportunities	www.bestfares.com
Travel opportunities	www.expedia.com
Travel opportunities	www.cheaptickets.com
Travel opportunities	www.orbitz.com
Travel opportunities	www.travelocity.com
U.S. State Department	www.travel.state.gov/travel
Visa Information	www.travel.state.gov/foreignentryreqs.html
Weather	www.weather.com
World current time zones	www.worldtimezone.com

While the Internet has a vast amount of travel information, other sources of travel information and arrangements are still very useful. Do not overlook travel agencies, toll-free phone numbers, travel guides, and auto clubs as valuable aids when planning business travel.

Travel Agencies

Travel agencies can be very helpful in planning a trip. The primary benefit of using a travel agent is the personal service and specialized knowledge that he or she may possess. Travel agents can use their computer systems to review schedules and prices of all the airlines flying to a destination, find pricing and alternative routes, and wade through the thicket of restrictions which apply to many airfares. Through their computer reservation systems, travel agents also can give you information about auto rentals, hotels, and other travel costs. You can request that the travel agency make a reservation on a specific flight, at a specific hotel, and with a specific auto-rental agency.

Travel agents can do more than just book an airline ticket or auto rental. Many travel agents specialize in travel to particular locations or in specific types of travel. In addition to their use of computer systems, these travel agencies may have personal knowledge of the destinations and hotels under consideration. Through their professional travel, feedback from their clients, and information from professional newsletters and associations, many travel agents may have in-depth knowledge and insights that are not found on the Internet. They can answer your specific questions and respond to the specific concerns of your traveler. They can also be helpful in making arrangements for complex travel. Some large travel agencies create their own air/hotel packages that are priced lower than purchasing the items separately.

Many companies have contracts with travel agencies to make reservations for all of their traveling personnel. In today's business climate, which stresses cost reduction, many businesses have eliminated their own travel office and no longer have contracts with travel agencies. Check to see if your company permits you to work with a travel agent and pay the agent's fees, if any.

Before using a travel agency that does not have a contract with your company, ask if there is a charge for services. Many travel agents now charge a service fee for each airline ticket they prepare because they no longer are paid by the airline for each ticket they book. Many of their other fees are paid by their bookings. If you find a travel agent who provides current information, good service, and reasonable airline prices, the agent's fees will be worthwhile. While you may be able to find a cheaper airfare yourself on the Internet, a good travel agent can prevent aggravation and save time for you and your office.

Toll-Free Telephone Numbers

Airlines, railroads, auto-rental agencies, hotels, and motels all have centralized reservations systems with toll-free telephone numbers. Agents at these toll-free numbers can answer your questions or help with complex bookings. These systems are often automated and you may have to wait until you get a live operator. Most airlines now charge an additional fee for purchase of tickets on the telephone. Lodging reservations can be made through a hotel chain's toll-free centralized system or directly with

Figure 9-2　A hotel lobby.

the hotel. You may be able to get a less expensive rate by calling the hotel directly since it may have special rates not in the central reservation computer. An efficient office employee should record frequently called numbers in a personal telephone directory or in a computer telephone/contact list.

Travel Guides

There are many travel guides that provide information and recommendations for visitors to a city or country. Travel guides recommend hotels, motels, and restaurants. The guides often discuss topics such as airlines serving an area, how to travel from the airport to downtown locations, traffic conditions, parking, and area attractions. There are travel guides available for specific cities, regions, and countries throughout the world. Many travel guides publish a new edition each year and also have Internet sites to supplement the guide. Travel guides are useful in gathering many types of information about a destination all in one book and in providing evaluations and recommendations regarding transportation, hotels, restaurants, and activities in the areas covered.

The following are examples of travel series that publish guides for many areas of the United States or the world.

- AAA TourBook (available to members of travel clubs affiliated with the American Automobile Association)
- Frommer's guides
- Fodor's travel guides
- Insiders' guide
- Michelin travel guides
- Mobil guides
- Rick Steves' guides

Since there are many other travel books available, check the travel department of your library or bookstore for additional sources.

Automobile Clubs

Automobile clubs such as the American Automobile Association (AAA), Allstate Motor Club, BP Motor Club, Chevron Travel Club, and the GM Motor Club offer travel information concerning hotels, motels, restaurants, places of interest, maps, roadside assistance, and towing services to their members. Some of them also publish travel guides and have their own travel agencies. Annual membership is usually less than $100 per year.

Computerized Maps

Computerized maps help orient travelers to new surroundings and are available from many Internet sites or on CD-ROMs and DVDs. When you use a computer-generated map, you can often select the exact area and scale you want to view. A computer-generated map can be customized to include the features most important to the traveler. County designations, roads, terrain profiles, schools, and museums can often be included or excluded from the map, depending on the traveler's need. The Web sites of many hotels have a link to a map that shows where the hotel is located.

Because the Internet is continuously updated, a map on a Web site can be more current than a printed map, which may have been created and printed a year ago. However, do not assume that a map, or any information on the Internet, is up to date; look for information on the Web page that indicates when it was last updated. Maps obtained from the Internet or from CD-ROMs and DVDs can be printed and often can be downloaded to notebook computers and handheld organizers.

AIRLINE TRAVEL

Air travel has undergone a revolution where airlines change fares, schedules, and even cities of service with little advance notice. Some changes are made seasonally in response to travel patterns; other changes are made in response to competing airlines or changing economic conditions.

Making Reservations

The quickest and cheapest way to purchase an airline ticket is through the Internet. Airline tickets may also be purchased through an airline toll-free number, from a travel agent, or at the airport counter. Tickets purchased through a travel agent or over the phone usually have a service fee; purchasing tickets at an airport ticket counter can require waiting in long lines and should be avoided except for last-minute travel.

When you first enter the Internet sites of most airlines and travel organizations, you will see a place where you can enter the name of the city you are traveling from, the name of the city you wish to visit, and the proposed travel dates. The program searches and provides a selection of airline schedules and prices. Often, these sites can sort airline flight schedules by time of departure or in order of increasing price. Some sites give you the option of comparing airfare over several days. Many of the cheapest flights may be available only for a short period of time or have restrictions that limit their use. Always check the restrictions before you book a flight and be aware that some third-party sites charge a booking fee. Also, several low-fare airlines do not participate in some of the multi-airline sites, but restrict their schedules to their own Web site. It is usually a good idea to check several Internet sites to compare rates and schedules before deciding on a flight.

Figure 9-3 An airline terminal.

Although airline travel today is often discounted, there are many restrictions on discount fares. Examples of airline restrictions include issuing nonrefundable tickets, requiring the immediate purchase of tickets or within twenty-four hours after the reservation is made, or purchasing tickets seven to thirty days in advance of travel to get a special fare. Since business travelers frequently do not have enough advance notice before traveling, they usually are not able to take advantage of the best discounts. A common restriction to secure a discount airfare is the requirement that the traveler stay at the destination city over a Saturday night. Many businesses now require that travelers include a Saturday night stay on their trips to obtain a lower airfare. Whether your traveler qualifies for a discount, you should read and understand the airline restrictions before making a reservation.

There are many types of services available from airlines. Several of these are discussed in the next section. After reviewing all possible schedules, prices, and services available, discuss the schedules with the traveler and then make a reservation. Always verify all information prior to paying for the tickets. Airline tickets may be paid for with cash, credit card, or check, but because most tickets are ordered over the phone or on the Internet, most airline travel is paid by credit card. On many airlines, once a reservation is made, it either cannot be canceled or there is a penalty for canceling.

When making reservations, be sure to give the airline the home, office, and cell phone numbers and email address of the traveler. Some airlines send email notifications of delayed or canceled flights. If there is a schedule change or flight cancellation, the airline may try to contact the traveler. Airline reservations should be reconfirmed a couple of days prior to traveling and again on the morning of departure. Airlines try to notify travelers of schedule changes, but it is best to verify flight times and reservations to avoid last-minute problems.

Choices of Airline Services

Types of Service

Most airlines offer at least two types of service. They are usually called *first-class* and *coach*, although some airlines call their two services business-class and coach. First-class service (or business-class service) is considerably more expensive than coach, but the seats are wider, and first-class service provides better quality food, free alcoholic beverages, and more service from flight attendants. First-class passengers sit at the front of the plane and can enter and exit the plane before other passengers. Companies usually purchase first-class seats only for top executives, and increasingly business travelers are not permitted to travel first-class at company expense. Some airlines offer a *business-class* service, which offers larger seats and more amenities than coach for a price between that of first-class and coach. The discount tickets widely advertised by the airlines are usually for coach seats. Airlines that fly smaller planes, such as commuter airlines, may offer only coach-class service.

Traveler Personal Preferences

Check with the travelers to determine their personal seating preferences when flying. Some people prefer to sit toward the front of the airplane, others over the wing, while others prefer to sit toward the back. Also determine whether a window or aisle seat is preferred. An aisle seat provides more leg room, and a window affords the traveler a sky view of the trip. Always avoid seating a business traveler in the middle seat of a three-seat row if at all possible. Smoking sections are no longer an option on flights in the United States and Canada. Many foreign airlines, however, continue to have a smoking section for their travelers.

HINT
Be aware of your traveler's preferences.

Types of Flights

Airline flights can be classified as nonstop, direct, and connecting. *Nonstop* service means that the flight flies directly between two cities with no intermediate stops. A *direct* flight means that the flight has an intermediate stop, but the passenger remains on the same plane the entire trip. A nonstop flight could, therefore, leave at 8:15 A.M. and arrive before a direct flight that left at 7:30 A.M. and made several stops along the way. The final type of flight is the *connecting* flight, on which the traveler must change planes at an intermediate city.

Many airlines encourage connecting flights by routing passengers through a hub where as many as twenty or more airplanes land and depart within an hour. Each airline has a minimum connecting time regarding the amount of time that must be available at a particular airport for a passenger to transfer from one flight to another. Airlines accept reservations only for connecting flights that meet their connecting time requirements. However, even with a flight itinerary meeting the minimum connecting time, there is always the danger that a delay in the first flight may cause a passenger to miss a subsequent flight. If you book a connecting flight, try to book an itinerary where both flights are on the same airline. If the first flight is late and the traveler misses the connecting flight, the traveler will deal with only a single airline to complete the trip. Unfortunately, flight delays occur, so be prepared. If your flight is canceled or delayed so you will miss your connection, use your cell phone while you are waiting on the tarmac or after you have landed to call the airline and rebook on another flight. The telephone call saves valuable time, avoids your standing in a long line to rebook on a new flight, and perhaps snags the last seat on a busy flight. Most airlines have a version of what is known as *Rule 240*, which spells out what the airline provides if a flight is canceled or delayed due to their actions (such as mechanical difficulty, but not weather delays). Under Rule 240, the airline is usually required to rebook you on the next available flight.

Meals

A wise traveler always tries to eat before getting on a flight rather than relying on airlines for food. Most airlines no longer provide a full meal service in coach, except on transcontinental or foreign flights. Food service on flights during a normal meal time may consist of a sandwich served in a tote bag. Some airlines provide only a beverage and snack service of pretzels or cookies, no matter the time of day. Some airlines now have a Buy-on-Board program and charge passengers an additional fee for meals. If you do not wish to purchase the airline meal, you can bring your own food.

Most airports have at an eatery where you can purchase a sandwich or snack food to eat during a flight. Some airports have restaurants that take reservations and deliver the order to the airline gate before your flight. Check with the airline to see what food service will be offered during the flight, then check with the airport Web site to see what other food alternatives may be available.

When airlines provide a meal service, they usually offer special meals such as kosher, vegetarian, fruit plate, low sodium, low-carb, and others. Since special meals must be ordered at least twenty-four hours prior to the flight, determine in advance if your traveler wants a special meal.

Airline Flight Guides

Airline schedules are available via the Internet, either from an individual airline or from travel reservation sites that list many airlines. Seasoned travelers often carry airline flight information on alternate flights in case they have a change in plans or flights are delayed. Many airlines provide electronic schedules that can be downloaded to desktop computers, notebook computers, or handheld computers. Travelers can also check airline schedules using handheld organizers that have wireless connections or cell phones that can access the Internet. Some airlines provide printed guides of their flights. These guides are usually sized to fit in a traveler's pocket and may be available at airline counters.

Electronic Airline Tickets

Electronic tickets (*etickets*) are less expensive for the airlines than the standard paper forms; thus, to encourage passengers to use electronic ticketing, most airlines charge an additional fee to write a paper ticket. When you purchase a ticket through the Internet, you will receive an electronic ticket. When you purchase a ticket over the phone or through a travel agent, you may have the option of receiving a paper ticket, but then you will have to pay additional fees for both the paper ticket and for the convenience of using either the ticket agent or airline telephone agent.

In electronic ticketing, the passenger receives a confirmation number for a flight itinerary and uses that confirmation number to board an airplane. Electronic ticketing is quicker than using paper forms because the entire booking and ticketing transaction can be done via phone or computer. There is no need to go to an airline or a travel agent, or wait for a ticket to arrive through the mail.

With an eticket, the passenger can check in with the airline and print his or her own boarding pass twenty-four hours prior to the flight. By going to the airline Internet site and entering the eticket confirmation number, the traveler can print out a sheet of paper with a bar code that serves as the boarding pass. This boarding pass will be scanned at the airline gate prior to entering the airplane. By printing out the boarding pass ahead of time, the traveler can bypass lines at the airline counters.

Frequent-Flyer Programs

Many airlines offer free, frequent-flyer bonus programs that encourage a traveler to use one particular airline. If the traveler has a frequent-flyer number, be sure to provide it to the airline when making an airline reservation. By frequently flying on one airline, the traveler accumulates points that may be used toward free travel, upgraded accommodations, or other gifts. Many airlines have joint programs with hotel and car-rental agencies where the traveler may earn extra points and obtain discounts for using those hotel or car-rental companies. Also, airlines have partnerships with credit card companies that award the traveler bonus points by using the credit card for restaurant meals, shopping, medical bills, and so on. Business travelers often use a particular airline to increase the number of frequent-flyer miles in their account to generate a free trip or upgrade to a better seat. Many companies permit the traveler to use the frequent-flyer miles earned on company travel for personal travel, but some companies require that frequent-flyer travel points be used only for business purposes.

In addition to the free, frequent-flyer programs, many airlines have membership clubs that provide quiet lounges in airports. In addition to a quite place to wait or work between flights, the lounges may provide free coffee and snacks, Internet access, fax machines, and travel assistance. The cost for these clubs may be several hundred dollars, but membership can also be purchased using frequent-flyer miles. If the traveler is a member of an airline club, check the airline's Web site to determine where the club lounges are located.

Luggage

Airline travelers on a trip lasting a few days face a choice regarding luggage: should they carry their luggage into the airplane cabin or check the luggage with the airline? The two main reasons for carrying luggage on the plane are to save the time spent waiting for luggage to arrive at the end of the trip and to ensure that the luggage does, in fact, arrive.

There are two disadvantage of taking luggage on the plane. The first is that you will have to transport heavy luggage, often down endless corridors through airports and then through security, and then try to find a place for the luggage on the plane. Suitcases with built-in wheels and briefcases with wheels are very popular to help people transport luggage through airports

There is very limited space on aircraft, and airlines restrict the size and amount of luggage they permit to be carried aboard the aircraft. Airlines differ on size limitations for carry-on luggage, so it is wise to contact the airline you are using or visit the Web site to determine its luggage standards. A typical airline limitation might be one carry-on bag and one personal item. Personal items include coats, purses, handbags, umbrellas, cameras, and notebook computers. The carry-on bag typically is limited to a combined dimension (length + width + height) of 45 inches. Most airlines have sizing boxes at airport counters that show the dimensions of luggage that are permitted on the plane. If planes are full, travelers may have to place the suitcase underneath the seat in front of them, thereby using most of their leg space. This can result in a very uncomfortable flight.

The second disadvantage of taking luggage on the plan relates to security procedures that now restrict the amount of liquids and gels that can be brought into an airplane cabin. Can the traveler take a trip only with liquids and gels that are less than 3 oz. each and that, in total, fit into a single, one-quart plastic zip-top bag? Security restrictions are subject to change and the traveler should check the Transportation Security Administration Web site, www.tsa.gov, for the latest information about security policies that affect air travelers.

Each airline has its own restrictions on the number, size, and weight of checked luggage. The limitations on checked luggage typically include the number of bags (usually two per person), the size per bag (such as 62 inches combined dimension), and weight per bag (such as 50 lbs per item). Most airlines charge travelers a fee from $50 to $100 for each piece of luggage over the airline's luggage limit, size limit, or weight limit.

When checking luggage with an airline, always have your personal identification tag on both the inside and outside of the luggage and be sure that the airline has placed a baggage tag with the proper airport code on the suitcase. Each airport in the world has a unique three letter identifier code. This is done to avoid confusion between airports serving cities with the same names: for example, Charleston, West Virginia (code CRW) and Charleston, South Carolina (code CHS). The code also distinguishes among multiple airports serving the same city. For example, three airports serve the Washington, D.C. area: Ronald Reagan Washington National Airport (code DCA), Washington Dulles International Airport (code IAD), and Baltimore-Washington International Thurgood Marshall Airport (code BWI). If a baggage tag with the wrong airport code is placed on your suitcase, it will have a nice trip without you.

Be sure you keep the luggage check receipts, which contain your luggage tracking bar code. Some airlines ask how many pieces of luggage you will be checking when you check in using the Internet, and then print the luggage receipt directly on your boarding pass. If your luggage does not arrive at the end of your trip, immediately go to the airline's baggage office, usually located next to the luggage pickup location. You will need the check receipts to complete a claim form, which the airline will use to trace your lost luggage. When the luggage is located, usually the airline will deliver it to your home or hotel.

If your luggage is lost, get the name and phone number of the agent who makes a record of the lost luggage. Call this person often to check on lost luggage. The toll-free number you are given on the printed sheet may not be as helpful in locating your lost luggage as the airport baggage agent.

Boarding Passes

Boarding passes are issued by the airline to reserve seating and to ensure that only ticketed passengers enter the plane. The airlines are required to check and verify your identity for security purposes prior to issuing a boarding pass. You can obtain a boarding pass in several ways. If you have an eticket, you can print a boarding pass from home or the office up to twenty-four hours in advance of a flight by entering passenger and flight information at the airline's Web site. Print boarding passes as soon as possible. If the flights are overbooked, the time you check in (via your boarding pass) may mean that you have a seat on the flight; also, some airlines assign seats in the order passengers check in. If your flight is at 7 A.M., try to print your boarding pass at 7:01 A.M. the day before.

You can receive a boarding pass at curbside when you check in your baggage or when you check in with the airline reservation agent at the ticket counter. Finally, you can often print a boarding pass from an automated kiosk near the airline ticket counter. The traveler may have to enter his or her airline mileage program account number into the keypad or insert a credit card for identification.

The boarding pass often indicates the airport gate from which the flight is scheduled to leave. Check the departure gate on monitors in the airport to see if there has been a change.

All travelers must have a boarding pass to go through airport security. If the airline denies a traveler a boarding pass, the traveler may be on the TSA No-Fly List or have a name similar to someone on the No-Fly List. To travel by air, these travelers should contact the TSA and complete the Travelers Identity Verification Form at the following Web site: http://rms.desyne.com/needtodo.htm.

Airport Security

After the terrorist attacks of September 11, 2001, the United States government instituted many changes in airport security that affect every airline traveler. All persons and items carried on an airplane must pass through a security inspection system operated by a U.S. government agency, the Transportation Security Administration (TSA). Only ticketed passengers are permitted in airline boarding areas, and to reach the boarding area, a traveler must pass through a TSA security checkpoint. To enter the airport security area, the traveler needs to display a boarding pass and a government-issued photo ID, such as driver's license or passport. After showing the boarding pass and photo ID, the traveler passes through a metal detector to search for weapons or items that can be used as a weapon, and carry-on luggage will be X-rayed. Items that can be used as weapons cannot be carried onboard an airplane. These include guns, knives, box cutters, baseball bats, spear guns, scissors, razor blades, hockey sticks, etc. As mentioned earlier, liquids and gels must be placed in 3 oz. containers that all fit into a single one-quart plastic zip-top bag. This plastic bag will also be X-rayed.

Before passing through the metal detector, you should place metal objects, such as watches, cell phones, personal digital assistants (PDAs), coins, and keys in a small basket available in the security area. Metal detectors also detect metal in clothing. If some of your clothing has metal, it is better to pack the clothing because it may set off the metal detector and delay your boarding. All passengers must remove their shoes so they can be X-rayed. If you travel with a computer or video camera, remove it from its carrying bag and place it on the X-ray conveyer belt. Since notebook computers look alike, always label your computer with your name, company address, and telephone number. TSA allows passengers with medical needs requiring diabetes-related supplies and equipment to carry the items if they are labeled with the manufacturer's name or pharmaceutical label. In addition to going through metal detectors, many travelers are asked to walk through *puffer machines*, which blow puffs of air on a traveler to detect explosive material. People who cannot be cleared by the metal detectors or puffer machines are asked to undergo a hand-wand inspection or a pat-down. The pat-down can be conducted in private.

In addition, checked baggage is examined by an electronic screening device and/or screened by TSA employees. TSA recommends that checked baggage not be locked to avoid breaking the locks for inspection. To secure the luggage, some travelers use small plastic cable-like stripes, which can be cut easily by TAS inspectors. There are now locks available that are TSA-compliant. TSA personnel have the keys or combinations to these locks, so if they need to open luggage, they can do so without destroying the locks. Packing suggestions for checked baggage include (1) not packing film or food; (2) spreading heavy items so the contents can easily be viewed; (3) putting personal items in plastic bags to reduce touching by TSA inspectors; and (4) not overstuffing the luggage so if it is opened for inspection, it can be closed by TSA personnel. Additional security information can be obtained from the TSA at www.tsa.gov.

To expedite travel, Registered Travel Programs, which provide prescreening background checks, are becoming available at selected airports. Special security lines are offered for travelers who sign up, supply personal data, and pay a fee of approximately $100. Since saving time is often important to the business traveler, the $100 annual fee may be worth the cost. Members of the Registered Travel Programs receive biometric cards that are used at Registered Travel kiosks. At the kiosks, iris scans and fingerprints are matched with the person's ID card.

While airport security measures have increased passenger safety, the screening process has created a haven for thieves. It is important to watch your personal possessions when passing through airport security scanning equipment. If you are not alert, someone could easily grab your personal items. Pay particular attention to your notebook computer as it moves on the conveyer belt because computers are attractive to thieves.

HINT

For travel security information, visit www.tsa.gov

Checking In

The traveler must check in with the airline prior to boarding, and check-in procedures vary at different airports. Travelers with etickets may complete check in when they obtain their boarding pass at curbside check-in, via the Web, or at the automated kiosk. Passengers with paper tickets may have to check in at the departure counter. Even with a boarding pass, travelers who are not at the departure counter well before flight time can lose their seat. The requirement for check-in time varies with the airline, and many airlines suggest that passengers arrive at the airline, departure gate very early. With increased security procedures and long lines, travelers are encouraged to arrive at the airport one and a half to two hours prior to their departure time. To improve their on-time schedule record, many airlines begin boarding passengers a half an hour before departure time and close the airplane doors ten minutes prior to departure. Therefore, late-arriving passengers may not be allowed to board the plane. Maintaining airline on-time arrival and departure schedules is important to the airlines and to their passengers. In addition, the United States Government Bureau of Transportation Statistics publishes airline on-time statistics, which indicates which airlines met their schedules and which flights are frequently late. This on-time information is available on the Internet.

For security reasons, check-in time for international flights can be several hours before the scheduled flight departure time. Always check with the airline regarding how long before the flight passengers should arrive.

Upon Arrival

After arriving at the destination and leaving the plane (*deplaning*), the traveler should first retrieve his or her luggage. Travel by air requires ground transportation to a hotel or a business meeting location. Most airports are served by a variety of ground transportation services, including taxis, auto rentals, or shuttle vans to and from downtown locations or the suburbs. Hotels near airports often have free shuttle service between the airport and the hotel. Call the hotel or check the hotel Web site to determine if it provides a courtesy van or if an airport shuttle service is available. Also, confirm the hours of operation of the courtesy van. This is particularly important if the flight leaves early in the morning or late in the evening.

Travel Safety and Security Precautions

- Do not divulge travel plans unnecessarily. For example, do not tell the grocery clerk, gas station attendant, restaurant personnel, etc., of your travel plans.
- Do not discuss travel plans where you can be overhead.
- Do not discuss travel plans with strangers.
- Be aware of pickpockets. Pickpockets may work in groups of adults or children and create diversions so you become an easy target. Techniques used include asking you for the time, a match, a cigarette, or extra change, or spilling food or drink on your clothing.
- Secure money using a hidden money belt worn under your slacks or shirt.
- Carefully watch and secure wallets that are in back pockets.
- Carefully secure purses and do not place them on the back of a chair or leave them unattended even for a moment.
- Keep your hotel/motel door locked at all times. Only open the door if you are expecting someone, and look through the peephole prior to opening the door.
- Know where the hotel stairways are located. Count the number of doors from your room to the closest exit. In an emergency, you may not be able to see the exit.
- If you are uncomfortable in an area, do not walk alone.
- If the area is questionable, limit your activities, especially at night.
- If you see a suspicious individual, do not enter an elevator or subway with him or her.
- Be alert to carjackers and thieves.

Packing for your business trip
- Take the least amount possible.
- Take neutral-colored clothing that mixes and matches, thus extending your wardrobe.
- Take sample-size cosmetics and put them in plastic zip bags so nothing will spill and soil your clothing. Since many hotels/motels provide shampoo and hair dryers, check with the hotel/motel to determine if you need to carry these items.
- Take a small folding suitcase to pack meeting handouts, souvenirs, etc.
- Since most luggage looks alike, attach a ribbon or other distinguishing item to the outside of your suitcase to quickly identify it.
- When flying you must follow the Transportation and Security Administration's 3-1-1 rule. This rule allows each traveler to carry liquids or gels on the plane in plastic containers no larger than 3 ounces. the containers must fit into a one-quart, clear plastic, zip-top bag, with a limit of one bag per passenger.

Figure 9-4 Airport waiting area.

Jet Lag

People who travel across time zones often experience *jet lag*, which is a change in the body clock. The symptoms include exhaustion, loss of sleep, too much sleep, disorientation, loss of appetite, lack of motivation, and lack of concentration. In some cases, the symptoms may last for several days or even weeks. Since jet lag muddles the thought processes, it can be a major problem for business travelers who must make business decisions upon arriving at the destination. Many travelers feel traveling east is worse than traveling west, but either direction can be a challenge. To help combat jet lag, some business travelers arrive the day before an important meeting to give the body time to adjust to the time change. Some experts believe when traveling east, it helps to go to sleep an hour earlier each night for several nights prior to the trip. Others recommend eliminating caffeine for several days to help the body adjust.

HINT

Jet lag can be a problem for travelers.

LODGING

Selecting a Hotel or Motel

Selecting lodging can be the most difficult part of preparing a travel plan. The choice of hotels and motels is usually greater than the choice of airlines or car-rental agencies. In a large metropolitan area, the choices can be overwhelming.

Very often, however, a traveler who visits a destination frequently has a preference regarding lodging. Travelers attending a convention or large meeting are usually given information about suggested hotels. If the traveler is attending a meeting and is unfamiliar with the area, ask the meeting host to recommend lodging. If an administrative assistant is not given specific hotel recommendations, the selection of a hotel is usually based on the following criteria: location, price, accessibility to clients or meeting sites, and accommodations desired.

Location and price are the two most important criteria in selecting accommodations. Usually, except in resort areas, the closer a hotel is to the city's central business district, the more expensive the room rate. Hotels that are convenient to an airport, particularly those hotels with courtesy transportation to the airport, can also command a premium room rate. Often the most reasonably priced accommodations are on the fringes of cities and are near major highways. However, a traveler staying in such a hotel or motel may need to rent a car to reach clients and meeting sites. People with meetings in a city center area can use taxis or mass transportation to travel from the hotel to meetings. Ideally, the hotel or motel should be accessible to the business appointments and to transportation. This, however, is not always possible.

Today some hotels and motels offer a free continental breakfast, which is both convenient for the traveler and saves time and money. The breakfast usually consists of at least juice, donuts, sweet rolls, and coffee. Some facilities offer more elaborate breakfasts that also include cereal, toast, bagels, eggs, fruit, yogurt, waffles, and other foods. Generally the free continental breakfast is not available at expensive hotels that cater to the business traveler.

Hotels

Hotels that cater to the business traveler are found in a city center, at resorts, near industrial parks, or near airports. They offer a variety of restaurants, meeting rooms, airport transportation, and additional services that are not found in most motels. Hotels are often used by travelers who do not arrive by car; therefore, they provide a variety of services and entertainment at one location. A hotel may include shops, travel desks, business center services (fax, photocopy, etc.), swimming pool, or health club. These services may be very important or have no value to the individual traveler. You should determine which of these amenities, if any, are important to your traveler.

Many hotels now have broadband computer access in each room. In some hotels, the cost of broadband is included in the nightly room charge; in other hotels, it is available for an additional charge, either on an hourly or daily basis.

As the travel industry redefines itself to find the perfect niche for each traveler, a new trend toward hotels with more luxurious amenities has emerged. The amenities include more lavish bedding, high-speed Internet access, flat-screen televisions, cordless phones, in-room exercise equipment and mini-bars, and enhanced lighting.

To accommodate the hectic schedules of business travelers, many convention centers and large hotels have reduced customer wait time by offering self-check-in and checkout services. This is a convenience often used by the busy traveler.

Call the hotel a few days prior to the arrival date and confirm that it has a reservation for the traveler. Get the name of the person you speak with in case there is a problem later with the reservation. If you have a reservation and arrive at a hotel and are told that it is overbooked, the hotel should "walk" you to another hotel, which means the hotel should pay your transportation costs to the another hotel. You can ask for additional compensation for your personal inconvenience.

Motels

Motels are usually smaller than hotels, with an informal atmosphere and limited food services or no food services on site. Motels are frequently located near major highways, and they usually offer extensive parking. Travelers planning to do a lot of driving to meeting facilities and appointments may prefer a motel convenient to major highways rather than a hotel in the center of a city.

Other Lodging

The lodging industry is continually developing new variations on the concept of hotels and motels. Some hotels offer two-room suites that may include a sitting room suite or kitchen facilities in addition to the usual bedroom. *Bed and Breakfast* (*B&B*) facilities, which are usually small inns or restored properties, are also available. *Extended-stay* facilities with kitchens and sitting rooms are being built throughout the country to cater to business travelers who may need to stay for extended periods.

Nationwide Lodging Chains

Many national hotel and motel chains specialize in a particular type of accommodation. These chains have toll-free central reservation services and Internet sites that provide directories with maps indicating the location and the services offered at each hotel or motel. Many of the national and worldwide lodging chains operate facilities in one or more of the following categories of lodging: luxury, medium priced, and budget. Examples of national chains are Hyatt, Marriott, Hilton, Holiday Inn, Hampton Inn, Fairfield Inn, Quality Inn, and Comfort Inn. The national lodging chains have frequent-stay programs similar to airline frequent-flyer programs, where guests earn points for each night's lodging. The national chains also work with airlines so guests can receive airline frequent-flyer miles from the hotel's partner airlines. Check with the traveler to determine whether he or she is a member of any of the frequent-stay programs and if this should be a factor in selecting lodging.

In additional to national chains, accommodations are available through regional chains and local hotels and motels. As an assistant who makes reservations for a supervisor, you should keep records for future trips regarding your supervisor's travel preferences, hotels and motels that were suitable, and car-rental agencies that were reasonable. In addition, keep records on problems the traveler encountered so you will know what to avoid.

Reservations

Hotel and motel reservations are usually made by visiting the Web site or calling the facility's toll-free telephone number. While it may be quicker to use the chain's centralized reservations number, less expensive rates can often be obtained by making reservations directly with the hotel or motel where the traveler will be staying. Hotels sometimes have lower rates that are only available on the Internet. Whether you call the central reservation number, call the hotel directly, or visit the Web site, never accept the first rate quoted; always ask if there is a lower rate available. Hotels often list many different prices for the same room. It is helpful to ask if the hotel has any special rates. Be sure to ask if there is a special convention rate or if the hotel has a corporate rate for your business. Ask if the supervisor belongs to any organizations or clubs that may qualify for travel discounts, such as the American Automobile Association (AAA), AARP, Costco, travel clubs, etc. If the traveler is a member of the hotel or motel frequent-guest program, the traveler may qualify for special discounts, upgrades, or other amenities. Hotels and motels often participate in airline frequent-flyer programs, and this information should also be checked when making a reservation.

Hotel reservations can also be made over the Internet, and it is wise to check the hotel's Web site for Internet special rates. Web travel sites have become some of the largest travel agencies in the country and, because of their buying power, can often book hotel rooms cheaper than you can reserve from the hotel itself. Some Web sites book rooms in general locations and then tell you which specific hotel is booked only after receiving payment. Check the Web site before you complete the reservation to be sure you reserve a specific hotel if location or a specific hotel is important.

> **HINT**
>
> When making a reservation, always ask for the best price.

There are many choices; therefore, an administrative assistant should know the supervisor's preferences in lodging accommodations. Nonsmoking rooms are available in most hotels and motels, and this choice can be an important health consideration for guests. Some travelers prefer one large king-size bed, while others prefer a queen-size bed or two double beds. If the traveler intends to work in the room, you should ask the reservation agent if the room contains a desk and if the room has a broadband computer hookup. Selecting appropriate accommodations creates the environment for a more comfortable and productive trip for your supervisor.

When making a reservation, request either a confirmation number or a written confirmation. Always verify the confirmation number by repeating it to the reservation agent. Written confirmations are now often sent by email. The traveler should be given a copy of the written confirmation or confirmation number and a second copy should be kept in the office file. All confirmation numbers should be included in the itinerary, which is discussed later in this chapter.

HINT
Confirmation numbers are important. Save confirmation numbers, and print email confirmations.

Guaranteed Reservations

Most hotel and motel reservations are held only until 4 P.M. or 6 P.M. on the day of arrival. As a precaution against having a reservation canceled, it is best to guarantee a reservation by using a major credit card. Giving the credit card number to the hotel guarantees that a room will be available regardless of how late in the evening the traveler arrives. This also means that the room must be paid for if the reservation is not canceled by the hotel's deadline. Always ask about the hotel's cancellation policy when making a guaranteed reservation and be sure to get a cancellation number from the hotel or motel if you must cancel a reservation. Also, be aware that some facilities have a policy requiring cancellations two or three days prior to the arrival date, and some charge a cancellation penalty.

HINT
By what time must you cancel the reservation? Is there a cancellation fee?

AUTOMOBILE TRAVEL

Personal Car

Many times a personal car is used for business purposes. In that case, the traveler completes an expense report form so the employee will be reimbursed for expenses. Reimbursement is usually based on a per-mile rate—usually not more than the Internal Revenue Service allows per mile traveled for business purposes. This amount usually changes each year. The employee should keep accurate records of the dates and purposes of business travel and the number of miles traveled. You will find information regarding expense accounts later in this chapter.

Auto Rental

Organizations frequently have a contract with a specific nationwide car-rental company, and they expect all traveling employees to use that company. In exchange, the company gets a better rate on the auto rental. If your company or the traveler does not prefer a specific auto-rental company, you can call a company's toll-free telephone number or search for a rate on the Internet. There are many nationwide auto-rental companies as well as local agencies, and they have toll-free phone numbers and/or Internet sites. Also, most airlines have partnerships with auto-rental companies and usually have direct links from the airline's Web site. The auto-rental rate quoted through an airline Web site may or may not be less expensive than making a reservation independently.

Auto Rental Base Rates

Auto rates are based on the size of the car and the number of days of the rental. The smallest size auto available for rental, the economy size, often has a trunk too small for the traveler's luggage or an uncovered trunk that can be seen from outside the vehicle. Most business travelers prefer to rent a compact or midsize auto. Cars may be rented by the hour and by the day, but the daily charge is usually the same as a few hours, and the weekly charge is usually equal to the charge for four days. Most auto-rental agencies check the driver's license. Furthermore, they may check driving records and may charger a higher rate for drivers who have poor driving records or who are under twenty-one or twenty-five years of age.

Auto-rental rates vary widely and often discounts are offered. As when making airline or hotel reservations, never accept the first rate quoted. Ask about corporate rates, discounts for membership in the company's auto club or other travel clubs such as AAA, membership in organizations such as AARP, buying clubs such as Costco, or others. Auto-rental companies often have coupons that provide an upgrade to a larger size car for the same price as a smaller vehicle. Coupons or other discount offers may be available from the Internet, enclosed with monthly credit card bills, or sent to persons subscribing to the auto-rental email list.

In addition to the base daily rate, the final auto-rental charges also include additional user taxes imposed by local governments and airport user fees. Make sure you know all the required fees and taxes before you make a reservation.

Additional Charges

Auto-rental companies offer and charge for a variety of other services. Some companies offer free mileage, while others charge for the number of miles traveled. An additional drop-off charge may be added if a car is left in a city other than the one where it was picked up. Also some companies charge an additional fee for a second driver. The major additional charges are for personal liability insurance and insurance to cover damages to the car. These charges can significantly increase the cost of the auto rental. Insurance coverage for rental car damage is often included in services provided by credit cards at the gold or platinum level. In addition, the insurance you have on your own car may cover personal liability on a rental car. The traveler should check with his or her insurance and credit card companies to determine their coverage. Accordingly, it is wise to confirm that the policies do not exclude cars used for business purposes. If coverage is available from either of these sources, it may not be necessary to purchase auto insurance from the rental company. In addition to insurance, gasoline is a standard auto-rental charge. Some companies ask the traveler to return the car empty of gas, while others ask the driver to fill the car before returning it. The traveler should be aware of which method is used by the rental company.

People traveling by auto can use the Internet or CD-ROMs to obtain maps with personalized driving directions to help them reach their destination. By entering the starting location and the desired destination, a computer program can provide both a map and written directions all along the route, including mileage and route numbers. Map programs can also calculate the driving distance and time that should be allotted for the trip. Some computer programs are very detailed in their maps and driving directions, and they pinpoint street addresses and provide detailed instructions such as "Turn left at Rt. 5, drive 1.4 miles, right on Rt. 343." These maps can be printed or can be downloaded to a PDA for use during a driving trip. Interactive maps can also be viewed on the Internet on mobile devices such as cell phones, notebook computers, and handheld organizers. Some sites include restaurants and other stopping points along the route. Three widely used Internet mapping sites are www.mapquest.com, maps.google.com, and maps.yahoo.com.

GPS Maps

Many auto-rental companies now provide automobiles that have GPS navigation systems (based on the satellite global positioning system) and built-in display screens that show an electronic map and highlight the car's current location. After entering a destination, the computer calculates the route to be followed, and the driver can follow the car's progress made during the journey.

Frequent Traveler Clubs

The company, or the traveler, may also participate in a program run by auto-rental companies that is similar to an airline frequent-flyer program. Membership in most auto-rental clubs is free and provides several benefits. Reservations can be made easily because the auto-rental company has information on file about the traveler and his or her auto preferences. Being a member of an auto-rental company's program allows the traveler to take advantage of speed check-in and checkout. Often travel club members can bypass the check-in procedure at the auto-rental counter and go directly to the car, which can easily save the traveler a half-hour when picking up a car.

Picking Up a Car

The primary location to rent a car is at an airport. In most airports, auto-rental check-in counters are located near luggage pickup. If a traveler does not have an auto-rental reservation, the traveler can try to locate a car at the airport. However, this will probably require standing in several long lines and, perhaps, not locating a car. While the auto-rental company may have a check-in counter inside the airport terminal, in larger airports the cars are often picked up and returned at a location that may be several miles away. The traveler must use a courtesy bus or van from the terminal to reach the auto-rental agency. Once at the rental location, the traveler is given directions with maps of the area and directions on how to return the car.

When making a reservation, you should confirm the operating hours at the auto rental location. This is particularly important if the auto-rental pickup or drop-off time is set for very early in the morning or very late in the evening. Most auto-rental agencies request the incoming flight number, and if the flight is delayed, the agency will continue to hold the car until the traveler arrives.

While most cars are rented at airports, auto rentals are also available in downtown areas, resorts, and suburban areas. The selection of rental companies in these areas, however, may be limited. If you need to rent a car for pickup other than at an airport, check the Web or call auto-rental companies and ask where they have rental sites. An auto-rental company that is within walking distance or a short taxi ride from where the traveler is staying is preferable.

Sample Auto Rental Agencies

Alamo Rent a Car
www.alamo.com

Avis Rent a Car
www.avis.com

Budget Rent a Car
www.budget.com

Dollar Rent a Car
www.dollar.com

Enterprise Car Rental
www.enterprise.com

Hertz
www.hertz.com

National Car Rental
www.nationalcar.com

Thrifty Car Rental
www.thrifty.com

RAIL TRAVEL

Rail travel for business is very convenient in several sections of the country. Rail service usually provides direct, downtown-to-downtown service. When considering the time and expense of traveling to distant airports in each city and the security requirements of air travel, railroads can provide an attractive alternative between many cities. Rail travel can also be less expensive than air travel, and there are usually fewer weather delays using a train.

Most passenger train service in the United States is operated by Amtrak. Its Web site, www.amtrak.com, is similar to the Internet sites operated by the airline, hotel, and auto-rental companies. You can check schedules and fares, make reservations on line, and then print out the ticket at a Quik-Trak kiosk at the train station or have it mailed.

Because most stations are located in the central city, many business travelers can conduct their meetings and return home in a single day. When you plan a trip for your traveler, don't overlook train travel as an option for cities that are in your region.

RESPONDING TO THE TECHNOLOGICAL DEMANDS OF BUSINESS

Business travelers rely on the Internet and cell phones to keep in touch with their offices and clients. Most cell phone companies now provide nationwide coverage, either through their own networks or in a roaming agreement with other companies. However, there are areas of the country where cell phone service may not be available. If cell phone availability is doubtful, it may be best to call the traveler's cell phone provider or check the Web site to determine if the cell phone operates in the area the traveler will be visiting. Special attention must be made for international travelers because, in many cases, the common cell phones people use in the United States will not work in Europe, Asia, South America, etc. Therefore, international travelers often rent a wireless phone in the country they are visiting or rent a phone in the United States specially designed to work in the region visited. In some states and in many areas outside the United States, cell phones cannot be used while driving, and this restriction includes hands-free wireless phones.

It is also important to verify how travelers access the Internet, if that is their intention. Hotels are meeting the demands of business clients by providing on-site technology in many ways. Since most business travelers want to check their email when they are away from the office, most hotels that cater to businesspeople provide connections in rooms where lodgers can easily connect to the Internet. Some business-oriented hotels now provide unlimited long-distance phone service or high-speed Internet connections for a fixed daily rate. Some hotels and motels have computers available for rent and have experts on staff that can solve computer problems in a meeting or guest room. Internet access is also available from many cell phones, from most notebook or handheld computers equipped with wireless or Wi-Fi cards, or from Internet cafés found in many areas.

Frequently hotels and motels that cater to business travelers have business centers that provide the following services: complete computer systems on movable carts; small offices with a computer, fax, telephone, and table; and fast Internet access. If these features are important to your traveler, check with the hotel prior to making a reservation.

Conventions are good opportunities to gather information and materials, but the materials must somehow get home. The business centers of many business hotels often provide services to mail material back to the office; this can be important because of weight and luggage restrictions when flying.

TRAVEL FUNDS

Expense Accounts

Travel can be a major cost, so companies limit the travel expenses that they pay. Usually, companies pay only for approved travel expenses for items such as transportation (including cabs, parking, or tolls), food, and lodging. At the completion of the trip, the traveler completes an expense account report and is reimbursed by the company for approved expenses. Companies may advance cash or travelers checks that employees use to cover anticipated costs of a trip. At the end of a trip, the expenses of the trip are compared with the funds given in advance to the traveler. If the approved expenses are more than the travel advance, the traveler receives additional money from the company. The traveler refunds money to the company when the cost of the trip is less than anticipated.

Some companies allow employees a *per diem*, which is a fixed amount for travel expenses per day. The per-diem amount usually includes meals but may also include lodging expenses. Employees generally do not have to submit receipts to their

Figure 9-5 A hotel registration.

employers for those items covered by the per-diem allowance. Many companies issue corporate credit cards to employees who travel, and these cards simplify employee travel records. Because the card is used solely for company travel and not used for personal expenses, the credit card statement can be submitted with an employee travel reimbursement request. Some companies pay the funds to the employee and then the employee pays the credit card company, while other companies pay the credit card invoice directly.

As mentioned earlier, business travelers often receive corporate rates at hotels, motels, and auto-rental agencies. These discounted rates are offered to frequent users. Often a corporate identification card is all that is necessary to qualify for these discounts. When making a reservation, ask if your company qualifies for a corporate discount.

Expense Reports

One of the duties of an assistant is to help the traveler prepare the expense report at the end of a business trip. A detailed list of expenses must be available to complete the expense report accurately. For that reason, a business traveler should make a daily listing of expenses while traveling.

Figure 9-7 is an example of a personal record of travel expenses that a traveler completes each day of a trip. Develop a similar sheet for your company and have your supervisor use it while traveling. If the traveler uses a handheld organizer, it usually includes expense account forms as one of the built-in features. If receipts are required, the traveler should take an envelope where receipts can be stored for later use when completing the expense record. After a trip, an administrative assistant completes the company expense reimbursement form using the information the traveler has provided. Company expense report forms vary, but the information required is essentially the same.

HINT
For reimbursement, keep detailed expense records.

Money for the Trip

Unfortunately thieves are always eager to steal credit cards, money, and wallets, and travelers are often easy targets. Therefore, the traveler needs to be aware of travel financial options.

Travelers can carry *traveler's checks*, which can be purchased from a bank, credit union, or auto club, or on the Internet. To ensure the validity of the check the purchaser signs each traveler's check twice—first when purchasing the check and then again when using the check to pay for an item. The merchant can then compare both signatures to determine the validity of the checks. Each traveler's check has a serial number printed on the front of the check.

In the last few years, *traveler's check cards*, which are prepaid cards with an account number, have become popular. They look like credit cards, are accepted in most places, are convenient to use, and can be refunded if lost. Most cards have a feature that allows additional money to be reloaded when necessary.

While traveling, many travelers withdraw cash as needed from *Automatic Teller Machines (ATMs)*. ATMs are located in banks, airports, businesses, and on many

Date	Beginning Mileage	Ending Mileage	Destination	Parking	Other Expenses
6/1/XXXX	32,457	32,489	Wood Inc.	2.00	
6/2/XXXX	32,489	32,529	B.K. Supplies	5.00	1.75 toll

Figure 9-6 An auto expense record.

Personal Record Travel Expenses

Date _____

Hotel/Motel _____   Amount _____

Mileage Begin _____   End _____

Breakfast _____

Lunch _____

Dinner _____

Taxi _____

Parking _____

Tips _____

Additional Expenses _____

_____

_____

_____

Figure 9-7   A personal daily expense worksheet.

Travel Expense Record

Date	Lodging	Meals	Mileage	Misc.	Daily Total
8/14	$60	$35		$5	$100
8/15	$60	$42		$8	$110
8/16	$60	$33		$9	$102

Method of Transportation: *airplane*
   Miles @.25
Airline Ticket: $300

Trip Total: $612

Traveler's Signature: Date:
Supervisor's Signature: Date:

Figure 9-8   A travel expense record.

streets around the world. ATMs that are not part of the traveler's banking network often carry user fees. ATMs in foreign countries may have high transaction fees and currency conversion charges. In some cases, using a convenient ATM outweighs the transaction costs and the safety issues involved in carrying cash.

Prior to each trip, verify that the assistant has a list of the numbers of all traveler's checks, traveler's check cards, and corporate credit cards as well as respective toll-free phone numbers. If the traveler's checks or cards are lost or stolen, the assistant can notify the traveler's check or credit card companies and obtain replacements.

Itinerary: Wilma Sugarman
6/1/XXXX to 6/4XXXX

June 1	Delta Airlines flight 347, Confirmation 3BG 4 TSLM
	Departs Baltimore-Washington International Airport (BWI) at 9:15 A.M.
	Arrives Los Angles Airport (LAX) at 11:02 A.M.
	Hertz car rental, confirmation #2988345S
	3 P.M. meet with Max Rodman at his office, 3400 Western Blvd. (map is enclosed)
	Reservation California Best Western, 3704 Western Blvd.
	Confirmation #BW43775, Telephone No. 831-555-6714
June 2	Meet with Bill Snowdon at 9 A.M., Telephone No. 831-555-2174
	Reservation Califorina Best Western, 3704 Western Blvd.
June 3	Drive to Newport Beach
	Meet at 11:30 A.M. with Marilyn Rose at 2380 Beach Way
	Reservation at Newport Beach Villa, 1215 Beach Drive Confirmation #2318LP, Telephone No. 831-555-8977
June 4	Delta Airlines flight 782
	Departs Los Angles (LAX) at 11:30 A.M.
	Arrives Baltimore-Washington International Airport (BWI) at 8:04 P.M.

Figure 9-9 An itinerary.

ITINERARY

An itinerary is a day-by-day travel plan. It includes dates, hotels, telephone numbers, times and locations of meetings, methods of transportation, airline schedule and flight numbers, hotel and car-rental agency rates and confirmation numbers, and any other information necessary to help the traveler. If the traveler is flying, transportation to and from the airport must also be considered; if special airport pickup service is used, it should be noted on the itinerary. Because some cities are served by more than one airport, the itinerary should indicate which airport is used. Copies of the itinerary should be given to the traveler, administrative assistant, and the traveler's family if so desired.

> **HINT**
> An itinerary is a day-by-day travel plan.

PASSPORTS AND VISAS

Travel to locations outside the United States requires a *passport*. A passport is used by a government to grant permission for international travel and also is the internationally recognized way to identify the traveler. Citizens of the United States obtain passports from the Department of State. Passport applications are available from passport agencies, major post offices, and some county and municipal offices. The first time an applicant applies for a passport, the applicant must appear in person. Applicants for a passport must furnish proof of citizenship with one of the following documents: certified birth certificate issued by a city, county, or state; consular report of birth abroad or certification of birth; a naturalization certificate; or certificate of citizenship. In addition, two 2- × 2-inch photographs taken within the past six months, showing current appearance, must be attached to a passport application. Applicants who do not supply a social security number are subject to a $500 fine enforced by the Internal Revenue Service.

U.S. Department of State
APPLICATION FOR A U.S. PASSPORT

OMB APPROVAL NO. 1405-0004
EXPIRATION DATE: 08/31/2008
ESTIMATED BURDEN: 85 Minutes
(See Instruction Page 3)

WARNING False statements made knowingly and willfully in passport applications, including affidavits or other supporting documents submitted therewith, are punishable by fine and/or imprisonment under provisions of 18 U.S.C. 1001, 18 U.S.C. 1542 and/or 18 U.S.C. 1621. Alteration or mutilation of a passport issued pursuant to this application is punishable by fine and/or imprisonment under the provisions of 18 U.S.C. 1543. The use of a passport in violation of the restrictions contained therein or of the passport regulations is punishable by fine and/or imprisonment under 18 U.S.C. 1544. All statements and documents are subject to verification.

☐ 5 Yr. ☐ 10 Yr. Issue Date _____
☐ R ☐ D ☐ O ☐ DP
End. # _____ Exp. _____

When completing this form, PRINT IN BLUE OR BLACK INK ONLY.

1. Name of Applicant

Last

Suffix (Jr., Sr., III)

2. Date of Birth (mm-dd-yyyy)

First

Middle

3. Sex ☐ M ☐ F

4. Place of Birth
(City & State OR City & Country)

5. Social Security Number
(See Federal Tax Law Notice on Instruction Page 3)

6. Alien Registration Number
(If Applicable)

7. Height Feet | Inches

8. Hair Color

9. Eye Color

10. Occupation

11. Employer

DS 11 06 2005

12. E-Mail Address (Optional)

13. Mailing Address

Street/RFD Number **OR** Post Office Box

Apartment Number

City

State

ZIP Code

Country (If Outside the U.S.)

In Care of (If Applicable)

14. Permanent Address or Residence (If same as mailing address write "Same As Above")

Street / RFD Number (DO NOT LIST P.O. BOX)

Apartment Number

City

State

ZIP Code

15. Home Telephone (Include Area Code)
( )

16. Business Telephone (Include Area Code)
( )

17. Have you ever applied for or been issued a U.S. passport? ☐ YES ☐ NO
If yes, complete the remaining items in block #17 and submit most recent passport.

Name in which your most recent passport was issued

Status of recent passport
☐ Submitted ☐ Stolen ☐ Lost ☐ Other _____

Most recent passport number

Approximate date your most recent U.S. passport was issued or date you applied. (mm-dd-yyyy)

18. Travel Plans

Date of Trip (mm-dd-yyyy)

Length of Trip

Countries to be Visited

19. Have you ever been married? ☐ YES ☐ NO If yes, complete the remaining items in block #19

Spouse's or Former Spouse's Full Name

Is your spouse (or former spouse) a U.S. citizen? ☐ YES ☐ NO

Date of Birth (mm-dd-yyyy)

Place of Birth

Date of Most Recent Marriage

Widowed? ☐ Divorced? ☐
Give Date

20. What other names have you used? (Include Name Changes, Maiden Name, & Former Married Names)

1)   2)   3)   4)

DS-11
06-2006

Page 1 of 2

Figure 9-10 A passport application. (continued on next page)

Passports are issued for a ten-year period for persons over eighteen years of age. Depending on the passport application location, the fee may be paid by check, cash, credit card, money order, or bank draft. Passports may be renewed by mail if (1) the passport is not damaged, (2) it was received within the past fifteen years, (3) if the applicant was over sixteen when it was issued, and (4) the name on the passport is the same as the new passport or you can legally document a name change. When renewing a passport, you must provide your old passport along with your application and fee.

Is your passport current?

Information on obtaining U.S. passports and current fee information is available via the Internet at www.travel.state.gov/passport. Airlines are now scanning passenger passports and comparing them with immigration and customs databases to identify

Name of Applicant (Last, First, Middle)			Date of Birth (mm-dd-yyyy)

21. Parental Information

Mother's Maiden Name			Date of Birth	Place of Birth
Last	First	Middle		

Father's Name			Date of Birth	Place of Birth
Last	First	Middle		

Is your mother a U.S. citizen? ☐ YES ☐ NO   Is your father a U.S. citizen? ☐ YES ☐ NO

22. Emergency Contact - Provide the information of a person not traveling with you to be contacted in the event of an emergency.

Name		Street / RFD Number	
Apartment Number	City	State	ZIP Code
Telephone ( )	E-Mail Address (Optional)	Relationship	

STOP DO NOT SIGN APPLICATION UNTIL REQUESTED TO DO SO BY PERSON ADMINISTERING OATH.

23. Oath & Signature

I declare under penalty of perjury that I am a United States citizen (or non-citizen national) and have not, since acquiring United State citizenship (or U.S. nationality), performed any of the acts listed under "Acts or Conditions" on this application form (unless explanatory statement is attached). I declare under penalty that the statements made on this application are true and correct.

X _____
Applicant's Signature - age 14 and older

X _____
Mother's Legal Guardian's Signature (If Identifying Minor)

X _____
Father's Legal Guardian's Signature (If Identifying Minor)

FOR ACCEPTANCE AGENT USE ONLY

Facility Identification Number _____
☐ Acceptance Agent; Facility Name & Location

☐ (Vice) Consul USA; Location _____

☐ Passport Services Staff Agent
Subscribed & Sworn to (Affirmed) before me

_____ Date (mm-dd-yyyy) _____
(Signature of Person Authorized to Accept Application)

Applicant's or Father's Identification Information

Type of Document   Issue Date _____
☐ Driver's License
☐ Passport   Expiration Date _____
☐ Military Identification   Place of Issue _____
☐ Other (Specify) _____
Name _____
ID Number _____

Mother's Identification Information

Type of Document   Issue Date _____
☐ Driver's License
☐ Passport   Expiration Date _____
☐ Military Identification   Place of Issue _____
☐ Other (Specify) _____
Name _____
ID Number _____

(SEAL)

For Issuing Office Use Only

Name as it appears on citizenship evidence _____

☐ Birth Certificate ☐ SR ☐ CR ☐ City   File Date _____ Issue Date _____
☐ Passport   Issue Date
☐ Report of Birth ☐ 240 ☐ 545 ☐ 1350   Issue Date
☐ Naturalization Certificate   Issue Date   Cert. #
☐ Citizenship Certificate   Issue Date   Cert. #
☐ Other
☐ Seen & Returned
☐ Attached

APPLICATION APPROVAL

FEE _____ EXEC. _____ EF _____ OTHER _____

DS-11   Page 2 of 2

Figure 9-10 A passport application. (continued)

forgeries and tampering. Due to post-9/11 security procedures, citizens of the United States, Canada, Mexico, and Bermuda now must present passports when entering the United States, even when returning from a day trip across the border.

A *visa* is a document permitting a visitor entry into a foreign country. Not all countries require a visa for entry. Information regarding visa requirements can be obtained from the Internet, travel books, travel agencies, and airlines serving foreign countries. Visas are usually obtained from the embassy of the foreign country a visitor plans to visit. Visa fees and the time required for processing applications varies, so it is best to check on visa requirements as soon as foreign travel is anticipated.

Before traveling to another country, it is prudent to investigate whether any medical precautions may be necessary. The U.S. Government's Centers for Disease Control and Prevention (CDC) maintains an Internet site (www.cdc.gov/travel), which is the standard reference for medical information of interest to travelers. The CDC Internet site includes information on vaccinations that may be required or medication recommended to be taken as a precaution when traveling to specific countries.

TRAVEL HINTS

- Take $1 and $5 bills for tipping.
- Take a list of credit card numbers and telephone contact numbers in case credit cards are stolen. Do not keep the list with the credit cards.
- Allow extra time to travel to the airport in case of an accident en route to the airport.
- Do not take the last flight of the day in case it is canceled.
- Carry all medicine on the plane. Do not put medicine in a checked bag.
- Know which airline seats work for you. The emergency row has more leg room. The seat in the row before the emergency row does not recline. Generally planes are boarded with the last rows first.
- Trains often have wider seats than planes do.
- Train stations are often located in downtown areas, while airports are away from the downtown area.
- Trains may require reservations.
- Carry an emergency first-aid kit, especially if you are traveling out of the country.
- Prior to foreign travel, check restricted areas.
- Check the weather forecast for your destination using newspapers, television, or the Internet. Because the weather may be unpredictable, it is wise to take a folding umbrella when you travel.
- Many hotels offer dry-cleaning services or have irons available for last-minute touch-ups. However, you can eliminate the need for ironing by carefully packing clothes.
- To avoid wrinkling your jacket while traveling, remove it and carefully fold it.
- It is wise to carry a small snack with you on a plane. Even if your flight has a meal service, meals are usually served a couple of hours after the departure time. If you have a 12 P.M. departure, you may not be served until 2 P.M.
- It is also a good idea to carry something to read or a work project to complete. With the uncertainty of airline travel, your travel time may be several hours longer than you anticipated.

- Always take a road map with you even if you are not going to drive. The map will assist you in becoming familiar with the area you are visiting.
- Be aware of your company's policy on telephone calls home. Some companies reimburse employees, within set limits, for calls made to the traveler's family.
- Wireless (Wi-Fi) Internet is now available in many airports. Wi-Fi does not mean cost-free. Accounts are available with companies such as T-Mobile and Sprint. Price plans include daily charges of about $8 and monthly charges of approximately $25.

CHAPTER REVIEW

1. Name four travel guides that would be helpful when planning trips.
2. What factors should be considered when renting a car?
3. What is meant by the term corporate travel rates?
4. Explain the term guaranteed reservation.
5. Explain how the Internet is involved in travel reservations.
6. What information should be included in an itinerary?
7. What is the purpose of a passport?
8. What is the purpose of a visa?

ACTIVITIES

1. Use the Internet to determine the time and cost of a trip from your home to the city of your choice. Include in your report three possible time schedules, airlines used, and a cost comparison for your trip.
2. Visit two airline Web sites and review information about their frequent-flyer travel program.
3. Visit two airline Web sites to determine what kinds of special meals are available.
4. Go to a library and look at the travel book section for books by Mobil, Frommer, Fodor, Michelin, or others. Select a city you would like to visit. Then select two hotels or motels that appeal to you. Also select three restaurants where you would like to eat. Explain why you made your selections.
5. Select two cities in different states about five hundred miles apart. You are planning a week-long trip. Use the Web to research information about two auto-rental agencies. You have not decided if you want an economy car or a midsize car. You are going to leave the car in the second city. What are the charges? Remember you must be concerned with drop-off charges, mileage charges, gasoline charges, and insurance fees. Explain why you made your final selection.
6. Download from the Internet a passport application and complete it. If you do not currently have a passport, you might actually apply for one.
7. Prepare a detailed itinerary for a three-day trip to a city of your choice. Contact several airlines to determine the best schedule and fare. Contact several car-rental agencies to compare rental costs. Select a hotel that is a member of a national chain. Determine if there is a limousine service to the

hotel from the airport. After deciding on the hotel, inquire about room costs and the reservation cancellation policy. Prepare a complete itinerary, including dates, times, locations, hotel and rental-car rates, telephone numbers, and method of transportation. You may use the Internet to research this activity.

8. Visit the Transportation Security Administration (TSA) Web site and review current travel security policies. Write a report of your findings.

PROJECTS

Project 17

Complete the following travel expense report from the receipts shown below. If needed, add additional rows to the table.

Travel Expense Report						
Date	City	Lodging	Food	Tips	Taxi	Daily Total
7-24	Tampa		27.00	5.50	22.00	49.50
7-25	Tampa		25.25	4.00		29.25
7-26	Tampa		23.95	4.00		27.95
7-27	Tampa	295.00				295.00
Total amount to be reimbursed:						401.70
Date:				Traveler's Signature:		
Date:				Supervisor's Signature:		

8230 87235 23789 2076
VISA
Lucy R. Castle
Three nights
$295
Inns of Tomorrow, Tampa, FL 33606
7/27/XXXX

8230 87235 23789 2076
VISA
Lucy R. Castle
Food $23.95, tip $4
The Sea's Delight, Tampa, FL 33607
7/26/XXXX

8230 87235 23789 2076
VISA
Lucy R. Castle
Food $27, tip $5.50
Hawaii at Night, Tampa, FL 33607
7/24/XXXX

295.00
27.95
29.25
49.50
401.70

8230 87235 23789 2076
VISA
Lucy R. Castle
Food $21, tip $4
Pedro's Best, Tampa, FL 33607
7/25/XXXX

Taxi receipt
$22
7/24/XXXX

Lunch at a fast-food restaurant $4.25
Tampa
I forgot to get a receipt
7/25/XXXX

Project 18

Prepare the following itinerary.

Mary, I am going to be traveling to Denver on May 1 (United Airlines flight #478). The flight leaves at 10:01 A.M. It arrives at 12.33 P.M. I will be staying at the Hyatt Convention Center (Confirmation #7182409). I will then fly to San Francisco on American Airlines (flight #326) and will stay three nights at the Mark Hopkins Hotel. The flight leaves Denver at 9:02 A.M. and arrives in San Francisco at 11:17 A.M. The confirmation number at the Mark Hopkins is #221684. After two nights in Denver and three nights in San Francisco, I will be returning on United's 8:07 A.M. flight (#602), arriving at Chicago O'Hare at 3:59 P.M.

HUMAN RELATIONS SKILL DEVELOPMENT

HR 9-1 Scents

Men and women who wear perfume, cologne, aftershave, scented hair-care products, or scented cosmetics can offend others without realizing it. Fragrances should be light enough so they do not disturb other workers. Working in close proximity to others and in closed or windowless offices can compound the problem of a heavy fragrance. In addition, people with allergies can become physically ill from breathing strong scents. After using a product for a period of time, the user becomes less sensitive to the smell and may not be aware that the scent is disturbing to others.

- Ask a friend to be honest and tell you if your fragrances can be smelled by a person near you. Are your fragrances too heavy or offensive?
- How would you tell a coworker diplomatically that you find a scent too heavy?

HR 9-2 Restoring an Injured Relationship

Getting along with other workers is important, but a relationship can be damaged by a misunderstanding or insensitivity to a situation. If a friendship existed and then cooled because of a problem, the problem must be solved before the friendship can continue. Unfortunately, one person may not be aware of what caused the problem, and getting the other person to talk about the problem may be difficult. To begin solving the problem, remove yourself from the office environment. Suggest meeting for lunch, going for a walk at lunch, or meeting after work to talk. Start by saying that you would like to continue your friendship and explain that you are not aware of what created the problem. Repairing a damaged relationship can take time, but it can be worth the effort.

- Have you lost a friendship?
- Discuss a friendship that you lost.
- How would you restore a damaged relationship with your supervisor?
- If your coworker was not interested in remaining friends, how would you handle the day-to-day work situation?

SITUATIONS

How would you handle the following situations?

- S 9-1 Your employer asks you to go to the airport to pick up Ms. Kahn, whom you have never met.
- S 9-2 Your supervisor is attending a business meeting in Cheyenne, Wyoming and immediately needs a folder that she did not take with her on the trip.
- S 9-3 Your employer is on the third day of a fourteen-day trip. You have just received a telephone call informing you that the hotel for day twelve has been destroyed by fire.

PUNCTUATION REVIEW

Punctuate each of the following sentences. For a review of punctuation rules, see the Appendix.

1. He wore a dark blue suit and he impressed the manager
2. The budget office estimated that because of the new regulations the cost of maintaining the equipment would be very expensive
3. Rodney who has a pleasing personality worked in a small office on the tenth floor
4. Because most persons who receive outplacement counseling are anxious to continue working they actively search for jobs
5. Penny has a large office with an impressive view of the city and a private elevator
6. At one time my mentor was Ted Lincoln the manager
7. With all of their credentials the applicants also have many shortcomings that must be considered
8. William I believe received the outstanding employee award at last years ceremony
9. Yes I saw the results of the advertising campaign
10. If business takes a hands off attitude the problem will not be solved by next June said the Mayor
11. The reigning theory about career development was discussed at the last board meeting and Samuel said lets stop talking and implement it
12. Such a policy would create what many of our departments drastically need a think tank

13. In our view Thomas Costello took the initiative developed the project and brought it to a successful conclusion

14. The petroleum company which is incorporated in Kentucky transferred the stock to three members of the board of directors

15. Joseph Peerless the witness stated I have never seen a corporation run with such a lack of courtesy

CD ASSIGNMENTS

CD Assignment 9-1

Open the file **CD9-1_MG** on your Student CD and follow the instructions to complete the job. You will also need the file **CD9TF**, which is on your Student CD.

CD Assignment 9-2

Open the file **CD9-1_LD** on your Student CD and follow the instructions to complete the job. You will also need the file **CD9TF**, which is on your Student CD.

CD Assignment 9-3

Open the file **CD9-3_JL** on your Student CD and follow the instructions to complete the job. You will also need the file **CD9TF**, which is on your Student CD.

CHAPTER 10

....

Business Terminology

Objectives

After studying this chapter, you should be able to:

1. Explain the impact of the globalization of business.
2. Explain ecommerce.
3. Explain market systems.
4. Explain the four types of business ownership.
5. Read and use a stock listing.

INTRODUCTION

If you hope to advance to a job with greater responsibilities, it is essential that you understand the business and economic terms used to describe the American economic system. Business and economic terms are not only important in the business world, but these terms also have become an integral part of modern society. An understanding of these terms, therefore, will help you to be successful in your personal life as well as in your professional career. While the professional terms used in a real estate office are quite different from the specialized terms used in a medical office, both offices use the same language for general business activities. In this chapter, you will review standard economic and business terms used by many offices, as well as specialized professional terms used in several types of businesses. Mastering the language of business will improve your ability to work in any office. This chapter discusses the language of several broad concepts common in today's business environment. In the Appendix, you will find a review of additional terms commonly used in business, accounting, law, and real estate.

IMPACT OF THE INTERNET

The Globalization of Business

The globalization of the world economy has created a new business culture and has changed businesses across the country. The rise of a global economy is the result of many political, technological, social, and economic factors, including the lowering of

Figure 10-1   A business executive. Courtesy of: Ruthi Postow Staffing.

HINT

Globalization has changed the business world.

trade barriers between nations, privatization of many nations' economies through the encouragement of private businesses, and an increase in telecommunications technologies such as the Internet. Business decisions made in Europe or Asia can affect the availability of supplies and raw materials for your business, can provide competition to your company, or can open new markets for your employer's product. Today, businesses are no longer limited to one locality and often operate in many countries. Businesses must have a global perspective when they create their business plans. Business globalization requires an interaction of people from numerous cultural backgrounds. Cultural diversity and its implications on business are discussed in Chapter 15.

MY SUCCESS STORY

My Name Is Rose

I really do not talk too much because I am a quiet kind of girl. Sure, I talk to my friends, but I am shy around older people. I let this personality trait affect my job performance. I was too scared to ask questions, so my work suffered. If I did not know how to do something, I tried to do it my way. Of course, my way was not always the best way. I should have asked my supervisor for assistance, but I was too scared of him. After again making a mistake about the proper way to do the task, my supervisor called me into his office. He said that he would prefer, if necessary, to explain the job task to me instead of my doing it wrong. He told me that I was a good worker, but I did not have to do everything myself. Then he asked me if I was afraid of him. I looked down at my feet and quietly said, "Yes." He then said we would work this out together because he did not want to fire a good worker like me. He said I needed to learn to talk to him and ask questions. It took a while, but I now ask for additional information when I do not know how to complete a job. I really have a great boss who is eager to help me solve my problem and succeed in my career.

Figure 10-2   An employee working in a global economy.

Ecommerce/Ebusiness and the Internet

The Internet provides an electronic marketplace where buyers and sellers meet to conduct business. This electronic marketplace has flourished and grown immensely in the last few years and, while it is expected to undergo changes, it will continue to grow in the future. *Electronic business* (*ebusiness*) is a broad term that relates to all aspects of a company's computerized activities, including its automated internal networks, use of the Internet in its business strategy, processing of orders and inventory control, and sale of goods to customers. The selling and buying of goods and services using the Internet is referred to as *electronic commerce* (*ecommerce*) and is changing the way business is conducted in this country and globally. Ecommerce has become very successful in the sale of retail goods and services throughout the country. There are two types of ecommerce: business-to-consumer transactions and business-to-business purchases.

Business-to-Consumer

Business-to-consumer (*B2C*) is the selling of products or services between business and the consumer using the Internet. Ecommerce has advantages for both the buyer and the seller. From the seller's viewpoint, ecommerce is an efficient way to present a business's goods and services to a large group of buyers. The cost to sell an item can be very low. Buyers appreciate the 24-hour-a-day, 7-day-a-week (24/7) easy access to a large selection of items. Purchases can be completed from the comfort of one's home or office. Payment can be made using a credit card and takes only a few minutes. B2C Web sites may combine products from many vendors in one location for easy consumer access. Once the consumer has purchased one product, Web links can be established to encourage the consumer to purchase further products. In addition to offering online buying, many online merchants enhance the Internet experience by supporting online chats, where customers have electronic real-time conversations to ask questions, discuss issues, or review products. Many Internet business Web sites also provide FAQ (Frequently Asked Questions), Q&A (Questions and Answers), support systems, and email customer support.

Ecommerce has empowered the purchaser in ways unheard of several years ago. Buyers use Web sites to obtain a wide array of product and service information. These might include product reviews from other users, information about financing the product, information from manufacturers' Web sites, or government-sponsored sites that contain safety information. Purchasers can easily check specifications and prices from competitors to determine the best item and price for their needs. Both purchasers and retailers appreciate the ability to use the Web to provide answers to questions and other public feedback.

Many traditional businesses have moved to ecommerce because the Internet has become a significant segment of today's technology-driven society. Traditional companies are rethinking their business practices to compete in a market in which communication and purchasing of products is accomplished over the Internet. There are many opportunities but also pitfalls for companies that enter the ecommerce arena. Companies that are innovative and successful will be the ecommerce leaders in the future. Ecommerce requires a redesign of how products are marketed and distributed. Moreover, ecommerce can alter an enterprise's entire sales approach and can dramatically change its records management process. In addition, business and computer security is very important to the conduct of ecommerce, both to protect a business's information and also to protect the consumer's privacy.

Business-to-Business

Government and private industry are joining the private consumer in purchasing through the Internet. This type of ecommerce has become known as business-to-business, also referred to as *Business 2 Business (B2B)*. B2B is the selling of products or services between businesses using the Internet. Businesses buy products, which they in turn use to build their own products, and then sell the product to another business or to the consumer. Ecommerce can help automate the production and distribution system for a company. In addition, B2B has the potential to decrease costs and increase revenue. Furthermore, B2B has created partners who both profit from the partnership while providing additional services to the customer. An example of a B2B partnership is an electronic catalog that sells products from many vendors. With this service, the customer can search the electronic catalog and view products from several vendors according to the item type, cost, and feature.

Internet Auctions

Online auctioning is another sales opportunity for the vendor to provide a product to the purchaser, and many companies such as eBay have embraced this opportunity. In an online auction, the highest bidder purchases products or services. The online marketplace auction has grown and has become very successful.

Global Ecommerce

Ecommerce is a business without the restrictions of a building, time, or place. Web sites can be viewed wherever the Internet is available around the world. Use of the Internet has opened new foreign markets to American businesses for the selling and purchasing of products and services. These markets are now available 24 hours a day (24/7). Since the Web page presents the company's image to the viewer, companies design their Web pages to increase sales and promote the company's objectives. Web sites for companies that wish to create an international business should be designed with a global perspective so they can be easily understood and used by people and diverse cultures all over the world. Therefore, slang words, which may not be understood in different parts of the United States or in foreign nations, should not be used. Many companies prepare their Web site so it may be viewed in several languages.

Egovernment and the Internet

Governments at all levels have joined business in using the Internet to improve their services and efficiently reach their clients. Government clients include both business and the general public.

Most businesses in the country interact with the government on several levels. Governments provide information that may be useful to the business, such as employment information, information about trends in the business's industry, or new research in the business's field. Governments now use the Internet for more than distribution of information about their services, and the range of government services on the Internet can vary widely. Most businesses can now file local, state, and federal taxes and reports using the Internet. The Internet can be a source of new opportunities for business because many governments list their major purchase procurements on the Internet and invite businesses to submit proposals or bids. Businesses can apply for many government benefits or permits using the Internet. Governments post proposed regulations or legislation on the Internet prior to adoption. Therefore, a wise business regularly checks the Web sites of government agencies that deal with business in the community.

SOURCES OF BUSINESS INFORMATION

Reading daily newspapers and business publications or their online services will help keep you informed of current events. A political or economic event in another part of the country or in another part of the world may affect the business where you work. A change in economic conditions or new legislation could alter the business environment in which your employer functions and therefore could affect your job and the operation of your office.

Many offices subscribe to well-known business publications, such as *The Wall Street Journal*, which contain news about business ventures, stocks, taxes, politics, marketing, and other subjects that affect the business environment. Important business publications include *Business Week, Fortune, Barron's, Financial World* and many other well-recognized publications. In addition, there are many specialized services such as Standard and Poor's, Bloomberg, and Moody's, which report on the stock, bond, and municipal markets. You should become familiar with these publications or their online services and skim them for information related to your business. If your office does not subscribe to the business newspapers or magazines that interest you, check the selection available at your library or purchase your own subscription.

Each industry also has specialized publications and newsletters that contain information directly related to that industry. These publications may be monthly, weekly, or daily, and some are available over the Internet or can be sent via email. Examples of these specialized publications are *Journal of Accountancy, Journal of Taxation, Accounting Review, Administrative Management, Telecommunications Reports, Communications Daily, Satellite News*, and *Best's Insurance Reports*. These publications are excellent sources of news about the industry specified. By reading specialized publications and newsletters, you will be well-informed about events in your field.

Television and radio provide up-to-date business and financial information by broadcasting programs about financial and business issues. There are several full-time financial news services such as CNBC, distributed by cable and by satellite television, and Bloomberg Radio, carried by the XM and Sirius satellite radio services, as well as daily business programs, such as *Nightly Business Report*.

Also, the Internet is an up-to-date reference for business information. Many business publications, newspapers, cable television networks, and financial television programs have created their own Web sites to extend their services to their readers and viewers. Additionally, many banks, financial institutions, mutual fund companies, and brokerage firms have established Web sites that contain business information. Data can be obtained from newsletters, newsgroups, and emails as well as individual company Web sites. Always bookmark interesting Web sites and click the links from site to site to expand your knowledge of a specific topic.

You should read as many business publications as you can. The following is a sample list of business publications.

- *Barron's*
- *Business Week*
- *Business Month*
- *Columbia Journal of World Business*
- *Commerce America*
- *Credit and Financial Management*
- Daily business sections of newspapers
- *Dunn and Bradstreet*
- *Electronic News*
- *Forbes*
- *Fortune*
- *Harvard Business Review*
- *High Technology Business*
- *Industrial and Labor Relations Review*
- *Money*
- *Nation's Business*
- *SmartMoney*
- *The Wall Street Journal*

ECONOMICS

Economics is the study of how a community manages its income, expenditures, labor, and natural resources. The production, distribution, and consumption of goods and services are all included in the study of economics. No person, business, or government can produce or purchase everything needed or desired. People and organizations continually make choices of how to spend their money. As individuals, we often have to choose whether to spend our money going to a movie, eating in a restaurant, or buying clothes. In the same sense, each business must make a choice concerning allocation of its resources of money, people, or raw materials. For example, to earn a greater profit, should a business continue production of an old, but successful item (and risk being overtaken by competitors with new products), or should it invest its money in the production of a new product (which may not be successful)? As this question implies, economic decisions can be very complex, with far-reaching results.

Market Systems

One aspect of economics is the *market system*. A market occurs when buyers and sellers exchange goods or services for money. In economic terms, a market is not simply one store but includes the entire community.

We live in a *free-market system* where people are free to go into whatever type of business they choose. A business tries to attract consumers to its products or services so the owners of the business will earn a profit. *Profit* is the difference between the cost to manufacture and sell an item and the price for which it is sold.

In a free-market system, businesses are free to set the price of any product or service they sell. Consumers are free to choose from any product or service available in the market. A sale occurs when a consumer is willing to buy an item at the same price at which the business is willing to sell it.

Consumers have a major role in deciding the type of products manufactured and their selling price. People will not purchase goods or services if they do not need or want them or if the price is higher than they are willing to pay. While a manufacturer chooses to make a product in the hope that it can be sold for a profit, the consumer has the final choice—deciding whether to purchase.

When a new product is developed, consumers have no knowledge of the item. Marketing involves the selling of goods and services and often uses advertising to influence consumers to purchase a product. Advertising the product informs the consumer of its benefits and creates demand. In many cases, consumers do not know that they want a product unless advertising convinces them that the product is desirable.

The price of most new products is very high because of the expense of developing and producing only a limited number of items. As larger numbers are produced through mass production, the price of the products can be reduced. As larger numbers of a product become available, and as additional people know about it through marketing, more people will want to purchase it.

Since the business owner, or *entrepreneur*, is in business to make a profit, the owner has an incentive to produce items efficiently in response to consumer demand. The more efficiently the product is produced, the greater the potential profit. Competition limits the profit of a company because it involves rivalry between companies selling the same products or offering similar services. *Competition* regulates the price that can be charged for a product or service. The producer or retailer can raise the selling price of a product when there is a lack of competition or when the limited quantity of a product is insufficient to meet consumer demand. If a consumer can find the same item at a lower cost, the consumer will purchase it at the lower cost. The entrepreneur, who is the most efficient producer or retailer of a product or service, can lower the selling price and attract more customers. Selling more of the item can then increase profits.

The free-market system encourages specialization, which results in the most efficient use of time and resources. Specialization is producing one particular item or delivering one type of service. Companies specialize in those products that are most profitable for them.

The government does not directly control the economy in a free-market system. A free-market system, however, does not mean a total absence of a governmental role in the nation's economy. Governments may regulate some industries, such as requiring the treatment of hazardous waste material or prohibiting the sale of dangerous toys to children. The government's ability to tax businesses and the government's own spending have a major effect on the nation's economy. The extent of government regulation, tax policies, and spending levels are major political and economic issues in our society.

Business provides goods and services for consumers to purchase. The income received from the sale of these goods and services allows a business to pay workers a salary. Workers spend their salaries for food, shelter, clothing, and other products. This spending, in turn, produces other jobs, and the money continues to flow through the economic system. This process is called the *circular flow of goods and services*. If jobs are terminated, workers do not receive a salary. Consequently, their ability to purchase goods and services must decrease. This change in spending patterns is felt throughout the business community.

Figure 10-3 An employee processing a charge using a credit card approval machine.

HINT

Types of business organizations:
  Sole proprietorship
  Partnership
  Corporation
  Cooperative

TYPES OF BUSINESS ORGANIZATIONS

Several types of business ownership have developed to meet the financial and management requirements of different businesses. Business ownership can be divided into four categories: sole proprietorship, partnership, corporation, and cooperative. Each of these types of businesses has different tax and liability implications for the business's owners or investors.

Sole Proprietorship

A *sole proprietorship* is a business owned by one individual. The owner provides all of the money for the investment in the business and receives all of the profits. The owner manages the business, makes all of the policy decisions, and is personally responsible for all of the business's debts. If the business has financial difficulties, the owner can be required to sell personal property to pay the debts. An example of a sole proprietorship may be a small business such as a photographer's studio, a farm, an accountant's office, or a business operated from a home.

Partnership

A *partnership* is a business owned by at least two people. Ownership in the business may or may not be equally divided. Ownership and profits are divided according to an agreement between the partners.

States have created several types of partnerships. In a *general partnership*, each partner is legally responsible for the debts of the business and the promises of the other partners. Therefore, one partner may be forced to pay the business debts of other partners. Many states permit two additional types of partnerships. In a *limited partnership*, partners with management authority are known as *general partners*; they can sign contracts for the partnership and they are liable for the partnerships debts. *Limited partners* are passive investors with no management authority and are liable only for the amount of their investment. In a *limited liability partnership* (*LLP*), all the partners have limited liability for the partnership's debts. LLPs are often used by professional groups such as attorneys and accountants. Examples of a partnership can also include a restaurant or a supply store.

Corporation

A *corporation* is a business created under state law and is a legal entity separate from its owners. Ownership in the corporation is represented by shares of stock. The stockholder can sell the stock to another individual at any time without the consent of the corporation. Stocks are often purchased through stock exchanges such as the New York Stock Exchange or the American Stock Exchange. Stockholders have no personal liability in the business. If a corporation fails, the stockholders only lose their investment. Their personal money is never used to pay the debts of the business.

People usually buy shares of stock in a company because they expect the company to grow and to earn a profit. The profit can be reinvested in the business or it can be returned to the stockholders in the form of a dividend. A *dividend* is similar to the interest you earn from a savings account at a bank—except that bank interest is guaranteed and a stock dividend depends on the company making a profit. Stockholders purchase stock with the expectation that the stock will increase in value or that dividends will be earned. A corporation pays taxes on its profits, and the stockholders pay taxes on the portion of the profits that they receive. IBM, General Motors, and ExxonMobil are all corporations, but corporations are not limited to large companies.

The stockholders control the corporation by selecting the *board of directors*, which operates the company. The board of directors manages the corporation and appoints the officers who run the company. The size of the board of directors varies. Generally, corporations have an annual meeting where stockholders vote on policy decisions. Each share of stock represents one vote. Stockholders who do not attend the annual meeting are asked to sign a document called a *proxy*, which gives written authorization for another person to vote on the issues.

There are two types of stock—*common stock* and *preferred stock*. Owners of *preferred stock* have preference over owners of common stock when a dividend is declared. A company must pay the owners of preferred stock their dividends before the owners of common stock receive their dividends. Owners of preferred stock usually receive a fixed rate of dividends, while owners of *common stock* do not receive dividends at a fixed rate. If a company does not have enough income to pay dividends to the owners of both preferred and common stock, the owners of common stock do not receive their dividends until the preferred stock dividends are paid.

In recent years, many small businesses in the United States have been formed under a type of corporation known as a Limited Liability Corporation (LLC). The LLC is a low-cost alternative to forming a regular corporation and combines many of the features of a corporation and a limited partnership. There are many tax advantages to operating as an LLC, and an owner's business interests are protected from personal creditors.

Cooperative

A *cooperative* is a business owned by its members. The members are not liable for the debts of the business, but the profits are returned to the members. A cooperative is managed by a board of directors elected by members of the cooperative. An example of a cooperative is a food cooperative, which provides low-cost food to its members.

BONDS AND TREASURY SECURITIES

Corporations raise money in several ways. You have already seen how they sell shares of stock, which represent ownership in the company and include the potential of sharing in the future profits of the corporation. They can, of course, go to a bank for a loan. A third way often used by private corporations—as well as the federal, state, and local governments—is to borrow money by selling bonds to investors. *Bonds* are loans made by individuals or financial institutions, and they do not receive ownership or a potential share in future profits. Repayment of a bond is the first obligation of a corporation, and bond payments must be made before any dividends or profits are distributed to shareholders.

Bonds are issued for a set period of time, known as the *maturity date*, which may be one year, ten years, or even thirty years in the future. The bondholder receives interest payments each year until the bond maturity date, and most bonds pay a fixed rate of interest. At the maturity date, the company pays back (*redeems*) the amount of the loan, which is the face value (*principal*) of the bond certificate. For example, a person may purchase a bond with a face value of $1,000, paying 5 percent, and with a maturity date ten years in the future. Each year for the next ten years, the bondholder (person who purchased the bond) will receive a check of $50 as interest from the company. At the end of the ten-year period, the company will redeem the bond and the bondholder receives a check for $1,000.

Bonds can be bought or sold at any time before the maturity date without the approval of the company. Older bonds can often be purchased for costs either above or below the face value. If a bond is paying an interest rate higher than that which can be obtained through the purchase of a new bond, people are willing to pay a higher price, a *premium*, to obtain the higher income. However, if the bond is paying an interest rate less than the interest rate that can be obtained through the purchase of a new bond, the bond will sell at a *discount* of the face value. Bonds selling at a discount will be redeemed at full face value if held to maturity.

Corporate bonds are certificates issued by corporations, and they are usually issued in $1,000 denominations. Investment bankers and brokers sell these bonds to their clients. Bonds represent a company's promise to pay interest to the bondholder. The stronger the financial condition of the company, the better chance the bondholder has of receiving repayment of the money. The financial strength of many companies is rated by independent companies such as Moody's.

When a city, state, or local government issues a bond, it is called a *municipal bond*. Interest income from municipal bonds is normally not taxed by the federal government or by the government in the state in which the bond is issued. People in high tax brackets have an incentive to purchase municipal bonds because the interest income is free of most income taxes.

One way the U.S. government meets its financial needs is through the sale of government securities. Treasury securities may be purchased by individuals or businesses directly from the twelve Federal Reserve banks across the country, the Bureau of Public Debt in Washington, commercial banks, other financial institutions, and via the Internet. Purchases made through commercial banks and other financial institutions usually include a fee in addition to the cost of the security. Additional information about government securities can be found on the Web.

Treasury securities are very safe investments because both the bonds and the interest to be paid on government securities are backed by the U.S. government. There is an active market for previously issued securities, and they are easily purchased or sold on the open market. Interest earned from Treasury securities is exempt from state and local income taxes. Payment of federal income tax on the earnings of several of the Treasury notes and bonds can be deferred until the security is redeemed.

Types of government securities

- *Treasury bills* (*T-bills*) are issued by the U.S. Treasury for thirteen weeks, twenty-six weeks, or one year. Treasury bills are sold at a discount from the face value, and the purchaser receives the face value upon maturity. The minimum amount of purchase has a face value of $1,000, and bills are sold in multiples of $1,000.

- *Treasury notes* are similar to T-bills because they also require a minimum purchase of $1,000. Treasury notes are issued for two, five, and ten years. Notes are sold near face value, and the purchaser receives interest every six months. Two types of notes are available: one that pays a fixed rate of interest, and one that is indexed with the rate of inflation.

- *Treasury bonds* are issued for thirty years. Bonds may be redeemed by the government before the maturity date, and they are sold with a minimum purchase of $1,000.

How to Read a Stock Listing

Many people own securities, either directly through ownership of stocks and bonds, through the ownership of a mutual fund, or indirectly through participation in a company retirement plan. Following the stock market is easy because most newspapers carry stock quotations. Some newspapers may print information only on those stocks

52-Week							Sales				
High	Low	Stock	Sym	Div	Yld.	PE	100s	High	Low	Last	Chg.
42.34	38	NorW	NXC	4.00	10.3	15	189	39	38.11	39	−.89
117	101	Otell	OWT	4.5	4.5	20	256	112	111	111	+1.34
32.46	19	PlaDa	PRP	2.8	2.8	18	123	31	30.12	31.35	. . .

Figure 10-4   A stock table.

of local interest or the ten most active stocks of the day, while other newspapers carry several pages of information about stocks. Because detailed information is readily available on the Internet, newspapers may not print all of the information discussed here. Most stock tables utilize a format similar to the one shown in Figure 10-4. Stock tables are read beginning with the left column.

52-week High	The highest price for the stock during the prior 52 weeks.
52-week Low	The lowest price for the stock during the prior 52 weeks.
Stock	The name of the stock, which is abbreviated.
Sym	A short code assigned to the stock.
Div	The amount of the dividend paid by the company for each share of stock for the past year.
Yld.	The yield on the stock is the dividend expressed as a percentage of the stock price.
PE	The price–earnings ratio of the stock is the ratio between the market price of the stock and its earnings per share.
Sales	The number of shares sold (in hundreds) during the day.
High	The highest price for the stock for that day.
Low	The lowest price paid for the stock for that day.
Last	The price of the stock when the stock exchange closed for that day.
Chg.	The change in price from the prior day's closing price.

Prices for stocks are now reported to the nearest cent. Newspapers usually report a stock trade of $45.34 as either 45.34 or $45\frac{34}{}$.

FINANCIAL STATEMENTS

Income Statement and Balance Sheet

In your role as an office employee, you may be asked to read, interpret, and keyboard an income statement or a balance sheet. An *income statement* is a financial statement that lists the income and expenses of a business over a particular period of time, often a month or year. A *balance sheet* is a financial statement that lists the assets, liabilities, and capital of the business on a specific date.

B & W Manufacturing
Balance Sheet
December 31, XXXX

	Assets	
Cash	200,000	
Office Equipment	56,000	
Building	350,000	
Total Assets		$606,000
	Liabilities	
Accounting Receivable	75,000	
Notes Payable	30,000	
Accounts Payable	12,000	
FICA Tax Payable	2,800	
Federal Income Tax Payable	5,000	
Total Liabilities		124,800
	Capital	
B & W Manufacturing Capital		481,200
Total Liabilities and Capital		$606,000

Figure 10-5   A balance sheet.

L & K Manufacturing
Income Statement
For Year Ended December 31, XXXX

Revenue		
Professional fees income		$150,780
Expenses		
Rent Expense	12,000	
Salary Expense	52,000	
Travel Expense	8,000	
Office Supplies	2,000	
Office Equipment	8,000	
Telephone Expense	1,000	
Electricity Expense	1,200	
Gasoline Expense	900	
Maintenance Expense	2,500	
Total Expenses		87,600
Net Income		$ 63,180

Figure 10-6   An income statement.

Budgets

One of your duties may be to help prepare or keyboard a department or office budget. In a large company, departmental budgets may be prepared in addition to company budgets. A budget includes a dollar figure for each anticipated item of income and expense and is usually prepared a year or more in advance. Before budgets are adopted, top management must approve them. When developing a new budget, a company usually considers last year's expenses, any new initiatives that may be

Purchasing Department
Budget for XXXX

Projected Income (Budget Allocation)

Base Operating Support	$800,000
Special Funds to Support Expansion Project	93,400
Total Projected Income	$893,400

Projected Expenses

Rent	$ 5,600
Utilities	1,000
Telephone	1,200
Travel	15,000
Insurance	600
Salary	600,000
Taxes and Benefits	220,000
Office Supplies	10,000
Office Equipment	40,000
Total Projected Expenses	$893,400

Figure 10-7   A department budget.

Figure 10-8   An employee working on a department budget.

undertaken, and an increase in anticipated income and expenses. The development of computer spreadsheet packages has made budget preparations and revisions an easier task and permits budget forecasting many years in advance.

Tax Forms

Taxes are a fact of life in every business. Most businesses must be responsible both for the collection of taxes from their customers and payment of various taxes to federal and local governments. Businesses often collect sales and use taxes from customers and are responsible for forwarding these funds to a government agency. In addition, businesses pay a variety of taxes based on their payroll and income. Business taxes are very complicated, and the office employees should be aware of any tax collection or reporting within their area of responsibility. The federal government and many state governments encourage the submission of taxes electronically via the Internet.

Common tax forms

941 The federal quarterly tax return prepared by businesses.

1040 The personal income tax return, not used by businesses.

1099 A tax form that lists interest earned at banks, savings institutions, and brokerage firms and is sent at the end of the year to each client.

W-2 The federal tax form provided to employees listing wages earned and taxes withheld.

W-4 The federal tax form used by an employee to notify the company regarding the employee's income tax withholding. This form is completed by the employee and is used by the employer to determine the amount of federal tax to be withheld.

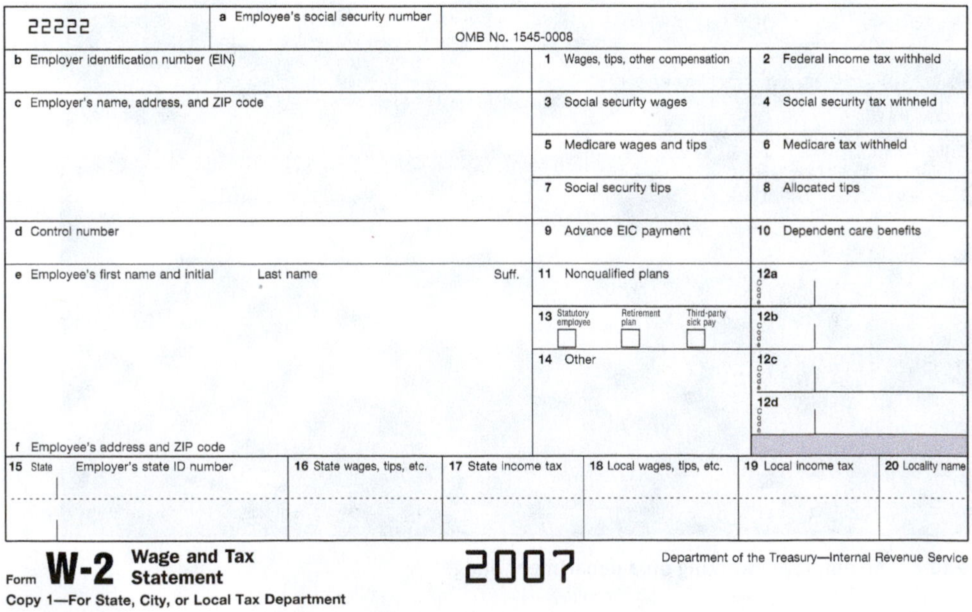
22222
a Employee's social security number
OMB No. 1545-0008
b Employer identification number (EIN)
1 Wages, tips, other compensation
2 Federal income tax withheld
c Employer's name, address, and ZIP code
3 Social security wages
4 Social security tax withheld
5 Medicare wages and tips
6 Medicare tax withheld
7 Social security tips
8 Allocated tips
d Control number
9 Advance EIC payment
10 Dependent care benefits
e Employee's first name and initial
Last name
Suff.
11 Nonqualified plans
12a
13 Statutory employee
Retirement plan
Third-party sick pay
12b
14 Other
12c
12d
f Employee's address and ZIP code
15 State
Employer's state ID number
16 State wages, tips, etc.
17 State income tax
18 Local wages, tips, etc.
19 Local income tax
20 Locality name
Form W-2 Wage and Tax Statement
2007
Department of the Treasury—Internal Revenue Service
Copy 1—For State, City, or Local Tax Department

Figure 10-9 A W-2 tax form.

Form W-4 (2007)

Purpose. Complete Form W-4 so that your employer can withhold the correct federal income tax from your pay. Because your tax situation may change, you may want to refigure your withholding each year.

Exemption from withholding. If you are exempt, complete **only** lines 1, 2, 3, 4, and 7 and sign the form to validate it. Your exemption for 2007 expires February 16, 2008. See Pub. 505, Tax Withholding and Estimated Tax.

Note. You cannot claim exemption from withholding if (a) your income exceeds $850 and includes more than $300 of unearned income (for example, interest and dividends) and (b) another person can claim you as a dependent on their tax return.

Basic instructions. If you are not exempt, complete the **Personal Allowances Worksheet** below. The worksheets on page 2 adjust your withholding allowances based on

itemized deductions, certain credits, adjustments to income, or two-earner/multiple job situations. Complete all worksheets that apply. However, you may claim fewer (or zero) allowances.

Head of household. Generally, you may claim head of household filing status on your tax return only if you are unmarried and pay more than 50% of the costs of keeping up a home for yourself and your dependent(s) or other qualifying individuals.

Tax credits. You can take projected tax credits into account in figuring your allowable number of withholding allowances. Credits for child or dependent care expenses and the child tax credit may be claimed using the **Personal Allowances Worksheet** below. See Pub. 919, How Do I Adjust My Tax Withholding, for information on converting your other credits into withholding allowances.

Nonwage income. If you have a large amount of nonwage income, such as interest or dividends, consider making estimated tax payments using Form 1040-ES, Estimated Tax

for Individuals. Otherwise, you may owe additional tax. If you have pension or annuity income, see Pub. 919 to find out if you should adjust your withholding on Form W-4 or W-4P.

Two earners/Multiple jobs. If you have a working spouse or more than one job, figure the total number of allowances you are entitled to claim on all jobs using worksheets from only one Form W-4. Your withholding usually will be most accurate when all allowances are claimed on the Form W-4 for the highest paying job and zero allowances are claimed on the others.

Nonresident alien. If you are a nonresident alien, see the Instructions for Form 8233 before completing this Form W-4.

Check your withholding. After your Form W-4 takes effect, use Pub. 919 to see how the dollar amount you are having withheld compares to your projected total tax for 2007. See Pub. 919, especially if your earnings exceed $130,000 (Single) or $180,000 (Married).

Personal Allowances Worksheet (Keep for your records.)

A Enter "1" for **yourself** if no one else can claim you as a dependent . . . . **A** ____

B Enter "1" if:
- You are single and have only one job; or
- You are married, have only one job, and your spouse does not work; or
- Your wages from a second job or your spouse's wages (or the total of both) are $1,000 or less.

. . **B** ____

C Enter "1" for your **spouse.** But, you may choose to enter "-0-" if you are married and have either a working spouse or more than one job. (Entering "-0-" may help you avoid having too little tax withheld.) . . . . **C** ____

D Enter number of **dependents** (other than your spouse or yourself) you will claim on your tax return . . . . . . **D** ____

E Enter "1" if you will file as **head of household** on your tax return (see conditions under **Head of household** above) . **E** ____

F Enter "1" if you have at least $1,500 of **child or dependent care expenses** for which you plan to claim a credit . . **F** ____
(**Note.** Do **not** include child support payments. See Pub. 503, Child and Dependent Care Expenses, for details.)

G **Child Tax Credit** (including additional child tax credit). See Pub 972, Child Tax Credit, for more information.
- If your total income will be less than $57,000 ($85,000 if married), enter "2" for each eligible child.
- If your total income will be between $57,000 and $84,000 ($85,000 and $119,000 if married), enter "1" for each eligible child plus "1" **additional** if you have 4 or more eligible children. . . . . **G** ____

H Add lines A through G and enter total here. (**Note.** This may be different from the number of exemptions you claim on your tax return.) ▶ **H** ____

For accuracy, complete all worksheets that apply.
- If you plan to **itemize or claim adjustments to income** and want to reduce your withholding, see the **Deductions and Adjustments Worksheet** on page 2.
- If you have **more than one job** or are **married and you and your spouse both work** and the combined earnings from all jobs exceed $40,000 ($25,000 if married) see the **Two-Earners/Multiple Jobs Worksheet** on page 2 to avoid having too little tax withheld.
- If **neither** of the above situations applies, **stop here** and enter the number from line H on line 5 of Form W-4 below.

- - - - - - - - - - - - - - - - - - - **Cut here and give Form W-4 to your employer. Keep the top part for your records.** - - - - - - - - - - - - - - - - - - -

---

Form **W-4**		**Employee's Withholding Allowance Certificate**		OMB No. 1545-0074
Department of the Treasury Internal Revenue Service		▶ Whether you are entitled to claim a certain number of allowances or exemption from withholding is subject to review by the IRS. Your employer may be required to send a copy of this form to the IRS.		**2007**

1 Type or print your first name and middle initial.	Last name		**2** Your social security number
Home address (number and street or rural route)		**3** ☐ Single ☐ Married ☐ Married, but withhold at higher Single rate. **Note.** If married, but legally separated, or spouse is a nonresident alien, check the "Single" box.	
City or town, state, and ZIP code		**4** If your last name differs from that shown on your social security card, check here. You must call 1-800-772-1213 for a replacement card. ▶ ☐	

5 Total number of allowances you are claiming (from line **H** above **or** from the applicable worksheet on page 2) **5** ____

6 Additional amount, if any, you want withheld from each paycheck **6** $ ____

7 I claim exemption from withholding for 2007, and I certify that I meet **both** of the following conditions for exemption.
- Last year I had a right to a refund of **all** federal income tax withheld because I had **no** tax liability **and**
- This year I expect a refund of **all** federal income tax withheld because I expect to have **no** tax liability.

If you meet both conditions, write "Exempt" here . . . . ▶ **7** ____

Under penalties of perjury, I declare that I have examined this certificate and to the best of my knowledge and belief, it is true, correct, and complete.

Employee's signature
(Form is not valid unless you sign it.) ▶ _____ Date ▶ _____

8 Employer's name and address (Employer: Complete lines 8 and 10 only if sending to the IRS.)	**9** Office code (optional)	**10** Employer identification number (EIN)

For Privacy Act and Paperwork Reduction Act Notice, see page 2. Cat. No. 10220Q Form **W-4** (2007)

Figure 10-10 A W-4 tax form.

CHAPTER REVIEW

1. Explain the term *economics*.
2. Explain the term *freedom of choice* as it refers to business.
3. Explain the term *marketing*.
4. Explain the term *entrepreneur*.
5. List the four types of business ownership and explain each.
6. List three types of government securities.

7. List three tax forms and explain the purpose of each.

8. Explain this stock quote:

52-week							Sales				
High	Low	Stock	Sym	Div	Yld.	PE	100s	High	Low	Last	Chg.
12	7	Hargo	HRX	.25	1.7	7	35	8.34	8.12	8.12	−.22

ACTIVITIES

1. Visit a stock brokerage firm, and prepare a written report describing what you saw.

2. Follow five stocks for three weeks, and prepare a written and oral report summarizing the progress of the stocks. You may use the Internet to research this activity.

3. Select three business publications and summarize one article from each. Also, present one summary orally to your class.

4. Read two articles about current economic forecasts and summarize each.

5. For a two-week period, read your local newspaper and clip all the investment advertisements you find.

6. Watch a financial television program and write a summary of it.

7. Talk with employees of two different types of businesses. Ask what business terms are used in their particular business. Then write a report about the types of companies, terms used, and the advantages of working in that type of business.

8. Watch three television news shows, and prepare oral and written summaries of the business and economic news discussed.

9. Search the Web for financial information about three companies. Write a report about your findings.

PROJECTS

Project 19

Key in the following letter. Change the style to modified block.

Joyce C. Kaplan
Purchasing Agent
R & W Manufacturing Company
2735 Franklin Lane
Charleston, WV 25311

Date

Dear Ms. Kaplan:

As we discussed, we are interested in saving your company money. Our office developed new organization software package last June, and installed it in twenty-five companies in your city. We would like your company to be number twenty-six.

The organization package will allow your company to save over eighty staff hours a week. As you can see, this package will save you the salary of two full-time employees.

Learning to use this package is simple. We will train your staff to use this package in our free one-day seminar, which is offered at your office immediately after purchasing the package.

I will call you next week so we can arrange a demonstration for you.

S. C. Rosen
Regional Sales Manager

Project 20

Send this memo to the staff and supply any additional necessary information. The memo is from Rhonda S. Brown, Chairperson, Company Innovation Development Team.

Please accept my congratulations for a job well completed. The Company Innovation Development Team has done an outstanding job, and every team member deserves our praise. Furthermore, we believe that the report created by the team will be a guide in charting our future. The recommendations will be discussed at the monthly Company Forum next week.

Attached is your copy of the final report. Please review the document prior to the forum so you will be ready to address any issues of concern.

In addition to the printed copy, an electronic version of this report is available on the network in the Innovation Directory.

I look forward to seeing you at the next forum.

HUMAN RELATIONS SKILL DEVELOPMENT

HR 10-1 Extra Hours

Working extra hours can be a daily occurrence or just a peak-time problem. Some employees enjoy working extra hours because of the extra money, prestige, or the chance for advancement. Other employees prefer not to work extra hours. Additional hours may cause personal problems because of schedule conflicts or childcare responsibilities.

- How would you tell your manager that you do not mind working extra hours occasionally, but that you do not wish to do so on a regular basis?
- How would you help a manager who frequently does not give advance notice of overtime understand that you need advance notice to make arrangements for care of an elderly relative?
- What would you do if you were asked to work overtime on a Saturday, and you had already planned to go away for the weekend?

HR 10-2 Another Job

Sometimes one job does not pay enough money to meet all of your financial requirements. While moonlighting at a second job may be an option to meet your financial needs, the stress of two jobs can become overwhelming. Persons working a second job can become irritable, argumentative, overwrought, and nonproductive. Exhaustion can turn an excellent employee into a mediocre employee at both jobs. Since some companies prohibit moonlighting, always review company policies prior to beginning a second job.

- As a supervisor, what would you say to an employee who you know is moonlighting and whose job performance has suffered?

SITUATIONS

How would you handle each of the following situations?

- S 10-1 As a supervisor, you have noticed that Mark, Wilma, and Barry are extending their lunch break so they can watch the conclusion of a television show.

- S 10-2 Today you received the sixth call this week from Harry Whitlock. Harry would like to talk with Tim Kendrick, your supervisor, but Tim refuses to talk with Mr. Whitlock.

- S 10-3 Harriet Peckman always arrives at the office by 8:15 A.M. and it is now 9:30 A.M. Dinora Pazimo has a 9 A.M. appointment with Harriet, and she is still waiting. You know that Harriet's husband works until 2 A.M., and he does not like to be disturbed early in the morning when he is sleeping.

PUNCTUATION REVIEW

Punctuate each of the following sentences. For a review of punctuation rules, see the Appendix.

1. As the meeting concluded she contacted the director and arranged another meeting

2. Jack who is retiring in June is going to England France and Germany

3. You will I think like the new line of appointment calendars

4. I do not have in my personal library the book you cited but it should be available from the department library county library or university library

5. However the meeting was rescheduled for next month

6. Before she left for her vacation she completed all of the jobs in the basket

7. Ted who recently became assistant director has been with the company for over twenty years

8. When she called I was in conference with Mr Epstein and Ms Chen

9. I am meeting Henry Rosen Junior on Monday and Tuesday I am meeting Henry Rosen Senior

10. The guest speaker is Elliott Jameson III and his topic is Business in the New Century

11. If your total payments to the IRS fall short of your estimate pay the revised estimate by January 15 which is the deadline for the December payment

12. In order to capitalize on the enormous demand for publication 205 Office Environments the price was raised from $15 to $20

13. I bought my personal digital assistant (PDA) and new computer software at Chips Inc which is located at 7th Avenue

14. The brokers offered advice but the stockholders didnt listen

15. While Joseph was manager he wrote a policy and procedures manual for his department

CD ASSIGNMENTS

CD Assignment 10-1

Open the file **CD10-1_IT1** on your Student CD and follow the instructions to complete the job.

CD Assignment 10-2

Open the file **CD10-1_IT2** on your Student CD and follow the instructions to complete the job.

CD Assignment 10-3

Open the file **CD10-1_IT3** on your Student CD and follow the instructions to complete the job.

CD Assignment 10-4

Open the file **CD10-1_IT4** on your Student CD and follow the instructions to complete the job.

CD Assignment 10-5

Open the file **CD10-1_IT5** on your Student CD and follow the instructions to complete the job.

CHAPTER 11

....

The Office Environment and Design

Objectives

After studying this chapter, you should be able to:

1. Handle situations involving the office landlord.
2. Explain security techniques used in an office.
3. Describe a favorable office environment.
4. Explain the important aspects of office design and layout.
5. Describe methods of purchasing office supplies.
6. Explain methods of inventory and their purposes.
7. Prepare a deposit slip and endorse checks.

INTRODUCTION

Working in an office can be challenging. While preparing for your profession, it is easy to overlook some activities that are vital to the successful operation of an office but are so common they are often invisible. This chapter deals with activities related to the office and the office environment. The mastery of these operational activities will keep an office running smoothly on a daily basis.

LANDLORD AND BUILDING STAFF

Dealing with Your Landlord

Most offices have a landlord. If your office is part of a large organization, the business may lease a floor of a large office building or may even occupy its own building. In these situations, the business has a professional staff to deal with landlord-tenant relationships or with the responsibilities of building ownership.

If the business is small, you or your supervisor may work directly with the landlord regarding the lease of space. A *lease* is a document that establishes a business's relationship with the landlord and specifies the amount of office space the business will occupy, the rental rate, and the services the landlord will provide. Landlord-supplied services may include heating, lighting, security, provisions for parking, office cleaning, and building maintenance. The lease also explains the conditions under which the business may occupy the leased space. The lease may include restrictions about the type of businesses, hours of operation, use of machinery, noise, and the number of people allowed in an office. If you work in a small office and must work with the landlord, you should become familiar with the terms of your business's office lease.

Building Staff and Maintenance Staff

While most employees do not interact directly with their landlord, every employee should have an interest in the building where he or she works. The maintenance of the building and of the individual offices affects the health, safety, and attitude of the people working in it. The *building staff* supervises the building and acts as the landlord's representative. They may or may not have an office in the building. The *maintenance staff* is responsible for the daily functioning of the building and its infrastructure, including heating, plumbing, and electricity. It is always best to develop a good relationship with the building and maintenance staff, and it is important to treat them with respect. Some offices even remember the members of maintenance or building staff with small gifts at holidays. Keep in mind that people are much more helpful if you are pleasant and ask for assistance rather than order them around and demand service. By developing a friendly, respectful relationship with members of the building and maintenance staff, you will get better service.

OFFICE SECURITY AND WORKPLACE VIOLENCE

Building Security

The topic of building security has become crucial since the terrorist attacks of September 11, 2001. Many building owners have taken measures to increase building security. These measures may include restricting public access to buildings by closing some of the entrances or constructing physical barriers to keep cars and trucks away

MY SUCCESS STORY

My Name Is Anna

Now it is my turn. I had my first baby when I was eighteen years old. My next two children arrived a few years later. I was busy raising my children, and I did not have time to think of a career for myself. I am happy to tell you that when my last child entered college, I did too. It was not easy because I thought I might be too old to learn. Actually, college was fun and stimulating for me. After I received my degree, I was ready for the next hurdle—a job. I was scared that I was too old for the job market, but I think I was hired because I brought maturity and business skills to the employer. I have now been employed for ten years and my job evaluations have all been terrific. In addition, my company and I have a great respect and concern for each other.

Figure 11-1 A security guard at a business office.

from the outside of buildings. Parking may be limited in underground garages or in areas adjacent to the building.

Office guards control access to many buildings and permit only authorized personnel to enter. Members of the staff may be required to display photo identification badges. Visitors may have to show identification and sign registers before entering a building and/or they may have to be escorted by employees. In addition, visitors and staff may be required to open purses and briefcases for inspection or even pass through airport-style metal detectors.

No business wants a visitor wandering alone through an office where that visitor could disturb employees, "accidentally" see confidential information, steal documents or equipment, or even have an accident for which the company would be liable. New technologies are being used to strengthen areas of office security. To improve security, many offices are replacing traditional keys with smartcards, often called *swipe cards*, which are plastic cards the size of credit cards encoded with door-locking codes. They provide increased security, can be recoded easily to provide entry or deny entry to specific individuals, and can keep track of which individuals lock or unlock a door.

Companies now include smartcard technology on identification passes or use bar codes as building entrance passes. Security is moving forward in the field with the use

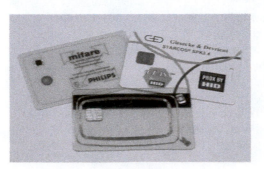

Figure 11-2 Smartcards for an office entrance. Courtesy of: Hirsch Electronics WeSecureBuildings. com.

Figure 11-3 A security guard screening visitors. Courtesy of: Hirsch Electronics WeSecureBuildings.com.

of *biometrics*, which is the study of recognizing individuals through unchangeable physical characteristics. Human characteristics such as voice, fingerprints, and face contours can be used to verify employee identity prior to entering a building or office. The biometric authentication software can be built into devices, eliminating the need for passwords, PINs, and keys. Many offices use fingerprint sensors instead of passwords for building entry or to log into computer systems. Another biometrics security system used to verify a person's identity is a system that scans a person's eye. Since a person's biometric characteristics are practically impossible to replicate, these technologies will become more widespread and will increase security for offices, employees, and computer systems.

Some of these security measures were in place before September 11 and were intended to protect confidential commercial information or sensitive government documents. As more companies become concerned about safety and security protection, the use of these technologies will continue to strengthen.

Fire Safety

One of the responsibilities of an office building manager is to provide a safe and secure environment for a business and its employees. Modern building codes and zoning regulations in many communities address the basic safety requirements of office buildings. These regulations address items such as emergency exits, electric and water requirements, the type of business, and the number of people who can safely work in a specific type of building.

What is your personal emergency plan?

Figure 11-5   A biometrics reader. Courtesy of: Courtesy of DigitalPersona, Inc.

Fire safety is a major workplace concern, and many localities mandate fire alarms and fire sprinkler systems. Fire alarms are regularly tested, and often you are notified of the test date. If you hear a fire alarm while working, evacuate the building for your own safety. It is important to walk away from the building. Frequently people evacuate a building and stand directly outside it, which is a dangerous location. Sprinkler systems generally have a sprinkler head located in individual offices or spaced at regular intervals in large areas; if a fire occurs, the individual heads are automatically activated as needed.

As an employee, it is your personal responsibility to know where the fire exits are and to ensure that those exits are never blocked in any way. Be sure you know several ways out of your building in case an exit cannot be used. Furthermore, if you see unsafe situations occurring in your building or in your office, immediately call the situation to your supervisor's attention.

Emergency Medical Equipment

Many companies have installed Automated External Defibrillators (AEDs) to provide prompt medical assistance to persons having a heart attack. The AEDs are generally mounted in a labeled and protective metal cabinet in a public area. Since state regulations often require that individuals be trained and certified to use AEDs, many companies now train employees to use them.

Workplace Violence

In the last several years, there has been an increase in violence in the workplace, which has shocked employers and employees and increased public awareness of the issue. Today workplace violence is no longer limited to dangerous occupations, such as law enforcement, but can occur in all fields. Regrettably, incidents of violence can be found in every workplace. Violence can be mental as well as physical and includes, but is not limited to, robbery, murder, stalking, threats, verbal harassment, and sexual harassment. Proactive preventive efforts are necessary but do not solve all problems; therefore, all employees should protect their own personal safety by maintaining a keen awareness of their physical surroundings and the people around them. Employees and employers should be alert to the warning signs of violence.

Statistics indicate that workplace violence is often committed by disgruntled employees. Although an individual may appear to be a model employee, there may be underlying signs of conditions that lead to violence such as drug abuse, alcohol dependence, depression, financial difficulties, mental unrest, loss of employment, or destructive behavior. It is difficult to anticipate internal workplace threats, but by increasing workplace security, some violent actions may be prevented. Installing a security guard or gate to control entrance to the workplace, glass partitions to separate employees from visitors, and security alarms at designated locations all may deter violent confrontations. Companies should establish a workplace violence-prevention program and train employees about workplace violence. Companies that provide employee assistance programs have procedures to deal with employee grievances, enforce policies against harassment, and offer personal counseling are better equipped to prevent workplace violence by coping with a problem before it becomes a violent issue. Additional prevention methods include educating the employees concerning unacceptable behavior, providing bright security lighting and alarms, installing video surveillance equipment, requiring the use of identification badges, and having security guards and electronic or password-protected entrance access. Information about preventing workplace violence can be obtained from the U.S. Department of Labor, Occupational Safety and Health Administration at 1-800-321-6742 or www.osha.gov.

> **HINT**
> Workplace violence can be directed toward anyone.

Monitoring Employees

Many businesses monitor employees and the workplace to improve security. Employees may be observed, sometimes without their knowledge, by small, concealed video cameras placed in hallways or offices. When companies use surveillance equipment, a safer and more secure workplace is provided to the employee because cameras can quickly alert security personnel to serious safety problems. However, while electronic monitoring may be a security safeguard for the employee, many employees feel that monitoring violates their personal rights and is an invasion of privacy.

Companies may also monitor employees to increase productivity or reduce theft. Some companies have spot-check procedures, while others have continuous organization-wide observation systems. Generally companies that monitor employees experience a reduction in theft and an increase in productivity from employees who would have slacked off on the job. In addition to personnel monitoring, companies may monitor employee communications such as email, telephone, and computer usage. Increasingly companies are monitoring employee Web traffic to determine if it is used for personal Web surfing. Employers are concerned about buying from eBay, shopping online, checking finances with online banking and stock/bond trades, reading and sending personal emails, and viewing pornography, which all squander away company time. Employee downloading of video and other large computer files can slow down a company's Internet and internal network connections and hinder required business activities.

While it may be legal for a company to monitor its employees, the company should specifically notify employees of policies regarding usage of company equipment and of its employee-monitoring activities.

> **HINT**
> Monitoring of employees has increased.

THE OFFICE FACILITY

Physical Environment

Your office is the single place where you spend most of your waking hours. Your office, therefore, should provide comfort and meet your needs as well as those of your employer.

With changes in office technology and design, and as companies reduce overhead costs, the amount of office space per employee has been reduced. As a result of this trend, employees who in the past had private offices may be asked to share office space. In some offices, a large room is divided into many individual workstations, which may be grouped or divided by partitions, shelves, or acoustic panels.

Many office workstations are designed using modular furniture systems, which are based on a family of interchangeable parts. Desks and storage units connect directly to freestanding walls and can be reconfigured to meet the changing needs of the office.

To combat the cramped office problem, office furniture designers have developed mobile file cabinets that roll out for usage and are stored under desks; storage boxes mounted on a pole; adjustable storage towers with multiple directional access for use by adjacent employees; and cubicle walls with grooves for shelves, binders, boxes, and desktop accessories. To further control employee space, some companies are using storage units to divide offices instead of movable walls.

When many people work in an open office environment, the result is often noise pollution. Reducing the level of noise caused by equipment, telephones, conversations, and traffic in an open office is a challenge. Acoustic tiles, partitions, carpeting, and draperies are often used to reduce the level of noise.

The quality of lighting in an office is important, especially for employees who spend much of their day working at a computer. Too much light is as visually disturbing as too little light. Lighting, sun-related lighting problems, and glare on a page or a computer terminal can cause eyestrain. Overhead lighting, task lighting, and desktop finishes may all produce a glare. Offices should use fluorescent lights and adjust windows and drapes to provide sufficient light and reduce glare. Glossy finishes on desks and countertops reflect more light and provide more glare than surfaces with a matte finishes. Eyestrain may be reduced by taking breaks from the computer, using eye drops, and using nonglare computer shields.

Indoor air pollution has become a problem in some offices because of improperly designed buildings or poorly ventilated air systems. Another source of indoor pollution is caused by office equipment that produces ozone (electrically charged air) that is inhaled into the body. Employees need to be aware of potential indoor pollution problems and alert the supervisor if they feel sick, become lightheaded, or experience a work-related illness.

Cleaning the Office

In some offices, a professional cleaning staff goes through the offices at night when the offices are vacant. In other offices, the cleaning staff cleans the offices during normal working hours. In either circumstance, be pleasant to the cleaning staff and know what you should do to help them in their work. The cleaning staff is instructed about how to clean offices and under what circumstances not to clean offices. If you make cleaning your office difficult, you will probably not be pleased with the way it looks.

Heat and Air Conditioning

Both employees and office electronic equipment are sensitive to temperature, humidity, air quality, and cigarette smoke. To control the climate within the office and maintain the health of the staff and the working condition of the equipment, modern office buildings are usually constructed as closed, controlled environments with sealed windows. Heating and air conditioning may be controlled for the entire building by the building maintenance staff. Some buildings may have temperature controls for specific floors, zones, or offices, but temperature control for individual office areas often is not offered. In addition, heat and air conditioning may not be available after traditional business hours or on weekends or holidays when the building is not normally used. Generally, heating and cooling should be set at a comfortable temperature of 68 to 75 degrees in winter and 73 to 79 degrees in summer. However, a temperature that is comfortable for one employee may be too hot or cold for another. Employees who work in controlled-environment buildings must often cope when the office temperature is beyond their immediate control or comfort level. An uncomfortable employee is not a productive employee.

Be aware of the general temperature of your office in relation to other offices. Because of their placement in the building, some offices may be warmer than others. Some offices are comfortable in winter but not in summer, while others are comfortable only in summer. If your office is consistently uncomfortable, there may be a problem with the heating/air-conditioning unit in your area. The building maintenance staff may be able to adjust the unit to provide a comfortable temperature. The temperature in offices that have windows can be adjusted to some degree by using the window blinds. Opening the blinds on a sunny day brings in heat as well as light, while closing the blinds reduces solar heat that warms the office. Some employees use small electric fans to cool their offices in the summer and electric heaters to warm their offices in the winter. When using electric appliances, be careful not to overload electrical circuits. Electric heaters can get very hot and should be used with caution. Also be careful about placing electrical cords for fans or heaters so they are not in a traffic area. Many employees dress for the temperature they expect to find in their office. To accommodate temperature changes, a sweater or suit jacket can be worn or removed as the office temperature changes. Therefore, a wise employee keeps a solid-color jacket or sweater in the office for the days when the office is cold.

What is your climate comfort level?

Plants

Plants are used in an office to bring the warmth of the outdoors inside, and they help to soothe an office environment by making it seem less harsh. The color that plants bring to the office can enliven a dull decorating scheme. Another function of interior landscaping is to separate work areas and create privacy. In addition, specific types of plants purify the office air and reduce indoor air contaminants. Even artificial silk plants may be used to create a pleasant environment, but most people prefer living plants. Because plants need frequent maintenance, they should be placed at an easily accessible level. Most plants prefer temperatures of 65 to 75 degrees, so it is important to consider room temperature and the location of blowing heating and cooling air when selecting and placing plants. A lack of water or sun causes plants to die, ruining the attractiveness of the office. Plant specialists can make recommendations regarding the type of plants suitable for a particular office, suggest where to place the plants for maximum enjoyment, and maintain the plants. The philodendron, schefflera, African violet, Jade, ivy, and spider plants require little light and minimum maintenance, so they are frequently used in the office to bring the texture and experience of the outdoors inside. In addition, studies have shown that several types of plants, including bamboo palm, dracaena, English ivy, and gerbera daisy, may be used to clean pollutants from the office air.

HINT
Plants improve the office environment.

Safety

Every employee should be on the alert for unsafe conditions in the office. Items placed in or near walk areas are a major cause of accidents. People walking through an office may not be familiar with the specific location of all office furniture or they may be thinking about their work and not watching every step. To prevent accidents, electrical wires and cords should be enclosed in tubes, taped to the floor, buried, or placed where people will not trip over them. Trash cans should be placed along walls or next to furniture and away from where people walk. In addition, when chairs are not in use, they should be placed close to the desk; if a desk or file cabinet has a pull-out shelf, it should be pushed in when not in use.

File cabinets can be a primary source of injuries. When not in use, the drawers of vertical file cabinets should be closed, not left open. If a file drawer is open, a person walking by could stumble or bump into the drawer. As another safety precaution, only one drawer of a vertical file cabinet should be open at a time. When several drawers are open, the weight of the cabinet shifts; thus, the cabinet may become top-heavy and tip over.

FILE AND COMPUTER SECURITY

File Security

Always be aware of the security requirements of your office and be responsible for the security of your area. When computers were first introduced, some people thought the electronic transfer of data would lead to the paperless office. Unfortunately, the ease and speed of information exchange using computers, word processors, photocopy machines, and facsimile machines have led to more paper in most offices, not less. Much of the information that is processed and stored on paper is of a confidential nature. To protect the privacy of individuals and the confidential nature of many business transactions, care must be taken to safeguard files and the information they contain.

Many offices require that file cabinets and drawers be locked when not in use. While this may appear inconvenient, it is essential that employees follow the company policy regarding security. Some organizations conduct surprise inspections to check the security of offices and files. Keys to locks should not be left out where they can easily be found. People often write down a lock's combination in case they forget it, and then they place the written combination in their desk drawer where it is easily found. While this may be convenient for the employee, it decreases the security of the files. If other persons know where the lock combination is located, the files are not really secure. If you have been given the combination of the office safe, do not divulge it to anyone. If you are working on sensitive material and you leave your office—even for a few minutes—secure the documents before leaving.

After confidential documents are no longer needed, they are often destroyed before they are thrown out. A *paper shredder* is used to cut the paper into very thin strips or to shred it to the size of confetti. Shredders are categorized according to the size of the shredded sheet, entrance sheet capacity, speed, and waste capacity. Shredders that cut paper into very small pieces provide a high degree of confidentiality. Most office-quality shredders can cut papers containing staples and paper clips. After the paper is shredded, it falls into a receptacle that keeps the documents confidential until proper disposal. For destruction of the most sensitive documents, the shredded paper may be placed in special bags and burned. While working at home, telecommuters who work with confidential documents should also shred and properly destroy materials.

Computer Security

Computer security is a major concern for a company, and it may have procedures addressing the security of computer equipment, limitations on access to computer files, and the safeguarding of computer data. The loss of computer information

Figure 11-6 A paper shredder.

would be a disaster for most offices, so be knowledgeable of and follow the computer security procedures in your office.

Computer systems are vulnerable to *hackers*, people who make unauthorized entry into computers and who may steal, disrupt, or destroy computer data. Hackers are usually people unknown to the company who enter computer systems via the Internet, but they may also be disgruntled present or former employees. The more information unauthorized people have about the company's computer system, the easier it is for them to break into the system and steal or destroy data. Office computer systems frequently require the user to have a login code and a password to gain access to the system. Remember that your password is confidential, so do not disclose it to others. Do not use a password that is easy for someone else to guess, such as your birthday. To safeguard your computer system, do not write down your computer password and leave it where others may see it. Furthermore, do not tell anyone outside your office how your office computer system operates.

Computer systems are also vulnerable to storms, which can cause electrical surges that destroy computers, computer data, printers, and other electrical equipment. *Surge protectors* are devices that protect computer equipment from damage by smoothing over sudden changes in the electric current. Always be sure that the surge protectors in your office are in use and operating properly.

Theft of computer hardware is a common occurrence; therefore, computers may be attached to their desks by special locks. Security hardware may be inconvenient, but the loss of a computer and its data can be very damaging to an office. Notebook and handheld computers are designed to be carried out of the office. In some offices, an employee must show written authorization before taking computer equipment out of the office. If you are authorized to take computer equipment out of the office, the equipment has been placed in your care, and you are held accountable for its return.

All offices should have a plan for recovery in the event that a disaster strikes the office or its computer system. The most common recovery plan involves storing data off-site. If the original files and all backups are kept at the same facility and the facility experiences a catastrophe (fire, water damage, explosion, etc.), all backups will also be destroyed. Off-site storage should be done on a regular basis, at least once a week. With the advances in technology, some companies send electronic backups to a Web server at an off-site location.

The Office Environment and Design

Securing computers against viruses is also an important part of a computer security plan. As discussed in Chapter 6, scanning for a computer virus is essential to prevent damage to the office computer system. Viruses caused by infectious emails have increased, so virus protection is vital for the safety of your computer.

When it is time to dispose of your desktop computer, notebook computer, personal digital assistant (PDA), or cell phone, the security of your data becomes a major issue. Because these devices often contain lists of passwords, personal data, telephone lists, personal files, confidential office files, and so on, they can be a gold mine for identity thieves. Simply erasing the data may not solve the problem because a knowledgeable thief can easily resurrect your personal information and steal your identity. It is very important, but also difficult, to wipe out all of the data prior to disposing of the device. Check with your company's computer department for recommendations on how to erase a hard drive. For further suggestions or steps to erase data from a hard drive, enter "erase a hard drive" in an Internet browser.

OFFICE FURNITURE, EQUIPMENT, AND SERVICES

Before new equipment is purchased, the decision of where to place it and on what to place it must be made. Frequently equipment is purchased and only later is consideration given to its location. Without prior planning, equipment is often simply placed where it fits, without consideration of proper lighting, the height of the table on which is it placed, or employee comfort during its use.

An assistant's desk should be large enough to accommodate all of the work and papers used each day. The desk should be placed for easy accessibility to the supervisor. It should be situated so that the assistant can greet clients and not be surprised by an unexpected visitor. In addition, the desk must be away from office traffic so work can be completed without being hindered by noise, conversations, or persons walking by.

A computer should be placed on a stand or desk that is the correct height for keyboarding documents. To save space and reduce wrist pain, many computer desks have pullout shelves for keyboards. In addition, a stand or desk area must be available for the printer.

Employees working in a multiperson office should have some personal space. Plants or filing cabinets can be used to create private areas. A multiperson office should be designed to accommodate the traffic caused by a large number of employees entering and leaving.

Studies have shown that office décor and color have an effect on an employee's moods. Color can be used to create enthusiasm and increase productivity. Generally, blue and green are calming and relaxing colors, red and orange are exciting and stimulating colors, and yellow makes a room seem bright and happy. In addition, color can be used to alter the perceived size of a room. Light colors create the appearance of a larger room, while dark colors make a room seem smaller. Creating an office that is comfortable includes the arrangement of furniture, personal belongings, and decor.

Ergonomic Furniture

Ergonomics is the study of the human body in relation to its work environment, that is, the study of how the physical environment affects employees. Employees come in different sizes—short, tall, thin, and not so thin. All employees do not fit comfortably at the same size chair or desk. To meet the changing needs of the office environment, office furniture has been developed to help employees be more comfortable. Prior to purchasing office furniture, look at each employee and determine the best furniture fit for that person. Sitting incorrectly, having an office chair that does not support your back, or having a desk that is not at the correct height all can cause back pain. Back

Figure 11-7 An ergonomically designed chair.

pain is one of the major causes of employee absenteeism and can affect the employee's ability to work efficiently.

To accommodate people's different heights, an office can purchase adjustable chairs, tables, and printer stands. A comfortable employee completes a task more accurately, more quickly, and more efficiently, and an employee who is comfortable is happier. A desk for computer keyboarding use should be about 27 inches high, while a desk for writing purposes may be 29 inches high. To accommodate leg movement under the desk, there should about 27 inches of space. It is helpful to have a keyboard tray that tilts and moves. When purchasing a chair, be sure it has an adjustable seat and backrest. The height of the chair should adjust so the person's arms are high enough for the desk, and the person's feet rest on the floor. For comfort, short people may require a footrest with a nonslip surface. The chair backrest should firmly support the lower back. Chair legs should have wheels so employees can easily move their chairs. The seat span should be about 18 inches, but this dimension may change depending on the size of the individual. The monitor height and location are also very important. The monitor should be at a comfortable distance while sitting in the chair, and the screen should be at eye level to avoid raising the neck to an uncomfortable position.

> **HINT**
> Ergonomics is the study of the human body in relation to its work setting.

The placement of furniture can also affect an employee's comfort and productivity. Avoid placing equipment at a location that requires the employee to twist around in the office chair to reach equipment. Twisting in a chair can cause a neck or back injury or can cause the employee to fall out of the chair. Preventing injuries is less expensive than the high medical costs and loss of personnel hours resulting from injuries.

A common office health problem frequently associated with computers is *carpal tunnel syndrome*. This injury, which is often caused by repetitive motions used in keyboarding documents, results in pain in the hands, wrists, or arms. Carpal tunnel syndrome can be reduced by taking breaks to rest your hands, using correct hand placement on the keyboards, using ergonomic keyboards, or using wrist supports when keyboarding.

Back and neck pain is often caused by incorrectly lifting items or by not properly supporting the back while seated. To avoid back injuries, always use safe lifting techniques such as lifting from a kneeling position instead of lifting by bending at the waist. It is better to use appropriate lifting techniques and prevent an injury than to treat an injured back.

Equipment Repairs

Office equipment does break and require repairs. One employee should be responsible for overseeing repair of office equipment. Detailed repair records should be kept because it may be important to know how often and what types of problems occurred on a specific piece of equipment.

Type of Equipment		
Serial Number		
Model Number		
Purchase Date		
Vendor	Vendor Address	Vendor Telephone No.
Repair		
Date Repair Requested	Date Repaired	Serviced By
Cost	Warranty	
Comments		

Figure 11-8 A repair record.

Before a repair is requested, the payment of the repair should be considered. Is the equipment under warranty? Is there a maintenance agreement on the equipment? A *maintenance agreement* is a contract for repair of the equipment, and usually a set fee is paid on an annual basis for the repairs. Some companies lease equipment instead of purchasing the equipment. A lease contract may or may not include maintenance of the equipment, so you should know the terms of the lease agreement before you repair equipment. You should have a file of equipment covered by maintenance contracts.

Repair for equipment under warranty or under lease, or when a maintenance agreement is in place, is handled by calling the appropriate vendor. When calling about a repair, indicate the nature of the problem and how often the problem occurs. It may take several telephone calls to have an item repaired. After the repair is completed, you will usually be asked to sign a receipt indicating that the work was completed.

If an office has no agreements regarding the repair of equipment, you must identify a source for repairs. You could contact the company from which the equipment was purchased, the manufacturer, or an authorized dealer, or search the Internet for a repair facility. Many areas have independent shops that can repair office equipment. Listings of possible repair facilities can be found in the yellow pages of the telephone directory. When contacting a company about the repair of equipment, you must determine whether it is qualified to do the repair, how your company will be billed for the service, all costs, and the length of the warranty on the repair.

Photocopiers

Digital technology has transformed the standard office photocopier into a flexible piece of equipment that can perform many functions. Older, nondigital photocopy machines did one task very well—copying correspondence, reports, and other documents for daily use in the office. A nondigital copier copies one page at a time and can

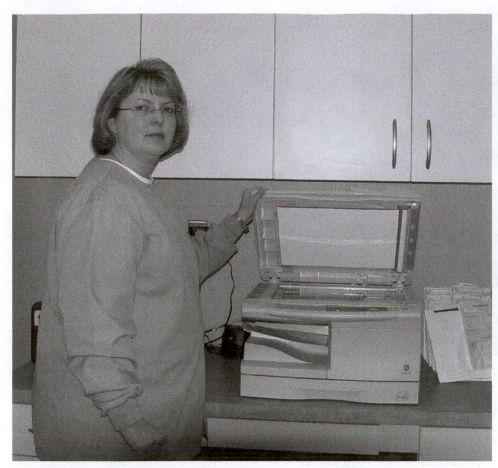

Figure 11-9   An employee using a small office copier.

make single or multiple copies of a document. Today most copy machines make copies on at least two sizes of paper—regular size 8.5- × 11-inch and legal size 8.5- × 14-inch paper. Larger copy machines can reduce or enlarge the size of the copy, collate and staple multiple copies, copy on both sides of the paper, automatically feed a stack of originals, allow interruption of copying at any time, reset the number of copies after the first set has been run, and diagnose and describe machine problems.

A *digital copier* is more flexible than a nondigital copier because it scans a page and then stores the page in memory, like a computer. Original documents are scanned once, and then multiple copies can be printed. Since the originals move through the machine only once, copies can be completed more quickly and with less paper movement than in a nondigital machine, resulting in greatly increased machine reliability and lower maintenance cost. Since pages are stored in memory, they can be handled like many other documents. Some digital copy machines enlarge the text or reduce it so four or more pages fit onto a single sheet of paper. The digital copier can be connected to a computer network and can then serve as a network printer. The quality of the printing is better than using a standard copier because the copies are original printed pages, not photocopies of originals. Sophisticated feeders, staplers, and folders are available as attachments to copiers. Some copiers can print on 11- × 17-inch paper, so a user can create and print a full 8.5- × 11-inch stapled booklet directly from a computer. (A piece of paper 11 × 17 inches folded in half results in a standard 8.5- × 11-inch booklet). Depending on the software available with the machine, sections of pages can be edited, deleted from the final copy, or centered. Scanning a page into a digital photocopier is identical to using a scanner on a computer, except it is

Figure 11-10   An employee using a large office copier.

faster because copiers have large-capacity feeders and operate at high speeds. Images can be scanned and files stored to computers on a local area network. When used with Optical Character Recognition (OCR) software, the images can be brought into a word processor or other software and edited. Finally, a digital copier can be connected to a telephone line and serve as a fax machine because it both scans and prints images. A digital copier can combine the functions of a photocopier, printer, scanner, and fax machine into one unit that can be connected to an office computer network and also to other computers via phone lines. In addition to having black-and-white copiers in the office, color copiers are becoming more prevalent because of the increased use of colored graphics, pictures, and images.

The operating instructions for most copy machines are attached to the machine or are built into small video displays on the machine. In addition to the general operating instructions, you need to learn how to replace paper in the machine. Efficient operators should also know how to clear a paper jam in the machine and how to add *toner*—the chemical used to print the text.

An *auditron* is used to count the number of copies made. A company can have an individual auditron for each department, so each department would be charged correctly for its use of the copy machine. Operators need to control the number of copies made because the annual costs for photocopying can be significant.

Copying and Shipping Centers

Need an odd-sized packaged shipped? Want to photocopy a newsletter in red ink? Want an oversized print, a photo mounted or laminated, a banner or sign printed? Need to print a photo from a memory card or memory stick? Your office may not have the materials, equipment, or know-how to handle these and many other unusual requests, but there are many businesses that may be able to help in an emergency or to do that once-a-year type of job. If a copy job cannot be completed at your office

Figure 11-11 A copy center.

location because of limited facilities, limited time, or broken equipment, it can be taken to a quick-copy store. Copying and shipping centers provide a wide variety of services, but the objective of most of these businesses is to provide quick service at a reasonable cost. The office employee should be familiar with the services offered by copy centers that are convenient to the office. Many of the projects can be sent directly from your office computer to the service center. Therefore, when you go to pick up the product, it is ready and waiting for you.

Copying centers may contain a variety of specialized photocopying equipment and supplies not found in many offices. They usually have high-speed machines that can photocopy at high volumes, do color photocopying, or use colored inks. They often do specialized printing, for example, printing on heavy paper for report covers, and have machines for binding thick documents. Copy centers can be lifesavers when your regular office photocopier is down and you must finish a critical job. Some copy centers are open twenty-four hours a day so those last-minute jobs can be completed.

Businesses that specialize in shipping have mailing materials such as boxes, wrapping, and packaging for fragile items. You can buy these specialized supplies or the shipping center can package the item and have it picked up by an overnight carrier service such as UPS, FedEx, or DHL. Many shipping centers have photocopying capability, and some rent mailboxes to business as an address of convenience.

Recycling

As society has become more concerned about the environment and the dilemma of disposing of materials, many offices have become involved in recycling. Workplaces often have bins to recycle paper, and many offices purchase recycled paper for copiers, printers, and folders. In addition, food facilities purchase napkins and cups made from recycled paper and have bins to collect beverage cans and bottles for recycling. Workplace dependency on computers and electronic equipment has created eCycling, which provides opportunities to recycle electronics. Recycling opportunities exist for computers, printers, printer cartridges, circuit boards, monitors, traditional and cell phones, batteries, etc. These items may contain lead and mercury, which are hazardous materials. Frequent technological changes make computer and electronics obsolete so recycling resources is a prudent management and environmental choice. Search the Web for local recycling options.

HINT

Join your in company's recycling effort.

Figure 11-12   A paper recycling bin.

Figure 11-13   A glass and metal recycling bin.

OFFICE SUPPLIES

Typical Office Supplies

The variety and quality of office supplies and equipment have expanded as a result of the introduction of new technology in the office. Supplies and equipment can be purchased from local vendors, out-of-town distributors, or via the Internet.

The following are a sample of supplies and equipment used in a modern office. If you are not familiar with any of them, go to an office supply store and review the types of supplies they carry.

- A selection of rubber stamps with the following imprints:
  As per your request
  Company's return address
  Completed
  Confidential
  Current date and time
  Faxed
  File copy
  Final notice
  For deposit only
  For your information
  Paid
  Received
  Rush
  Urgent
- Binder clips in several sizes
- Bookends
- Business card stationery
- Business card holders
- Card file boxes—3- × 5-inch, 4- × 6-inch, or 5- × 8-inch, with built-in dividers
- Cartridges for printers, fax machines, and photocopiers
- Coil pens with stand
- Color-coded labels in a variety of colors, shapes, and sizes
- Color-indexed protector sheets
- Colored markers
- Columnar pads
- Copy holders
- Computer data storage
  Disks
  CD-R, CD-RW, DVD+R, DVD−R
  Memory sticks and memory cards
- Computer disk mailers
- Daily reminders and planners

- Desk and wall calendars
- Desk rack systems for hanging binders and folders
- Electric hole punches
- Expanding accordion file boxes
- Flipcharts and markers
- Get-acquainted badges
- Invitation stationery
- Locator boards to indicate if an employee is in or out of the office
- Magazine and literature storage systems
- Mailing boxes with bubble or plastic peanuts for packing
- Mailing tubes
- Message boards
- Paper clips (regular size, jumbo, and nonskid)
- Paper for printers, fax machines, and photocopiers
- Paper trimmers to cut paper to a desired size
- Platform footrests for computer users
- Portfolios
- Postal scales
- Rubber chair mats—mats placed on top of carpets to allow chairs to slide easily
- Scheduling boards
- Staplers, staples, and staple removers
- Stationery trays
- Stick-on notes and flags
- Wall or desk cordless electric pencil sharpeners
- Wall- or door-mounted file folder holders

Storing Supplies

Large offices often maintain a *storeroom* or *stock room* where supplies are kept. Small offices often have a supply cabinet or drawer where commonly used supplies are kept. In some businesses, employees must use a form to request supplies stocked in the company storeroom. In other organizations, employees can pick up supplies as needed.

Inventory

A well-run office has an individual who is responsible for ordering and distributing supplies. Since essential supplies should always be available, it is important to check the supply inventory frequently. Some offices keep a *perpetual inventory* where every major item purchased or removed from the supply room is recorded. For example, for small items such as paper clips, the inventory tracks how many boxes of an item have been purchased or used. The advantage of a perpetual inventory is that it is easy to determine how many of an item is still on the shelf and the chance of running out of an item is decreased. If a supply is needed quickly, it can be purchased from a local store, but last-minute purchases should be kept to a minimum. It is helpful to maintain a file of local office supply catalogs and to bookmark favorite office supply Web sites. These catalogs and Web sites are useful when you need to buy supplies.

> **HINT**
> To make installing new equipment easier, label all cords and adapters.

PURCHASES AND PAYMENTS

Offices must purchase supplies and equipment to support the operation of the business. Large companies may have a department of several people who purchase supplies for the entire company. In smaller companies, purchasing of supplies is often the responsibility of an administrative assistant.

Purchasing

Each office has its own specific procedures and forms to be used for the purchase of supplies, services, and equipment. These procedures are often outlined in a purchasing handbook. Study the office purchasing handbook to learn your company's purchasing policies and requirements. In some organizations, purchasing requirements may depend on the type of product or service requested, or the amount of the purchase. For example, purchases under a set amount (such as $500, $1,000 or $2,000) may be made with a company credit card and minimal documentation. In these cases, however, the person using the credit card may undergo special training to ensure that he or she is aware of and responsible for following company policies.

The purchasing procedures in most offices have two goals. The first is to ensure that the purchase is made at the best price for the quality of the item required for the job. The second goal is to have well-documented records to support the purchase and to prevent fraud. Companies often require multiple copies of all purchasing documents so each step in the purchase and payment process can be recorded for possible review by the company's auditor.

Requisition

When the company needs an item, the first step usually is a request for purchase. A *purchase requisition* is completed and sent to the supervisor or to the company's purchasing department. The purchase requisition lists the item required and the reason for the purchase. If the purchase is unusual or the cost is above a preset dollar limit, a detailed justification may be required.

For the purchase of small items, a listing of several vendors and the price of each item required often accompanies the purchase requisition. Price quotations may be obtained from catalogs, by making telephone calls to vendors, or by viewing office supply Web sites. For an online or telephone quote, the source of the price quote and the name, date, and title of the person providing the quote all should be recorded. Each company has its own policy regarding the dollar limit of purchases that can be made using telephone quotations.

Price information for larger purchases may be requested by telephone, but often the vendor must provide a *written quotation* regarding the price and terms of the sale. For the largest purchases, vendors are customarily mailed detailed specifications of the items required, and they must return their *bids* by a specific date and time. The use of specifications and bids is a very formal process and is generally supervised by a company's purchasing department.

Purchase Order

After a purchase has been approved, a *purchase order* is prepared and is sent to the vendor to order the item. In reviewing price quotations, be aware of the vendor's return and payment policies. Some vendors have a *no return* policy, others have a return policy that requires payment of a percentage of the purchase price for reshelving the items, and others issue a full refund.

Purchase Requisition

L & M Hardware
1556 Lindberg Avenue
Jefferson City, MO 67443-9890

Deliver To: Joseph Walker   Requisition No.: 672890

Location: Purchasing   Date: June 15, XXXX

Job No.:   12424   Date Required: July 25, XXXX

Quantity	Description
1	Adjustable posture chair
1	Executive desk

Justification: To set up office for new assistant director of the Purchasing Department

See attached quotations: Eastman $1,125

                         Miami Equipment $1,400

                         Levy Supplies $1,750

Figure 11-14   A purchase requisition.

Purchase Order

L & M HARDWARE
1556 Lindberg Avenue
Jefferson City, MO 67443-9890

EASTMAN CORPORATION   Purchase Order No.: 91-3434
3500 Jefferson Drive
St. Louis, MO 67234-7880   Date: July 25, XXXX

Deliver To: Joseph Walker
Delivery Required By: Aug. 25, XXXX

Quantity	Item No.	Description	Cost
1	CH345-A	Adjustable posture chair	275
1	DK8C	Executive desk	850
			Total $1,125

Figure 11-15   A purchase order.

MANAGING MONEY IN THE OFFICE

Banking

As an office employee, your duties may include making bank deposits, endorsing checks, and writing checks for payment of bills.

Bank Deposits and Check Writing

When making a bank deposit, a *deposit slip* must be completed. Deposits can be made in person, by mail, at an automatic teller machine (ATM), and at a night deposit facility. Deposits that include cash should not be made by mail, and coins should not be included in ATM deposits.

Computer software packages are available that write checks and reconcile a bank account. Using computer software is a quick and accurate way of writing checks. The computer prints the checks and also records the payment for accounting purposes. Accounting statements and bank reconciliations are then prepared from the information entered on the check payments. The use of computer-prepared checks has simplified the bookkeeping in many offices.

Endorsing a Check

Prior to depositing a check, it must be signed by the payee, or *endorsed*. The payee is the name of the person or company to whom payment is made. There are specific rules governing the location of the endorsement of a check. The endorsement should be written on the back of the check. With the check facing you so you can read it, flip it up (or down), then place the endorsement not more than 1.5 inches from the left edge of the check.

There are three common ways to endorse checks. Businesses should endorse a check with what is known as an *endorsement in full*. When using this endorsement, a person writes the words "for deposit only" or "pay to the order of [payee]" and the name of the payee on the back of the check; then the check is signed by the person to whom the check is made out. To speed depositing checks, many offices use rubber stamps with "for deposit only," the company name, and the account number to which the check will be deposited. Using this rubber stamp, company checks can quickly be endorsed and deposited to the company's bank account.

A *restrictive endorsement* uses the words "for deposit only" on the back of the check, which indicates that the check can be deposited only to an account. The third type of endorsement is a *blank endorsement*, which contains only the signature of the payee. This endorsement is risky because anyone who finds a check with a blank endorsement can cash it.

Paying Bills by Computer

Using a desktop computer, a business can pay bills electronically without writing a check. After setting up an account with a financial institution, the company enters a list of vendors to be paid through the electronic bill-paying system. When payments are made, the company connects via the Internet to the bank's electronic bill-paying system. Security is extremely important when paying bills by computer. Passwords and identification numbers open a company's bank account, so they should never be left where unauthorized staff or the public can see them.

Electronic Funds Transfer

Electronic funds transfer (EFT) has been a common practice for many years. Many organizations directly deposit salary to their employees' checking or saving accounts and electronically send withheld taxes to the federal and state governments. The United States federal government uses electronic funds transfer for almost all payments to employees, vendors, and grant recipients.

Electronic funds transfers can be set up between banks that are members of the National Automated Clearing House Association (NACHA). (Almost all banks in the United States are NACHA members.) To set up an EFT account, an organization must authorize the electronic transfer of funds from its bank account. The organization

```
Voucher Number _____

Date _____

Paid To _____

Purpose _____

Account Title _____

Amount _____

Approved By _____

Signature of Recipient _____
```

Figure 11-16   A petty cash voucher form.

must complete an EFT authorization form for each organization that will receive funds electronically. Electronic funds transfer payments are often authorized for reoccurring expenses such as taxes, rent, utilities, and salaries but are also used for payment to vendors. Businesses can use EFT to accept payments from the public, and charities can use EFT to receive donations.

Organizations use EFT because the system reduces the time and expense of processing paper checks, funds are available sooner, and there is less chance of fraud or of paper checks being lost. If your organization uses EFT, you may be required to prepare EFT payments or review EFT reports to confirm their accuracy.

Petty Cash

A *petty cash fund* is used to pay for small expenses that occur in the office. Offices usually set a maximum amount for withdrawals from the fund. Depending on the office, the limit can be for purchases below $25, $50, or $100. When an expense is incurred, the purchase receipt is given to the petty cash officer. After signing a petty cash voucher, the employee is reimbursed for the expense, and the receipt is attached to the petty cash voucher. Typical expenses include emergency supply purchases, taxi fares, and inexpensive office purchases.

CHAPTER REVIEW

1. How can the noise in an office be reduced?
2. List three suggestions to improve office safety.
3. Why are plants used in an office?
4. Define *ergonomics* and explain how it is used in the office.
5. Define a restrictive endorsement, an endorsement in full, and a blank endorsement.
6. Explain how a petty cash system is used in an office.

ACTIVITIES

1. Visit an office supply store and write a report describing ten office supplies or pieces of equipment that you were not aware of prior to your visit. Include in your report how each item is used.

2. Visit two offices and prepare a written report describing the office layout, use of color, use of plants, the effect of sunlight, and placement of equipment. Be prepared to give an oral summary of your report to the class.

PROJECTS

Project 21

Send this letter to Mr. A. J. Lockreim, 1142 Madison Heights, Albuquerque, NM 87109. Use the modified block style with open punctuation. Make a file copy and send a copy to Diane Percy, Associate Director. Set the columns up as a table, and center the table. Spell in full all abbreviations. Use an appropriate closing and sign it from Katie L. Barrington, Manager. Use proper formatting and make the document attractive.

We received your Oct. order and have attempted to fill it immediately. Unfortunately, some of the items are out of stock, but they will be sent by the end of the month.

The following items will be sent immediately:

Item	Stock Number	Quantity
Chairs	357NM02	6
Desks	982SRC2	10
Lamps	7243KR1	2

The following items are back-ordered:

Items	Stock Number	Quantity
Stands	432158JM	2
Charts	21256CC5	5
Fans	41694PS4	8

We appreciate the opportunity to serve you.

Project 22

Send this memo from Julie R. Stuart, Budget Director, to all department heads.

I have reviewed the expenditures that you submitted in September. After careful consideration, the budget team and I have developed a projected expense budget for the next several years. The projections are listed below.

Current Year	Projected Year 1 ($)	Projected Year 2 ($)	Projected Year 3 ($)
Rent	8,400	10,500	12,000
Utilities	1,800	2,200	2,500
Travel expense	12,400	15,000	18,000
Administration	40,000	45,000	49,000
Temp agency	5,000	7,500	9,000

HUMAN RELATIONS SKILL DEVELOPMENT

HR 11-1 Worker Who Has Too Much to Do

Keeping up with all job responsibilities can be difficult. Improving organizational skills, becoming more knowledgeable about the job, increasing efficiency, and eliminating wasted time all enhance the ability to complete more work in less time. Unfortunately, it may be impossible to complete all of the work to be done because the workload is too heavy for the amount of time in the workday. If this is the case, review your workload with your supervisor. Before discussing the problem, view the situation from the supervisor's viewpoint and prepare a detailed list of all your duties. Several questions to consider are: (1) Can some job duties be dropped because they are no longer necessary? (2) Can some job assignments be delayed? (3) Can job duties be assigned to another employee? and (4) Can a new employee be hired?

- What criteria would you use to determine if you have too many job responsibilities?
- You approached your manager and discussed the overload in your work. Your manager said your job responsibilities are not too heavy, but you waste too much time. What would you say to the manager?

HR 11-2 Do Not Underestimate Your Supervisor

Appearances can be deceiving, so it is easy to underestimate the importance of your supervisor. It is possible to have a preconceived idea of the "important" supervisor. Do not permit your conceptions to rule your thoughts. Remind yourself that in your job as a new employee, you are not in a position to judge your supervisor's power and influence.

- Describe what you believe to be the appearance of the "important" supervisor. Include a description of the supervisor's office.
- Have you met an influential businessperson who did not meet your idea of the influential businessperson? Describe the appearance of this person.
- From the company's viewpoint, list three criteria that would demonstrate the effectiveness of a supervisor.

SITUATIONS

How would you handle the following situations?

- **S 11-1** Several times, you have requested that an electrical cord be removed because of a potential safety problem. Today a client tripped and fell because of the electrical cord.
- **S 11-2** You have an assigned parking spot at your office. Mark, a coworker, frequently parks in your spot, and you have difficulty finding a place to park.
- **S 11-3** As you walked past the petty cash drawer, you saw Daniel take money and not sign a petty cash form.

GRAMMAR REVIEW

Select the correct word from the word in parentheses.

1. Alexis (is, are) the director of the new project.
2. Bob and Malcolm (is, are) attending the seminar at Georgetown University.

3. Audrey (was, were) late for the staff meeting.

4. Ms. Moore and Mr. Wong (was, were) qualified for the new position.

5. Alan and Allison (is, are) members of the Boston Business Association.

6. The bus (was, were) late arriving downtown.

7. All of the managers at the meeting (was, were) from the Southeast region.

8. Everybody (was, were) satisfied with the results of the research.

9. What (is, are) the result of the advertising campaign?

10. Either Herbert or Carlos (was, were) a management trainee at the bank.

11. Both of the managers (was, were) ready to go to the airport.

12. Chan (write, writes) a newspaper article each week.

13. Hung and Jennifer (donate, donates) to the office flower fund.

14. Vicky and Mary (represent, represents) the department at the annual meeting.

15. Each of the employees (is, are) responsible for a segment of the budget.

CD ASSIGNMENTS

CD Assignment 11-1

Open the file **CD11-1_RS** on your Student CD and follow the instructions to complete the job. You will also need the file **CD11-1_RR,** which is on your Student CD.

CD Assignment 11-2

Open the file **CD11-2_RP** on your Student CD and follow the instructions to complete the job. You will also need the file **CD11-1_RR,** which is on your Student CD.

CD Assignment 11-3

Open the file **CD11-3_IOS** on your Student CD and follow the instructions to complete the job.

CD Assignment 11-4

Open the file **CD11-3_IOF** on your Student CD and follow the instructions to complete the job.

CHAPTER 12

Seeking Employment

Objectives

After studying this chapter, you should be able to:

1. Conduct a job search.
2. Use the Internet to assist in a job search.
3. Write a letter of application.
4. Write your résumé.
5. Complete a job application.

Are you ready to look for a job?

GETTING STARTED

Your employment attitude and mind-set are essential for you to find employment successfully. Before you begin your job search, it is very important that you understand the job selection process from the employer's viewpoint. The company's objective is to sell a product or provide a service and in order to meet this objective, the company must hire employees. Hiring managers want to hire qualified professionals as quickly as possible, and they want to recruit from a large pool of qualified applicants. As budgets are tightened, low recruitment costs become more important. Therefore, recruiters want to avoid hiring mistakes, which are costly. Most organizations prefer to spend the least amount of time and money advertising, interviewing, and training applicants.

Interviewers are looking for an employee who can contribute to their organization. Throughout your job search, you should focus on the skills, ideas, and qualifications you can bring to a prospective employer. Your objective is to let a business know what you can do for it, not what you would like it to do for you. Consequently, you must emphasize what you can contribute to the company. In addition to the fundamental skills required for the job, employers want to hire smart and energetic employees who have strong social skills. Conduct your job search and interview so the employer knows that you are the best person for the job. Stress to the employer that your goal is to add value to the company, not just work there and be paid.

Prior to responding to a job posting, ask yourself if you have the required skills for the job. If you are definitely not qualified, do not waste your time and the employer's time. If you have some skills, apply for the position. The recruiter may decide that you can be trained for the position or find another position for which you are qualified.

What credentials are required for the job you want?

PLANNING FOR YOUR CAREER

A variety of positions are available for the office assistant, and they all require superior office skills, good grammar and punctuation skills, attention to detail, and excellent human relations skills. There are positions in accounting, education, government, law, medicine, real estate, retailing, science, technology, and many other fields. Also, careers are available in small businesses such as auto repair, construction, or lawn service. Consider jobs in non-profit organizations and government. Furthermore, each community has a variety of businesses that reflect the economy of that area. Your goal in finding a job is to match your interests and skills with an employer's needs. Finding the perfect job may require you to reevaluate your goals and to accept a position that is almost perfect. Do not be afraid to take a chance on a position. It may be your path to success.

Jobs are obtainable in most fields because every company, regardless of size, needs to manage its operations. While a good background in office procedures is essential for getting the job you want, it is also helpful if you know the terminology used in that business and, better yet, have some prior experience in the field. As you search for the types of companies where you would like to work, learn some of the terminology used in those fields. Suggestions on how to become familiar with terms used in various fields and examples of some business terms were discussed in Chapter 10. For example, an assistant in a law office must be knowledgeable about legal terminology, while an assistant in a medical office must know medical terminology. Displaying knowledge of the business where you are applying for a job will help you during job interviews and will increase your chances for getting the job you want.

Do you have technological expertise?

The First Step

The first step in seeking employment is to determine what kind of a job you would like. If you do not carefully think through this question, you may not find a job that will suit your needs. The correct answer to the question, "What kind of job would I like?" is not, "Any job that pays well."

What kind of job do you want? What is your passion?

MY SUCCESS STORY

My Name Is Rahul

I always wanted to open my own business. I am the kind of guy who does not want to work for another person. I want to make all my decisions and be responsible for myself. I graduated from college with a degree in business and then started my own company. During the summer, while in high school and college, I worked in construction to pay my car expenses and to learn about the type of business I wanted to own. The first day I officially opened my company, I was hesitant but eager because I thought this career is my life's work. I have had my own company for six years now. My customer base grew slowly but steadily, and now I am doing well. I always focus on superior customer service and good communications skills. The business courses in human relations skills helped prepare me to work with clients from all walks of life.

Before beginning your job search, ask yourself the following questions:

- Am I interested in part-time or full-time employment?
- What are my career goals?
- Do I have personal interests that I would like to incorporate into my job (for example, interests in music, art, finance, politics, journalism, photography, the environment, etc.)?
- Do I want to work in a specific type of office, such as a legal, medical, insurance, advertising, or real estate office?
- Do I want to work for a large, medium, or small company? Is the size of the company important to me?
- Do I want a job with many responsibilities?
- Do I want a job with a defined path for advancement?
- Can I work under pressure? Which jobs would have more pressure?
- Do I want a job near my home?
- Am I willing to commute farther for a higher salary?
- Am I willing to move to another city? If so, where?
- Am I willing to travel overnight on business? Am I willing to be away from my family for several days at a time?
- Do I want to work overtime?
- Am I willing to work overtime occasionally to complete a project?
- Do I need advance notice of overtime because of personal commitments?
- What personal responsibilities will I have to juggle?
- What are the barriers to my career advancement?
- Can I work on an established time schedule or, because of personal requirements, must I have flexible hours?
- Can I work equally well with a male or a female supervisor?
- Do I have difficulty working with certain personality types? If so, what personality types create problems for me?
- What salary do I expect? What is the least salary that I would be willing to accept? (This is an important issue that must be carefully thought through.)
- What benefits are important to me?
- Is medical insurance coverage especially important? Do I or does someone in my family have a medical problem that must be covered by insurance?
- Are investment benefits important?
- Is the type of retirement plan important?
- What amount of sick leave or vacation time can I expect?
- Is the availability of educational assistance important for my future goals?
- Is the availability of recreational or exercise facilities at the office important to me?

Does this job match my personal expectations?

Take the time now to answer each of these questions as honestly as you can. Then review your answers. Your answers should provide guidance in selecting the job that will satisfy your needs.

Job Satisfaction

HINT

A great career can transform your life.

A career choice is not an easy decision to make. Your decision should be based on whether the career can bring you both personal and economic satisfaction. In addition to salary, your profession must satisfy your personal goals. Does your job make you happy? Do you leave at the end of the day and want to return to work the next day? We do not live in a perfect world. There is no perfect employer and no perfect job, but your job should make you happy and create an environment where you enjoy the hours you spend working.

How an organization treats its staff influences the happiness and fulfillment a worker receives from a job. Employee satisfaction is vital to employee and company success, and it may be one of the criteria you use when seeking a job. Many organizations survey employees regarding their job satisfaction and publish the results. *Fortune Magazine* publishes an annual list of the "100 Best Companies to Work For." Search the Web for employee-friendly companies.

What are your personal job-hunting blockades?

HOW TO FIND EMPLOYERS

No single method is the best way to find an employer. There is some truth in the adage that a successful applicant must be at the right place at the right time. Therefore, you must expand your job search to contact the largest number of potential employers. When seeking employment, find companies that are hiring. Look in the newspapers for companies that are "hot" or "growth companies." Read the local business pages to see which companies are expanding. Using a variety of job-seeking methods will help you find a job that meets your goals.

When seeking employment, it is wise to look for a company with a stable future. Before accepting a position at a company that has recently experienced restructuring or downsizing, try to determine the business climate for that company and the morale of its employees. Does the company have a future and do the employees enjoy working there? If the business will soon merge with another organization, you might be reassigned to another position or you might even be laid off.

Friends and Networks

Because some jobs are never advertised, contacts through friends are good ways to hear about available positions. Tell everyone you know that you are looking for a job. When you tell people that you are looking for a job, also tell them about your skills and training. Ask people to pass your name on to others. Employee referrals often increase the chance of being hired, so identify where your friends work and use this knowledge to your advantage. Some companies prefer to hire from employee referrals because the current employee has already done the initial screening of the new applicant.

Many people believe finding a job through a network of friends and contacts is the best way to obtain a job. In response to online job searching, networking sites have appeared that build professional relationships between employees and job seekers. Networking sites allow the user to create a profile, which is a background summary, and then search for associates with similar career interests. When a match is made, an email relationship can begin. Networking contacts may provide the connection you need to obtain a job. Prior to applying for a position, search your network for persons employed at the company. Then when you apply for a position via the company Web site or by traditional mail, include a referral from the company employee. This referral may be the extra push you need to get the job.

HINT

Networking is a terrific technique for finding a job.

College Placement Offices, Career Centers, and Job-Counseling Centers

Most educational institutions have a placement office to assist their students in job hunting. The offices may be called a placement office, career center, or job-counseling center. While the services of each office vary, they may guide students in selecting a career, help prepare a résumé, and assist in finding a job. Many colleges have on-campus recruitment or job fairs. When you talk with recruiters, have a copy of your résumé with you. (A *résumé* is a brief summary of your background, education, and experience; preparation of a résumé is discussed in detail later in this chapter.) While college job fairs are generally casual, a specific appointment with an on-campus recruiter is more formal. Therefore, you should wear your interview outfit for that meeting.

College Internships

An internship is a terrific entrance into the job market because it provides an employment experience, an opportunity for working in the desired field, and the opportunity for networking connections. Some internships may be volunteer positions, while others may bring a modest salary. Salary is not the most important part of an internship. Internships provide exposure to different types of jobs and real-world work experience that will help you get a full-time job later. Internships are also a way of getting into a company, and many internships evolve into full-time jobs.

Employment Agencies (Free and Fee-Paid)

The purpose of an employment agency is to bring together a job seeker and an employer. Employment agencies screen applicants before referring them to clients because employers do not want to waste time talking with unqualified applicants. Some employment agencies are run by nonprofit institutions or governments, others are private businesses. If the employment agency is not a nonprofit or government-sponsored agency, either you or the employer pay the agency's fee. Many jobs are listed as *fee-paid*, which means that the employer pays the fee. If the job is not listed as fee-paid, you, the job applicant, must pay the fee.

Read an employment agency contract carefully before you sign it. While you should talk with the employment counselor in great detail before you sign anything, remember that only what is in the written contract is binding. Be sure to ask in advance if the jobs are fee-paid by the employer or if you will pay the fee. If the fee is paid by the applicant, the fee is normally a percentage of the first year's salary. If you decide to use an employment agency, ask employers and friends to recommend reputable employment agencies.

Temporary Employment Agencies

Working for a temporary employment agency is a way to learn about job openings and gain valuable job experience while receiving a salary. Companies like hiring temporary workers (*temps*) because they help out during busy times and avoid over-staffing, which may result in layoffs and poor morale. A temporary job may be only for a few days, during a company's busy season, or be for longer-term employment while a regular employee is out on extended medical leave. Working for a temporary employment agency often gives an employee the flexibility to determine when, where, and how long to work. A temporary employee also has the opportunity of working for a variety of companies. This can be a chance to gain valuable experience in a particular field, a method of deciding what kind of a job you want, and an opportunity to meet people in your field. A temporary worker must be adaptable and knowledgeable. Studies have indicated that jobs for temporary workers will grow because companies are using more temporary workers to meet their peak-time staffing requirements. Many employment agencies provide temporary workers with vacation, holiday, or sick-leave benefit packages and other opportunities that in the past were associated only with full-time employment. Because the temporary agency is the employer, it is responsible for paying the employee and withholding the appropriate taxes. Furthermore, some positions are considered *temp-to-hire*, which means that if the supervisor is satisfied with the employee's work performance, the employee is later hired as a full-time employee of the company and ceases to be an employee of the temporary employment agency.

Part-Time Employment

A part-time job can be several hours a day, eight hours a day for only a couple of days a week, or a few hours a day for several days a week. Working part-time sounds like the best of all worlds because the individual has a fulfilling job experience and free time to pursue other activities. Unfortunately, part-time employment can have drawbacks because of the lower salary for fewer hours worked, and many part-time employees do not receive medical coverage, retirement benefits, paid vacations, or paid holidays. Working part-time for an organization can be an entrance into the company or a way of learning whether you are interested in working in a particular type of business.

Newspaper Advertisements

The classified ad sections of city and local newspapers can provide the job seeker with information about a wide selection of jobs. Carefully read the qualifications printed for each position. Often telephone numbers are included in the ad so an interview can be arranged quickly. Since the employer may use the call as a screening device to eliminate applicants, prepare in advance what you are going to say during the telephone call. If the newspaper advertisement requests a résumé, you should send it immediately because your procrastination could result in another applicant being hired. A cover letter, which is discussed later in this chapter, should be sent with your résumé. Newspaper advertisements often ask that a response be sent to a post office box to keep the name of the company confidential and to allow the company to screen applicants. Today, many employers request that the résumé be faxed or emailed to them. If you do not have a fax machine, copy centers offer faxing at a nominal fee.

In addition, newspapers generally have online job postings, which are available at the newspaper Web site. From the newspaper Web site, click the job link, and then search for a job title that meets your qualifications. When you find a job that interests you, click the job title for details of the position, which also includes the application procedure.

Job Searches Through the Internet

Another way to search for a job is through the Internet. Jobs can be located on the Internet in several ways. Many businesses and governments post job openings on their Web pages. If you think you are interested in working for a specific company, go to its Web page and view the job openings listed. Usually the home page will have a link for "job openings" or "employment." While at the Web site, carefully review its other pages to obtain background information about the organization and its products or services. Many companies believe they hire more employees through their own Web site than through general résumé posting.

There are also many Internet sites that specialize in matching the job seeker with the best employer. Some sites post job openings, while other sites are set up so job seekers post résumés to an online job board where employers can view their qualifications. If you post your résumé, you must be comfortable with others viewing your skills, previous employers, home address, telephone number, and email address. Furthermore, some online job sites share personal data, so your privacy may be in jeopardy.

Because security may be an issue when job seeking on the Web, be careful about sending personal information over the Internet, even if you think you know the company. Identity theft and scams from postings to online job boards have increased. Avoid providing any personal information by email or telephone. As a security feature, some job boards allow the applicant to hide all personal information. Personal information includes your name, address, telephone number, social security number, account numbers, driver's license number, passport number, martial status, financial records, and so on. To obtain personal information, thieves post phony job ads. Consequently, it is important to protect yourself.

If confidentiality is a concern, you can (1) list only your skills and job experiences without listing employer names, (2) use a rented mailbox as your address, or (3) use a new email address designated for your job search. To preserve your privacy whenever you seek a job using the Internet, do not give out your social security number until you have accepted a job, and never provide credit card numbers. In addition, set your Internet browser to nullify cookies so advertisers cannot follow you with advertisements. Remember to remove your résumé from all sites upon acceptance of a job and cancel any job email address accounts you may have created for your job search.

There are also many Internet sites that list thousands of job openings, either locally or from across the country, as well as sites that list résumés for employers to review. Job listings posted on the Internet can change daily and can be accessed by many job seekers. Check Web sites often if you are seriously interested in finding a job.

Technology has made Web-based automated hiring practices common. Accordingly, many businesses now require that applications and résumés be submitted electronically via the Internet. The Web-based job opening may include a link to the company Web site where the company mission statement, office locations, benefits packages, and additional employee information are shown.

To complete an application form, called an eform, you may need to copy and paste information from your résumé into the form and keyboard answers to any additional questions. Include all information required by the online application instructions. Omitting even one item may disqualify you from consideration. After completing an application, print a copy of it for your records. Some systems ask you to send a short email message with two attachments, a cover letter, and a résumé. The résumé can be sent as a Word document attachment or as a plain text attachment. If you have a choice, send the résumé as a Word attachment because it will retain the original formatting. If the résumé is sent as a plain text attachment, it could lose some of its formatting and will not look as attractive as the original document.

Many companies believe online recruitment has made job vacancy fulfillment less expensive and more efficient. As a general rule, the Web has eliminated the paper delay associated with a job hunt and has decreased the time needed for the job search.

Depending on the circumstances, it may be wiser to send a well-written résumé and cover letter through the mail than to submit an application via the Internet. In some instances, it may be appropriate to send an electronic résumé and cover letter and then follow up with a paper résumé and cover letter sent by traditional mail.

Before you search for a job, create your résumé, cover letter, and thank-you letter using word processing software. This will allow you to organize and prepare your materials in advance, to format your documents, and to use spell-checking features so the documents look polished. These documents can often be stored on job-seeking Web sites to email to prospective employers when you find an opening that interests you. Then when you find a job, customize the cover letter and send it to the hiring manager.

Job applicants may find the following employment-related Web sites helpful.

Federal government jobs	www.usajobs.gov
CareerBuilder	www.careerbuilder.com
HotJobs	www.hotjobs.com
Monster	www.monster.com
9to5, National Association of Working Women	www.9to5.org
National Partnership for Women and Families	www.nationalpartnership.org

Other Employment Options

Many professional organizations assist in matching employees and employers through job announcements in a monthly publication, sponsoring job fairs at a conference, posting job openings on a Web site, and providing contacts about jobs from the members of the organization.

Professional journals list positions that are available locally or nationally, and these publications can be found at the library or through professional organizations. Entry-level positions are usually not found through professional journals, but these journals may provide information on companies that are expanding and may also be helpful when seeking career advancement.

Many communities have a chamber of commerce that maintains a list of its business members. You could call or send letters of application to members of the chamber of commerce. Because unsolicited applications are considered a *cold call* on a business, the response rate may be low. On the other hand, you may find the one company that is interested in you.

If you are interested in working for a particular type of business, the yellow pages of the telephone book or an Internet search may provide lists of businesses by the type of service or product they offer. If you know you want to work for a specific company, research the company, complete your résumé, and then contact the company and request an interview.

If you cannot find the job you want and you are financially able, you may be able to volunteer your time. Many nonprofit organizations accept volunteers to assist in their daily activities. Volunteering is a terrific entrance into a career and a great way to meet top-notch professionals. Moreover, a volunteer job may develop into a paid position.

LETTER OF APPLICATION

When a résumé is sent, a letter of application must accompany it. A letter of application, which is also called a *cover letter*, should be sent with résumés that are mailed or faxed to prospective employers. The letter of application should *never* be sent on the letterhead stationery of your current employer. Since you probably do not have printed personal letterhead stationery, you must include your address at the top of the letter. Because your name is included in the complimentary close at the bottom of the letter, your name should not be included with your address at the top of the letter. Letter formatting information is provided in Chapter 3.

A letter of application should include the following information:

- The position for which you are applying.
- Where you heard about the job.
- Why you think you are qualified for the job.
- A brief description of your qualifications.
- A request for an interview.

A letter of application should be short and to the point. It should encourage the reader to read your résumé and contact you to arrange an interview. In the beginning of the letter, indicate why you want this particular job, and include how your qualifications match the job description. Give enough details in the letter to create interest, but save information for the résumé and for an interview. The cover letter is your opportunity to win an interview, so use the letter to your advantage. If there is something in your background or personality that makes you the perfect person for the job, say it. Always remember that your résumé must be accurate and truthful; do not exaggerate.

If possible, address the letter to a specific person at the company where you are applying. If you do not have a specific name, call the company and ask for the name of the person who will receive the application. When writing the letter of application, verify the spelling of all names because misspelling the company name or interviewer's name may immediately disqualify you from the position.

The letter of application must sell your skills and abilities, and it must focus special attention on your résumé. Therefore, customize the letter to spotlight the skills you have that the potential employer is seeking.

Furthermore, emphasize what you can do for the company, not what you want from the employer. Keep in mind that the business is interested in the service it

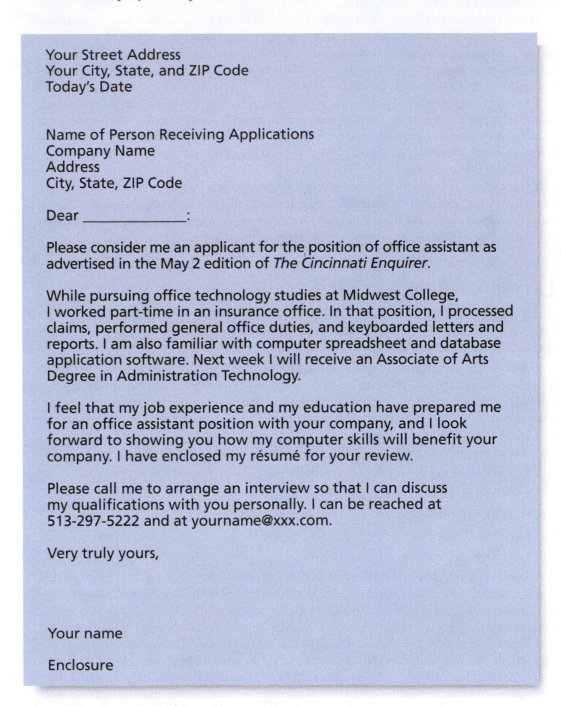

Your Street Address
Your City, State, and ZIP Code
Today's Date

Name of Person Receiving Applications
Company Name
Address
City, State, ZIP Code

Dear _____:

Please consider me an applicant for the position of office assistant as advertised in the May 2 edition of *The Cincinnati Enquirer*.

While pursuing office technology studies at Midwest College, I worked part-time in an insurance office. In that position, I processed claims, performed general office duties, and keyboarded letters and reports. I am also familiar with computer spreadsheet and database application software. Next week I will receive an Associate of Arts Degree in Administration Technology.

I feel that my job experience and my education have prepared me for an office assistant position with your company, and I look forward to showing you how my computer skills will benefit your company. I have enclosed my résumé for your review.

Please call me to arrange an interview so that I can discuss my qualifications with you personally. I can be reached at 513-297-5222 and at yourname@xxx.com.

Very truly yours,

Your name

Enclosure

Figure 12-1 Letter of application.

performs or in the product it sells, and is not concerned with what it can do for you.

When writing your cover letter, be specific about your accomplishments but be brief. Details can be included in your résumé or they can be discussed at the interview. However, do not overstate your skills because discrepancies on your application will place your credibility in doubt—always be honest.

The letter of application should look attractive, and it should be one page in length. A page crammed with type, long paragraphs, and small margins will not make a good impression on the reader. In addition, proofread the letter for spelling, grammar, and punctuation. Always keep a copy of everything you submit to a prospective employer— including a copy of the letter of application.

Your letter of application should include your email address and your home telephone number so the employer can contact you to arrange an interview. If you do not want a prospective employer to call you at your current job, do not put your current employer's telephone in the letter of application, and do not include your cell phone number. Since you may not be home when the employer calls, it would be best to have a telephone answering system take your messages. The first contact an employer may have with you may be your phone answering message system, so create a professional greeting for your messages.

You do not want your current employer to be aware of your job search, so include a sentence in your letter of application stating that you are submitting the résumé in confidence. The prospective employer should respect your request.

The days after you submit your letter of application and résumé are one of the most frustrating stages in searching for a job: waiting to hear from a prospective employer. The time lag between submitting the application and receiving a response from the company can range from a few days to months. Unfortunately, many applicants never receive a response to their letter of application. Some employers never acknowledge receiving an application, even if it was sent by email or traditional mail.

REFERENCES

Even before you prepare your résumé or begin an active job search, you should identify at least three people to serve as your references. Selecting references is very important because potential employers will want to contact your personal references, and the comments made about you by your references can help or hinder your ability to obtain a job. When you select a reference, choose someone who knows your work ability. Do not ask your minister, friends, or next-door neighbor unless these people are familiar with your work, job skills, or business accomplishments. Instead, you should seek references from teachers, coworkers, or people you have worked with in a volunteer organization. Former supervisors are usually listed on a job application, so they should not be used as references.

Talk with your references and obtain permission before you use their names. It could be very embarrassing to you if a prospective employer contacts a reference who does not remember you. If your reference is not familiar with all of your accomplishments, send the person a copy of your résumé. The better informed your references are, the better chance you have for the job. Furthermore, select references who will make positive comments about your abilities because a poor reference could destroy a potential job offer. You should be aware that some references are reluctant to say anything negative about an applicant because of fear of legal action.

If your references are not listed on your résumé, take a printed sheet to the interview with their names, addresses, email addresses, and telephone numbers.

Who are your references?

RÉSUMÉ

A résumé is a summary of your background, education, work experience, accomplishments, and interests. In the business world, the terms *résumé* and *data sheet* are used interchangeably. Most résumés for entry-level jobs are limited to one page, but a person who has been employed for many years may have a two-page résumé.

Since your résumé is the major initial contact a prospective employer has with you, it must convince the employer that you are the right person for the job. Most job listings receive many responses, so companies use résumés to screen out less qualified applicants. Research the company prior to sending a résumé because your knowledge of the company can influence and alter the writing of your letter of application and résumé. Always review the job listing to determine what specific qualifications and skills the employer is seeking, and emphasize those items in your résumé. It is important that your résumé be included in those that are considered for the position, not those that are quickly eliminated.

Companies that post job openings on the Internet often request that the applicant apply via the Internet. With this procedure, the applicant completes an application form directly on the Web. The responses are evaluated and those candidates who are ranked high are considered for an interview. In most cases, this process eliminates sending a letter of application and résumé. Consequently, the résumé is provided at the interview.

Formatting the Résumé

Computer software packages and word processing templates can assist in the creation of a résumé. Do not, however, just fill in the blanks in these programs. The key to creating a successful résumé is analyzing your strengths and deciding what information to include.

Today, many companies scan résumés electronically to reduce time and the costs of the job-hiring process. In general, computer scanning of résumés relies on the computer's recognition of key words that relate to the required and desired skills included in the job-opening announcement. The software is written to filter, which means that it seeks specific key words. The computer software performs a key word search based on artificial intelligence to select qualified candidates, and the applicants who have high rankings are then considered for the position.

Prior to submitting your résumé, ask if it will be scanned by computer. For a résumé to be properly scanned into the computer, it must be prepared in a scannable format. Guidelines for preparing résumés for scanning may be found on a company's Web site or included with its application. Your résumé must contain enough detail about your skills and background and the key words appropriate for the position you are seeking. It is also essential to use only the abbreviations used in the announcement. Scannable résumés may require that skills and education be described in only a few words, not complete sentences, so they can be recognized by the computer software. When preparing a résumé that is to be scanned, use a common nondecorative font and short phrases such as *wrote manual, designed system, planned meetings*, and so on. Do not use bullets and columns and avoid using italics, underlining, lines, shadows, or graphics if the résumé is to be scanned. In addition, if the résumé is to be scanned, educational degrees should be written as A.A., not as Associate of Arts degree. The résumé should be mailed in a flat envelope and not folded because folding may result in the scanner being unable to read the résumé.

It is important to market only the skills you want to use. Persons who have been employed for many years have a variety of skills, some of which may not pertain to the job they are seeking. Target the job you want, and develop realistic employment goals applicable in today's high-technology world.

Suggestions for formatting a résumé to be printed

- Place the résumé on standard 8.5- × 11-inch white bond paper.
- Print the résumé on one side.
- The résumé should be limited to one or two pages.
- Use a good printer.
- Use plain type fonts, such as Helvetica, Arial, Courier, or Times New Roman.
- Make the appearance attractive.
- Make the résumé easy to read.
- Proofread—never send a résumé with misspelled words or grammatical errors.
- Use action verbs such as the following:

administered	analyzed
arranged	completed
conducted	coordinated
created	developed
enlarged	established
evaluated	examined
expanded	formulated
generated	improved
increased	instructed
launched	organized
performed	presented
processed	promoted
represented	researched
unified	wrote

What to Include in Your Résumé

The standard résumé usually consists of seven parts, each of which is discussed in this section. The order of the parts of the résumé can vary according to your credentials. Generally your most important qualifications are listed immediately following the personal data and objective. Because a person's résumé reflects that person's background, the type of information included on a résumé varies widely from one individual to another. Furthermore, your résumé should be tailored to demonstrate your life experiences to a prospective employer. Carefully read the job description and focus on your talents and experiences that apply to the position. A résumé prepared by someone who has had several years of work experience or by someone who is returning to the workplace after not working for many years may look very different from the résumé of someone who has recently graduated.

There are two basic styles of résumés: (1) *chronological* and (2) *experience-based, skill-based,* or *competency-based*. If you have been employed and have a background of experiences, an experience- or competency-based résumé is probably preferable. An experience-based résumé focuses on your key job duties. Therefore, this type of résumé may not include all of the characteristics or elements of a chronological résumé. The decision of what to include is determined by the experiences you are highlighting.

People who have been out of the workplace for several years raising children or pursuing other goals often have gaps in their employment experience, so an experienced-based

HINT

Your chronological résumé includes:

Personal data
Objective
Skills
Work Experience
Education
Accomplishments
References

What does your résumé say about you?

résumé is probably their best choice. To avoid emphasizing that the last year of employment was, for example, ten years ago or that there are gaps in your employment history, do not list dates on the resume. From an employer's perspective, short-term employment or an employment lapse may be an area for concern. A résumé for a person returning to the workplace instead lists years of experience and job duties with the specific employer, thus, eliminating specific dates.

In this chapter, you will find several very different résumé formats that you may find helpful when creating your own résumé emphasizing your background. Design the résumé to capture the employer's attention so you will be called for an interview. Accordingly, each item included or omitted from the résumé creates a picture in the recruiter's mind and tells the company something about the applicant. As you review the sections of the résumé, consider how you are going to design your résumé to present yourself to prospective employers.

Personal Data

This section includes your name, street address, city, state, ZIP Code, email address, and telephone number. The personal data section is usually centered at the top of the page, but it can be keyed at the left or right margin. You should *not* include your marital status, sex, height, weight, or age.

Objective

Write an objective that shows the employer the type of job you are seeking. The focus of the objective should not be too limiting, however, or you may be eliminated from consideration for a position. The objective should be customized for the specific job. Therefore, it may be necessary to revise your résumé and adapt the objective to meet the criteria of each job.

Sample job objectives

An administrative assistant's position with growth potential and the opportunity to use office technology skills.

To obtain a position as an entry-level manager in a forward-thinking company, where my background and experiences will be utilized.

To obtain an assistant position in a marketing company that emphasizes creativity, strong work ethics, and client interest.

An assistant position that offers challenges and career growth while utilizing my education and experiences.

An office assistant's position with a large legal firm where my legal and office administration skills will be used.

An entry-level management position using my communication, leadership, and customer-service skills to benefit the employer.

An executive assistant position with a nonprofit organization where I can use my interpersonal relations skills in addition to my business skills to manage the office.

An assistant position with a high-tech company where I can use my computer skills to perform the functions of running an office while developing and monitoring the company Web site.

Education

Include any information pertinent to the job. List schools with the most recent experience first.

College	Include the following for each college attended:
	Name of college; date of graduation or dates of attendance
	Course of study (also list specific classes pertinent to the job)
	Degrees or diplomas received
High school	Include the following:
	Name of high school, community, date of graduation
	Course of study (list specific classes pertinent to the job)
	Degrees or diplomas received
	(The high school section is included only by recent high school graduates. It is logical to assume you attended high school if you attended college; therefore, do not include high school on your résumé.)
Other	List any other relevant educational experiences such as:
	Seminars
	Short courses
	Evening classes
	Courses by software companies and professional organizations

Skills

Include specific information such as:

- Keyboarding speed
- Knowledge of specific software programs
- Any unusual skills that may be of interest to an employer
- Foreign language fluency

Work Experience

List your work experience and dates of employment with the most recent experience first. If most of your experience is not full-time, include part-time experience and indicate that it is part-time. Employers are interested in the job duties you performed, so explain the duties of each job that you list. Volunteer jobs may also be included in a résumé if they are relevant to the type of job you are seeking or if you have minimal paid work experience. Volunteer experience is looked upon favorably by many companies because they appreciate employees who are involved in community activities.

Personal Interests and/or Accomplishments

Some people feel that listing your interests is a waste of time, while others feel that your personal interests describe you to an employer. Whether or not you list your interests is your decision. If you decide to list your interests, include activities that show that you are able to work productively both alone and as a member of a team. For example, volleyball is a team activity and reading is a solo activity, so listing both on a résumé demonstrates that you function well as a member of a team as well as in individual activities. Any awards or recognitions that you have received should be listed under accomplishments. Examples of accomplishments include dean's list, scholarship awards, honor societies, etc.

References

If you have space on your résumé, include information regarding three references. If space is not available, indicate "References available upon request."

Maria S. Williams
8725 Churchill Drive
Gatlinburg, TN 37738
931-555-4522 (Home)
931-555-4396 (Cell)
mwilliams@mailmy.com

Objective: To obtain an office assistant position in an organization where my office and computer application skills can be utilized.

Education: Associate of Arts degree, 2006
Western Community College
Major—Computer Applications
Courses:

Computer Applications	Computer Literacy
Computer Presentations	Web Design
Keyboarding	Word Processing
Office Procedures	Accounting
Management	Psychology
Communication Skills	Business Statistics

Seminar 2007, Changes in Office Computers
Seminar 2008, Global Technology

Skills: Keyboarding 80 wpm
Knowledge of:
  Word, Excel, Access, PowerPoint,
    DreamWeaver, HTML
  Fluent in Spanish

Experiences: 2007–Present   Memorial Community Hospital
Assistant to Vice President;
Duties—planning conferences, writing and editing reports, and general office jobs. Wrote a desk manual for the new computer application software.

2005–2007   Lawrence Health Center
Part-time position while in college;
Duties—greeting clients, answering telephones, keyboarding, and filing.

Interests: Tennis, jogging, and classical music

References: Available upon request

Figure 12-2   A résumé—in chronological order emphasizing education.

Patrick J. Fishman
7802 E. Jefferson Drive
Cincinnati, OH
513-555-6807 (Home)
513-555-4399 (Cell)
pjfishman@worldtoday.com

Objective

To obtain an assistant position in a company that stresses professional responsibilities in the workplace.

Relevant Experience

Administrative Responsibilities
- Responded to multiple telephone calls in high-traffic office
- Maintained calendars for ten managers
- Greeted clients
- Developed a new office filing system
- Maintained office supply inventory
- Planned meetings
- Trained new employees
- Planned travel for ten managers
- Completed travel expenditure forms

Work History

- Cosmo and Sons 2007–present
- L & L Enterprises 2005–2007
- Joseph Accountants Inc. 2003–2005

Personal Skills

- Proficient in Microsoft Word, Excel, Access, and PowerPoint
- Excellent oral and written communications skills
- Strong work ethic
- Well organized
- Detail oriented
- Team player

Education

Central Community College, Columbus, Ohio
- Associate of Applied Science (A.A.S) 2003, in Computer Applications
- Certificate 2002, in Office Skills

Seminars
- Workplace Skills 2008
- Human Relations in Office 2008
- Responding to the Demands of Technology 2007
- Web Designing 2007

References Available Upon Request

Figure 12-3 Experienced-based résumé.

Wilma F. Shadow
812 Century Lane
Missoula, MT 59801
406-555-9807 (Home) 406-555-9662 (Cell)
wfshadow@mailmy.com

Objective: An administrative assistant position using my soft skills and computer application knowledge in an office environment.

Profile:
- Willing and eager to learn
- Mature and dependable; can work without supervision
- Professional work ethic
- Conscientious
- Knowledge of grammar and punctuation rules
- Knowledge of Word, Excel, Access, PowerPoint, Publisher, and HTML

Work Experience
- Administrative Assistant, Michael Communications
  Duties: answered telephone, processed mail, prepared payroll, conducted marketing research

- Administrative Assistant, Maverick and Associates
  Duties: greeted clients, prepared travel documents, ordered supplies, managed petty cash fund

- Administrative Assistant, Great Mountain Enterprises
  Duties: answered telephone, managed fax machine, processed mail, keyboarded letters and memos

Additional Experiences
- Managed charity ball for six years
- Treasurer of home owners association
- Hospital volunteer

References Available Upon Request

Figure 12-4   A functional résumé emphasizing skills and experience for a person returning to the workforce.

Barry J. Clifton
20 Silver Lane
Houston, TX 77582
281-555-8896 (Home) 281-555-6732 (Cell)
barryjc@theworld.net

Objective

To obtain a position in a mortgage company where I can effectively use my accounting, event planning, and communication skills to support the director.

Qualifications

- Diligent team player
- Detail oriented
- Strong work ethic
- Decision maker
- Self-directed
- Professional business demeanor
- Excellent interpersonal skills
- Excellent oral and written communications skills
- Proficient in Microsoft Office Suite

Experience

- Windy River Industries
  - Prepared monthly and quarterly accounting reports
  - Liaison with Board of Directors
  - Scheduled meetings
  - Handled multiple projects

- M & T Research
  - Prepared accounting reports
  - Planned special events
  - Supervised staff of ten
  - Wrote and keyboarded documents

- B & C Service Center
  - Maintained payroll records
  - Answered telephones
  - Tracked report status
  - Dispatched repair personnel

Education

B.S., Central University
  - Double major in Accounting and Business

Seminars
  - Tax Law Changes
  - Event Planning for the Executives
  - Program Coordinator Projects
  - Supporting Multiple Directors
  - Accounting for Professionals

References Available Upon Request

Figure 12-5 Résumé for someone who has worked many years.

PENELOPE J. PATRICK

104 BERMAN PLACE
BETHESDA, MD
PJP6609@YAHOO.COM
202-555-8622

Objective

My objective is to work in a forward-thinking company where my customer service, computer, and management skills can be effectively utilized. My passion for achievement drives my approach to business.

Education

North Central University—Bachelor of Science in Business/Management

Employment

City Associates
Supervised daily office operation
Managed move to new office space
Designed office layout
Prepared annual budgets
Represented company on state advisory board

Charles & Lewis Associates
Supervised daily office operation
Ordered all equipment and supplies
Managed and filed travel expenses
Developed monthly training plan
Conducted training classes
Hired and trained staff

Skills

Computer skills in Microsoft Excel, PowerPoint, and Word
Goal oriented with strong organizational skills
Work well in culturally diverse environment

Seminars

Crisis Management Essential Skills
Office Skills for Now
Managing Your Office

Awards

Employee of the Month, Charles & Lewis Associates
Dean's List four years, North Central University
Student of the Year, North Central University

Interests

Volunteering: Literacy for Children, Health for All
Tennis, photography, painting, and chess

References Available Upon Request

Figure 12-6   A Functional résumé with an alternate personal information format.

APPLICATION FOR EMPLOYMENT

Generally employers request that all candidates they are seriously considering for employment complete the company's standard application form. Some companies require applications to be submitted online, while other organizations use the traditional paper application form. If you are asked to complete an application for employment prior to the interview, make a copy of the application before you begin keyboarding or writing on it. Practice keyboarding or writing on the copy to determine how many words fit on a line. Your practice will indicate if you must omit something or abbreviate words.

When you have completed keyboarding or writing the entire practice application, complete the original application and proofread it carefully. Before submitting the application, make a copy for your files.

THE INTERVIEW

If you have successfully located a job opening and prepared a résumé that has impressed a recruiter, you are ready for the most important stage in getting a job: a personal interview with a hiring manager. How you should prepare for and conduct yourself during the personal interview is the subject of the next chapter.

Figure 12-7 A hiring manager ready to interview an applicant.

CHAPTER REVIEW

1. Name three fields in which office assistants are employed.
2. Name four methods for finding a job.
3. What should be included in the letter of application?
4. List five of the suggestions given in this chapter for preparing a résumé.
5. List the types of information that should be included in your résumé.

ACTIVITIES

1. Find a partner and practice a firm handshake. A weak handshake often indicates that you have no interest in the person.
2. If you have responsibility for the care of a child or elderly parent, decide how you will handle last-minute illnesses or problems. Locate a backup person if your regular care provider is not available.
3. Even if you plan to drive to work, investigate the potential of using mass transportation. Your car may not always be operable.
4. Research the local newspapers for jobs for which you are qualified. Write a summary of the qualifications, types of jobs, benefits, salary, and locations.
5. Using the Internet, research the local businesses for jobs for which you are qualified. Write a summary of the qualifications, types of jobs, benefits, salary, and locations.

PROJECTS

Project 23

Prepare the following letter and make all decisions concerning the letter style. Supply any additional information required to complete the letter.

Send this letter to Thomas O'Malley, Attorney at Law, 710 Cherry Hill Court, Denver, CO 80204. The letter is from Robert Rosenblot.

Dear Tom:

How is life in Denver? As you know, we enjoyed seeing you while we vacationed there last year.

I have a favor to ask. My friend's daughter is moving to Denver, and I thought you might be able to help her. I have known Terri Tabber and her family for years. Terri's father and I attended college together and have continued our friendship all of these years. Terri is getting married in April and is moving to Denver after the wedding.

She graduated from college with a degree in business and a 3.4 average. During the summers in college she worked for temporary agencies to improve her basic skills. She also had a nine-month internship with a worldwide marketing corporation, which helped to sharpen her talent. In addition, she is intelligent, willing to work, and creative.

I think she would be a benefit to your company because she has the ability to grow and learn with you. I hope you will call her and arrange an interview. Her phone number is 716-555-8924.

Tina and I send regards to you and Suzanne. We should plan to get together again soon.

Project 24

Send this letter to Hanna J. Bluemont Office Manager, Sade & Uriz, Inc., 5207 Colony Lane, Nashville, TN 37901. The letter is from Emanuel W. Giegerick, Plant Director. Use block style with mixed punctuation.

Are you aware of the health benefits of plants in your office? Plants remove harmful pollutants from the air and make our office a healthier environment. Now that we are an environmentally conscious society, we are aware of the pollutants that grow in our offices.

Our plant service will plant, arrange, water, and maintain your plants. All you have to do is enjoy the plants.

We base the charge for our service on the number of plants in the office. If you have more than twelve plants, we have a special plan that is very cost effective. Below is a sample of our costs.

Number of Plants	Costs per Visit
1–3	$10
4–7	$12
8–12	$26

We have contracts with many businesses in your area, and would like you to join our family of customers. Please call us at 615-555-7844 to make arrangements for a free consultation. We hope to hear from you soon.

HUMAN RELATIONS SKILL DEVELOPMENT

HR 12-1 Bragging Workers

An office environment where one individual is constantly bragging about something can become uncomfortable for others. Learning to tolerate a person who boasts is easier than attempting to change the other person's personality. Sometimes people brag in order to gain attention. Agreeing with and listening to a person is a passive way to tolerate the situation. Also, changing the subject, but allowing the other person to speak, may solve the problem.

- How would you handle the situation where coworkers constantly tell you how brilliant their children are?
- What would you say to a coworker who brags about job successes?
- What would you say to a supervisor who wastes time telling you about job successes?

HR 12-2 Increasing Your Self-Confidence

Increasing your self-confidence is important for your professional growth. A low opinion of yourself can be transmitted to others, and they can adopt the same opinion of you. To increase your self-confidence, make a list of your attributes, review past evaluations, review your letters of recommendation, and review favorable comments that you have received from employers and peers.

- Name three people who believe that you are a success.
- Do you have confidence in your abilities?
- List five of your successes.

SITUATIONS

How would you handle the following situations?

- **S 12-1** Next week at 3 P.M. the office is having a retirement party for Bart, and everyone wants to attend. Your supervisor has said that the office must be staffed. Because you are the receptionist, you will be the person staying at the office. What options do you have?

- **S 12-2** Ms. Kathryn Leadman, the director, has asked you to plan the annual picnic again this year. You are very busy with your high-priority assignments, and you feel that you do not have enough time to do everything.

- **S 12-3** It is 12:30 P.M. and everyone is at lunch. Your supervisor's 1 P.M. appointment has arrived, and the client speaks a language that you do not understand.

PUNCTUATION REVIEW

Punctuate each of the following sentences. For a review of punctuation rules, see the Appendix.

1. Linda Meyers president of Golds Inc was my mentor
2. Dr Levitt cannot see you at 12 however she can see you at 1 PM
3. At Mollys Gallery we pride ourselves on offering the best quality art and customer service to our family of clients.
4. Charleston West Virginia Columbus Ohio and Harrisburg Pennsylvania are all capitals of states
5. His finances are in poor condition however he is not concerned
6. The cost of living is increasing and interest rates are rising
7. There are many jobs available in the computer industry therefore Bill decided to attend several seminars
8. The new telephone system was installed however there are problems with two office telephones
9. We recently completed a five year study examining the effects of employee training programs and have published the report on our Web site
10. If you own $20,000 worth of stock with an average dividend yield of 5 percent you can now save $475 after federal taxes
11. I just met Mr Hoover who is the assistant
12. In effect you will build market share and increase your profits by expanding your sales force
13. Would you rather meet at 10 AM or would you rather meet at 12 noon
14. Most savings and loan institutions are solvent but a few fail each year
15. Jennifer Minks the lawyer questioned the witness then she requested a delay in the trial

CD ASSIGNMENT

CD Assignment 12-1

Open the file **CD12-1_EAI** on your Student CD and follow the instructions to complete the job. You will also need the file **CD12_EAF** which is on your Student CD.

CHAPTER 13

The Interview and Job Offer

Objectives

After studying this chapter, you should be able to:

1. Conduct yourself in a professional manner during an interview.
2. Write a thank-you letter after an interview.
3. Explain the types of health insurance discussed in this chapter.
4. Explain EAP.
5. Explain a stock option.

PLANNING FOR THE INTERVIEW

The personal interview is the most important step in the hiring process. Recruiters use the résumé and letter of application to narrow the pool of applicants down to a few candidates they want to interview. They usually do not have time to interview more than three to five candidates. If you are asked to come in for a personal interview, you already stand out from the other candidates. At the interview, you must sell yourself to the employer to be offered the position.

Most interviews are scheduled by telephone, and some companies conduct a telephone interview prior to an in-person interview. Suggestions for handling a telephone interview are discussed later in this chapter.

If you hope to work for a specific company, try not to interview with that company first. You will be less nervous when you interview with your targeted company if you have already practiced and honed your skills by interviewing with other companies. By talking with other companies first, you will also have a better perspective regarding your favored company. You may decide that the company you originally preferred is not the company for you

Making an Appointment

Be calm and polite when making the appointment, and be sure to obtain clear directions to the business location. If you are invited to an interview and have not completed the company's application form, request that an application be sent to you or ask if it may be downloaded from the company Web site. You will then have the

> **HINT**
> New hires may be recent graduates, job changers, or employees rejoining the workforce after experiencing a layoff or having a baby.

opportunity to prepare your application form before the interview, as discussed in the previous chapter.

After you have made the appointment, prepare a file folder for the interview and place the following information in your interview file:

- Name of the interviewer.
- Name of the company.
- Date and time of the interview.
- Location of the company, including its street address.
- Building and room number of the interview.
- Directions to the company.
- Directions to the building if it is in a large office complex.
- Background information on the company.

Research the Company

HINT

Research the company prior to the interview.

Before you go to an interview, learn about the company. Never walk into an interview without knowing something about the employer. Doing research on the company not only gives you background for the interview, but it also demonstrates to the interviewer your initiative and interest in the business. Understanding the organization and its products, services, and goals help you during the interview to relate and match your experiences to the company's needs.

The same sources used in researching the position can be used to obtain information about the company. The Web sites of most companies are excellent resources for current information about the company's products, services, staff, and goals. Also, search the Internet for other information about the business. If the prospective employer is a national company, information about the company may be found in reference books contained in the reference department of your local library. In addition, the chamber of commerce may have information about local businesses. Newspapers are also a good source of information about local businesses through both articles and advertisements. Also, ask friends who work at the company for information. As a last resort, call the company's main telephone number and ask about the company's business.

The Telephone Interview

In the interest of time and reducing costs, some companies conduct preliminary and sometimes final interviews by telephone or speakerphone. You should try to schedule a telephone interview just as you would schedule an in-person interview, but sometimes a

---

MY SUCCESS STORY

My Name Is Jonah

I am a twenty-four-year-old guy and computers are my life and passion. Yes, I am an obvious member of the Internet generation. I grew up using computers so I knew I wanted a job working with computer Web sites and having fun. My degree is in Web programming, and I have a terrific job with a midsize company developing and maintaining client Web sites. My days are filled with work, which I describe as fun. We use a team approach in my organization, and my team members strive to create a quality product while focusing on the client's individual needs. I have my dream job.

recruiter will call and ask if it is convenient for you to talk about the job at that time. It is probably better to respond that it is a convenient time; however, if you are truly given the option of scheduling a better time, do so. By scheduling a time, you will have the opportunity to prepare yourself for the telephone interview.

A telephone interview allows the interviewee the luxury of creating the interview setting. Therefore, gather your notes, set your mind for a professional conference, remove noise and distractions such as children and television, and use a telephone with good reception. If during a telephone interview questions are presented by several members of a screening panel, the applicant may have difficulty identifying the panel member and not recognize a follow-up question. Since gestures and body language are not visible on a telephone call, it is difficult to interpret and respond to interviewer's questions. In addition, it is important to allow time for the interviewer to consider your response or to make notes about your comments. An interview requires your full attention, and it is not a good idea to use your cell phone for the interview while driving. Use the telephone interview to your advantage so you can make the screening cut and be invited to an on-site interview.

PREPARING FOR THE INTERVIEW

The interview is your opportunity to sell yourself to the company, and you must promote yourself quickly because most hiring decisions are made during the *first few seconds* of the interview. The first impression you make is very important, so appear confident, smile, be enthusiastic, stand or sit straight, use positive body language, use eye contact, and use a reasonably firm handshake.

The Practice Session

Prior to the interview, do a practice session in front of the mirror or ask friends or family members to do a mock interview with you so you will have the opportunity to rehearse answering interview questions. Rehearsing your answers should improve your interviewing skills. Be prepared, during the interview, to emphasize what you can do for the employer, not what the employer can do for you. Your experiences may have landed you the opportunity for an interview, but the interview is the time to discuss your potential with the employer. Do not dwell on your past experiences; concentrate on the future.

Dress as you would dress for the interview and look at yourself in the mirror—at your clothing, facial expressions, and body language. Body language demonstrates your feelings and attitudes by gestures and posture. For example, sitting forward demonstrates interest and attention, while folding your arms across your chest demonstrates a defensive attitude.

> **HINT**
> Rehearse an interview in front of friends or the mirror.

Later in this chapter, you will find a list of possible questions that a hiring manager may ask. Since you want to make a good impression, practice answering customary questions that you think the interviewer might ask you. Also, review your résumé and determine what questions it may prompt.

Your Personal Appearance

Several years ago, an office clothing transformation began in the technology industry and spread to traditional businesses. The casual atmosphere of the technology industry coupled with the young age of many of the employees changed the way workers dressed in the office. In the past, proper office clothing meant a suit. Consequently, a business suit was appropriate for the interview. Today in many high-tech companies, casual attire is the norm. Therefore, a job applicant dressed in a suit would be inappropriately

Figure 13-1 Dressed for an interview.

HINT

Hiring managers expect that you will wear your best and most appropriate clothing for the interview. This is your chance to make your best impression.

dressed. Over dressing for a casually attired company is as much of a problem as under dressing for a professionally attired company. Because of uncertainty about today's business dress code, call the company prior to the interview and inquire about their clothing style or visit the company parking lot to see what the employees are wearing. You want to be appropriately dressed for the interview because your attire may influence the hiring decision. If you decide it is appropriate to wear the traditional interview clothing of a suit, enliven the outfit with a brightly colored tie for the man or a snappy colored blouse for the woman. An outfit that is devoid of color and interest can create a boring image of you in the recruiter's eye.

Personal appearance for the interview

- Your hair should be clean and combed.
- Your clothing should be pressed.
- Job candidates should wear interview-appropriate clothing, which may be a suit, depending on the company's dress code.
- You should appear rested, so get a good night's sleep the night before the interview.
- Smile.

What to Take with You

You want to make a positive first impression, so do not carry any more to the interview than you absolutely need. Leave as much as possible in the car or at home if you are using public transportation. If you are nervous (most applicants are nervous), you could drop everything, which can be extremely embarrassing. It is better for female applicants not to carry a purse because it may be difficult to hold your purse, coat, briefcase, and so on, while shaking hands. The less you have to carry the better. Put your keys, money, ID, etc., in your briefcase, which also has a copy of your résumé. Use a folder or small briefcase to carry your résumé and your list of references. Also, take several copies of your résumé to the interview.

Take the following items to the interview

- Pen.
- Small notebook.
- Résumé.
- List of references.
- Copy of grades.
- Proof of citizenship or work permit.
- Social security number.
- Sample portfolio.

You should create a portfolio showcasing your knowledge, skills, talents, and writing abilities. The following are examples of documents that might be included in your portfolio: letters and memos you have written, reports you have created, surveys you have conducted, and other business documents you have written. To maintain confidentiality, it is acceptable to block out names and sensitive information in documents in your sample portfolio. Since students may not have work-related documents, they may substitute copies of assignments. After you have selected your portfolio documents, arrange them attractively in a binder with an appropriate cover sheet. By creating a portfolio of work samples, you demonstrate to a prospective employer your organizational skills and the quality of work they can expect from you.

> **HINT**
> Create a portfolio and take it the interview.

Going to the Interview

A day or two before the interview, make a trial run if necessary to locate the building and determine how long it will take you to travel to the company during typical business-hour traffic.

Go *alone* to the interview. Do not make plans to meet friends after the interview because you do not know how long the interview will last. You may be asked to complete an application, take a test, meet other staff, or tour the company's facilities as part of the interview process. If you have a friend waiting for you after the interview, you may hurry through the interview and you may not make a good impression.

Arrive at the interview fifteen minutes early. If you arrive too far ahead of schedule, walk around outside or sit in your car. You do not want to be too early, but *never* arrive late for an interview. When you arrive at the building, locate a restroom and straighten your hair and clothing.

THE INTERVIEW

Your interview starts the moment you walk through the door, so put a smile on your face and look confident as soon as you enter the building. Always be pleasant to the receptionist and everyone you meet because you do not know who will be asked to

> **HINT**
> Make a positive impression from the moment you walk through the company's front door by treating everyone courteously.

Figure 13-2 Employer conducting an interview.

evaluate your job suitability. Consequently, never ask indiscreet questions of or gossip with other employees. If possible, leave your coat in the reception office. Never use your cell phone, Blackberry, or personal music system in the reception area while you are waiting for the interviewer. Do not check messages, make a call, or send a text message. You should be focused on the interview and the possible job. Asking the interviewer to wait while you finish a cell phone conversation or put away your music player creates a poor first impression and may destroy your chance of getting the job.

If you were unable to complete an application form at home, you may be asked to complete a company application prior to the interview. If you must complete an application form by hand at the time of the interview, use a pen and print your answers carefully so the application can be easily read. Interviewers are becoming concerned about handwriting legibility, and some interviewers believe that handwriting reflects a person's personality.

Interviews may be conducted by one person or a team and may last a few minutes or all day. Most interviewers have techniques that they use to encourage you to answer their questions. Some will be very pleasant to help you relax so that you do not realize how much you are telling about yourself. However, other interviewers may be very rude and abrasive. The rude behavior may be used to determine how you react in a stressful situation. In addition, some recruiters will ask off-the-wall questions to determine how quickly you think and can respond to a situation.

The hiring manager may say that he or she is taking notes during the interview. Do not be upset; you cannot expect the interviewer to remember everything that you say. Some companies have interview screening rounds. If you make the first screening cut, you go to the first interview; if you make the second screening cut, you go to the second interview; etc. If you do not make one of the screening cuts, you can always write a letter reinforcing your qualifications for the position.

Many businesses now require drug testing of prospective and current employees because persons using drugs or abusing alcohol perform below expected work levels and may cause harm to other employees. You may be asked to take a drug test as part of the interview process.

During the Interview

Although interviews can be stressful, try to be upbeat and positive during an interview. When possible, answer questions in a conversational manner instead of with one-syllable responses such as yes or no. This is your opportunity to use your friendly personality to your advantage.

- Do not sit until you are invited to sit.
- If the interviewer wishes to shake hands, do so with a firm handshake.
- Smile.
- Be pleasant.
- Do not smoke or chew gum.
- Do not wear heavy perfume.
- Look the interviewer in the eye.
- Listen carefully to the interviewer.
- Do not allow nervous gestures to show.
- Do not giggle—this is a sign of nervousness.
- Do not slouch in the chair.
- It is better not to accept coffee or a soft drink—you could spill it.
- Never put your personal items on the interviewer's desk.
- Use positive, not negative, body language.
- Do not interrupt the interviewer.
- Do not appear arrogant or act like a know-it-all.
- At the end of the interview, ask specific questions about the job or the company. (Do not ask questions about benefits, sick time, vacation, pay, etc. These questions should be saved until a specific job offer is made because they indicate a personal, not company, concern.)
- When the interview is over, leave immediately.

When you go to an interview, accentuate your positive skills and talents. The interview is the time to emphasize your strengths and play down your weak points. You will be compared to other candidates, and you must demonstrate that you are the best employee for the job.

Questions That May Be Asked During an Interview

The following requests and questions are often asked during interviews. How would you respond to each?

- Tell me about yourself.
- What are your personal goals?
- Why should I hire you?
- What can you do for me?
- Why did you choose this company?
- Where do you plan to be five years from today?

- Why did you select this field?
- What was wrong with your last job?
- Why did you leave your last job?
- Did you get along with your supervisor and coworkers?
- Are you punctual?
- What personal characteristics are necessary for success in your field?
- What were your favorite subjects and least favorite subjects in school?
- How do you spend your leisure time?
- What are your strengths?
- What are your weaknesses?
- How do you rank yourself as an employee?
- What gives you the greatest satisfaction?
- What is your ideal job description?
- What kinds of projects interest you?
- What do human relations skills in the workplace mean to you?
- What was the last book that you read?
- What do you know about my company?
- What are your future plans?
- What have you learned from other jobs?
- What personal characteristics do you have that will help you in this position?
- What have you done that shows initiative?
- How did you learn about this job?
- What salary do you expect?
- Do you like to work?
- Are you more comfortable working alone or in a group?
- Why do you job hop?
- Will you fit in here?
- What does being a team member mean to you?
- Explain how you use common sense in the workplace.
- How do you manage stress?

Answer all questions honestly. Try to emphasize your positive, not negative, characteristics.

In addition to basic interview questions, some recruiters present a scenario, and the applicant is then judged on the ability to respond quickly to a hypothetical, office-related case study. Some hiring managers use behavior interviewing, which concentrates on instances of past behavior as a predictor of future efforts. You may be asked to describe in detail an incident you experienced in the workplace. To prepare for this type of interview question, you should review how you have resolved various problems in your office and how you would address the types of problems presented in the Human Relations Skill Development sections at the end of each chapter in this book.

If you are asked to submit writing samples or employment documentation, respond in a timely manner. It is very important to be pleasant when responding to all requests. Your personality and ability to work with people is also being evaluated. Employers are not eager to hire persons who they believe will create conflict in the workplace.

HINT

Use positive body language such as sitting forward in your seat. Do not use negative body language such as crossing your arms over your body.

Questions the Interviewer Should Not Ask

Some people who conduct interviews know the techniques of interviewing, while others are not aware of them. Federal and many state laws prohibit discrimination in employment; most employers today are familiar with antidiscrimination laws and ask only job-related questions. If you are asked questions on the following topics, you will have to decide how to respond. You could say that the question is illegal or that you would rather not answer it.

Questions on the following topics are *not* usually relevant to the position and, therefore, may be illegal:

- Age.
- Skin color.
- Religion.
- Limitations because of gender.
- Marital status.
- Number of children or whether you are planning to have children.
- Race.
- Ethnic background.
- Credit rating.
- Employment of spouse.

Federal laws prohibit discrimination in the workplace based on race, color, national origin, religion, gender, age, pregnancy, and disability. For more information on anti-discrimination laws, see Chapter 15.

HINT

Stress what you can do for company, not what the company can do for you.

Questions an Applicant Might Ask

During the interview, you will probably be given an opportunity to ask questions regarding the position. The questions you ask should reflect your interest in the job and the company.

Questions to ask during an interview
- Who would be my supervisor?
- How would my work be evaluated?
- How often would my work be evaluated?
- What are the opportunities for advancement?
- Are there educational opportunities?
- What would my duties be?
- Describe a typical day.
- How would I be trained for the job?
- What duties are most important for the position?
- How would I receive job feedback?
- What are the barriers to advancement?
- If hired, would I fill a newly created position or would I replace someone?
- Was my predecessor promoted?
- What is your management style?
- Is this department team-oriented?
- What is the next step in the interview process?

If an employer does not have an opening that fits your qualifications, ask if the employer knows of another department within the company or another company that might have a job for someone with your qualifications and talents.

Questions that should be be deferred until after the job is offered

- What is the salary for the position?
- What are the hours?
- Is there overtime?
- What are the medical benefits?
- What are vacation and sick-leave policies?
- What other benefits are provided?

Reasons Applicants Are Not Hired

The following are reasons that applicants for jobs are not hired. How would you measure up during your interview?

- Insincere.
- Too interested in money.
- Too interested in what the company can do for them.
- Poor appearance.
- Impolite.
- Inability to speak clearly.
- Not interested in working.
- No enthusiasm for the job.
- Spoke badly of past employer.
- Lack of skills.
- Late for interview.
- No job goals.
- Too aggressive.
- Failure to look at the interviewer.
- Lazy.
- Too nervous.
- Did not smile.
- Past history of job hopping.
- No experience.
- Bad manners.
- Overblown ego.
- Demanding personality.
- Poor responses to questions.

HINT

When interviewing you, the employer is attempting to evaluate your leadership and problem-solving abilities.

AFTER THE INTERVIEW

Interview Review

It is impolite and unprofessional of you to take notes during an interview. Therefore, shortly after arriving home, you should record your impressions of the interview. Create an interview review sheet similar to the sample in Figure 13-3 and complete it after every interview.

Name of company _____

Address _____

Phone _____

Name of interviewer _____

Title of interviewer _____

Duties of job _____

Beginning date _____

Salary _____

Benefits _____

Atmosphere of company _____

Transportation/parking _____

Positive aspects of job _____

Negative aspects of job _____

Would I like to work there? _____

Do I think the position will be offered to me? _____

Date of the interview _____

Date I sent thank-you letter _____

Personal evaluation

   Was I nervous? _____

   Did I answer all of the questions effectively? _____

   Did I look the interviewer in the eye? _____

   Did I sell myself? _____

   Was I courteous? _____

   What did I do right? _____

   What did I do wrong? _____

   What could I have done better? _____

   Did I ask questions? _____

Figure 13-3 Interview review sheet.

Thank-You Letter

Within a couple of days after each interview, you should write a thank-you letter to the interviewer. Few applicants write a thank-you letter after an interview, so writing one will impress employers; this letter may be the slight push you need to obtain the job. A thank-you letter is also your opportunity to express interest in the job and to emphasize any qualifications that are pertinent to it. Stress a qualification to which the interviewer seemed particularly responsive. It is also an opportunity to mention anything you forgot to express at the interview and to emphasize your written communication

Your Street Address
Your City, State, and ZIP Code
Today's Date

Interviewer
Interviewer's Title
Company Name
Address
City, State, ZIP Code

Dear _____ :

Thank you very much for the opportunity to interview for the administrative assistant position you have available. I believe my education and job experiences have prepared me for the responsibilities of your administrative assistant position, and I am eager to become a member of your team.

As I mentioned at the interview, I feel my recent experience in writing the manual for the computer applications software at my company demonstrates my ability to use many computer software programs. I would like the opportunity to use my office skills and my computer software knowledge for your company.

If I can provide you with additional information, please call me at 513-555-5222. I hope that you will consider me for the position of administrative assistant in the marketing department, and I look forward to hearing from you soon.

Sincerely,

Your Name

Figure 13-4 Thank-you letter.

skills. If you were asked to submit writing samples or employment documentation, you should mention them and enclose them with your thank-you letter.

Do not wait too long to write the letter because an employment decision could be made quickly. In today's technology-driven world, some applicants immediately send a short thank-you email and then send a traditional thank-you letter. If a hiring decision will be made quickly and time is of the essence, it may be acceptable to fax the thank-you letter. If the letter is faxed, mention in the letter your reason for faxing it.

> **HINT**
> Always write a thank-you letter.

Call Back

At the end of the interview, most interviewers say they will call you. If you have not heard from the interviewer in a couple of weeks, you could call and ask if a decision has been made. (*Caution*: Some interviewers indicate that *frequent* telephone calls are overly aggressive.)

Reference Checks

After the interview, the company may check the references you provided and verify past work experience. In addition, the recruiter may confirm that you have responded truthfully about your education, experience, and achievements.

JOB OFFER

Success

If you are offered a job, you must make the decision whether or not to accept it. If you have interviewed with several companies, you may be offered a job that is not your first choice. Within a day or two of being offered the job, you may have to make a decision about accepting the offer. Carefully choose your job. Do not rush and accept an offer if you are uncertain about it. You do have the option of thinking about the job offer before you accept it. Ask yourself if the offer fits your criteria.

After receiving a job offer, you are in a position to ask the questions regarding salary and benefits.

- What is the salary for the position?
- What are the hours?
- Is overtime required?
- What are the medical benefits?
- What are vacation and sick-leave policies?
- What other benefits are available?

The next section reviews common employee benefits that may be offered.

Questions to ask *yourself* before accepting or declining a job offer

- Is this job right for me?
- Do I have the knowledge and skills to perform the duties of the position?
- Does the job fulfill my needs?
- Would I be happy with this job?
- Would I be happy with this company?
- Do I think that I can work with the supervisor and the other employees?
- Am I satisfied with the salary offer?
- Is the company financially stable?

> Is the job offer a good fit for you and the employer?

When you are offered a new job, ask to receive a written and signed employment offer that details the starting salary, starting date, and company employment policies. If the job meets your personal and financial requirements, you should send a letter accepting the job offer and indicating the starting date.

Disappointment

> **HINT**
> Before accepting a job, consider all of the positive and negative aspects.

Of course, if you did not receive a job offer that you hoped to receive, your ego can suffer a blow. Ask yourself why you did not receive the offer. If you did not receive the offer because of your limited qualifications or negative personal characteristics, take appropriate action to improve. Remember, finding the perfect job and employer takes time and effort. The stress of job hunting can cause you to feel frustrated, angry, depressed, and discouraged. Always boost your ego with positive comments and reduce your stress level with the suggestions discussed in Chapter 16.

BENEFITS

Whether you are seeking your first job or considering a job change, many factors other than salary should be considered before making your final decision. In addition to the starting salary, you should review factors such as opportunities for promotion, working hours, commuting time, quality of the working conditions, and your interest in the job.

Fringe Benefits

While the issues discussed in the previous paragraph are important, you should also consider the other benefits that a job has to offer, such as medical and life insurance, retirement plans, annual and sick-leave policies, and opportunities for further training. These benefits are referred to as fringe benefits and are usually offered to all employees of the business. Some benefits, such as the amount of annual and sick leave, may be standard for all employees although the amount of annual leave may increase the longer the employee works with the organization.

Even if these benefits are not an important consideration in accepting a job offer, you should carefully review the benefits material that is usually given to new employees. As a new employee, you may be asked to make a decision about benefits that cannot be changed easily while you work for that organization. Changes may be permitted only during limited times during the year or when the employee undergoes a life-changing event such as a marriage, divorce, or the birth of a child.

> What fringe benefits are important to you?

Medical Benefits

The major benefit frequently provided to employees is medical insurance. The employer often contributes a portion of the cost of a medical insurance plan, with the employee paying the balance. Some companies have a single health plan, while other companies may give employees the option of selecting from a number of medical insurance plans. Plans may include health maintenance organizations (HMOs), preferred provider organizations (PPOs), and direct-pay plans. While the differences among the three plans are complex, in general, the differences occur between the amount the employee must pay and the flexibility the employee has in choosing a doctor. Those enrolled in an *HMO plan*, usually the least expensive plan, must go to doctors who are members of the HMO. In addition, HMO members are required to obtain a referral from their primary-care doctor prior to seeing a specialist. The insurance premium that employees pay for a PPO is usually more than the premium paid for an HMO. Those enrolled in a *PPO plan* can pick any doctor, but employees pay a higher percentage of the medical bill when the doctor they choose is not a preferred provider for the PPO. Employees pay the highest premiums in a *direct-pay plan*, but they can choose any medical provider. Generally, you will be given the option of selecting medical insurance for yourself (single plan) or for yourself and members of your family (family plan).

Some companies offer dental or vision insurance. This insurance provides additional coverage because the dental or vision coverage under most general medical insurance plans is not very comprehensive or is nonexistent. The cost of this additional insurance can be high, so carefully review your own situation before deciding whether to take either of these additional plans.

As a cost-reduction measure, some companies are reducing their contribution for family health insurance; in some cases, they are not insuring a working spouse but are requiring the working spouse to obtain health insurance from his or her employer.

The costs and types of medical coverage vary widely. You may only be given thirty or sixty days in which to make a choice, so this is something that you should consider promptly when given the opportunity.

Under federal law, many employees are required to receive two medically related benefits. The Family and Medical Leave Act of 1993 permits most employees to take unpaid leave up to twelve weeks for family- and health-related circumstances without losing their jobs. Information about the Family and Medical Leave Act can be found on the Department of Labor Web site at http://www.dol.gov/esa/whd/fmla/. The Pregnancy Discrimination Act is an amendment to Title VII of the Civil Rights Act of 1964 and protects employees and applicants for employment from discrimination on the basis of pregnancy or childbirth. An employer cannot refuse to hire a woman because of her pregnancy and must treat a woman who cannot perform her job because of her pregnancy as any employee who is temporarily disabled. Information about the Pregnancy Discrimination Act can be found at the Equal Employment Opportunity Commission Web site at http://www.eeoc.gov/facts/fs-preg.html.

Flexible Spending Accounts

Some employers offer *flexible spending accounts* (*FSAs*) where you can have money taken from your salary and placed in a special FSA for either health care or dependent care. These deductions are taken before taxes, which means that the deductions reduce your salary for income tax purposes. Funds in the FSA health care account are used to cover out-of-pocket expenses that are not covered by your insurance. Sample expenses covered under a health care FSA are medical insurance copays and deductibles, eyeglasses, contact lenses, medical hearing aids, and prescription drugs. Funds in an FSA dependent-care account are used to pay for childcare or adult dependent-care expenses. In most instances, however, you must use the amount deducted within the calendar year. If you deduct $500 for childcare expenses and do not use the full $500 within the year, you lose the balance. If you know you are going to have certain types of expenses, these plans are a good way of putting money aside for the expense; in addition, they reduce your taxes.

Retirement Plans

An important benefit of most jobs is being able to participate in a retirement plan. You were just hired, why worry about retirement? You will not have to worry about how you will live during retirement if you regularly save money through a retirement plan. Although it's best to start saving money while you are young, it's never too late to put money into a retirement fund. Someone who won't retire for thirty or forty years can benefit from the miracle of compounding. If you can save $1,000 in a retirement account and invest it at only 5 percent for forty years, it will grow to become $7,000. If the $1,000 is invested at 7 percent, it grows to become $14,000.

Many employers will put money into a retirement plan in addition to paying your salary. Money in the retirement plan earns tax-free income until it is taken out, though there may be a penalty to withdraw the money before you retire. In some organizations, the employer also matches contributions made to the retirement plan by the employee. Some companies run their own pension plans, while others offer plans in conjunction with banks, mutual funds, or other financial institutions. Perhaps the best type of retirement plan is known as a 401(k) plan, which refers to a section of the Internal Revenue Service law. Under a 401(k) plan, you can ask your employer to make a deduction from your salary for a contribution to the pension plan. The deduction reduces your salary for tax purposes. If you invest $500 in a 401(k) plan, not only does your money earn tax-free income over the years, you also save the income taxes you would have paid on the $500 for that year.

In addition, you may be eligible to invest in an *Individual Retirement Account* (*IRA*). An IRA is a special account permitted by the federal government to encourage people to save money for retirement. There are two types of IRA accounts, and both types allow people to earn income on their investments in the IRA account without paying taxes each year. Money invested in a traditional IRA can be deducted from a person's gross income for income tax purposes, and payment of taxes on income earned in the IRA account is delayed until the person withdraws the money, usually at retirement. In a Roth IRA, taxes are paid on the funds that are placed in the Roth IRA, but no taxes are paid on the earnings while they are in the IRA account or when they are withdrawn. An IRA must be established with an approved financial institution and can be invested in a variety of securities, including CDs, stocks, bonds, and mutual funds.

Other Benefits

The range of other fringe benefits can vary widely. Some employers provide *low-cost life insurance*. You can purchase life insurance, usually in multiples of your salary and frequently without having to undergo a physical exam. In some instances, you can also purchase life insurance for your spouse.

As companies increasingly realize the importance of happy and well employees, Employee Assistance Programs (EAPs) are becoming popular. These programs may offer counseling (personal or business), day care, elder care, health benefits, or wellness programs, including exercise facilities. As the population ages, employers are beginning to focus on providing more elder-care options for adult day-care on a daily or emergency basis. In addition to health-related activities, companies frequently provide work-related training opportunities as a component of Employee Assistance Programs. Educational opportunities help update employee skills and teach employees new skills applicable to other jobs within the company, thus allowing the company to retain good employees. Furthermore, under the Employee Assistance Program, some employers provide free parking or provide funds, tax-free, to underwrite commuting costs using mass transportation such as the bus, train, or subway.

Optical, legal, and personal identity insurance coverage is now being offered through some employers. In many cases, the cost of this insurance is paid for solely by the employee. Because coverage is based on a group rate, the fee is generally reasonable.

In addition, many companies have added bereavement leave to their employee benefits. In today's mobile society, employees often live thousands of miles away from the rest of their family, and a bereavement trip may require several days of leave.

Employee Stock Options

A *stock option* is an increasingly available benefit that gives an employee the right to buy company stock at less than the market price. The employee is given the right to purchase the stock at a fixed price at a future date. When using or *exercising the stock option*, the employee purchases the stock for the set price and then can keep the stock or sell the stock on the open market, hopefully for a higher price. Stock options permit employees to share in the success of the company. The more successful the business, the higher the stock price and the greater the profit the employee can make on selling the stock.

Cafeteria Benefits

Some employers offer a variety of employee options called *cafeteria benefits*. Cafeteria-style benefits allow the employee to select specific benefits the employee wishes to receive from a predefined group. For example, an employer may offer an employee $1,000 in benefits, and let the employee choose to use the money to purchase a more expensive medical plan, purchase stock options, or invest in a retirement plan. With this type of plan, the employee can tailor the benefits to best fit the employee's requirements.

CHAPTER REVIEW

1. What items should you take to an interview?
2. What types of questions are illegal for an interviewer to ask?
3. What types of questions might an applicant want to ask during an interview?
4. List five reasons why applicants may be rejected for a job.
5. Discuss medical insurance as explained in this chapter.

ACTIVITIES

1. At home, practice your interview in front of a mirror. Watch your body movements, gestures, and facial expressions.
2. Listen to an audiotape of your voice. If your voice is whiny or high-pitched, it may be necessary to lower the pitch of your voice. Notice words that you continually repeat, such as *ah*, *huh*, and *ok*.
3. Videotape a mock interview, and then critique it either privately or in class. Use a partner and trade being the interviewee and being the interviewer. Prepare a list of questions that you will ask when you interview the other person.
4. Practice sitting. Are you sitting in a graceful, professional way? Is your body slouched? Is your body language demonstrating a positive or a negative attitude?
5. Practice smiling. Remember, a friendly employee is valued.
6. Practice walking in an assured manner. Keep your head high.
7. Talk with a member of your class and look the person in the eye.
8. Make a list of the questions you plan to ask a potential employer.
9. Ask a friend in business to do a mock interview with you and then critique it. Write a summary of the interview and the critique.
10. Invite a wardrobe consultant to talk with your class.
11. Go to two stores and look at appropriate clothing for an interview. Select two interview outfits and determine their cost. Talk with a sales representative about building an appropriate work wardrobe for yourself and determine the cost of this new wardrobe. Decide which purchases you would make immediately and which would be deferred to a later date. You are not actually purchasing the clothing. You are researching clothing availability, price, and style.
12. Select a job from the newspaper or an online source and prepare the following for that job.
    a. Letter of application
    b. Résumé
    c. Thank-you letter
13. Ask a company about the accommodations it has made for disabled persons.
14. Ask a company how it handles family medical leave requests.

PROJECTS

Project 25

Send this memo to the staff. It is from Annabel Lambton, Telecommunications Director.

Our long-awaited telephone system will be installed in three months. When the new telephone system is activated, all employee telephone numbers will change. To learn your new telephone number, click on the link www.R&JEnterprise.com/telephoneorder and key in your current number.

We have negotiated a special discounted business card order rate with our supplier. Each employee will receive 500 business cards at no charge to his or her department. The cost of the cards will be paid out of the Telecommunications budget. All business cards will follow the company established format. Business card orders must by received by February 20. Send an email with your name, new office telephone number, cell phone number, and fax number to Gesumwa Zhou.

Project 26

Write an email to all employees announcing an employee contest to name the company mascot. Create a flyer to attach to the email. You make all of the decisions.

HUMAN RELATIONS SKILL DEVELOPMENT

HR 13-1 Where Is My Coworker?

Although Josie comes to the office every day, after lunch she disappears for about an hour. Monday around 2 P.M. your supervisor walked past your office and asked if you had seen Josie, who works in the cubical next door to you. You replied no and continued to work. Tuesday at 2 P.M. your supervisor asked if you had seen Josie and again you replied no. Wednesday the same situation occurred. Now is it is 2:30 and Josie is still not in her office, so your supervisor asked you to look for her. You discover her taking a nap on the sofa in the conference room. When you walked into the room, Josie awakened. You then told her that your supervisor was looking for her.

- What do you say to your supervisor?
- How do you feel about the situation?
- What do you say to Josie?

HR 13-2 Budget

On June 1, all employees received an email from the Accounting Department informing them that the fiscal year was almost over and there were unexpended funds. You were asked to submit to your supervisor a list of items you wanted to purchase. The email from the Accounting Department indicated that all budget requests must be submitted by June 20. On June 2, you sent your list to your supervisor, who responded in an abrupt and curt tone of voice. He said he was busy with more important tasks and would get around to it later. Today is June 16. You really would like to have the items on your list.

- How do you handle the problem?

SITUATIONS

How would you handle the following situations?

- S 13-1 You continually receive brusque, angry, and short-tempered emails from a coworker. In last two weeks, you have received seven such emails. What options do you have?

- **S 13-2** Three weeks ago, you worked ten extra hours to complete an important rush project for which you were supposed to receive overtime pay. Your current pay stub does not include the overtime pay. Therefore on Monday, February 1, you sent Tiffany, who does the payroll for your department, a polite email asking that she check into the issue. Since you have not received a response by the following Monday, you again sent her an email. Instead of responding to you directly, she copied you on an email sent to the payroll department, asking that they confirm receiving an email from her on February 1 with your revised pay. The email paints you in a negative way. This copy is the only response you have received from Tiffany. You did not receive an earlier response telling you she had received the original email and was investigating the problem. How do you feel? What options do you have?

- **S 13-3** You are working on a team project and your co-chair is not pulling her weight. What options do you have?

PUNCTUATION REVIEW

Punctuate each of the following sentences. For a review of punctuation rules, see the Appendix.

1. If you have more than four attachments use form 704

2. Mr Rollins is always available to answer questions to provide advice and to guide his staff

3. In addition she returns phone calls immediately so that problems can be quickly resolved

4. Mr Biltmore who is from Chicago anticipates questions to avoid negative repercussions

5. During the evaluation period she worked six days a week to complete the work

6. In all of these activities she applied the knowledge and experiences she has gained throughout her career

7. As a result of consulting with the staff prior to the move the transition was less traumatic

8. To be considered for this position the applicant must apply online

9. Responsibilities will include leadership in planning organizing and evaluating proposals and budget forecasting

10. The Search Community which meets every Monday afternoon, is comprised of dedicated supervisors

11. Dr Mendez who is a graduate of the University of North Florida is the CEO of Wilmer Industries

12. Upon completion of the interviews the committee will forward five names to the President for review

13. In the past five years Dr Theodore has provided executive oversight and strategic leadership to all divisions

14. While serving as CEO Dr Solomon spearheaded the initiative

15. If you need a login form email me today

CD Assignments

CD Assignment 13-1

Open the file **CD13-1_IGS** on your Student CD and follow the instructions to complete the job.

CD Assignment 13-2

Open the file **CD13-2_MSV** on your Student CD and follow the instructions to complete the job.

CHAPTER 14

Career Advancement to Management

Objectives

After studying this chapter, you should be able to:

1. Understand downsizing and outsourcing.
2. Obtain a promotion.
3. Understand the procedures for changing jobs.
4. Negotiate a raise.
5. Work with a new supervisor.
6. Define and use the term *networking*.

CHANGES IN YOUR COMPANY

HINT

It is unusual to spend an entire career with only one employer.

It is rare today for an employee to spend a lifetime of work with only one company. Even if you intend to work with a firm for many years, changes in your personal life may result in the need to change jobs. Also, organizations experience change, and while some companies grow financially stronger over the years, others weaken. A company that was financially secure a few years ago may experience financial problems due to increasing competition, a slowdown in the economy, or other changes in the business climate. Furthermore, companies restructure and *downsize* or lay off employees, to reduce their costs and remain competitive with other businesses in their industry. The restructuring of a company may create an awkward working environment for the employees who remain after a downsizing because they often must perform the work of departed workers. In addition, the morale at the companies that have experienced restructuring may be very low.

As a way to reduce operating costs, some firms hire independent contractors who are not paid full benefits. A company may also engage in outsourcing job duties. *Outsourcing* is a method of shifting an office function from regular staff to an outside company. Usually the intent is to reduce costs and sometimes also to increase the level of service. For example, a small office may shift its payroll function from its own clerk to a business that specializes in processing payrolls. Because it specializes in preparing payrolls for many organizations, the outsource organization may be very experienced and proficient, and therefore may charge less than the original company

HINT

Outsourcing moves a job duty to an outside company.

would have to pay to complete its own payroll. Outsourcing often results in loss of jobs for the company's employees, though employees may be given the opportunity to join the organization that received the outsource contract. Job losses may also occur because in today's economic atmosphere, there is a trend to move jobs to other countries where labor and operating costs are less. This movement of jobs outside the country is called *offshoring*. As a result of the global telecommunications capabilities discussed earlier, many office-related jobs can be relocated off shore with no reduction in customer services.

In a rapidly changing business environment, no employee is guaranteed a job. Always be aware of your options for growth, training, advancement, and change. Keep your opportunities open and plan for your future.

GROWING IN YOUR PROFESSION

HINT
Stay on track.

With the passage of time, your career goals or job duties may change. You may decide that the first job you accepted was perfect at the time, but as you grew in job knowledge and proficiency, it no longer meets your expectations. Moving to a new job can be a lateral or vertical career change. A *lateral* career change is a change in duties but with the same level of responsibility as the current job, while a *vertical* career change is the acceptance of a position with more responsibilities than your present job. Both lateral and vertical career changes can result in an increase in salary.

Your education should not stop because you have a job. Employees must continually upgrade their skills. Some employers encourage their staff to take courses, while others require that a specific number of courses be taken each year, and many pay for training or retraining. Numerous avenues are available for retraining or updating your knowledge. They include college courses, seminars, workshops, CDs, DVDs, Internet courses, and audio and videotapes. Being successful in the workplace depends on a lifetime of learning.

HINT
Create a career map for yourself. Develop your career goals and objectives.

Perhaps you have continued to grow in your profession by taking courses or attending seminars. Furthermore, it is reasonable that you now want to use the knowledge that you have recently acquired. You may have to inform your employer about your new skills and your desire to use them in the office. If you cannot use these new skills in your current position, you may have to obtain another position either with your current employer or at another company. Listed below is a framework for planning your career.

Develop your own career plan
- Identify new duties that you would like to perform.
- List courses that you have taken.
- Summarize knowledge that you have gained.
- Search for courses that you should take to advance your career.
- Determine the knowledge that you must obtain through on-the-job training.
- Set your future goals.

HINT
Make a difference in your career by expanding and updating your knowledge and leadership skills.

This is not a once-a-year project but a continuous process that you should conduct throughout your professional career. When you have reached your goals or when you have become bored with your job, it is time to seek a change. A job without a challenge can be humdrum and dull. If you are not challenged, you will not produce to the best of your ability. It is important to remember that you do not want to become stagnant in your job. The potential for advancement is up to you, but you must show initiative and a desire to be promoted to a new and challenging job.

The opportunity for professional advancement is only one reason for you to seek a new assignment. You may have taken your present job knowing that it was not the career of your dreams, but you had to accept it for financial reasons. There may be a personality conflict between you and your supervisor or between you and a coworker. Your present job may not be giving you enough responsibility or you may be disenchanted with the duties. Your personal situation may require that you have a position with a higher salary. Any of these reasons may be motivation for your desire for advancement.

Before you talk with your employer, decide what kind of a change you want. Do you want new responsibilities with your current firm, or do you want to move to a new company? By analyzing your career plan, you will be able to discuss your concerns intelligently with your supervisor.

Demonstrate Your Excellence

HINT
Show your supervisor that you are a top-notch employee.

Not everyone deserves a promotion. In today's business climate, you must prove that you deserve any promotion, job change, or salary increase. To obtain the change you desire, you must demonstrate outstanding performance in two critical areas—initiative and excellence of work. Demonstrate that you are a top-level person who is valuable to the company and earns the salary you are being paid.

To establish a reputation for initiative and excellence of work:

- Read and comprehend the information you work with on your job. This is a good way to learn about the company and its projects.
- Offer to draft reports for your supervisor. Also offer to edit reports written by other employees.
- Be financially responsible and develop money-saving techniques that increase efficiency.
- Do not be a clock watcher. Be willing to arrive early or stay late if it is necessary to complete an important project on time.
- Be courteous to the clients and to all employees regardless of their job status.
- Take advantage of company training programs to learn new skills. Also, update your present skills as technology changes.
- Learn about something that no one has yet learned. After you become an expert, you can train the other employees.
- Learn new software packages and offer to train other employees in their use.
- Let your supervisor know that you are active in professional activities.
- Always be professional in the way you dress and act.

MY SUCCESS STORY

My Name Is Laura

I love music, and it is my life. I always wanted to work in the music field, but I must face reality: I am just not that talented. Therefore, I decided to combine my love of music with my career in business. After getting my education, I landed an entry-level job with my local symphony. I have worked my way up, and now I am the assistant to the managing director of the symphony. My job is dynamic and awesome because it combines my passion for music with my business skills. My job allows me to earn a living while pursing my ambition of working in the performing arts.

- Complete each project accurately and promptly. Always meet every deadline.
- Read professional journals so you are aware of developments in your field.
- Be consistent with your excellent performance. Do not allow yourself to slip even for one day.
- Tell your supervisor that you are ready for a new and challenging project. Then develop the project and obtain the desired results.

As you establish a reputation for initiative and excellent work, make yourself more visible to management by letting others know about your accomplishments. When you meet a goal or successfully complete a project, diplomatically let your coworkers know about it. Management usually hears news through the grapevine. If your company has a staff newsletter, send a note to the editor listing your recent achievement.

Indicate that you are planning to stay with the company for a long time. Discreetly inform your supervisor that you have no desire to find a new job because you enjoy your current and anticipated responsibilities. In addition, talk with your supervisor about your desire for advancement and your willingness to try other challenging assignments. Present your supervisor with a detailed plan for your advancement, and include in your plan projects on which you would like to work so you may grow in your job responsibilities.

Carefully analyze your present job description and work with your supervisor to redesign your current position into the career you want. Then rewrite the job description, including the new tasks you plan to complete, but omit the tasks that you feel are no longer important. Prepare a justification that supports your recommendation that those tasks be omitted entirely or reassigned to another colleague.

> **HINT**
> Set your goals and follow through.

Certification of Competency

One way to demonstrate your excellence is to pass national tests that document your office skills. There are several organizations that will certify your office skills. Passing the tests developed by these organizations is solid evidence of your competency in these areas.

Microsoft Office Specialist Certification

Microsoft has developed many software packages that are used in businesses and has created an opportunity for office employees to validate their desktop computer skills. The Microsoft Office Specialist certification is a comprehensive testing program designed to test Microsoft Office skills. The examinations are given in many languages and at sites throughout the world. Tests are given for Word, Excel, Outlook, PowerPoint, Access, and Project. Employers use Microsoft Office Specialist certification as a screening tool to validate a job candidate's knowledge and to promote employees to new positions. Additional information can be obtained from Microsoft's Web site.

International Association of Administrative Professionals

One avenue for advancement in your career is to become a Certified Professional Secretary (CPS) or a Certified Administrative Professional (CAP). The CPS and CAP are professional titles granted only to those individuals who meet the educational and work-experience requirements developed by the International Association of Administrative Professionals.

Employers may look for CPS or CAP certification as verification of your knowledge and skills and may recognize this achievement with an increase in salary. Many colleges offer credit for passing the CPS and CAP exams. The CPS and CAP exams are given twice a year, in May and November. Prior to taking the exam it would be wise to take a CPS or CAP review course and to study the CPS and CAP Review Modules. Information about the CPS and CAP exams is available from the International Association of Administrative Professionals at www.iaap-hq.org.

Asking for a Raise

A *raise* is an increase in salary, and a *promotion* brings changes such as better benefits, a preferable job assignment, a more desirable office, a new title, or improved working conditions. A promotion may occur either with or without a salary increase, and a salary increase does not imply a promotion. A salary increase can be given to all employees to reflect inflation, often called a *cost-of-living adjustment*, or may be the result of having worked at the company for a fixed period of time.

An employee can ask for a salary increase or promotion as a reward for his or her level of performance. Employees can also ask for a salary increase because the employee believes that he or she is being paid less than comparable employees. Before you ask for a raise or promotion, research the job market to determine the accepted salary range for the duties you perform. As you research salary ranges for the type of job you have, remember that salary ranges can vary considerably from one geographic area to another. Also, survey the job market to determine what types of jobs are available for people with your qualifications. In addition, maintain a file of your accomplishments, positive comments from colleagues and supervisors, and review this file prior to your performance evaluation.

Prepare a detailed list of your achievements, including problems that you solved as well as projects you organized, developed, and completed. Now that you have decided to request a raise or promotion, hand your list of achievements to the supervisor when you discuss the potential for a raise.

Before you make the decision to negotiate a raise or promotion, consider all of your options first. Do not go into your supervisor's office without considering the fact that your request may not be granted. Listed below are issues to think about prior to requesting a raise or promotion.

- If you do not get the raise or promotion you want, how would you feel?
- Would not receiving the salary increase or promotion cause a strained relationship between you and your supervisor?
- Would an improvement in benefits, a better office, or improved working conditions be an acceptable alternative to you?
- Would the promise of a raise or promotion in a few months be acceptable to you?
- What amount is acceptable to you in terms of a raise and what is not acceptable?
- What other alternatives would you consider? Would you consider resigning from the position?

If your request is turned down, ask why. If your supervisor states that you do not deserve a raise or promotion, ask what job tasks and objectives you must fulfill. Indicate that you plan to meet those objectives by your next job evaluation. Although you feel you are ready for a raise or promotion, you supervisor may not agree. If that is the case, you may receive the following comment: "I am sorry that I cannot grant your request now, but I am training you for your career advancement by giving you additional assignments and projects." This response may indicate that as soon as you have the knowledge and experience, you have the opportunity for a promotion.

If you did not receive the salary increase or promotion you requested, do not resign immediately. There are many considerations to be made before resigning a job.

In some businesses, salary increases are granted as part of a group compensation package. Persons employed by government agencies generally fall into this category. This type of package provides all employees who have satisfactory evaluations a cost of living increase and/or a step increase based on length of employment. Furthermore, in some companies, employees have an annual performance review, and at that time a salary increase may be discussed.

Do you deserve a raise or promotion?

HINT

Carefully weigh your decision to seek a new job.

MAKING A JOB CHANGE

Is It Time to Change Employers?

If you are thinking of resigning your job, do not make a hasty decision to leave. Everyone has bad days and thinks of quitting. Make a list of the positive and negative aspects of the job. Which list is longer? Which list contains the most important items? Weigh the decision to leave very carefully.

Before you change jobs, it is important to understand why you want to leave your job. The traditional reason for changing jobs is for a higher salary or more responsibilities. But there are also other reasons. Sometimes workers leave a company when they no longer feel part of the "family." This loss can result from colleagues leaving the company or from a feeling of dissatisfaction. When employees are not rewarded and are not respected, they lose pride in the company and in their work. This discontentment and disappointment can become the impetus for the move.

Before changing a job, ask yourself the following questions.

HINT

Take charge of your life.

- What do I expect from a new position?
- Am I satisfied with my present job? Why not?
- What changes would I like to make?
- What do I like about my supervisor?
- What do I dislike about my supervisor?
- What characteristics would I like to see in a supervisor?
- Is my present salary reasonable?
- What should my salary be?
- What types of projects do I like doing?
- What types of projects do I dislike doing?
- What opportunities are there for advancement in my present job?
- Which companies have better opportunities for me?
- Whom do I know who works for a company that might provide opportunities for me?
- Am I satisfied with my job location?
- Would a better job location be important enough to prompt me to change jobs?
- Am I willing to commute a longer distance for a better job?
- If I have a personality conflict with my supervisor or with a coworker, is it serious enough to cause me to seek another job?
- Am I better off staying with this job a little while longer or looking for a new job?

Thoroughly research other positions in the same company and decide if there are openings for which you might qualify. If the reason you are leaving your job is for more money, discuss this with your supervisor because you may be offered a higher salary.

If you are leaving because of a problem with a coworker, your job responsibilities, or poor working conditions, discuss the problem with your supervisor. The supervisor may be able to resolve the problem so you will not have to change your job.

If you do decide to leave, wait before you notify anyone because you may change your mind. Quitting immediately will not solve all of your problems, and you will face the challenge of looking for a new job. In addition, you may not leave until you have a new job. After you announce your decision to leave, stick with the decision. You will appear ambivalent if you constantly change your mind about leaving and will weaken your credibility if you stay.

When you decide to change jobs, assess your skills. Examine all of the opportunities available without limiting yourself to your current type of position. Most employees have skills that are common to all jobs and therefore can be transferred to a position in another field. These transferable skills include the areas of management, human relations, training, organization, computers, teamwork, oral and written communications, public speaking, etc. When seeking a new position, do not limit yourself to your current job type. By using your transferable skills, you can explore all options regardless of the job category.

HINT
Compare salaries for similar positions in comparably sized companies.

Looking for a New Job

After you have made the decision to seek other employment, you must decide whether to give immediate notice of your resignation or to begin your job search while you are still employed. Most people simply cannot go without a salary for a long period of time between jobs and must begin their search for a new position while continuing with their current employer.

If you continue in your old job while searching for a new one, you must handle your job search with discretion. You should not tell coworkers you are looking for other employment, work on your résumé at the office, or use the office telephone to set up interviews. Job-seeking phone calls can be made during your lunch break from your cell phone or from a pay phone outside your office complex. Once your decision to seek other employment is known by your supervisor, you may not receive choice assignments. People will think you are no longer interested in your present job, and your supervisor's attitude toward you may change. Therefore, keep the news of your job search away from your coworkers as long as possible because it may take an extended period of time to find a new position.

Keeping your job hunt a secret may require planning on your part. Interviews should be set after work, but some recruiters may not accommodate your schedule. It may be necessary to take a day of leave from your current job to interview for a new position. If you frequently take leave, your current employer may discover that you are seeking a new job. Also, dressing for the interview can focus unwanted attention on you. If your workplace is casual and you appear at work in a suit, your supervisor may guess that you are looking for a job. One solution is to dress in casual attire and change before you go to the interview. Another option is to dress up for several weeks so people will not suspect that you are looking for a job.

Your job search should include the techniques discussed in Chapter 12. Additionally, talk with others in your field, and let your contacts know that you are ready for a new challenge. You should also use two techniques discussed later in this chapter: networking and becoming active with professional organizations.

What are the roadblocks to your career advancement?

The Trailing Spouse

In a two-career family, a problem occurs when one person's career requires relocation to another city. The remaining spouse may be perfectly content with his or her current job but will usually want to move to be with the spouse. If the employee is being transferred to another location of a large company, the company may be able to provide job assistance to the trailing spouse. Even if an employee is moving to a new community to accept a position with a new employer, that employer may offer assistance to place the trailing spouse in a suitable position. If your relocation will create a trailing spouse in your house, speak to the personnel office of the new employer about whether they can provide job assistance to reunite your family.

LEAVING THE OLD JOB

Letter of Resignation

Since considerable time and money is spent training employees, most employers would like good employees to stay in their job forever. That is not a realistic situation in our mobile society. Although employers frown upon job hopping, it is acceptable to change a job after two years. In large metropolitan cities, it may be acceptable to stay in a job for only one year. However, a record of constant job-hopping may jeopardize your chances of future employment.

If you do decide to change employers, do it courteously and graciously. When you leave a job, do not voice all of your grievances and past problems with the office and your coworkers. Leaving on a negative note will influence how people remember you. They will remember the negative comments, not the terrific job skills you had. You may need help from your coworkers as future references, or they could eventually be employed at the same company where you work, so their thoughts about you are important. You reputation is valuable; do not tarnish it.

Tell your supervisor about your decision to leave before you tell your friends and coworkers. It would be embarrassing for you if your supervisor heard from another source of your decision to leave the company. Select the right time and atmosphere in which to tell your supervisor of your new job. Indicate that you have enjoyed working with the supervisor and the company, but you have received an employment offer that you cannot refuse. Since your leaving may present a problem for the supervisor, be prepared for the possibility that your supervisor may not be happy with your decision to leave.

It is customary to give at least two weeks' notice before leaving a position. To demonstrate your professionalism, always offer to train your replacement and complete any projects in progress. A letter of resignation should be given to your supervisor when you resign. The letter should express your satisfaction with the company, demonstrate your professionalism, and indicate the date you intend to leave. You do not need to include the name of your new company or when you will begin working at the new job.

Although you have made the decision to leave and have notified your employer, you are still employed by the company. Therefore, you still are still working and have job duties to complete. This is not the time to slack off the job.

After you leave the company, continue to maintain contact with your supervisor and colleagues. Later you may need to ask for advice or even a reference for another job. Email is an easy way to continue contact. It is also a good idea to meet for lunch or an after-work drink.

Leaving a job is not easy—whether you enjoyed the job or hated it. Because of emotional attachments at your current organization, you probably have a feeling of belonging to the company, pride in your job, and camaraderie with your colleagues. Leaving a job and moving to a new endeavor can create stress and a sense of uncertainty, but you will also be able to look forward to a new future and a stimulating new job.

Will you miss your coworkers?

HINT
Inform your supervisor of your new job prior to telling your colleagues.

HINT
When leaving a job, give at least two weeks' notice.

September 10, XXXX

Mr. Jerry Edens, Director
Watson, Inc.
3000 Running Brook
Forest Grove, OR 97116

Dear Mr. Edens:

I have enjoyed the three years that I have been employed by Watson Inc., but the time has come for me to accept another position. I have been offered a position too promising for me to decline so my last day of employment at Watson, Inc. will be September 27.

I realize how important it is to have continuity for my projects; therefore, I will complete all current projects prior to my last day here at Waston's. In addition, I will be glad to train my replacement so all ongoing projects will continue in a satisfactory manner.

Because of the many opportunities I have experienced here, I have grown a great deal in my field. I know that I will miss everyone at Watson's. Thank you for your help and consideration during the last three years.

Sincerely,

Alicia Webster

Figure 14-1 Letter of resignation.

The Employer's Perspective of Employee Turnover

Leaving a job is hard on both the employee and the employer. When an employee leaves a company voluntarily or is asked to leave, turnover occurs, and turnover is costly—regardless of the reason for leaving. As you deal with the reaction of your supervisor and coworkers to your leaving, remember that they are considering the following:

Costs of employee turnover
- Hiring and training of replacements.
- Necessity of covering the position before a new person is hired.
- Loss of expertise.
- Negative effect on current employees and their morale.
- Clients may leave and follow an employee.
- Loss of time, knowledge of, and proficiency of ongoing projects.
- Employees often leave jobs when their coworkers leave the company because they experience a loss of family, so they in turn look for other opportunities.

Job Dismissal

In today's complex business world, people are released from a job for a variety of reasons. The traditional reasons for being fired are poor work habits and personality conflicts, but a company reorganization plan may result in a change of duties and dismissals. Furthermore as budgets are reduced, company cost-saving initiatives may trigger layoffs. It is important to remember that losing a job does not mean you were incompetent.

If you are released from your job, assess why you lost the job. If the situation occurred because of circumstances that you could not control, such as companywide layoffs, accept the situation and seek another position.

If you were fired because of problems you could change, you should evaluate the situation carefully and alter your behavior. For example, if you lost your job because you were rude to someone, make an effort to improve your personality. Do not carry the same problems to a new job. If a prospective employer asks why you were fired, be honest. State the reason for the dismissal, and then state how you have corrected the problem.

The loss of a job, even if it was not your fault, is a still a blow to your ego and self-esteem. Always try to leave the company on a positive note, even if you have negative feelings about the job or you were dismissed. After you have recovered from the initial shock of the job dismissal, spend time building your self-confidence and doing something you enjoy. Spend time with your family and friends, and relax a little to gain a positive and optimistic attitude. Then accept the challenge of a job search and go on with your life. Maintain a positive outlook on your job search and notify business associates, friends, and everyone you know that you are now career transitioning.

> **HINT**
> Do not let a job loss destroy your self-confidence.

Departure Procedures

Leaving a job does not mean just walking out the door and saying goodbye. Most companies have specific procedures that must be followed whether the employee left the job because of a new job, layoff, dismissal, illness, or retirement.

The following are typical procedures that employees must follow when leaving jobs:

- The immediate supervisor must sign off that the employee is leaving.
- Building security must sign off that all keys have been returned.
- The company library must sign off that all books have been returned.
- Human Resources must sign off that leave, health, or retirement benefits have been applied for and discussed.
- Computer staff must delete passwords.
- The travel department must confirm that there are no outstanding travel advances.
- The property department must confirm that the employee does not have company property at home. The same department must confirm that all of the employee's equipment on the inventory is on company grounds.

To expedite the sign-off procedures, a form may be hand-carried from one person to another. In the case of an emergency illness where the employee is unable to hand-carry the forms, another employee may be asked to perform this duty. If all discharge forms are not completed appropriately, the final paycheck may be held.

Retirement

Although you hope to start a promising career with a new company, some of your colleagues may be ready for the next stage in their careers—retirement or reduced-workload retirement. It is important for a new employee to understand the feelings and concerns of employees at the other end of the work spectrum. Employees nearing retirement may be reluctant to end their career and jump into the next step, which they have not fully defined. While some employees are excited about and looking forward to retirement, others are reluctant. Therefore, some companies are offering an ease-into-retirement option with reduced workloads. This can be a winning situation for both the employee and the employer. The employer maintains a secure and stable workforce while providing flexibility and more freedom to the employee. This decision also permits established employees the opportunity to train and mentor new employees, which benefits the company.

Continuation of Health Insurance Under COBRA

For many people, the second greatest impact of the loss of a job (the first being loss of salary) is the loss of health insurance. In 1986 Congress passed the Consolidated Omnibus Budget Reconciliation Act, often identified as COBRA, which gives some former employees, retirees, spouses, and dependent children the ability to continue their employee group health coverage after they lose their jobs. While the entire COBRA continuation insurance premium is paid by the employee (without employer copayment), the premium will be at a group rate and therefore will be less expensive than purchasing coverage at an individual policy rate. Health insurance under COBRA is generally available for eighteen months, but the period may be extended for persons with disabilities. Further information about COBRA continuation insurance can be found on the Internet at www.dol.gov/dol/topic/health-plans/cobra.htm.

> **HINT**
> COBRA allows workers to maintain health insurance benefits.

OBTAINING ASSISTANCE

Networking

Growing in your chosen career includes meeting other professionals. One of the terms used today for meeting and forming your own group of professional contacts is networking. A *network* is an informal association of business associates who can provide assistance to each other. A group of business associates meeting and sharing ideas at a business meeting, at home, or at a party can be a network. A network is not a formal organization and may consist of only one or two other people who, in turn, know a few other people. When you attend business or social meetings and parties, talk with other professionals and exchange business cards. Then arrange to meet for lunch or after work. Become friendly with people and periodically speak to them on the telephone. When you or another member of your network needs business assistance, you have friends, or friends of friends, to contact who can make helpful suggestions and recommendations. A network would be advantageous to you if you are looking for a job because people in your network can recommend companies and employers to you. Since people like to assist, ask members of your network for suggestions to improve your career and to move up the corporate ladder. In our time-crunch world, most people still feel that they can spare at least a couple of minutes to help guide their friends and associates.

> **HINT**
> Think about your professional development tools.

Professional Organizations

A professional organization can help you grow in your field. Professional organizations expose their members to new and changing ideas, provide discussions on and solutions to important problems, and provide a means of meeting other professionals in the field. There are professional organizations for persons interested in almost every field, and attending meetings of professional organizations is an excellent opportunity to network.

WORKING WITH A NEW SUPERVISOR

Starting on the Right Foot with a New Supervisor

Employee turnover at all levels is very common in the workplace. At some time in your career, it is likely that your supervisor will change jobs while you remain in the same position. A new supervisor will have different ideas about how to manage situations. You will have to relate to the new supervisor's operating style and personality, so give yourself time to adapt to the restructured office environment.

Suggestions for success with a new supervisor

- Do not indicate that the former supervisor did something in a certain way and that method was the only correct procedure. Accept the fact that two managers do not have the same work style or ideas. You should realize that there are many ways to reach the same goal.
- Accept the change and decide that you will profit and learn from the new situation.
- Always be courteous.

Figure 14-2   A Successful employee.

- As soon as possible, make an appointment to talk with the new supervisor about your job responsibilities. Have a copy of your job description with you so you and your supervisor can compare your current job description with the new supervisor's expectations.

- Let your supervisor know that you are ready and willing to work as part of the team.

- Offer to answer any questions you can to acquaint the supervisor with ongoing projects.

- Do not relay stories about your impressions of the new supervisor to other coworkers. Do not gossip with your coworkers about your supervisor.

- Give the new supervisor time to meet the challenges of the job. If you are unhappy with the new supervisor's attitude or performance, wait. It may take a few months for the supervisor to adjust to his or her new responsibilities. If you are dissatisfied with the new supervisor's management style, it is a good idea to wait at least six months before you consider looking for another job.

Observe how the new manager assumes the responsibilities of leadership. You can learn from observing two different managers' styles and approaches to the problems present in your office. The more you learn from your supervisors, the easier it will be for you to become a supervisor or manager.

BECOMING A MANAGER OR SUPERVISOR

If you are in an entry-level position, your goal may be to advance to the position of *supervisor* or *manager*. The two terms are often used interchangeably. Both terms refer to people who direct or administer the activities of a business. Some businesses have many layers of management, with each level of management responsible for increasingly larger portions of the organization. But whether a person manages a division or just a single project with no employees to supervise, managers at all levels must deal with many of the same concerns—motivating and guiding.

As you advance to a position of supervision, your perspective, your duties, and your responsibilities will change. Many of the techniques discussed earlier in this chapter will help build the experience, reputation for excellence, and initiative you will need to move into management.

> Do you have management potential?

> What is your leadership style?

A Manager's Duties

Supervise a staff

- Guide employees during normal daily business activities and through periods of chaos. Generally, employees want someone to assist them in solving problems.

- When possible, empower your employees to make decisions.

- Encourage employees to work to the peak of their abilities and capitalize on each person's strength.

- Encourage employees to grow, retrain, and update their skills. Although employees want to improve, they often need direction and leadership to reach their goals.

- Plan and supervise training for employees in a fast-changing technological world.

- Encourage each employee to become more knowledgeable of company policies and to grow within the company.

HINT

Engage your employees in the job.

- Be objective, not critical, when an employee discusses a concern with you.
- Be an advocate for your staff.
- Demonstrate that you are proud of your staff.
- Do not show partiality or favoritism.
- If a conflict arises, listen to each employee's comments before making a decision
- Treat each employee with dignity and courtesy.
- Do not betray employee confidences.
- Encourage the employee to communicate with you and to seek assistance when necessary.
- Create effective teams.
- Encourage competent employees to be acting supervisors while you are on a vacation or traveling on business. It is in your best interests to prepare employees to accept the responsibilities associated with higher-level jobs and become potential supervisors.
- Recognize that employees may have personal or family problems that may occasionally interfere with their work. These problems might include personality conflicts, being unqualified to complete some jobs, having negative feelings about the office, and allowing personal problems to affect the ability to produce effectively on the job. Depending on the problem, it may be necessary for the supervisor to refer the employee to a counselor or physician.

Develop departmental plans

- Support the company's mission and philosophy.
- Know the company's written and unwritten polices to ensure that they are properly followed.
- Create performance objectives for your department that fulfill the company's mission.
- Identify the human and financial resources required to meet the objectives for next year's proposed budget plan.
- Ask your staff members what you can do to make their work experience more upbeat and positive.

Set goals and deadlines

Are you a good supervisor?

- Plan work schedules so that all work is completed by the due date. To reach this objective, you must be knowledgeable of the project and have the ability to realistically determine the amount of time necessary to complete a project.
- Establish an equitable division of the workload.
- Design, implement, and work within the framework of a department budget.
- Review assignments with employees before the completion date of a project. A periodic review of projects reduces the chance of a last-minute crisis. By monitoring the progress of a project, there will be time to take corrective action if the project is not progressing toward its planned goals, if the employee needs assistance, or if the job requires additional staff.

Implement procedures to improve productivity and customer service

- Purchasing supplies and equipment is necessary for the efficient operation of your office.

- Manage department and company resources.

- Do not ignore a problem, because dismissing it may allow it to escalate.

- Mediate office problems

- Listen to employees' suggestions, accept the best ideas, and reject less favorable recommendations without damaging employee morale.

- Discuss your plans and goals for the company with the employees.

- Inform employees of any changes you anticipate.

- Understand the duties and skills involved in all of the projects that you assign to your employees.

- Monitor employee and customer interaction.

Hiring and disciplining employees

- Hiring employees requires selecting the best person for the job, which includes knowing the objectives and skills necessary for the position.

- Employee evaluation may require the development of assessment forms and a personal conference with the employee.

- Disciplining subordinates is a difficult job, requiring diplomacy and objectivity. It is easy to become involved in the personal life of an employee and overlook negative work situations.

- As a supervisor, you must decide when to reprimand an employee or make remarks that criticize his or her performance. Furthermore, reprimands or suggestions for improvement should be delivered in private, not in front of other staff members. These instances should conclude on a positive note, such as, "I know you have the ability to make the appropriate changes."

A good manager always remembers that excellent employees reflect positively on the manager, the entire department, and the company.

HINT
Are you a forward-thinking manager?

Figure 14-3   Dressed for a meeting with a client.

Problem-Solving Techniques

An important skill for office supervisors is the ability to understand and apply problem-solving techniques. A manager who cannot solve problems is ineffective.

Suggestions for solving problems

- Define the problem.
- Develop several possible solutions.
- Write the positive and negative points of each possible solution.
- Analyze and consider each point.
- Study the ramifications of each possible solution.
- Make a list of the people who will be affected by the decision.
- Consider how this type of problem was solved in the past.
- Consider whether the solution being considered may set a precedent. After making this decision, would it be difficult to reach a different decision in the future for a similar problem?

Distance Managing

In today's technology-driven workplace, employees often work and are managed from a distance. Administrators who telecommute or who manage employees who telecommute have special issues with which to contend. The success of the employee or manager depends on the ability to create a working environment without the traditional walls, office chats, and comaraderie. Employees who work outside the traditional office need to be part of the office community, and creating a workable office community is the responsibility of the manager supervising the employee.

Suggestions for managing a telecommuting staff

- Make sure the telecommuting employee has the proper telecommunications equipment.
- Employees who telecommute must be kept informed of all office actions but not overloaded with nonessential information.
- Do not overload the telecommuting employee with email.
- Employees who work off-site need immediate feedback on all projects. Without accurate and worthwhile feedback, employees cannot fulfill the company's objectives.
- Check periodically with the telecommuting employee. Always try to be available when they call or email.

Motivation Incentives

Employees should be recognized and rewarded as often as possible. A thank you from the supervisor for a job well done can occur daily. Furthermore, recognition is not something that should be given once a year during the performance evaluation process. Praising an employee reinforces positive conduct and encourages the employee to succeed. Recognition should be given in private and also before peers. Supervisors should praise all employees, not only the best or favorite employee. Sometimes it is difficult to find something positive to say about the mediocre employee, but the supervisor who does find something positive to say may raise the employee's self-esteem and encourage the employee to become a better worker.

When praise is used properly, it can be a motivational tool. Praise is a reward that the supervisor gives the employee, but the supervisor must be comfortable commending the employee for it to be beneficial. If the supervisor is uncomfortable praising an employee, the supervisor's attitude will be apparent to the employee. In addition, the supervisor's feelings and attitudes will be evident in gestures and other nonverbal messages. The motivational advantage of the acknowledgment will be worthless if the praise is not given in a positive manner. Recognition motivates employees to achieve success, improves employee morale, and creates an employee-oriented work environment. Companies who reward their people gain employee respect and gratitude.

The following is a list of employee morale boosters that can be used if permitted by company policy. Some of these morale boosters require small outlays of money; some do not.

Recognize employees with special privileges

- Permission to leave a few hours early before a holiday.
- Morning or afternoon off after completing an important project.
- Frequent-flyer miles.
- Special parking space.
- Employee-of-the-month award.
- Stars of the Department display with pictures of the employee.
- Great Employee certificates or trophies.
- Permission to wear casual clothing for a week.

Recognize employees with food

- Have lunch delivered to the office.
- Provide a pizza, ice cream, or popcorn party.
- Give gifts of candy, cake, cookies, fruit, turkey, ham, etc.
- Provide snacks of cookies, pastries, or bagels.
- Invite the employee to a private lunch.
- Have a birthday lunch.

Give gifts of recognition

- Company T-shirts, hats, or mugs.
- Gifts of flowers and plants.
- Holiday parties (Halloween, Thanksgiving, Valentine's Day, Groundhog Day, etc.).
- Company-provided weekend getaway packages.
- Calendar with employees' pictures.
- Company-provided home computers.
- DVD or CD gift.
- Gift certificate for lunch, dinner, movies, video store, shopping mall, etc.
- Inexpensive gift from a business trip.
- Conduct a contest to design the company bumper sticker, mug, or T-shirt contest and award a prize to the winner.
- Create a company mascot contest and award a prize to the winner.
- Day at a spa.
- On-site neck and back massage.
- A monetary reward of $25, $50, or $100.

Use written recognition

- Place a "thank you" in the company newsletter.
- Place a letter of recognition in the employee's file.
- Email a "thank you" to the employee with a copy to coworkers.

Communities and growth opportunities

- Create a workplace community where employees become a family and work together. In so doing, members of a community help each other during the challenging times of life. This caring environment also encourages employees to talk about their families and share their cultural backgrounds.
- Create a "lunch and chat program" as part of a workplace community. During the lunch break, employees share tips about the office or home, or their personal ideas.
- Company-sponsored sabbaticals provide opportunities to study or reinvigorate the employee.
- Company-subsidized release time for employees to work on community projects. Giving back to the community is a rewarding experience and looked upon with favor by employers and communities.

The motivational incentives discussed can perk up employee moral and make a humdrum office setting more amiable, congenial, and employee friendly.

Welcoming a New Employee

HINT

Making a new employee feel comfortable can help him or her quickly become a member of the team.

One of the responsibilities of the supervisor is to welcome new employees and introduce them to their workplace and coworkers. The following are suggestions to help you orient new employees:

- Provide a tour of the department.
- Introduce the employee to department members.
- Assign a mentor from the department.
- Explain the daily work routine.
- Explain when and where breaks and lunch are taken.
- Explain the department's objectives.
- Explain how the employee's job relates to other jobs in the department and in the company.
- Explain the company organization chart.
- Explain building fire and safety procedures.

Evaluation

One of the duties of the supervisor is evaluating employees' job performance. Evaluations should be based on realistic criteria, not on subjective thoughts. The supervisor should keep running records of employee successes in a file, as well as instances when an employee performed poorly or had to be reprimanded. Prior to the evaluation, the supervisor should review the employee's file. In today's team-driven workplace, an evaluation may include the outcome of team projects in addition to personal tasks. Review the sample evaluation form in Figure 14-4 and revise it to meet the specific objectives of your office. The specific duties of each employee as listed on the job description would be placed on that employee's evaluation form. The performance evaluation should rate how well the employee is performing the job duties contained in the job description. Prior to completing an employee's evaluation,

EMPLOYEE EVALUATION FORM

Name: _____

Job Title: _____

Date: _____

Supervisor: _____

Complete the following for each duty in the job description
1 = Unsatisfactory   2 = Marginal   3 = Acceptable
4 = Commendable   5 = Outstanding

Duty: _____   Rating: 1 2 3 4 5
Comments: _____

Duty: _____   Rating: 1 2 3 4 5
Comments: _____

Duty: _____   Rating: 1 2 3 4 5
Comments: _____

Duty: _____   Rating: 1 2 3 4 5
Comments: _____

Duty: _____   Rating: 1 2 3 4 5
Comments: _____

Work Habits: _____   Rating: 1 2 3 4 5
Comments: _____

Cooperativeness: _____   Rating: 1 2 3 4 5
Comments: _____

Flexibility: _____   Rating: 1 2 3 4 5
Comments: _____

Initiative: _____   Rating: 1 2 3 4 5
Comments: _____

Overall Rating: _____   Rating: 1 2 3 4 5
Comments: _____

Figure 14-4   An employee evaluation form.

the supervisor should review past performance evaluations and compare past evaluations with current performance. The supervisor should also review whether there are changes in the employee's duties or changes in the workplace that could impact employee performance. While company policy determines how often a review is conducted, standard times for reviews are three months, six months, or yearly.

BUSINESS STRATEGIES

Conflict Resolution

Conflict resolution is a term often used to describe a process used for solving conflicts. For supervisors, solving conflicts may be a daily occurrence. Even if you are not a supervisor, you will often be placed in situations where you will have to resolve conflicts between employees or between clients and employees. Petty disagreements may evolve into long-term conflicts if they are not resolved quickly and diplomatically. As an office employee, it is important to become an expert at conflict resolution and to learn to use a nonaccusatory and constructive approach to resolving problems. Always remember that a cooperative workplace is a more productive workplace, and the ability to solve conflicts can be a step toward your advancement.

Conflicts between people can erupt for numerous reasons. Sometimes people bring their personal problems and attitudes to the office and create an environment that results in conflicts with coworkers. Many arguments begin without malicious intent but continue to grow and create a destructive climate. One person can be insulted or feel taken advantage of, while the other person is oblivious to the situation. All employees should understand the reasons conflicts occur so they can reconcile them immediately. Listed below are circumstances that may cause conflicts.

- Needs are ignored.
- Needs are incompatible.
- Misperceptions exist.
- Guidelines have not been established.
- People do not listen to what others say.
- People have different ideas.
- People have differences in values and principles.

To resolve arguments, it is essential to understand the origin of the disagreement and to recognize that conflicts are part of an overall relationship. Prior to solving the problem, there must be a clarification of ideas and an identification of hidden conflicts or thoughts. Without this component, the dilemma may never be resolved. A nonargumentive conversation with all concerned parties may be the first step in solving a conflict. The parties need to be open-minded and interested in altering their attitudes. The workplace atmosphere, timing, and comments from involved parties all join together to resolve or ignite a conflict. To be successful, conflict resolution must address each party's underlying concerns, improve their relationship, and provide benefits to both parties. In addition, it is important to learn from past experience and realize what can and cannot be accomplished.

Conflict resolution suggestions

- Be objective.
- Identify the issue.
- Identify the results each person wants.
- Do not become emotionally involved in the issue.
- Offer suggestions to solve the problem.

Your Personal Conflict-Resolution Style

It is important that you understand and, if necessary, modify your own behavior prior to attempting to resolve problems in your office. Critically answer each question below and evaluate your personality style. Then review your answers and devise a plan to improve your temperament.

- Do you know when not to express your opinion?
- Do you sometimes not express your opinions as a method of avoiding conflict?
- Do you shout when you are angry?
- Do you overreact to situations?
- Do you like to antagonize others?
- Do you make sarcastic comments?
- Can you control your emotions?
- Do you enjoy arguments?
- When angry, do you make negative comments unrelated to the real issues?
- Do you allow irritation to hinder important business relationships?
- Do you blame your colleagues for your problems?
- Do you have a negative personality?

If you are aware of your conflict-management style, you can make changes to improve it so you will be more successful when working with others.

Critical Thinking

Critical thinking is a thought process often used to solve problems. In critical thinking, the first step is to define the issue and then to design a creative, preliminary solution to the problem. One of the goals of critical thinking is create an accurate statement of the problem. This is very important because if the problem is not correctly defined, the solution will not solve the problem and the result will fail. Since all employees may not see the problem the same way and may not agree on what the problem really is, it is often difficult to reach agreement on how to clearly define the problem.

After the problem is defined, the next step is to develop a solution. Critical thinking uses an unlimited imagination to create inventive alternatives to problem solving rather than being limited to the obvious solution to a problem.

Mission Statement

Companies write mission statements to describe the purpose or reason the company is in business. The following are two examples of typical mission statements.

The Arts and Design Corporation exists to encourage and engage the community through experiencing the arts. The Arts and Design Board of Directors is committed to providing quality products that will last a lifetime and will be passed down to future generations. In addition, the Arts and Design Corporation hopes to establish a sharing of the value of art in our daily lives.

Our company was organized to provide our customers with the highest-quality bicycles at the lowest price. We believe that customer service is an integral aspect of our business, and we demonstrate this belief in every encounter with our patrons.

It is important to reexamine the mission statement periodically because the corporate objectives and policies may have changed.

CHAPTER REVIEW

1. List three suggestions for obtaining a promotion.
2. List five questions that employees should ask of themselves before changing jobs.
3. Define the term *networking*.
4. Describe two reasons employees are dismissed from jobs.
5. List five duties of a manager.
6. List two suggestions for managing a telecommuting staff.
7. List three motivational incentives.
8. List two suggestions for welcoming a new employee.

ACTIVITIES

1. Review local newspapers for meetings of professional organizations. The chamber of commerce and library may have a list of professional organizations in your area. Contact three organizations that interest you and ask for information concerning the scope of the organization, frequency of meetings, location of meetings, cost of membership, and requirements for membership.
2. List ten people who are members of your network. Indicate how you have helped them and how they have helped you. Also, indicate the future assistance you expect to receive from them and how you expect to help them.
3. Observe an office environment and write a report describing either how time was used efficiently or how time was wasted.
4. Videotape a role-playing situation where you request a raise in salary. Include the following situations: the raise is given; it is denied; it is denied, but a job-title change is offered with the promise of a raise later.
5. Prepare a videotape of a role-playing situation in which you notify your supervisor that you have accepted another job.
6. Write a letter of resignation for a position you have held for three years.

PROJECTS

Project 27

Write a memorandum to the staff requesting completion, by the end of the month, of the following survey form. The memo is from you and your title is Benefits Officer. Create a survey form that provides space for responses to the questions. If possible, insert an appropriate graphic on your survey form.

Do You Need Childcare or Elder Care?
   Name
   Home address
   Home telephone number
   Department
   Department telephone number
   How many children need care?

Ages of children
How are children cared for now?
What arrangements have you made if the child is ill?
Is your spouse employed?
Does your spouse's employer offer childcare or elder care?
Do you need elder care?
Age of adult
Comments

Project 28

Send the following letter to Danielle Levine. It is from Maxine R. Woodman, Director of Employee Development. Provide any information necessary to complete the letter and use a modified block style with open punctuation.

Developing your management skills is essential to your professional and personal growth. We are offering several seminars to help you reach your potential and grow professionally.

Listed below are titles and dates of the seminars.

Assertiveness Training	Sept. 2, 3, 4
Decision Making	Sept. 18, 19, 20
New Computer Techniques	Oct. 2, 3, 4
Review of Basic Skills	Oct. 10, 11, 12
Writing for the Future	Nov. 6, 7, 8

Contact Sharon McKinley at 800-286-5175 to reserve your place at the seminar.

HUMAN RELATIONS SKILL DEVELOPMENT

HR 14-1 Anger in the Office

The ability to control anger is an important skill to develop. There are many office-related situations that can cause the most even-tempered person to become angry. A temper tantrum, however, is not professional behavior for an office. Removing the frustrations a person feels can be a healthy release for the body; internalizing anger can cause problems, including physical illness. Outlets for anger include tearing up paper, physical exercise, talking with a friend, writing a nasty note and destroying it, performing an activity that you enjoy, or deciding that the anger is not worth the bother. In the workplace, do not allow others to see your anger. If you are furious about something, go for a walk, get a drink of water, or close your door and rest for a few moments. Understanding and responding appropriately to your own anger and the anger of clients, supervisors, coworkers, and others will help you create a better working environment.

- Do you lose your temper easily?
- What causes you to lose your temper?
- In the office, how are you going to manage your anger?
- You are the manager, and an employee approaches you in a fit of anger. How are you going to handle the situation?
- Describe an incident where a coworker showed great anger.

HR 14-2 Emotions in the Office

Some people are very sensitive and become hurt easily. They may have difficulty accepting criticism—either justified or unjustified. A negative comment about a project may be taken personally, although the comment was meant to be constructive criticism. A nasty remark from a coworker may make a person feel worthless. All of these situations can cause a person to cry. Telling someone to control their emotions is easy, but it may be difficult for them to do so. If you feel your emotions are out of control and if you feel you are going to cry, walk quickly to the restroom. This should give you the privacy you need to regain your composure. If the restroom does not give you privacy, walk to another floor, walk outside, or sit in your car. Most supervisors do not like to deal with tears and do not know how to cope with the situation.

- How would you handle the situation if your supervisor screamed at you in front of a client?
- How would you handle the situation if your supervisor has personal problems at home and takes the frustration out on you by telling you that everything you do is wrong?
- How would you handle the problem of an employee crying as you discuss the employee's poor performance?

SITUATIONS

As the supervisor of the department, how would you handle the following situations?

- **S 14-1** Katie used to be a good team worker and would do her share of the work. For the last three months, she has not been doing her share of the work, and other employees have begun to complain to you.
- **S 14-2** Daniel is habitually late for work. During the last seven days, he has been late four times. When he arrives, he always has an excuse.
- **S 14-3** Marsha has a negative attitude, and she constantly exhibits it by being rude and snapping at clients and coworkers.

PUNCTUATION REVIEW

Punctuate each of the following sentences. For a review of punctuation rules, see the Appendix.

1. Did the computers arrive Mary asked
2. Yes Ms Cheung we can repair the copying machine before 2 PM on Friday January 16 so you can print the report by your due date
3. Ms Patterson the realtor works most weekends but she enjoys her job
4. After work we are going to a professional meeting
5. Our efficient easy to learn computer software base package will take only eight hours to learn and you do not need prior computer experience to understand it
6. My vacation time has been changed from August to September
7. According to an industry survey JoLib was ranked No 1 in client service among midsize accounting firms
8. Mr Ford said I had approval to take my vacation in July
9. If you study the Martin Report carefully you will see the error on page 12 therefore you will understand the problems we are now experiencing

10. When the computer crashed I lost the document I was creating

11. Dr Mason cannot see you on Wednesday but Dr Johnson is available then

12. The top two floors of the Champagne Office Complex which is located at Joseph Avenue have been renovated

13. Todays staff meeting is canceled but we will reschedule it for tomorrow

14. When I travel on business I usually fly northern airlines

15. Because of the court decision the company changed its name

CD ASSIGNMENTS

CD Assignment 14-1

Open the file **CD14-1_EE** on your Student CD and follow the instructions to complete the job. You will also need the file **CD14-1_EEF,** Employee Evaluation Form, which is on your Student CD.

CD Assignment 14-2

Open the file **CD14-2_EIC** on your Student CD and follow the instructions to complete the job.

CHAPTER 15

Diversity in the Workplace: Understanding Those You Work With

Objectives

After studying this chapter, you should be able to:

1. Explain cultural diversity.
2. Explain a mixed-generation workplace.
3. Explain business travel in a global society.
4. Be familiar with government employment regulations.

DIVERSITY

Today's workplace gathers workers born in many countries and raised in numerous regions across the United States; they follow different religions, display various health conditions, and reflect scores of cultural traditions. The employer expects these diverse people to work effortlessly together as a team for the success of the business. For people to work well together, they must respect, understand, and accept each other. This model of a workplace environment is often referred to as diversity in the workplace.

As evidenced by the people we see and interact with, the American workforce is quickly growing more diverse each day. This is due in part to federal laws that overturned barriers of discrimination that unfairly kept many qualified people from the workplace. Federal antidiscrimination laws regarding race, color, national origin, sexual orientation, age, and physical disabilities are discussed later in this chapter. In this chapter, the term *cultural diversity* is often used to refer to the groups that are covered by the federal antidiscrimination laws.

Another reason for the changing diversity of the workplace is the result of the increase in immigration into America from other countries. Immigration has brought employees from new cultures into many businesses and has changed the demographic makeup of numerous American communities. The clients and customers you work with will be as diverse as the community in which you live. Your ability to work effectively with both coworkers and clients from diverse communities is an important factor in the success of your professional career.

HINT
Employees today work in a culturally diverse environment.

RESPONDING TO DIVERSITY

Fear of the unknown can be a source of strife. Employees often fear and are uncomfortable working with coworkers who are different from themselves. In addition, when workers are faced with cultures and customs that are unfamiliar to them, they frequently do not know how to respond. When people understand, they are less fearful, which reduces tension and anxiety. In many cases, cultural ignorance is a barrier to a productive workplace. A misunderstanding can create apprehension and disputes, which can escalate into major office conflicts.

Individuals who act or look different from the majority culture, who have medical conditions, or who have religious beliefs different from others often feel they are constantly on display for others to see and criticize. They may believe that they are not viewed as individuals but as representatives of a race, religion, or medical condition. They feel that assumptions are made about their feelings, beliefs, and viewpoints, all without knowing or understanding them. Understanding others creates a more receptive atmosphere and diminishes negative opinions.

HINT
Have consideration for people from other cultures.

Stereotyping is wrong, although individuals often do it because they think it makes dealing with someone easier. A person who stereotypes anticipates a specific response because he or she believes everyone responds that way. It is important to realize that not all people react the same way. If a group is perceived to have certain skills or to lack particular skills, the members of the group are often identified in a specific way. Supervisors should create an open and tolerant workplace that avoids stereotyping.

People are not totally different; they are really similar. To thrive in today's business community, you must recognize and benefit from the differences of others and learn from and share in them. People with dissimilar backgrounds bring distinctive approaches and values to the workplace. As a result, you must be sensitive to the feelings of others and not offend them. Employees often unintentionally make remarks or show negative feelings toward coworkers who are unlike themselves. Therefore, a greater comprehension and appreciation of a coworker's culture helps minimize hostility and resentment.

To solve budding problems, employers must reduce friction between employees by promoting understanding and acceptance. Business must emphasize the importance of using the abilities, talents, and positive traits of all employees, regardless of their

Are you culturally savvy?

MY SUCCESS STORY

My Name Is Nhu

For several years, I had a part-time position in my organization, but then I decided that I wanted a full-time position. To make myself indispensable to my company, I decided to use my expertise to become more visible to my supervisors. I took software training classes and offered to train my coworkers. My training sessions were cost effective for the company, and the participants learned to use the software packages. In addition, I became proficient at creating PowerPoint presentations. When anyone in the organization needed software or PowerPoint presentation help, I volunteered. My ideas and diligence paid off. A position became available, and the department supervisor suggested that I apply for the position. Yes, I got the job. Now I have a full-time position in a terrific organization.

background. For cultural diversity to be successful, business should build a positive awareness of the similarities of all people. The workplace must grow into a home of cultural harmony. In addition, employers and employees should learn to appreciate the differences each worker brings to the workplace and to respond positively to each employee's cultural background. A diverse working community provides a diverse learning environment for all employees. A multicultural environment brings the best of the world together for the enjoyment and benefit of all.

Education can be used to reverse negative employee behavior and attitudes. Most coworkers are not prejudiced, intolerant, or cruel; they are just uneducated about the cultures of others. When workers become well-informed of the cultural way of life of others, they become more respectful and considerate. A good adage for all employees is to honor your coworkers, and they will admire and respect you. If you appreciate and have a high opinion of everyone, they will return the feeling. Acceptance of all employees, regardless of their background, is crucial for a culturally diverse workplace to thrive.

To promote cultural appreciation, employers and employees must create an opportunity to share and celebrate the culture of each person. Enjoying the traditions of others brings people together. A social setting such as an office party is a perfect opportunity to bridge the cultural gap. A potluck lunch is an excellent occasion because each employee brings a favorite dish of his or her country or family and shares with the group the food, the recipe, and the reason the food it important. Everyone benefits from this experience because they learn more about the cuisine and culture of all employees. If employees are secure and comfortable working together, the office is not a tense and stressful zone.

Diversity awareness is a goal shared by many businesses because administrators realize the importance of working together for a successful future. To meet this objective, companies are developing training programs that, if used properly, can teach employees about the many cultures and customs of the world. These are long-term projects that are continually revised to meet the challenges and changes of the workplace community. In addition to improving cultural consciousness, employees must be trained to manage destructive diversity issues so they will be prepared if an incident arises.

This new culturally diverse, client-based and customer-based workplace has forced business into considering the impact of a diverse employee or client community in the workplace. The focus is on the specific workplace site and business. After the office administration has answered the question, it must rapidly move forward to create an interrelated workplace environment to foster a new worldwide community where all employees are secure and at ease. The success of this venture is based on and created from the efforts and determination of employers, employees, and clients.

How would you describe your cultural background?

HINT
Learn to communicate and share across cultures.

DIFFERING CULTURAL ATTITUDES

Your understanding and appreciation of the attitudes or outlooks of different cultures is one of the keys to working successfully in a culturally diverse workplace. The following list includes a few observations about how differences in cultural background may influence how a coworker or customer acts. Observations such as these are only the beginning to understanding the numerous cultures that share our world, and you must not assume that everyone in a group belongs to a stereotype; everyone is an individual.

- Some cultures respect authority automatically.
- In some cultures, rejection is the same as disgrace. Therefore, an employee does not request or call attention to him- or herself because he or she could

be rejected. The culture requires the employee to be quiet and do the job as requested.

If the manager is not aware of the cultural expectation, the manager may not recognize the ability of the employee.

- In some cultures, the supervisor is expected to automatically recognize the skills of the employee; therefore, an employee will not request or volunteer for a job assignment. The employee waits for the employer to tell him or her to do a job.

  If the manager is not aware of the cultural expectation, the manager may not understand the employee's seeming lack of initiative.

- In some cultures, when it is time for a promotion, employees automatically expect the promotion without talking to the supervisor and without applying for it. The culture believes that it is best to be modest.

  If the employee does not get the hoped-for promotion, he or she can become unhappy and disillusioned. If the manager is not aware of the cultural thought process, the manager is not aware that there is a problem and therefore cannot solve it. If the employee becomes dejected because of the lack of promotion and consequently seeks another job, the manager has lost an employee who could have grown into a top-rated staff member.

- In some cultures, it is not polite to call attention to accomplishments; therefore, the employee will downplay an accomplishment or award.

- In some cultures, conflict and contradiction are frowned upon, so the employee will not make any suggestions that may be contrary to those of the supervisor. These individuals do not speak at meetings because their comments may interfere with the comments of a supervisor.

  To solve this problem, the supervisor needs to explain to all employees that their ideas are important and should be shared.

- In some cultures, persons have tendencies to be more active and more vocal.

  Without an understanding of the cultural background, the manager may feel the employee is just loud and arrogant.

- In some cultures, persons have tendencies be more personal and appear to be friendly.

- In some cultures, persons have tendencies to be noncommunicative.

  Without an understanding of the cultural background, the manager may feel that the employee is not interested in the job.

- In some cultures, persons often do not work well with women or young adults.

  Without an understanding of the cultural background, the employee's behavior may be difficult to interpret.

HINT
Show respect for all cultures.

- Some employees work best in a company that has a family environment, where everyone is treated as a member of the family unit.

BACKGROUND IMPACT ON BEHAVIOR

Cultural diversity may affect personal communication styles, which may force people to behave in a particular way. A coworker or customer's background can influence how an employee reacts to a situation. Shown below are statements expressed by members of some cultures and the comments or feelings expressed by some individuals. Read the comments below so you can better understand your colleagues and clients. What do you think are the attitudes of the people making these comments? How would you react if someone made these statements to you?

Comments made by immigrants

- "I am an immigrant. When things go wrong and there are problems, I ask myself if it was worth it to come to this country. Am I going to make it here? I have many doubts."
- "I pretend to understand, but I really do not."
- "Working in a different culture with a new language has increased my workplace stress level. I am always afraid of making a mistake."
- "Sometimes I do not understand the language. I do not understand the slang."
- "I feel that my coworkers do not understand and differentiate my culture. There are many cultures, dialects, and differences, even if we are from a similar area. Not all people in the same region have the exact same cultural background."
- "My education from my country is not accepted here. Therefore, I must again start at the bottom of the workplace ladder. It is very depressing because I have studied and am knowledgeable."
- "I feel that my coworkers and clients are impatient with me. I feel inadequate and powerless to compete in the workplace."
- "I have trouble understanding the language, so I just smile at people. It seems to help."
- "It was difficult for me to move to America and give up my former way of life. It is hard to accept the American way of life and culture. My family and friends are in my country and I miss them. I still have ties to my country. I miss my country."
- "I think in my own language, and then translate to English. Sometime the ideas and concepts do not translate well. Some English words are not part of my culture."
- "I do not make special requests of my supervisor because in my culture that is considered argumentative. My coworkers ask for days off work for holidays and special events. I do not."
- "My culture requires that I not look the person in the eye, so I always look away."
- "Although my family has been in the United Stated for many years, I feel I am treated as though I just arrived today from another country."
- "In my culture, we have strong family ties, and my coworkers do not understand my feelings."
- "I like the way I dress, but it is too colorful for my coworkers."
- "I have been looked upon as having minimal competencies because of my cultural background."
- "I do not feel comfortable explaining why I am dressed as I am. In my culture, this is the appropriate dress."
- "I feel that my current job is at the bottom of the work scale. I have lost all that I was worth."
- "I feel that I am different from my coworkers and am not part of the group."

- "My coworkers do not understand my background, so they make negative comments concerning my dress or customs. This creates a tense situation for me."
- "Time and punctuality are important in America but not important in my country. We are more relaxed."
- "In my country, we know we are going to get together with friends. We do not plan to get together. It just happens. In the United States, everyone plans to get together. In my country, we just get together for coffee. Here people set a date and time to meet for coffee. I just do not understand all of the planning."
- "In my country when two people are sitting on a sofa, they sit near each other. In this country, they sit at opposite ends of the sofa. I thought they were friends, but I guess not."
- "I am not rude. We just talk in a straightforward manner."
- "We do not say something just to be nice. We really mean what we say. If I offer to help you, I really mean it."

Some employers believe
- All members of an ethnic group have the same goals and abilities.
- If one employee from a particular culture did not work out, all employees from that culture will not work out.
- Because of the employee's cultural background and quiet mannerisms, the employee could do only one type of job; therefore, the employee could never advance to a position of higher responsibility.
- They like to work with certain ethnic groups because they will do anything without complaining.

    The immigrant is willing to do almost any job with the hope of later being promoted.

What mistakes have you made in your relationships with coworkers, supervisors, and clients? Can you see yourself in any of the above examples?

WORKING WITH PEOPLE WITH DISABILITIES

The Americans with Disability Act has had a tremendous impact on the workplace. The Act requires employers to make reasonable accommodations so persons with disabilities will be able to function effectively in the workplace. Disabilities include physical and emotional illnesses.

To accommodate the needs of employees, the employer may be required to remove physical obstacles or provide alternatives to accommodate the disabled worker. The elimination of physical and technical barriers provides an opportunity for employment success. The required modifications may be visible to all employees or seen and used only by the disabled person. Most people are familiar with a ramp as a mobility accommodation, but they may not be familiar with other accommodations. To assist a blind employee, the employer may provide voice-activated software or audio recordings. To assist an employee who has physical limitations, ADA-compliant restrooms, water faucets, and facilities may have to be installed. Automatically opened doors remove entrance and exit worries for physically restricted employees. By providing these adjustments, a knowledgeable employee with physical limitations is able to function effectively in the workplace.

People often react unfavorably to what they see. Their reaction may be driven by fear and misunderstanding. Since a physical ailment may be viewed by coworkers, coworkers may have a judgmental mind-set that is displayed and directed toward the disabled person. Employees need to be educated concerning the reason for and limitations caused by disabilities. In addition, all employees should be trained so they will know how to work with a disabled person. Employees need to know when to provide extra help and when not to.

It is important to think from the perspective of another person. This skill is particularly helpful when working with a disabled person. An example of insensitivity occurs when a person stands while talking with a wheelchair-bound individual. The height difference forces the person in the wheelchair to raise his or her head and neck to have a conversation. If the persons are at the same level, this problem is eliminated. The standing individual was not trying to create a difficulty but just did not understand the height difference.

Persons who have a total or partial hearing loss may experience an awkward situation because of another person's lack of awareness. A person who has a hearing disability may also read lips while having a conversation. Therefore, if the speaker turns his or her head so the lips are not visible, the disabled person may be prohibited from participating in the conversation. Similar problems occur when a speaker gestures and covers his mouth with his hands. The speaker was not trying to hide the conversation but was unaware of the ramifications of covering his or her mouth. Improving diversity knowledge and perception would easily solve this dilemma.

Not all disabilities are visible; you must be sensitive to the needs of everyone. Be aware of mobility limitations that may not be visible. Therefore, never make comments that may offend anyone. Persons with heart, leg, or knee aliments may look

Figure 15-1 Physical limitations should not be workplace barriers.

healthy but may have difficulty with stairs. Therefore, it is inappropriate to make comments about being too lazy to walk the stairs.

Shown below are statements expressed by several workers with physical disabilities. Read the comments below so you can better understand your colleagues and clients and work together more cohesively. What do you think are the attitudes of the people making these comments? How would you react if someone made these statements to you?

Figure 15-2 An entrance button allows easy access for all.

Comments from persons with physical disabilities

- "I do not want to discuss my physical disability with anyone. Do not ask me what happened."
- "Since I am in a wheelchair, I am not considered part of the group standing around chatting. I am in the area, but I am not in the group."
- "I am in a wheelchair, but that does not mean I can't hear."
- "I am blind. When people finish a conversation with me, they often walk away from me. Since I am blind, I do not know that they have left so I continue to talk, and no one is there. This is very embarrassing."
- "I am blind. I wish people would tell me when my hair is standing up. I can't see it."

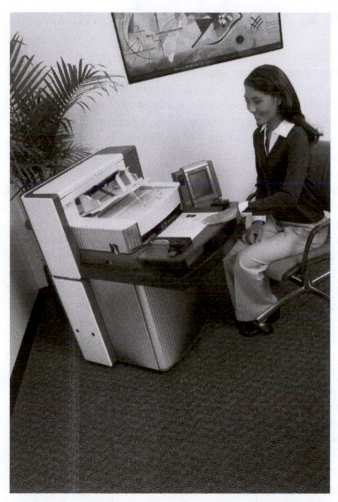

Figure 15-3 A printer that allows the employee to sit while using it. Courtesy of Eastman Kodak Company.

- "I am blind. Sometime my clothes do not match. I can't help it."

- "I am blind. It does not mean that I cannot hear."

- "I am deaf. Since I read lips, it is important for an individual to face me. During a conversation, people turn away."

- "It is raining today. Since I walk with two arm supports, I hope I do not slip and fall. I wish someone will help me with the doors."

- "I am a little slow, but that does not mean I am stupid. It would help if people would be patient with me."

- "I have a facial injury. Please ignore it. I do."

- "I am getting older and a little slower, but I am not dead yet."

- "For over a year, I have been going to a gym and seeing the same people. Then one day I was injured, which resulted in a huge scar on my leg. I did not go back to the gym for several weeks because of my injury. When I returned to the gym, I was surprised and disappointed because no one said anything to me. They did not ask where I had been, and they did not ask about the huge scar on my leg. In my country, someone would have rushed over to comment on the scar and my health. They would have asked what happened. They would have cared about me. I guess no one here cares about me."

GENERATIONS IN THE WORKPLACE: AGE-RELATED WORK VIEWS

Today's business world is a mixed-generation workplace. The modern workplace blends the young employee, the middle-aged employee, and the older employee into one workforce. Working together with people of different ages can present the same challenges as working with people from different cultural backgrounds. Employees of different ages frequently have different outlooks on life and often do not understand the values and lifestyles of those older or younger than themselves. To be successful in your career and help achieve your company's objectives, you must be able to understand and work with supervisors, employees, and clients who may be vastly different in age.

In a multigenerational workplace, age differences may become an issue for management and employees to take into account when understanding workplace communications and actions. Generally employees who are the same age and have comparable cultural backgrounds grew up sharing similar life experiences and life expectations. Therefore, those who grew up in another decade have life events that shaped their outlooks and created distinctive dreams and beliefs. Employees in their twenties grew up in a very different world from their coworkers who are in their fifties and sixties. As expected, the younger workers probably do not have the depth of job experience as older workers. In some instances, the older worker may not be as comfortable with technology or as informed about recent developments in the field because his or her formal education was probably many years ago.

Employees of dissimilar ages may not have the same personal desires and life objectives. For example, may be older employees may want to eliminate some of the job stress and extended employment hours, while new hires may be high-energy task-oriented employees who feel compelled to work long hours.

Furthermore, younger employees may gather together to talk and share personal and work experiences and may use language that is foreign to the older worker. Moreover, if the older worker tries to join the conversation, he or she may feel out of place and unwelcome. Therefore, the age difference may create an office division. If younger workers and older workers each associate primarily with their own age groups and ignore the advantages of working with people of all ages, the office ceases to be a team-focused environment. The employer's goal should be to create a setting where all employees, regardless of their ages, can meet their personal and professional objectives.

It is important that you recognize and respect the variety in ages within your office and overcome the natural differences between the older and younger worker. In addition, employees must work together to understand each person's viewpoint and workplace motivation. The following are observations about how age differences may influence how a coworker or customer will behave. Observations such as these are only a beginning to understanding differences in age, and you must not assume that everyone in a group belongs to a stereotype; everyone is an individual. What do you think are the attitudes of the people making these comments? How would you react if someone made these statements to you?

The Younger Worker

It is often felt that young workers have the energy and personal drive to devote to their careers, but they also value their leisure time. Furthermore, they expect to have a personal life and enjoy it. Although many work hard and play hard, some play hard but have little motivation to work. Although work and pleasure are divided into two separate worlds, they have business friends who have crossed the line and have become personal friends. They are often laid back and relaxed about situations that cause others stress and anxiety.

Common workplace beliefs held by younger workers
- We are more technologically oriented.
- We are attached to the Web, email, and cell phones.
- We must be in constant communication.
- We plan to change jobs often.
- We are less afraid of change.
- We desire and expect to move quickly up the corporate ladder.
- We are full of innovative and exciting ideas.
- We are savvy.
- We question everything.
- We have high energy.
- We are constantly on the move.
- We know we have a lot to learn, but give us a chance.

What some older workers think about younger workers
- They do not have a work ethic.
- They are not willing to put all of the hours and effort into the job.
- They are too casual.
- They do not respect experience.
- They have it too easy.
- They only play computer games.
- They get everything that they want without working and waiting for it.
- They are spoiled.
- They are commitment-shy.

- They do not know how to write a thank-you note
- They use words I do not understand
- They dress too casually, do not know when to dress up, do not know how to wear a suit and tie.
- They only wear flip flops and no stockings.
- They just don't get it.
- In my day, we did it this way . . . .
- They always wear jeans.
- They have no regard for punctuality.
- We paid our dues to get ahead in the business world; why do they feel it is unnecessary for them to pay their dues?

The Mid-Career Employee

Mid-career employees have been in the workforce for several years and often concentrate on their careers while putting great emphasis on managing their family responsibilities. Although they spend hours working, they also want freedom to enjoy themselves. Their leisure activities are family-oriented. They may experience a feeling of loss that they no longer are part of the younger worker generation but are fearful of becoming an older worker.

The Older Employee

Generally older employees have been employed for thirty years and many now have reached a life of relative financial success. This is the time when their life values are changing. They are not less dedicated to a job but are becoming more committed to enjoying life because of the realization that life is short. They desire more time for personal enjoyment and family activities. Regrettably this is also the time when their personal responsibilities may escalate. Many feel overwhelmed with caring for elderly parents while continuing responsibilities for college-age children. Although they feel life is getting shorter and it is time for them to enjoy themselves, they are suddenly faced with caring for elderly parents. Those nearing retirement may desire a more flexible schedule to manage their elder-care responsibilities. In addition, because of today's longer life expectancy, many older persons desire to be active and remain in the workplace in a full- or part-time capacity. This is a change from previous generations where age and health motivated workers to retire.

Common workplace beliefs held by older workers
- We remember when the world was not driven by technology.
- We know the history of the company and other companies.
- We work well with rules and policies.
- We know how the system works and how to get things done.
- We are reliable.
- We built this company into what it is today.
- We are the institutional memory of this organization.

What some younger workers think about older workers
- They are out of touch.
- The do not know what is happening.

- They are unresponsive to new ideas.
- They are too stiff.
- They should move out of the workplace to make room for the younger generation.
- They are afraid to take a risk or try something new.
- They put too much importance on past experience and past history.
- They are outmoded.
- They wear ties.
- They just don't get it.
- They are can't use a DVD player or an iPod.
- They are afraid of technology.
- They are too slow.
- They are out of step with the world.
- They are out of step with reality.
- They are just like my parents, and they don't know anything.

Inter-generational Success

For a company to be successful, the employees must work to achieve the objectives of the company. All employees, regardless of age or ethnicity, should recognize the positive values of working with everyone and avoid generational conflicts. When employees get along in the workplace, they are more successful and happy. The challenge for companies is to create a work environment where everyone is working together for the success of the company.

For a winning workplace, do not:
- Base a workplace decision on the appearance of an employee.
- Think an employee cannot do the job because he or she has gray hair and wears glasses.
- Think an employee cannot do the job because he or she is not wearing a traditional suit.
- Think an employee cannot do the job because he is wearing an earring.
- Think an employee cannot do the job because she has pink hair.
- Think an employee over fifty is not computer savvy.
- Think a young employee who wears cutoffs cannot do the job.

Employers and employees should turn the generation gap to their advantage and create a successful working environment where everyone uses their individual strengths and skills to work together to achieve the company's objectives.

FUNCTIONING AND TRAVELING IN THE GLOBAL SOCIETY

The globalization of products and services brings people and business from various cultures into contact with each other. Companies should recognize the potential for conflicts with foreign business cultures and should create a cultural diversity plan to encourage a working relationship with international clients and partners. Employees who have international business skills or who have knowledge of the cultures or the economic systems of other countries are assets to an organization.

Not understanding a culture can create barriers to communications. Cultural differences exist in oral and written communications, and one untactful remark can destroy a relationship that took many months to establish. Even when an employee of your company speaks the language of another country, cultural differences may alter the interpretation or meaning of what is said. Earning the trust and respect of members of all cultures can be vital to a business's success. Learning to share and enjoy the cultures of the world can be a personally rewarding experience for you and a bonus for your company.

Employees who work in a global company must adapt to new customs and economic practices so they will be able to execute their job responsibilities successfully. To create a good impression with foreign business associates and let them know that you are interested in them and their company, learn a few words of their language. Learning simple words and phrases such as *hello*, *good morning*, and *thank you* is not difficult and demonstrates your interest in working with international clients.

Prior to traveling to another country or working with foreign businesses, research the customs of the country. Become knowledgeable of the proper behavior and protocol of the country. In some countries, shaking hands is not acceptable, while in other countries it is expected. Also, taking business gifts when visiting one culture may be expected, and in other societies it may be inappropriate. Although a slang expression may be common to you, it should not be used because it may not be understood by persons from other cultures. Remember that a joke that you find very funny may offend a person from another culture.

You can find information on foreign cultures by consulting cultural relations books or searching the Web. In addition you can locate cultural information about many countries by visiting the U.S. State Department Web site at www.state.gov and following the links to U.S. embassies around the world.

Listed below are suggestions for working with international clients in the United States or in foreign countries.

- Always show respect for and interest in the culture of others.

- Be aware of religious and national holidays and their customs.

- Be aware that some businesses in foreign nations close for a few hours during the afternoon so that employees and customers can rest.

- Be aware of business attire in foreign countries. In some countries, professional business attire is expected; in others, casual clothes may be appropriate. Some countries dress very elegantly, and in others the dress is cosmopolitan. Casual attire such as shorts may not be appropriate. Adapt your clothing so you do not look out of place.

- Translate your business cards into the language of the foreign country. Some business travelers print their card in English on one side and in the local language on the other side.

- Know when it is appropriate to discuss business. In some foreign countries, business matters are discussed only while entertaining and dining.

- Know the etiquette of gifts. Gift-giving may be an important ritual in the foreign country.

- Know when to shake hands, hug, or kiss. Cultures differ on how to greet people.

- Be aware of where to stand. In some countries, people stand very close to each other, so do not automatically move back if a person stands close to you.

- Know the etiquette of time. In some countries, being late is accepted and expected. It may be inappropriate to be on time. In other countries, people are very punctual.

- Know when to toast the host at a meal. In some cultures, toasting is a form of respect.

- Always bring a gift if you visit someone's home.

- Do not criticize the country or the people.

- In some countries, avoiding eye contact may be perceived as being dishonest, while in other cultures, looking someone in the eye is frowned upon.

- In some countries, a business referral or introduction may be very important and may be the only means of meeting someone.

- Business moves very slowly in some countries, so do not expect to rush meetings or business conversations.

- Seating at a dining table may be arranged according to the highest-ranking person.

- Do not whisper to one person, because others may think you are talking about them.

- It may be inappropriate to eat food with your fingers. Conversely, be aware that in some cultures, eating with your fingers is appropriate.

- Know the proper time to eat. Some countries eat a late lunch or late dinner. A late dinner may start at 10 P.M.

- Be aware of the cultural issues relating to hand gestures because it is easy to offend someone with an inappropriate hand gesture.

- Always ask permission prior to taking a picture.

- Be aware of how the culture addresses people. Americans may prefer informal business discussions and often like to be called by their first names; persons from some countries may prefer a formal business discussion and prefer to be addressed by a title such as Mr., Ms., Dr., or Professor.

- Be aware of culture differences regarding the human body. For example, in some cultures, touching someone's head is inappropriate because the head is sacred.

- Always be aware of the etiquette used in the foreign country.

EMPLOYMENT PROTECTION IN THE WORKPLACE

Discrimination in the workplace not only creates tension in an office and interferes with the efficient operation of a company, it is illegal. Several federal laws protect employees and applicants for employment from discrimination or harassment in the workplace. Most of these antidiscrimination laws are part of the Civil Rights Act of 1964.

Race or Color Discrimination

Title VII of the Civil Rights Act of 1964 protects employees and applicants for employment against discrimination because of race or color with regard to hiring, termination, promotion, and any condition of employment. Job policies that disproportionately exclude minorities and policies that are not job-related are prohibited by Title VII. Title VII also prohibits harassment on the basis of color or race and prohibits behavior that creates intimidating, hostile, or offensive working conditions.

National Origin Discrimination

Title VII of the Civil Rights Act of 1964 also protects employees and applicants for employment against discrimination because of national origin with regard to hiring, termination, promotion, and any condition of employment. National origin includes an individual's birthplace, ancestry, culture, or linguistic characteristics. In addition, a workplace rule requiring employees to speak only English on the job may violate Title VII unless the employer shows that it is necessary for the conduct of business. Employers should maintain a workplace free of national origin harassment.

Religious Discrimination

Another function of Title VII of the Civil Rights Act of 1964 is to protect employees and applicants for employment against discrimination because of their religion with regard to hiring, termination, promotion, and any condition of employment. Employers must also make reasonable accommodation for the religious practices of employees unless the accommodations would cause an undue hardship on the employer.

Gender Discrimination

Title VII of the Civil Rights Act of 1964 also protects employees and applicants for employment against discrimination because of their gender with regard to hiring, termination, promotion, and any condition of employment. Sexual harassment is also prohibited by Title VII. Sexual harassment is defined by a federal government agency, the Equal Employment Opportunity Commission, as unwelcome sexual advances, requests for sexual favors, and other verbal or physical conduct of a sexual nature. Hostile or intimidating work environments can be created by sexual comments or jokes. The harasser can be a man or woman and can be the same gender as the victim. Sexual harassment can occur between coworkers as well as between employees and supervisors. Both forms are against the law.

Sexual harassment occurs when:

- Submission to such conduct is made either explicitly or implicitly as a term or condition of a person's employment.
- Submission to or rejection of such conduct by a person is used as the basis for employment decisions affecting that person.
- Such conduct has the purpose or effect of unreasonably interfering with a person's work performance or creating an intimidating, hostile, or offensive working environment.

The law requires all employers to provide their employees with a workplace that is free from sexual harassment. The law also requires employers to give prompt attention to sexual harassment complaints.

Age Discrimination

The Age Discrimination in Employment Act (ADEA) of 1967 protects employees and applicants for employment over age forty against discrimination based on age. The Older Workers Benefit Protection Act of 1990 amended the ADEA to prohibit employers from denying benefits to older workers. It is unlawful to discriminate against a person because of his or her age with respect to any term, condition, or privilege of employment, including hiring, firing, promotion, layoff, compensation, benefits, job assignments, and training.

Disability Discrimination

The Americans with Disabilities Act of 1990 protects qualified individuals with disabilities from discrimination in hiring, termination, promotion, and any condition of employment. Disabilities are defined as mental or physical impairments that substantially limit one or more major life activities. Employers must make reasonable accommodations for disabled workers unless accommodations would impose undue hardships on the operation of the employer's business.

Equal Pay and Compensation Discrimination

The Equal Pay Act of 1963 requires that men and women be given equal pay for work when jobs require substantially equal skill, effort, and responsibility under similar work conditions in the same establishment. Jobs must be substantially equal but do not need to be identical. Differences in pay are permitted due to seniority, quality or quantity of work, merit, or factors other than the employee's sex.

Pregnancy Discrimination

The Pregnancy Discrimination Act is an amendment to Title VII of the Civil Rights Act of 1964 and protects employees and applicants for employment from discrimination on the basis of pregnancy or childbirth. An employer cannot refuse to hire a woman because of her pregnancy and must treat a woman who cannot perform her job because of her pregnancy as any employee who is temporarily disabled. Information about the Pregnancy Discrimination Act can be found at the Equal Employment Opportunity Commission Web site at http://www.eeoc.gov/facts/fs-preg.html.

The Equal Employment Opportunity Commission (EEOC)

The EEOC is the federal agency that enforces many of the antidiscrimination laws described above. Many states also have state agencies that provide protection to employees and applicants for employment from discrimination.

Information about the EEOC and discrimination protection for employees can be found at the EEOC Internet site, www.eeoc.gov. This Internet site also provides information on how to file complaints with the EEOC.

CHAPTER REVIEW

1. What is cultural diversity, and why is it important?
2. Why is stereotyping wrong?
3. What is meant by a mixed-generation workplace?
4. List two suggestions for working with international clients.
5. Discuss three types of antidiscrimination protection in the workplace.

ACTIVITIES

1. Interview three people whose cultural backgrounds are different from yours. Ask them to share interesting facts about their culture. Ask them to share the recipes for some of their favorite foods.

2. Use the Internet and books to research two counties you would like to visit. Describe the culture of the country. Include a discussion on proper business attire and business behavior. Write a two-page paper on your research.

3. Write a one-page paper with suggestions for working with persons who are at least one generation older or younger than you. Use the Internet for research and include your personal experiences.

PROJECTS

Project 29

Send a memo to the office community. It is from Wilma Gomez, Chief Information Officer.

> I am happy to announce the appointment of our new Information Technology Client Services Director, Ms. Sassy Rodriguez. Ms. Rodriguez comes to us from Rodella Services where she held progressively responsible technical and management positions over the past twenty-five years. She has wide experience in networking, telecommunications, systems integration, and security engineering. She holds a B.A. in Information Science from the University of Southern California. While employed at Rodella Services, she was the recipient of the Employee of the Year Award for performance, initiative, and distinguished contributions.
>
> In the next few months, Ms Rodriguez will be responsible for upgrading the telephone systems, updating computer security, and centralizing the computing and help desk facilities.
>
> Please join me in welcoming Ms. Rodriguez to our community of distinguished employees.

Project 30

Write an email to all employees inviting them to attend the monthly lunchtime book discussion. This month's book is titled, *The Cultural Advantages of Life*. Create a flyer to attach to the email. You decide on the time, date, and location, and make all necessary decisions.

HUMAN RELATIONS SKILL DEVELOPMENT

HR 15-1 Customer Service

Your company is upgrading its customer-service support and has asked employees to volunteer to work a few Saturdays for the next few months to be available to help clients. You have been told that later you will receive comp time as a compensation for your assistance on Saturdays. Daniela, whose office is next door to yours, agreed to work the same Saturdays as you, but she has never appeared. Since a Saturday sign-in sheet is not used, she will receive the same comp time as you. You feel it is unfair for her to receive comp time when she has not been at work.

- Should you talk with your supervisor? What should you say?
- Should you talk with Daniela? What should you say?

HR 15-2 Telephone Comment

Several times you have heard the new receptionist make the following comments when answering the telephone. "S & K Consultants. You will have to wait. I am busy." You feel her comments are rude and unprofessional. Also, you believe the comment will alienate your clients.

- Should you talk with the new receptionist? What should you say?
- Should you talk with your supervisor? What should you say?

SITUATIONS

How would you handle the following situations?

- **S 15-1**   You submitted a résumé for a job. While you are rushing to leave the house, the recruiter calls you and begins the interview. Describe your feelings. What options do you have?

- **S 15-2**   You are standing in the office elevator when another individual enters. You say "Good morning," and expect a similar reply. The individual says to you, "You are standing in my elevator spot." You are surprised about the response but think the person is making a joke. After looking at the person's face, you quickly discover that the person is very serious.

- **S 15-3**   When someone has a personal problem in your office, you have become the person he or she runs to for advice. You are happy to help by listening to your coworkers, but you do not want to act as everyone's counselor.

PUNCTUATION REVIEW

Punctuate each of the following sentences. For a review of punctuation rules, see the Appendix.

1. As of today the employment figures show that jobs postings are increasing at a faster rate than in previous years
2. However a closer look at the project showed a decrease of 10 percent
3. To get that number we increased the budget by 20 percent
4. While the Web site showed 200 hits the revenue was down
5. No one knows when this upsurge in housing may end but it must end
6. In the shorter term the company outlook is favorable
7. When the company profits needed a boost the director met with investors
8. The management team leader L L Vancho is seen as visionary in the industry
9. On Friday the board of directors met to discuss the CEOs retirement
10. In 2008 the company recruited Mr Garedi to become the next director
11. The tight labor market which is seen as an investment factor is the topic of the next meeting
12. Before long the top three executives will retire which leaves the company with a shortage of advisers
13. Mollie Allen the former director is now the CEO for Charles West Industries
14. As member of the team he requested additional funds for the budget
15. Most of his staff was recruited and trained by him said Flora

CD Assignments

CD Assignment 15-1

Open the file **CD15-1_DIV** on your Student CD and follow the instructions to complete the job.

CD Assignment 15-2

Open the file **CD15-2_EPC** on your Student CD and follow the instructions to complete the job.

CHAPTER 16

....

Stress Management

Objectives

After studying this chapter, you should be able to:

1. List and discuss the causes of stress.
2. List and discuss the symptoms of stress.
3. List and discuss techniques to reduce stress.
4. List and discuss suggestions for avoiding job burnout.

THE DANGERS OF STRESS

Tension and worry go hand in hand and can destroy your health, job, and personal relationships. Everyone feels some tension, but excessive stress can be damaging. When you are in a pressure situation, your body sends you a message—stress. You must decide how to interpret the message and how to manage your anxiety. Your personal behavior patterns and personal characteristics influence your ability to manage stress. Some people are better at ignoring an irritating incident than others are. But your ability to manage stress is crucial. If you allow stress to control your personality and cloud your professional judgment, you may damage your reputation in the eyes of your supervisor and coworkers.

Stress can be felt in or derived from your work life and your personal life, and it may be difficult to separate the two. Home-inspired tension generally does not cease just because you are entering your office, and work-created pressure does not stop at the front door of your home. Therefore, stress must be prevented and managed wherever you are.

Are you stressed?

HINT
Manage stress before it controls you.

CAUSES OF STRESS

Unfortunately, stress will probably be part of your everyday work life, so learning to handle stress is important to your physical and emotional well-being. The biggest causes of stress usually are other people and their actions. Of course, you cannot eliminate your contact with other people, but you can learn to manage the people you come in contact with so you can reduce stress. Furthermore, you must learn how to deal effectively with your supervisor, coworkers, and the public when they are under a great deal of stress. Other factors that cause stress in the office are too much to do and too little time to do it; lack of advancement opportunities; little input into decisions; lack of communication from supervisors; conflicting assignments from several supervisors; and the constant interruptions caused by emails, home telephone, office telephone, and cell phone.

Having too much to do can increase your stress level, so do not overschedule yourself with work and personal activities. For your personal well-being and health, give yourself time to breath and catch up before you jump into another project or interest. Do not exceed your personal activity comfort level. To be a successful person, you need downtime, which means you need time to relax. By incorporating enjoyment time into your personal life, you will create more balance to your life.

Are you a negative person? Do your negative feelings make your environment more stressful? Learn to look at the positive side of each incident. Focusing on the negative aspects can cause more stress for you. Do not permit each minor incident or confrontation to escalate into a major issue and then to aggravate you.

SYMPTONS OF STRESS

To be able to manage stress, it is important to recognize physical symptoms of stress. Awareness of your personal reactions can help you control the tension you experience.

Symptoms of stress

- Upset stomach.
- Breathing rapidly.
- Heart pounding rapidly.
- Heavy perspiration.
- Tense muscles, often in the neck, back, arms, or legs.
- Tightening in the throat; difficulty swallowing.
- Exhaustion.
- Inability to sleep.
- Irritability.
- Lack of appetite.
- Weight gain or loss.

MY SUCCESS STORY

My Name Is Leslie

I am a nurse, and some people think I do not work in business. They are wrong. Daily I supervise a nursing staff of 25 people. In addition to medical responsibilities, my staff and I must be knowledgeable of company and insurance policies, have a flair for working with patients, and have excellent computer skills. Since some members of my staff have minimal business and computer experience, I must guide them through the basics of their duties. My job keeps me focused on patient needs and the business responsibilities of my department. The constantly changing technology in medicine and business keeps me on my toes.

- Nausea.
- Sweaty palms.
- Crying.
- Fears.
- Lack of attention to details.
- Perfectionism.
- Feelings of worthlessness.

PERSONAL STRESS EVALUATION QUESTIONS

Answer the following questions by carefully thinking about your personality, workplace, and home environment.

- Do you feel overwhelmed?
- Do you allow minor problems to become major problems?
- Can you laugh about your mistakes?
- What do you give up by being aggravated?
- Do you demand perfection of yourself?
- Do you allow others to diminish your worth?
- Do you react to unfounded negative comments?
- Do you often feel rushed?
- Do you feel that you are weak?
- Do you allow others to control your thoughts?
- Do you expect approval from others?
- Are you often tired?
- Do you feel worthless?
- Can you forget the mistakes you have made?
- Can you forget arguments?
- Do you feel insecure?
- Do you overreact?
- Do you feel buried under piles of tension?
- Do you have physical symptoms of stress?
- Have you lost your zest for life?
- Have you lost your tolerance of your coworkers, family, and friends?
- Do you want to hide?
- Do feel like you are drowning?
- Do you frequently feel unhappy?
- Do you often feel you have too many projects and too little time?
- Have you lost your appetite?
- Have you recently lost your temper?
- Do you feel you have lost your ability to cope?
- Have you lost your ability to enjoy your leisure activities?
- Do you feel trapped and unable to get out?
- Do you feel that others think you are stupid?

- Do you feel that the obstacles you encounter are insurmountable?
- Do you allow others to make decisions for you?
- Do you feel that you never get to do what you want?
- Have you lost your desire to fight for what you want?
- Do you feel caught in the middle of a problem?
- Do you think you can never win?
- Do you feel that your life is a whirlwind of immediate crisis?
- Does chaos make you feel stressed?
- Does a noisy environment make your feel stressed?
- Have you recently had a life-altering experience such as divorce or death of a family member or close friend?
- Are you the caregiver for an elderly family member?

After realistically answering the previous questions, what changes must you personally make to control your life? After changing your behavior, how will your life be improved?

MANAGING STRESS

For your personal welfare and job success, it is important that you are aware of how you react to stress and how to improve your ability to diminish the anxiety you feel. Your personal behavior style influences your ability to control pressure. Do not allow previous experiences to become personal baggage and influence your ability to manage stress. Therefore, evaluate each situation on its current merits, not how you felt last year about someone or an aggravating situation.

In stressful situations, individuals often want another person to solve the problem. Generally the individual feels overwhelmed and wants to be removed from the situation. Understanding how and why you react in a specific manner improves your ability to cope with the circumstance. When requests from coworkers, supervisors, and individuals involved in your personal life overwhelm you, set priorities and make your priorities clear to yourself and others.

To keep problems in the proper perspective, remember that today's problem will probably be forgotten and unimportant by next week, next month, or next year. Focus on what you can control, not what you cannot control.

There are many techniques that you can use to reduce or deal with stress before you go to a professional for medication or psychological assistance.

What does your stress meter say?

Techniques to reduce stress
- Recognize stress before it is too late.
- Stop and tell yourself to relax when you feel stress.
- Make a list of the times when you feel stress.
- Attack stress at its source. Be aware of what caused the stress.
- Do not create stress by procrastinating on a project.
- Do not try to do everything at the office. Delegate responsibility and permit other employees to work on projects.
- Do not let anger control you and create more stress for you.
- Eat a well-balanced diet.
- If caffeine makes you hyperactive, reduce or eliminate it.

- Get a reasonable amount of sleep each night. If you are sleep-deprived, you will feel more stress.
- Create a balance between work and home.
- See the humor in a situation. Tell yourself to laugh about the problem that is causing your anxiety.
- Learn to relax.
- Find something you enjoy and then do it.
- Make a list of the small pleasures in your life; when stressed, remind yourself of them.
- Tell yourself that the stressful situation or problem is important only for a short time and then it will be over.
- Tell yourself that the stressful problem is just not worth the aggravation.
- Ask yourself why you are upset. Then alter or accept the situation that caused the stress.
- Ask yourself why you are hurrying.
- Ask yourself if what you are doing is really essential.
- Stop and ask yourself if the problem is really worth all of the trouble it is causing you. If the problem is not worth the trouble, modify the situation or ignore it.
- Exercise—swim, walk, run, dance, bike, do aerobics, or do any exercise that relieves tension.
- Develop a hobby that captures your attention and relaxes you.
- Squeeze a stress-reducer ball.
- Visualize an activity that provides pleasure.
- Meditate or perform yoga exercises.
- Remind yourself that today's problems will probably be unimportant next week.
- Keep your workspace organized. A messy workplace can increase your stress level.
- Reduce workplace stress by controlling the clutter at home.

You can take actions at home that should reduce your stress at the office. Create a relaxing home oasis for yourself by decorating and furnishing a room that is peaceful and soothing. If every room is filled with clutter, you have nowhere to take a break from the stress. At home each evening, manage your personal clutter by sorting and processing the mail. Also, pick up and put away all clothing, dishes, magazines, newspapers, and so on. If your home gives you a peaceful feeling, you have a greater chance of beginning your workday in a calm mode. Before you leave for work in the morning, make your bed and when you arrive home, you will not immediately be faced with a disorganized mess. A mess can create stress for you and raise your anxiety level. If your anxiety level is elevated, you will react more quickly and in a negative way to issues at home. The stress you feel at home will continue to snowball, and the next morning you will be provoked and aggravated before you go to work. Thus, the cycle continues. Manage home clutter and stress before they destroy your workday.

Many companies have a support network established to help employees manage stress. The assistance may be from employees in the health or human resources departments or from an outside source. In many cases, the costs are covered by employee health-care plans.

> **HINT**
> It is your life. Don't let another person or event have power over you.

Stress can have long-term implications for your life. Therefore, it is important that you manage stress before you run out of options. What stress-reduction techniques do you think will work for you?

Job Burnout

Stress, boredom, and general life dissatisfaction can alter how you feel about your job. If you are unhappy with your job or life in general, your discontentment can evolve into job burnout.

To avoid job burnout

- Become involved in a new office project or personal activity.
- Make your office more inviting by rearranging the furniture and equipment and painting the walls.
- Adjust your office hours or lunchtime to add variety to your day.
- If you bring your lunch, bring something new. If you buy your lunch, try a new restaurant.
- Make your lunch break a time to look forward to by taking a walk, reading a book, shopping, or attending a concert.
- Update your work wardrobe and add sparkle to yourself.
- Bring to the office an object that gives you pleasure. Bring a favorite photo, CD, plant, and so on.
- Take a new route to work and enjoy the trip.
- Mentor a new employee and professionally grow yourself.
- Remind yourself of the reasons you originally accepted your job. Look at the bright side of your job.

To reduce on-the-job stress and burnout, regularly take vacations to rejuvenate yourself. If possible, take a two-week vacation. It takes some people a week just to begin the deep relaxation process, so one week may not be enough time to reduce stress. In addition, schedule minivacations because long weekends away provide the necessary fuel to continue in a fast-paced environment.

Sample Stressful Situations

Take a few minutes to review the following examples of stressful situations. How would you react to the following stressful situations? What could you have done to prevent the problem from occurring? How should you solve the problem? How can you reduce your stress level?

- You spent all day completing a rush job for your supervisor. When you took the completed project to your supervisor, you were told that he did not really need the completed job until tomorrow.
- You canceled your doctor's appointment so you could attend a mandatory staff meeting. An hour before the scheduled meeting, you received an email informing you that the meeting was canceled and rescheduled for the following week. You are angry.
- You have an 8 A.M. meeting with clients from out of town. You had a flat tire on your way to work so you called the office assistant and left a voice message asking that a note be put on the conference room door informing everyone that you would be late. When you arrive at 9 A.M., you find angry clients waiting for you. They were not informed of your flat tire. After you meet with the clients, you ask the assistant why a note was not placed on the

door. She tells you that she did not get around to listening to the voice mail. You are furious.

- Your office is on the fourth floor of the building with two elevators. It is a busy building and you often wait five or more minutes for the elevators. You do not walk the stairs because your briefcase is heavy, and you have a knee injury. You just received an email informing you that both of the elevators will be renovated. It will take six months to renovate each elevator. Therefore, only one elevator will be operating for the next six months. How do you feel?

- Your child wanted you to attend a school event today, but because of a meeting with an important client you declined. It is now a half hour after your scheduled meeting time, and the client has not arrived so you call him on his cell phone. He tells you that he is running late from an earlier meeting, so he will reschedule your appointment for next week. He says, "It's no problem."

- You are in a hurry to leave work because the long awaited repairperson has agreed to come to your house to repair your appliance. You rush to the office parking lot and jump into your car. At this moment, the security van appears in front of your car. The guard leaves the van to talk with someone getting into a car. You gently honk your car's horn, and the security guard ignores you.

- You arrived early at work to print several big and important jobs. Your printer prints one page and stops. You call the technical assistance department and hear a voice mail message saying that this is a busy time, and they will process your request tomorrow.

- As always, your weekly staff meeting is dominated by the same three loud and talkative coworkers. You rarely make any comments because you cannot get a word into the conversation. The latest comment made is absolutely ridiculous, so you feel compelled to voice your opinion. In addition, the suggestion requires completing a project, which means more work for you. As soon as you start to talk, your supervisor says that it is terrific idea and concludes the meeting. You are irritated.

- During a staff meeting in front of your colleagues, your supervisor berates you for not completing a job task. When you start to comment, the supervisor says this is not the time to discuss the issue. You are at a loss to understand the situation. You were never given the particular job task to complete.

- Today you are nervous about speaking at a meeting but you hope that, by being prepared and organized, the speech will go well. As part of your meeting preparation, yesterday you had a ten-page document copied for distribution. When you place the materials at the door for everyone to take, you discover that you have a five-page document of even numbered pages only. Apparently the odd-numbered pages were not copied. You are shocked, angry, and dismayed.

- Beatrice, one of your coworkers, is very friendly toward you. You like her, but you really do not feel comfortable with her. Whenever possible, Beatrice has to one-up everything that you do. If your supervisor praises you, Beatrice immediately reminds you of the praise she received from her supervisor. If you buy a new outfit, she tells you that it is pretty, and then tells you about the new outfit she bought. If you tell her about an exciting project you are doing, she tells her about her exciting project. If you discuss a problem with her, she listens and then jumps into the conversation with her problem. You do not object to her comments, but you object to her attitude of one-upsmanship.

What situations can you add to the sample situations? What are your experiences?

CHAPTER REVIEW

1. Why is it important for you to manage stress?
2. List three symptoms of stress.
3. List three techniques to reduce stress.

ACTIVITIES

1. For two weeks, maintain a personal stress-related diary.
   a. Show at what time of day you felt stress, how you felt it, and what caused the stress.
   b. Also include when you felt happy, and excited, and what caused the pleasurable feelings.
   c. At the end of the two weeks, review your findings and write a summary.
   d. Provide situation-by-situation suggestions for managing the stress you felt.
   e. Provide situation-by-situation comments for increasing your feelings of exuberance so they will carry over to your stressful periods.
   f. Select five stressful activities from your diary. Rate them on a scale of one to five with five as the most stressful. Comment on the importance of each activity at the time you experienced it. Comment on the importance of each stressful event two weeks after the incident.
   g. Share your findings with your partner. Ask your partner for suggestions for improvement.
2. What physical symptoms of stress have you felt?
3. Ask yourself what lifestyle changes are essential for your health.
4. Have you experienced burnout? Describe your feelings.
5. What management styles cause stress for you?
6. Describe three work-related incidents that were stressful for you.
7. Describe three non–work-related incidents that were stressful for you.
8. List three people who cause stress for you. Include why they make you tense and how you should manage the situation.
9. What career fears do you have? Do they cause stress for you?
10. What kinds of relationships create tension for you?
11. How would you change your workplace environment to prevent stress?

PROJECTS

Project 31

Write an email to all employees announcing an employee Information Technology Update Session for May 19 at 9 A.M. in the Main Conference Center. The agenda includes demonstration of the new employee security system, projectors, shared software, and computer password requirements. Create a flyer to attach to the email. You make all of the decisions.

Project 32

Send this memo to all employees. It is from Joseph C. Lewis, Director of Employee Benefits.

Is this the year you take control of your life? Join us in our newly created Personal Challenge Project, which begins next month.

Sessions in taking control of your life will be offered before work, during lunch, and after work. The following sessions will be offered during the first month.

Basketball to Move It
Cooking for Your Health
Let's Get out from Under
Drop Those Ten Pounds Now
Exercise for Your Life
Let's Enjoy Now

I hope you will call Monica at 4577 for all of the details and registration information.

HUMAN RELATIONS SKILL DEVELOPMENT

HR 16-1 Personal Safety

Your supervisor asked you to do a job that you feel endangers your personal safety. It is Thursday at almost 6 P.M. on a dark rainy night. The top news story is about a dozen dangerous criminals who have just escaped from a prison, which is located two blocks from your office. People are asked to take all necessary precautions to protect their personal safety. Your supervisor has asked that you wait outside your office building for a client who may drop off a file. Although, the client was uncertain if he would actually bring the file, you are asked to wait outside from 6 to 7 P.M. to receive the file. If the file is delivered, you are then supposed to return to your office and modify the documents to have ready for a meeting next Monday. You are very uncomfortable working late tonight because of security issues.

- How does the situation make you feel?
- What would you say to your supervisor to explain your feelings?

HR 16-2 Team Project

You and James, who is a member of your team, are working on a project together. James is pleasant but very difficult to work with on the project. When you share an idea with James, he says that the project cannot be done that way. Last week you met to prepare a summary for your current project, which will be distributed at the next team meeting. You expected the meeting to last fifteen minutes, but James insisted on including all possible details and scenarios saying that the details could be deleted prior to distributing the project at the next team meeting. You wonder why the details have to be included if they are going to be deleted. The meeting lasted over two hours. You feel that James likes to expand every project and create more work than is necessary. You will be working with James on future projects and would like to solve this problem.

- How does the situation make you feel?
- What options to you have to solve the problem?

SITUATIONS

How would you handle the following situations?

- **S 16-1** You want to work, but sending your two young children to day care has its drawbacks because of the expense, and your day care does not allow sick children to attend. You have managed your childcare responsibilities because you make arrangements, have backup plans, and are a dependable and conscientious employee. One of your coworkers frequently brings her child to work with her. Unfortunately, the child is noisy and disruptive.

- **S 16-2** You have been employed longer than any other employee, and you are now the keeper of the keys. This means that you have keys to all offices. Louise frequently loses her keys. In the last month, you have opened Louise's door at least twelve times. You are happy to assist your coworkers, but Louise interrupts your meetings and projects to have her door opened. She is taking advantage of you.

- **S 16-3** To avoid the stress of fighting traffic and to save money on gas, you take the subway (or bus) to work each morning. Your morning commute is the perfect time to read the newspaper or your favorite book and mentally plan your workday. Recently cell phones have invaded your personal commuter time. Every morning for the last few months, the same individual has sat beside you, in front of you, or behind you. Each day you are treated to a loud and lively conversation about the intimate details of her personal life. You find the conversation very distracting and annoying.

PUNCTUATION REVIEW

Punctuate each of the following sentences. For a review of punctuation rules, see the Appendix.

1. During the preparatory activities for this proposal Mr Davis reorganized the entire Web site

2. She initiated and created a spreadsheet which contains all the pertinent information about budget request

3. Ms Nugyen serves as the main contact person for budget requests and she ensures that all employee needs and concerns are addressed promptly and satisfactorily

4. During her temporary employment period Ms Joseph successfully completed the negotiations for and processing of three major projects

5. Mr Garcia who is from Texas provided significant input into the new projects

6. Julie works well with all members of the team anticipates team projects and is liaison to the director

7. She is a consistently reliable employee in terms of attendance paperwork travel vouchers etc

8. Mr Sanchez welcomed the new assignments and had a key leadership role in the team accomplishment of the six year plan

9. She proposed an on site visit to the San Diego regional office but due to budget restrictions the trip was not approved

10. The challenge of course was maintaining and motivating a staff during the downsizing of the department

11. Despite the downsizing which affected every employee the department had a very successful year in meeting all of its goals

12. Therefore the fundamental strategy was to develop and accelerate the regional revision proposal

13. By the end of July the department had met its quota

14. When designing the proposal I made sure that the project reflected the corporations goals

15. During the second half of the fiscal year she received an outstanding evaluation

CD ASSIGNMENT

CD Assignment 16-1

Open the file **CD16-1_ISP** on your Student CD and follow the instructions to complete the job.

CHAPTER 17

Business Etiquette

Objectives

After studying this chapter, you should be able to:

1. Use proper business etiquette.
2. Greet business associates properly.
3. Dress properly for business functions.
4. Use correct table manners.
5. Tip appropriately.
6. Write social business communications.

THE IMPORTANCE OF BUSINESS ETIQUETTE

Do you have good manners?

Are you savvy about business etiquette? Have you felt uncomfortable in a social setting? Have you felt awkward and clumsy at a business party? Have you felt anxious and unsure of yourself? Are you at ease mingling with people you do not know at a meeting or business reception? Have you agonized over which fork to use, how to introduce someone, how to greet your supervisor in a social setting, how to express your condolences, how to dress for a business-social event, how to order in a restaurant, how much to tip, or other essentials of business interaction? Do you know the ground rules for business etiquette? Ignorance is not an excuse for poor manners. Do you have the knowledge and expertise to survive in a competitive business world? Your lack of manners and decorum can affect your relationship with business associates and colleagues.

Social and personal relations skills are important to your ability to manage any situation in the workplace. Knowing how to survive in an informal social setting with your friends is not enough. In addition, knowing the right time and the proper way to act in a business setting may mean the difference between success and failure. If you are socially inept, you could damage your career and opportunities for success. Moreover, proper business etiquette improves your professional image and may help your career advancement. Your professional aura reflects your thoughts, your knowledge, and your

HINT

An etiquette blunder may be difficult for your business acquaintances to forget.

Figure 17-1 A setting for a business luncheon.

skills. If you are knowledgeable about good manners and proper etiquette, you have the tools for success and will be more confident in business-social settings. Furthermore, you want to present a professional impression to your clients, business associates, colleagues, and supervisors. Although times have changed and our social interactions are more informal than in previous generations, it is still important to know the essentials of social etiquette.

Do you know how to respond to respond to each of the following workplace situations?

- Expressing your condolences to someone who has experienced the loss of a family member.
- Expressing congratulations to a supervisor or coworker upon receiving an award, recent engagement, marriage, or birth of a child or grandchild.
- What to say to the newly separated or divorced coworker.
- Who pays a restaurant bill for a business lunch or dinner?
- How to pay the restaurant bill.
- When and how much to tip.
- How to respect or acknowledge religious customs of clients and coworkers.
- Use of proper table manners.
- Proper conduct during an office party.
- Attending a business banquet.
- Purchasing an appropriate business gift.
- Writing a thank-you letter for gifts and meals.

HINT
Good manners are important for your professional future.

HINT
Knowing business etiquette is essential.

Business Etiquette   365

ETIQUETTE AT BUSINESS EVENTS

Greeting Associates

We all know how we greet our friends, but do you know the proper way to greet business associates? Is it appropriate to hug, shake hands, slap the person on the back or shoulder, or high-five the person? If you make a mistake, you could embarrass yourself and make everyone uncomfortable. There are two customary ways to greet business associates.

Shaking Hands

Shaking hands is the accepted business greeting and is always used when you are introduced to a person for the first time. A handshake is friendly and shows you are interested in the individual. In today's contemporary business world, either the man or woman may initiate the handshake. Each person extends his or her right hand. Use a firm handshake, but do not squeeze too hard or you will hurt the person. Conversely, do not use a limp handshake because it exemplifies a weak and unprofessional person.

Hugging

When business associates have not seen each other in a while, a hug may be the perfect greeting. In the United States, it is acceptable for two women to hug and for members of the opposite sex to hug. In foreign countries, a hug between men is acceptable. If you are unsure if a hug is proper, it is a good idea to ask, "May I hug you?" In the last several years, hugs have become common greetings between business associates.

Introducing Two People to Each Other

You will often have the task of introducing two people to each other. This may be a visitor to your office, a person attending a meeting, or someone who has an appointment with your supervisor. You should be knowledgeable of the proper etiquette involved in introductions so when you introduce people, you appear calm and professional, not frazzled. When making an introduction, speak slowly and clearly so both people can hear each other's name.

When introducing a younger person to an older person, it is helpful to say a few words about one or both people. Your comments provide the opening dialog for the conversation between the persons. In this example, Joseph is older than Libby.

Joseph, I would like you to meet Libby, who recently moved to our area from Roanoke. Joseph plans the monthly motivation parties, so he is a good person to know.

Present the person in the lower job category to the person in the upper job category. In this example, Patrick is the Executive Vice President, and Hal is the coordinator.

Patrick, please meet Hal, who recently joined our team. Patrick is the Executive Vice-President.

Conversations

Knowing what to say in a one-to-one or group conversation can be a challenge. Dead silence after the hello can be an awkward experience. Therefore, plan in advance basic conversation openers to use when needed.

Generally conversations begin on a nonbusiness topic and proceed slowly to a business topic. Conversations in social-business situations should be polite and cordial. If the topic is highly controversial, it probably should not be discussed in a social setting. Shown below are suggestions for making conversation when you do not know what to say.

The art of small talk
- Chat about the event you are attending.
- People like to talk about themselves, so ask a question. If you are attending a business event, ask about the person's job.
- Chat about the weather.
- Chat about a movie you have seen or a book you have read.
- Chat about a recent article in the newspaper.
- Ask where the person comes from.
- Ask the person where he or she went to college.
- Give the person your attention.
- Listen to what people say and ask follow-up questions.

Conversation topics to avoid
- Medical procedures.
- Gruesome subjects.
- Politics.
- Indecent stories.
- Gossip.
- Offensive jokes.

Although it is sometimes difficult to end a conversation, it is important to do so politely because an abrupt ending can destroy what everyone thought was a pleasant and productive conversation. Therefore, in addition to conversation openers, have basic conversation closers preplanned. You do not want to appear to just walk away or to leave the other person hanging. You need a conversation conclusion, such as "I enjoyed talking. Let's get together soon," "Let's talk about this later," or "I see Bill, and I need to chat with him for a minute. Please excuse me." It is very important to end the conversation on a cordial note, even if the conversation topic was disagreeable.

Attending a reception

The purpose of a reception is to meet and socialize with many people and make new contacts. Therefore, do not chat just with the persons you came with or those you know. A reception is the perfect opportunity for you to introduce yourself to someone new because generally everyone is friendly and open to meeting new people. For that reason, circulate and expand your network of business associates. Do not interrupt a conversation to join it, but stand close by and when the opportunity presents itself, make an appropriate comment.

Although the primary goal of the business reception is to meet business associates, receptions are also opportunities to enjoy tasty foods and drinks. The food served may be something simple like chips, dip, and veggies, or it may be more elaborate and include cheeses and hot hors d'oeuvres. In addition to easy-to-eat foods, receptions frequently serve messy-to-eat foods like wings. Eating, drinking, or holding your food, all while chatting, can be challenge. Therefore, do not have a plate of food in one hand and a drink in the other because then you do not have a hand with which to eat. For easy maneuverability, it may be wise to eat something first and then have a drink. More important, you cannot shake hands if both your hands are full. Always remember that one of the primary purposes of a reception is to mingle, not just eat. Since you do not want to shake hands with messy fingers, use your silverware and napkin to keep your hands clean for greetings.

Receiving Line

Some events have a receiving line where you are greeted by the hosts or very important persons (VIPs). The procedure is to say hello, introduce yourself if necessary, and shake each person's hand. When you introduce yourself, say your name and where you are employed. When proceeding through the receiving line, keep your comments short because there are probably other people waiting to say hello.

Gifts

If you are attending an event at a person's home, it is proper to take a gift. If you do not take a gift, you may be considered rude and impolite. If you know your host's taste, you can take something special, such as a book or CD that he or she would enjoy. Of course, the time-honored gifts shown below are always appropriate.

Traditional gift suggestions
- Candy
- Wine
- Flowers or plants
- Basket of fruit, cheese, crackers, or jellies

PROPER DRESS

Do you know how to dress appropriately for business-social occasions? We live in an informal world, but dressing too casually can be a blunder. First impressions are important and people remember appearances. Therefore, carefully choose your attire. The way you dress paints a picture of you, your personality, and your business knowledge. Dressing inappropriately provides a poor image of yourself and your company; it also can affect your career.

In a social-business setting, dress modestly with clothing that is not too tight, too short, too low in the front, or too low in the back. Provocative clothing is inappropriate in a workplace social setting.

- What should you wear to an office holiday party?

Holiday party attire can be casual, business professional, or dressy.

If casual clothing is worn, it should be upscale and snappy. A nice pair of slacks with an attractive shirt or blouse is appropriate for a man or woman. To make the outfit more chic, a jacket or blazer may be worn.

A business professional holiday outfit for a woman is a dress, skirt suit, or pants suit accessorized with jewelry. A business professional holiday outfit for a man is a traditional suit or blazer with a bright or holiday tie.

If dressy clothing is worn, the man wears a business professional suit. A dressy holiday outfit for a woman is probably a black dress or fancy black pants suit. Women should not wear dresses or tops that are too revealing.

- What should you wear to an office picnic?

Picnics are casual, but do not wear torn or ragged clothing. Do not wear T-shirts with sayings that could offend someone. Also, do not wear your tightest and shortest shorts. Women's tops should not be cut too low.

- What should you wear to an after-work office reception?

Receptions can be either business professional or business casual attire. Most people will probably wear what they wore to work the day of the reception. When in doubt about what to wear, it is better to be more professional than casual. If you wear casual, it should be upscale, not sloppy.

BUSINESS LUNCHES AND DINNERS

Business lunches and dinners are part of the working day and an integral aspect of your professional life, so do not feel that they infringe on your personal time. It is common for business professionals to meet for breakfast, lunch, dinner, or drinks to

Figure 17-2   Dinner meetings are common in the business world.

socialize or discuss business topics. Use the opportunity of a business lunch or dinner to your advantage. Meet coworkers and supervisors away from the office and demonstrate your knowledge and skills. Attending a business lunch or dinner may also be an opportunity to show that you are an individual who has interests outside the office. Mention a book you recently read or a play you attended. You want your office colleagues to know that you are a well-informed and social person. Business lunches and dinners are also an important opportunity to network. These business meetings generally begin with a few minutes of nonbusiness chatter prior to beginning the business discussion. Be aware that poor table manners can damage your chances for a successful meeting and business project.

A social-business lunch or dinner may be held in a restaurant or a person's home. Be polite and courteous to the host, regardless of where the meal is served. Upon arriving, greet the host or hostess. At the end of the event, thank the host or hostess and mention that you had an enjoyable time.

If alcoholic beverages are served, limit what you drink. You do not want to become drunk and make inappropriate comments that could destroy your career. The type of drink you have is an easy way to stereotype you in someone's eyes. If you are attending an upscale event, your drink should reflect the event. Beer is generally casual, while wine is more sophisticated. Depending on the circumstances, it may be better to order a sparkling water instead of a beer or wine because you do not want to be the only person drinking an alcoholic beverage.

If you have food allergies, religious beliefs, or other factors that limit your food selections, politely tell your host about your concern. If it is a sitdown meal, it is helpful for the host to be informed of your food limitations prior to the event. Naturally, you should stress that you will be happy to eat something simple like a salad. If your food issue is not major, you can eat the other foods on the plate and ignore the offending item. If you are attending a meeting with a pre-ordered meal, generally the wait-service staff can make a last-minute food substitution to meet your food needs.

When ordering from a menu, make your food selection in the same price range as that of your host. Do not order the most expensive item on the menu. Do not order the same food as your supervisor unless it is something that you really enjoy. Use some originality when you select your food and remember to eat slowly. Nervousness may make you eat too fast, and then you will have nothing to do while the others are still eating. Furthermore, always order something you can easily eat, not something messy. In addition, do not be the only person to order dessert because everyone will watch you eat, and someone may even make comments about your consuming too many calories. If it is a small group, speak with each person at the table, not just the people seated near you.

At a buffet table, do not overload your plate because you do not want people to make disparaging remarks about your eating habits. Furthermore, most buffets allow guests to return for a second plate, so do not overstuff your plate.

Foods to avoid
- Sticky foods that you eat with your fingers.
- Seafood that is difficult to cut and eat.
- Foods that have strong aromas that may upset other guests.

Table Manners

What do your manners say about you? Shown below are some suggestions to improve your table manners.
- When all guests are seated at your table, put your napkin on your lap. At the end of the meal, place your napkin on the right side of the dinner plate. Do not put the napkin on the dinner plate.

Figure 17-3   A table setting.

- The silverware on the outside is used first. Forks are placed to the left of the plate. If you have two forks, the fork on the far left is used first. If a salad and an entrée are both served, the salad fork is on the far left side and should be used first. In today's informal world, some restaurants provide only one fork. Therefore, when the salad plate is removed, you may be asked to keep the fork. If you have a bread plate, put your fork on the bread plate until your entrée arrives. Otherwise, put the fork on the left side of table.

- Your beverage is placed to your right.

- Your salad plate is placed to your left.

- Your bread and butter plate is placed to your left. The bread and butter plate is placed above the salad plate.

- Wait until everyone at your table has been served before you begin eating. If there is a delay in the service and those without plates tell you to begin, you may begin to eat. Eat slowly or you may finish before the other guests. If you finish early, you will have nothing to do while the other guests are eating.

- When eating soup, move the spoon away from you in the bowl. Then carefully place the side of the spoon into your mouth. Do not put too much soup on the spoon or you will spill it.

- Only cut a few bites of your food at one time. Do not cut the entire dish into bite-size pieces.

- Food such as bread, butter, salad dressing, salt, pepper, and so on, are generally passed to the right.

- To avoid the problem of embarrassing yourself and destroying your food by oversalting, taste the food prior to salting it.

- Do not butter an entire bread or a roll. Break bread and rolls into small pieces prior to eating.

Poor table manners

- Do not reach across the table for a plate of food.
- Do not stab your steak.
- Do not put your elbows on the table.
- Do not talk with food in your mouth.
- Do not make noise when you eat.
- Do not chew with your mouth open.
- Do not wear heavy, long jewelry that will fall into the food.
- Do not wear long flowing shirts or blouses that will fall into the food.
- Do not use your napkin as a tissue.
- Do not comb your hair, apply lipstick, remove a contact lens, or insert eye drops in the presence of others. All personal toiletries should be attended to in the restroom.

Dinner Mishaps

What happens if you:

- Drop your plate?
- Spill coffee?
- Spill wine?
- Drop your fork?
- Drop your napkin?

Suggestions

- If you drop your fork, ask for another one.
- If you drop your napkin, pick it up and put it back on your lap.
- If you are in a restaurant and you spill something, try to stop the spill with a napkin. Then request assistance from the wait-service staff.
- If you are at dinner in a private home and you spill something, wipe it up immediately. Then offer to help clean it.
  - If it is an easy-to-clean spot on the tablecloth, do not worry about it.
  - If it is a spot on the carpet or a damaging spot on the tablecloth, the guest should offer to pay to have it cleaned. If the host declines the offer, the guest should send a small gift with a note of apology.

Arriving and Leaving

Shown below are hints to make you a first-class guest.

- For lunch and dinner, guests should arrive on time. For parties and receptions, guest should arrive on time or within fifteen minutes of the scheduled time.
- Guests in restaurants should leave shortly after everyone has finished eating and drinking. Coffee after the meal is an additional opportunity for chatting.
- Lunch or dinner guests at a home should wait at least twenty to thirty minutes after the meal before leaving.
- Within a couple of days after the event, write a note thanking the host for the lovely party, evening, and so on. In today's technology-driven world, email notes are acceptable, but handwritten thank-you notes are often appreciated.

Toasts

Happy occasions often include a toast to someone. When someone makes a toast, raise your glass of wine or water in honor of the person and take a sip. If you are asked to make a toast, make a pleasant comment about the person, and keep the toast short. Long tributes are often embarrassing to the honoree.

TIPPING SUGGESTIONS

If you are going to succeed in business, it is important know when, whom, and how to tip. It is often customary to give a tip for good service, and ignorance is no excuse for inappropriate tipping. Not tipping is rude. Shown below are typical tipping guidelines.

- In a restaurant, give the wait-service staff 15 percent to 20 percent of the bill. In a more expensive restaurant, the going rate is generally 20 percent.
- In an expensive restaurant, give the wine steward 15 percent of the wine bill.
- If there is a coat check employee, give $1 per coat. If an umbrella and briefcase are also checked, add a $1 for each item.
- Restroom attendants are generally given $1. The tip may be left in a glass vase or bowl on the counter.
- The tip for valet parking is from $1 to $3, depending on the location. For example, a basic garage attendant receives $1, but an attendant in an upscale hotel receives $3.
- Skycaps and bellmen are generally tipped $1 to $2 per bag.
- When tipping, fold the dollar bills so the money is easily identified when handed to the person. You want the person to know how much tip he or she is receiving. If you are giving $4, show all four ones when you hand the tip. If you are giving a $5 bill, show the five.
- Always say thank you when you hand the tip.

INTERNATIONAL ETIQUETTE

Since we live in an intercultural environment, social-business skills must be international in scope. You must know how to behave in a setting with guests from many countries and with a variety of cultural backgrounds. Your lack of awareness of social customs could offend international guests.

Shown below are general suggestions regarding international guests. You should also review Chapter 16. Prior to an event, it is wise to research the cultural customs of the specific country so you will not offend anyone.

- Be aware of personal space concerns. In some foreign countries, people stand very close to each other, which people in the United States may feel is an invasion of personal space.
- If visiting a home in a foreign country, the guest usually brings a gift.
- Equality between men and women in business is often not as accepted as it is in the United State.
- In some countries, the standard greeting for known associates includes three air kisses on alternating cheeks.
- Smoking is often an acceptable practice in foreign countries.

- Being late is the accepted practice in many countries.
- In some countries, people touch on the shoulders or arms.
- Gestures may have a meaning you are not accustomed to.
- In some countries, leaving a little food on your plate shows that you enjoyed the meal.

WRITTEN SOCIAL-BUSINESS LETTERS

Condolence Note

Business situations often require written communications to express condolences or congratulations. Shown below are samples you can use as models for your own letters.

Condolence Note 1

We at L & J Enterprises were very saddened to hear of the passing of Jason. Please accept our deepest sympathy.

Jason and I served on many committees together, so I knew him well. He was always a terrific person to work with and an inspiration to everyone. Furthermore, we will always remember his many years of leadership, service, and dedication to the business community. He was a dear friend to all of us and will truly be missed.

We are sharing in your great loss and feel that we have also lost a dear family member. Please accept our deepest condolences, and may knowing that we care provide comfort to you and your family.

Condolence Note 2

We were shocked and saddened to learn of your great loss. The news was so hard for us to accept. Nathan had a zest for life that we loved and admired. His passing will be felt by all who knew him, and he will be mourned by everyone.

He was a personal friend in addition to being a member of our workplace community, and we will genuinely miss him.

We are sending our deepest sympathy to you and your family. May your happy memories be a comfort to you during this difficult time, and may time help heal the sense of loss you feel.

Congratulatory Note

Congratulatory Note 1

Best wishes to you and your family on the happy occasion of your daughter's wedding. We have fond memories of Maria when, as a young child, she accompanied you to our office. She has now grown into a delightful young woman. We wish Maria and her fiancé health and happiness as they begin a new life together.

Again congratulations to you and your wife on this joyous event.

Congratulatory Note 2

Congratulations on your new position as director of P & J Enterprises. I am happy that your hard work and dedication are now being recognized. As I have said previously, you have all of the qualifications needed to succeed as director. Your past experiences have prepared you well for the new job, and I know that you are up to the challenges of the position. As we know, you have the tools for success in your pocket.

The only downside to the new position is that you are moving to the West Coast, and we live on the East Coast. Please stop by to visit whenever you are in this area.

Best regards to you and your family.

Thank-You Note

Thank-You Note 1

Thank you for the lovely blue vase. I know that I will treasure the vase because it is a reminder of the enjoyable times we had together. As you know, I love to garden, so I will cut some of my favorite flowers and put them in my beautiful new vase.

Thank you again for thinking of me.

Thank-You Note 2

Please accept the goodie basket as a token of our appreciation for speaking at our annual Children's Benefit luncheon. Your speech was caring and inspirational, but your presence and support were of utmost importance. Thank you for taking time from your hectic schedule to be with us. I know how busy you are.

As always, we are thankful for your encouragement and assistance.

Retirement Note

Retirement Note 1

Best wishes to you on your retirement. Everyone at SoBe Associates enjoyed working with you and benefited from your many years of experience. It is difficult to imagine how we will manage without your guidance.

As you begin this new stage of your life, we want to wish you many years of enjoyment, health, and happiness. Now you will have plenty of time to play all of the golf games we often discussed.

We want to keep in touch with you, so call us to arrange a date for lunch.

CONCLUSION

Business etiquette is a powerful tool to help you climb the corporate ladder. Unfortunately, inappropriate behavior can damage your reputation and chances for success. Good manners, courtesy, and appropriate clothing all work together with your knowledge, education, and experience to provide the framework for a flourishing career.

Therefore, do not embarrass yourself by making a mistake in etiquette. Use good social skills to your advantage and be a well-bred and polite person. Conducting yourself properly is essential for your career advancement. Good manners are essential, and the following key phrases will help express your good manners:

- Please
- Thank you
- You are welcome
- My pleasure

CHAPTER REVIEW

1. Describe an appropriate handshake.
2. List three suggestions, as discussed in the chapter, for topics for small talk.
3. Who greets you in a receiving line and what do you do?
4. List three traditional host gifts, as discussed in the chapter.
5. Describe a table setting. Indicate where the plates, silverware, and glasses are placed.
6. List two tipping suggestions, as discussed in the chapter.

ACTIVITIES

1. Describe two social functions you attended.
2. Write a paragraph discussing why you think good manners are important.
3. Ask two office employees to describe a business-social event (holiday party, picnic, etc.) that they attended.
4. Your supervisor is a grandmother for the first time. Express your congratulations to her. Write a paragraph discussing your conversation.
5. Your coworker told you that she is getting divorced. What would you say to her? Write a paragraph discussing your conversation.
6. Your coworker's husband is going to have major surgery. What would you say to her? Write a paragraph discussing your conversation.
7. Your supervisor's mother passed away. Express your condolences to him. Would you send a gift? Write a paragraph discussing your comments and describe the gift if you decide to send one.

PROJECTS

Project 33

Send this memo to the staff. It is from Bridget Valle, Human Resources Director.

You are invited to attend this year's Employee Awards Ceremony, which will be held in the auditorium. This is our annual opportunity to recognize some of our valued employees. Please join us on this special day for your friends and colleagues. After the ceremony, there will be a reception in honor of all employees. At L & J Industries, we acknowledge and appreciate all employees.

We look forward to seeing you at the ceremony. Share in the opportunity to personally thank your coworkers for their dedication to all of us.

Project 34

Send an email to the staff and attach this memo. The memo is from Rhonda Maxwell, Training Director.

Additional End-of-the-Year Budget Training sessions are now being offered.

The hands-on session will focus on preparing the end-of-year budget reports. Attendees will be able to perform a budget query and create monthly, quarterly, and yearly reports. Attendees will be shown how to view the availability of funds by account number and how to download budget queries into a spreadsheet.

All training sessions will be from 1 to 4 P.M. Training sessions will be offered as shown below.

January 18	Room 607
January 25	Room 607
January 30	Room 725
February 2	Room 607
February 5	Room 725

Each training session will end with a question-and-answer period, so bring your questions.

To register for the sessions:

Go to the company Web site.
Click Professional Development
Click Budget Training
Key in your name and department
If you have any questions, contact Trong Nugyen at 2377 or email her.

HUMAN RELATIONS SKILL DEVELOPMENT

HR 17-1 Your Wardrobe

You decided to update your work wardrobe and improve your professional image, so you have been shopping. Since your budget is limited, you spent time and effort planning, looking at magazine articles, and seeking clothing bargains.

When you dressed this morning, you very were excited about your new persona because today is the introduction of your new wardrobe. You decided to wear one of your favorite new professional outfits, which includes a trendy peacock-blue-colored blouse. Upon arriving at work, your spirits were quickly dampened. At your early morning meeting, two of your colleagues were also dressed in peacock blue, and a third colleague made a snide remark about everyone dressing as bluebirds. You now feel that your efforts to update your professional image were a total waste of time.

- How do you feel?
- What should you do to cope with the situation?
- How should you respond to your colleague who made the spiteful remark?

HR 17-2 Reception Behavior

You are attending an all-day conference which includes a buffet lunch. It is now 12:30, and you are hungry. You have been patiently waiting in the long buffet line for fifteen minutes. When it is your turn to reach the food tables, three people enter the line and start talking to the person in front of you. You overhear their conversation and one person says, "We're going to get in line with you so we can continue brainstorming ideas for next month's awards ceremony."

- How do you feel?
- How should you handle the situation?

SITUATIONS

How would you handle the following situations?

- S 17-1 Periodically you speak at meetings and must transport your files. Over the last year, you have requested a memory stick from the supplies supervisor many times, but you have not received one. Each time you ask for a memory stick, the supplies supervisor makes excuses and discourteous comments to you. You have noticed that at least 50 percent of the members of your department have received new memory sticks, but you cannot get one.

- S 17-2 It is obvious that your supervisor does not like you. She berates you whenever she has the opportunity. Her latest tactic is not to respond to your emails. Recently you have sent several emails requesting information on a project you are completing. You have not received any responses. You know that the email system is working because you receive emails that your supervisor sends to the entire staff.

- S 17-3 Several weeks ago, you ordered new business cards for your supervisor. Tomorrow your supervisor is leaving on a three-week business trip, and the cards have not arrived. You call the printer and are told the cards will arrive in a day or two.

PUNCTUATION REVIEW

Punctuate each of the following sentences. For a review of punctuation rules, see the Appendix.

1. As recent events have shown it is critical to have a large budget reserve
2. Because of the slowdown of the economy we recommended that four projects be delayed
3. The Board of Directors which is led by Mr Martinez has been proactive in dealing with the crisis
4. In both cases the crisis was quickly resolved
5. The position requires five years experience in the development and marketing of new technologies
6. Ms Hopkins who recently joined the company will be working in a multicultural environment
7. This is evidenced in the richness of the applicant pool the willingness of applicants to relocate and general interest from the community
8. An overview of the seminar which will be held on Monday is available on our Web site
9. Rick who is actively involved in community service is a fourth generation director of the company
10. If you do not complete the form correctly we will be unable to process your request

11. To prevent delays include your email address and telephone number

12. She has completed negotiations for a $50 million project which is waiting for final approval from the board of directors

13. Hanna is very energetic enthusiastic and personable in her dealings with the public

14. If you do not want to miss a call use your voice-mail system

15. His responsibilities include supervising mentoring and guiding the professional development of the staff

CD ASSIGNMENTS

CD Assignment 17-1

Open the file **CD17-1_AR** on your Student CD and follow the instructions to complete the job.

CD Assignment 17-2

Open the file **CD17-1_IT** on your Student CD and follow the instructions to complete the job.

CHAPTER 18

Tips of the Trade

Objectives

After studying this chapter, you should be able to:

1. Improve your office efficiency.
2. Dress appropriately for the office.
3. Improve your map-reading skills.
4. Handle work-related problems.

INTRODUCTION

This final chapter is different from the other chapters in this book. Rather than discussing another specific area of office procedures, this chapter will concentrate on *you* and how you can improve your office efficiency and handle work-related problems. This chapter is filled with hints and techniques that usually come only with years of on-the-job experience. Many of the techniques discussed in this chapter are as applicable to your personal life as they are to your professional career. Mastery of these skills, therefore, will aid in your personal as well as your professional growth.

> What are your personal tips for success?

PERSONAL HINTS

- Be a productive member of the team.
- Be a catalyst for innovation.
- Build a consensus for implementing your ideas.
- Use feedback from coworkers to fine-tune your projects.
- Anticipate problems so you are ready to solve them.
- Prioritize your jobs and constantly review your priorities.

- Keep yourself focused on your objectives.
- Look for projects that will spotlight your talents.
- Avoid statements that trigger a negative response.
- Repair damaged professional relationships before it is too late.
- A smile can help you win the support you need for an idea.
- Redirect anger in a positive way.
- Change your mind-set to see obstacles as opportunities to succeed.
- Always be nonjudgmental.
- Always have a positive attitude.
- Inspire creative thinking and inspire employees.
- Understand that learning is an ongoing process. Do not limit yourself to what you know today. Learn for the future. Realize that your skills are quickly outmoded and need to be updated frequently.
- Expect interruptions and do not allow them to irritate you. Interruptions are a daily occurrence in the life of an office employee. Do not allow interruptions to sabotage your productivity.
- In your role of office assistant, people will think you have answers for everything. They may expect you to be able to answer questions that are not pertinent to your job. Never be rude to anyone. Always answer questions in a courteous manner and to the best of your ability. If you do not know the answer to a question, indicate that you will try to locate the requested information.
- Read the newspaper daily to be informed about the political and business environment in your area. The business world changes frequently and it is essential that you read articles in newspapers and professional journals to keep current in your field. Read about your competitors to learn as much about them as you can. Learn what they are planning, their goals, their image, who their clients are, and their financial position.
- Use sick leave when it is appropriate. Do not expose your colleagues to germs, but do not use sick leave because you want a day free from work.
- Join professional organizations so your name will become familiar to business associates inside and outside your company. By increasing your visibility, you may reap the benefits professionally.

Separating Your Personal and Office Lives

Leave your personal life and problems at home, and leave your office life and problems at the office. Make a conscious effort to separate the two phases of your life. Taking your office problems home every day will interfere with the enjoyment of your personal life. The relaxation and stimulation you receive from your personal life will enhance your ability to handle office problems. Separating office problems and home problems is not easy, but with practice it can work.

Pick Yourself Up

Everyone has days when nothing seems to go right. To boost your morale, remember your strong points and the positive comments you have received. Also, remind yourself that there will be good days again.

Do not become upset or become defensive after receiving constructive criticism; accept it and learn from it. Consider the validity of the comments and modify your behavior accordingly.

Compliments

If someone gives you a compliment, accept it and say thank you. Some people respond with a denial of the compliment. For example, if you receive a compliment on your presentation, do not say, "I did not think that I made a good presentation."

Recognition

Employee recognition is motivating and uplifting. People like to know that their contributions to the workplace are valued, and they like to feel that they are important and appreciated. Offices often remember employees on Bosses Day, during the second full week in October, and Administrative Professionals Week®, during the last full week (Sunday to Saturday) in April.

Rumors

Use rumors to your advantage. For example, if you hear that your department or company will be restructuring, talk with your supervisor about accepting responsibility for a new project that will allow you to improve your skills and demonstrate your capabilities. Then when a new opportunity arises, you will have the required knowledge to step into the job.

Mentor

A mentor is a person who advises and guides. For the mentoring process to flourish, the mentor and the worker both must be on the same wavelength. Frequently a mentor is a person who has obtained a position higher than yours and who is willing to provide advice. A mentor can make your career advance more quickly and can steer you in the proper direction when a career choice must be made. Generally, the selection of a mentor is an informal process, and the relationship often is not directly stated between the parties. Rather, the mentoring relationship develops gradually through mutual understanding and trust. Sometimes mentoring is more formal, and some organizations establish mentoring programs for new employees who are guided by a senior employee. One of the major advantages of mentoring is the exposure to new ideas and opportunities, which may not have been possible without the guidance of a mentor.

MY SUCCESS STORY

My Name Is Maria

I am so excited that I have a good job, but when I started the job, I had concerns about the job and my coworkers. You see, I was not born in this country. Life is not the same here as it was in my country. Coming to this country was a cultural shock for me. My family and I moved here for a better life. I knew the best way to get ahead was to get an education, so I did. My job is with a family-owned company, which I like. The idea of working together with family is kind of like working in my country. I thought that my coworkers would laugh at the way I speak or my cultural background. I was wrong. They were interested in learning about my culture, and they did not laugh. They encouraged me to share with them and explain our way of life. I have the best coworkers who have turned into my best friends. Life is good.

Thank-You Notes

Write thank-you letters to people, such as teachers, mentors, and supervisors, who have helped you. Also write to colleagues and employees who have assisted you because people enjoy knowing that their help is appreciated.

Positive Thinking

Change your mental attitude, be positive, and improve your life. Do not be pessimistic. Negative feelings can weigh you down. Find the positive in each situation and emphasize it. It is possible to modify your pessimistic attitude and be optimistic.

Office Attire

Let your voice, appearance, and personal characteristics create the stage for your professional image. A professional is aware of the importance the business community attaches to appearance. When first entering the working world, you may have to adjust your wardrobe from that of a college student to clothing appropriate for a working person. It is wise not to completely change your wardrobe at one time. Buy a few things and decide if they are appropriate. Look at how the others in your office dress, and give special attention to the wardrobes of people who have jobs to which you would like to advance. Do the men wear ties, suits, or sport coats? Do the women wear suits, dresses, blazers, or separates—slacks, skirts, and sweaters? Then try to dress like those who have the job you would like in the future, rather than dressing for your present job. Executives may see that you are a candidate for advancement if your professional appearance supports your professional work.

In some traditional office settings, jackets must be worn by men and women. The jacket may be removed while employees are working, but it should be worn when a client comes in the office. When wearing jewelry, keep it classic; if you can hear it, too much is being worn.

In the last few years, the clothing worn in the workplace has become more casual. In some offices where the employees dress daily in traditional business attire, employees dress casually on Fridays. On Fridays, the employees wear *business casual*, casual clothing with a professional appearance—not jeans or sweat outfits. Dress-down days have become more popular, particularly in the summer months. Offices that have a casual Friday policy may have a provision that if there is a meeting with clients on a Friday, traditional business attire is appropriate instead of casual attire. In some offices, dress-down Fridays have evolved into business casual every day. Furthermore, workers in many high-tech companies wear casual clothing daily instead of business professional attire.

Some employers feel that the clothing worn today is too casual and inappropriate for the office. In most offices, jeans are not acceptable, and T-shirts with ludicrous remarks are unsuitable. For women, skirts that are too short or blouses that are cut too low are not appropriate office attire.

Sometimes it is more difficult to decide how to dress in the summer because most people feel more casual. While sandals, flip flops, and capris may fit into your summer lifestyle, the office dress code determines if they are acceptable. However, low-rise jeans and slacks that expose too much skin are not appropriate for the workplace. When in doubt about what is appropriate, check your company standards. It would be embarrassing to be sent home to change your clothes.

Always dress appropriately for the office. The one day that you dress in a nonbusiness manner will unexpectedly be the day that it is important for you to look professional. In bad weather, some people are tempted to dress in a sloppy manner. Do not embarrass yourself by dressing in a messy and unprofessional style.

Figure 18-1   An employee dressed for casual Friday. Courtesy of Eastman Kodak Company.

In addition, dress appropriately for your age. The trendy clothes worn by employees who are in their twenties are not appropriate for employees who are in their fifties. It is important to dress age appropriately so you do not look out of place. Dressing appropriately for your age does not mean wearing old and out-dated clothing. It means wearing clothing suitable for your workplace and age.

Furthermore, plan your outfit the night before so you do not waste precious morning hours selecting an outfit. To save time, organize your closet so that it is easy to coordinate outfits.

Always buy good-quality clothing that will last rather than buy fad items that quickly go out of style, but update your wardrobe each season with a few fashionable purchases.

What is the proper attire for your workplace?

An important aspect of appearance is a rested body. Always allow sufficient time for rest and sleep because you cannot function properly in the office if you are drowsy and exhausted.

Humor in the Workplace

As adults, we have learned to control our humor and often do not allow it to enter the workplace. Today the trend is changing. Humor has a respectable place in the world of work. Humor encourages people to see fun and laughter in difficult or tiresome situations, and it can help dissipate an angry confrontation. In addition, humor can help relieve stress, put people at ease, improve morale, and boost your ability to focus on the issue at hand. However, do not laugh at or exploit the plight or background of others.

Is humor a part of your lifestyle?

- Do you often see the humor in a situation?
- Do you laugh at jokes?
- Do you tell jokes?
- Do you sparkle when you hear a funny story?
- Do you share humorous situations or stories with others?
- Would your friends and colleagues say you have a sense of humor?
- Would your supervisor say you have a sense of humor?
- Do you take yourself too seriously?

HINTS FOR YOUR OFFICE

Write It Down

One of the most important hints for the office is *read*, *watch*, *listen*, and *take notes on everything*. Pay particular attention to details. Handheld computer organizers are very helpful for note taking and personal organization because they are easily accessible. If you do not take notes, you will not remember how to do something the next time the same situation occurs. Write notes about a project and, most important, organize your notes so you can find them later. To organize your notes, use a 3- × 5-inch card file box, a notebook with dividers, file folders, or a computer software package. A year later you may have a question about something you did. If you cannot find your notes, you will be lost. In addition, back up all computer note files.

Make Notes Now

If it was inappropriate for you to take notes during a meeting outside the office, jot down your thoughts as soon as you leave, before you forget the details of the meeting. Do not wait until you return to your office to make your notes. Immediately make notes after getting into your car or onto the bus.

Know Your Office Location

Be able to give directions to your office from public transportation, main roads, or interstate highways. Be able to explain to others the location of your office by describing the distinctive features and color of your building as well as the landmarks, street intersections, restaurants, and stores near it. Can you describe where a visitor should park, how to enter the building, or how to walk through a large building to find your office?

Employee Notification

An emergency situation or weather-related problem could require the unexpected closing of the office before employees leave home for work in the morning. There are several ways an office can create an employee at-home emergency notification system. Information about the closing can be posted on a company's public Web site or on an Internet site available only to employees. If the office has each employee's home email address, a group email can be sent regarding the office closure. You might place a voice-mail message about the closing on a phone number that employees are instructed to call in case of emergency or inclement weather. In addition, employees could call their voice mailbox and retrieve a message distributed to all employees. Another alternative is to establish a telephone tree. In a *telephone tree*, each employee is given the home phone numbers of several other employees. For example, the first person calls four people, and then each of the four people call four additional people, and so on. Telephone trees may not be reliable because if one person is not contacted, many people further down the tree will be affected and not get the message.

Employee Suggestion Box

Create an employee suggestion box. Read the suggestions, discuss them with your supervisor, and use all reasonable suggestions. Of course, never ridicule any suggestions.

Leaving the Office

Do not be the first person to leave the office each day or the first to leave office-related functions such as holiday parties or luncheons. If you continually are the first to leave, you may appear disinterested in your work or dismissive of your colleagues.

Elevators

An elevator conversation can be overheard by everyone riding in the elevator. If your conversation can be overhead by others, discuss only casual, nonsensitive subjects. Conversely, if you are with only one other person in the elevator, it may be the perfect opportunity to discuss a project or reinforce an idea.

The Lost Supervisor

Be able to locate your supervisor at all times. If the supervisor is going to be out of the office, know when he or she is expected to return.

Where Is It?

It is important to remember where you put items. If you cannot remember where everything is located, keep a "Where is it?" book. The "Where is it?" book can be a computer file with a printed copy for easy accessibility.

Food at Your Desk

Avoid eating at your desk. If a client walks in, food scattered across your desk looks messy and may even have a strong aroma. Also, you might spill food on important papers or on your computer. If you must eat at your desk, keep food in a desk drawer and remove a bite at a time. Keep all food out of sight.

Unknown Title

Sometimes it can be difficult to determine if a name is male or female. If you are unsure of a person's gender when writing a letter, call the person's office and ask. Also, if you are unsure of a person's title, verify your information. Some people are offended if an incorrect title is used.

Check the Desk

Because of illness or unanticipated problems, an employee may not come to work. The absence of an employee should not be an excuse for delay in a project. The absent employee's desk, in-basket, and out-basket should be checked to determine if there is a project that must be handled or a telephone call that must be made. Many offices have a policy that coworkers check the desk of an absent employee. If there is no policy, you should ask your supervisor whether you should check the desk of another coworker. The courtesy of checking a desk is a shared responsibility among employees.

Clean-Up Day

Designate a clean-up or organize-it day. Employees dress casually and spend the day cleaning offices by organizing, filing, or throwing out office clutter. A designated clean-up day may be the motivation necessary to inspire everyone to organize their offices.

List of Employees

A list of all employees should be available to all persons answering the telephones. Use the list so you do not have to ask important company officials what their titles are or how to spell their names. Also, be able to correctly pronounce the names of all employees.

Commitments

When you say you will do something, do it. Make a commitment and adhere to it. Always be responsible.

Assistance

When you receive a telephone call or someone approaches you with a question, say, "Hello. How can I help you?" This indicates your in interest in the individual and displays a courteous manner.

Response

After you are thanked for helping to solve a problem or to answer a question, a good response for you to make is "You are welcome" or "My pleasure." This comeback sets a pleasant tone and shows that you actually care about the person and are eager to help him or her. Do not say, "Huh," "Whatever," "No problem," or "Ok."

Ending a Conversation

When you are busy working on a project and a coworker stops at your desk to chat, end the conversation politely by saying, "I am sorry, but I need to work on this project. I will stop by later to chat with you. Thanks so much for understanding."

Remembering People

Prepare a card file or use computer software to record the names and addresses of all clients, business associates, and coworkers. Include important information about these people, such as descriptions (so you will recognize them the next time they come to the office), important dates in their lives, their preferences about restaurants and foods, and their spouses' and children's names. Do not pry for this information, but if they mention these details, you can enter them into your file. People like to feel important. Review the information prior to the person's next visit to your office.

Employees like to be remembered, and computers have made remembering easier. One way to show interest is to develop an employee birthday list and add it to your calendar. Then send computer-designed or store-purchased cards to each person on the appropriate date. Offices often celebrate birthdays with parties for each person or a party for all persons with a birthday in that month. In some companies, the person celebrating the birthday provides the food for the party.

Addressing Clients by Name

When clients call on the telephone or visit the office, call them by name. Say, "Good morning, Ms. Sanchez. It is nice to see you."

Meeting People

If you meet people at a party and you do not feel it is an appropriate location or time to discuss business or the possibility of a new job, tell them that you would like to arrange a time at their convenience to talk with them about a job, business, etc.

Keep a Contact List

Always keep a file of people you meet, and put everyone you meet in your file. These contacts can be very helpful if you have a problem. A last-minute crisis may be solved by a person on your contact list. This list can be kept in your computer software contact list, computer or written address book, personal digital assistant (PDA), business card file, 3- × 5-inch card index system, or database file. The list should include a telephone number and email address.

Smoking in the Office

Because of concerns about indoor air pollution and health risks, many organizations now restrict smoking in offices. In some areas of the country, it is illegal to smoke in public buildings. Many companies even restrict smoking to designated areas outside

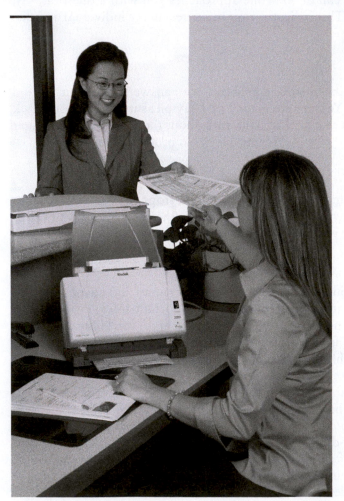

Figure 18-2 An employee assisting a client. Courtesy of Eastman Kodak Company.

the building, usually away from the main entrance. Be aware of your company's policy regarding smoking. Knowledge of this policy is important if you smoke or if you have clients who smoke.

Serial Numbers

Maintain a list of serial numbers and model numbers for equipment in your office as well as computer software. You may have to supply a serial number to receive authorization for repair of equipment that is under warranty. To upgrade software, the serial number of the current version is frequently required.

Desk Organization

Organize your desk for easy accessibility. Always be able to quickly locate supplies and working materials, such as project files. Use desk organizers and dividers to arrange supplies in your desk. Place dictionaries and frequently used reference materials on the top of your desk or in another easy-to-reach area. Dictionaries and reference manuals should not be hidden in the bottom desk drawer. You may not be motivated to use these reference materials if they are not easily accessible.

Work Area

Keep your work area neat. Some people believe that a neat workplace means a neat and efficient person. Do not allow your desk to accumulate stacks of papers and folders. Use a desk file drawer as a temporary location for folders frequently used. If your office becomes cluttered with papers and files while you are working on a crucial project and you do not have time to file the documents, find another desk or unoccupied space where you can work. Some people become agitated when working in a cluttered

Figure 18-3 An employee working at an organized desk.

What does your
work area say
about you?

environment. Furthermore, it is very easy to misplace a paper when your work surface is covered with papers and file folders.

Place only a couple of personal items on your desk. These items should reflect your personal taste but continue to demonstrate your professional image. Your office and desk are good display areas for certificates or awards you have received.

Throw Folder

Create a throw folder as part of your computer file organization system. When you think you no longer need a file, move it to your throw folder, which will contain files you no longer need, files that have been saved with new names, last year's version of a file, older versions of files you are currently using, and so on. With this method, only the latest version of a file is in your working folder. This eliminates confusion and errors about which file is the current file. Of course, you can delete unneeded files, but you might want them at a later date. Throw folders are easy to back up to permanent storage using CDs or DVDs.

Tape Dispenser

When refilling an adhesive tape dispenser, do not throw away the roller that holds the tape in the dispenser When hurrying to replace the tape, many people throw away the roller.

Proofread

Proofread everything—even if you use a computerized spelling or grammar package. The spell check built into your word processing software checks only if the word you keyed is in its dictionary, not if it is the correct word. It is very difficult to proofread a document you have keyed. Because you are already familiar with the document, you eyes will read words that are not even there. The secret to proofreading is to read every document three times. First, read the document in the normal order. Then read the document backwards—reading from the bottom right of the page to the top left of the page. It is easier to spot an error if the words are not in their proper context. Proofread the third time in the proper sequence. Since it is easy to overlook an error, it is helpful to proofread the document again another day or to exchange proofreading duties with a coworker.

Reviewing a Document

It is important to read an entire document before making comments on it. Do not make handwritten notes to yourself on the document. The last paragraph may change your original thoughts. If you feel compelled to write notes immediately, write your comments on a sticky note that can be removed easily.

Envelopes

Remember that all correspondence needs an envelope. Because instructors do not always require an envelope for each assignment, students sometimes forget that envelopes are required for mailing documents. When keyboarding a document, prepare the envelope for it.

Pinch Hit

In any office, but particularly a small office, be prepared to do any job. If someone is absent or if there is a rush job, be willing to help complete a project. Be a team player and work together with others. Getting along with people in the office and advancing in your position means doing any job that is necessary.

Great Idea

You have a great idea, but your colleagues or supervisor resists it. At a later date, have a member of your department who embraces the idea present the idea to the group.

Company Policy on Personal Use

Be aware of your company's policies on personal use of the office email, telephone, voice mail, and the Internet. Many companies have increased their surveillance of employee usage. If you are uncertain about allowed use, do not do it.

Email Attachment

When sending an email attachment, attach the document prior to keying in your message. It is easy to key in the message and in haste click Send without attaching the document. By attaching the document first, you can avoid embarrassing yourself.

Charitable Activities

Many companies participate in communitywide charitable fundraising activities, such as the United Way, and may match employee contributions with company funds. Also, companies sponsor volunteer activities so employees may contribute to their community. Office-sponsored activities could include adopting local families in need, visiting sick children or elderly persons, working with schools, rehabilitating old houses, participating in community clean-up days, working in homeless shelters, big-brother and big-sister programs, and so on. Some organizations allow employees to perform community outreach projects on company time. While involvement in these charitable activities is usually voluntary, you may receive subtle pressure from your coworkers or from your supervisor. Carefully consider whether you wish to contribute funds or participate in these activities. Participating in these extra activities may result in your being part of the team and advancing in an organization. Generally, companies look favorably on employees who give back to the community.

Civility

One of the new communication buzz words is *civility*, which means a polite and considerate code of conduct. Employers, employees, coworkers, and clients all expect to be treated with respect and courtesy. The philosophy is that if you respect them, they will respect you. "Treat me well and I will treat you well."

Turn a Negative into a Positive—Do Not Demand

Instead of demanding something, politely make a suggestion or request instead. For example, instead of demanding that a coworker complete a portion of a project, request assistance with the project. Say, "It would be very helpful if you could complete your portion by tomorrow so I can work on my part. As you know, it is important that we meet the deadline." If your coworker sets the radio volume too high, solve the problem in a nonconfrontational way. Do not shout, "Turn down the radio." It might be better to say, "I need to concentrate to finish this project on time, so it would be great if you could lower the radio. It would really help me."

YOUR DAY

Organize Yourself the Night Before

Home responsibilities can make mornings hectic. To reduce stress, use the following suggestions to organize yourself the night before.

- Check the weather forecast.
- If you need an umbrella, locate one.
- If it is winter, gather your coat, scarf, hat, and gloves.
- Select your clothing and accessories.
- Have alternative clothing cleaned and pressed in the event you decide that you cannot wear your original outfit.
- Put money in your wallet.
- Put everything that you need into your briefcase.
- If you must make personal telephone calls during the day, place the telephone numbers in your briefcase.
- If you take your lunch, make it the night before.
- If you take nonperishable food, put it in your briefcase at night.
- Set the breakfast table, place coffee in the filter, place cereal bowls on the table, and place the pans you need on the stove.
- Buy a coffee maker with a timer.
- Rinse breakfast dishes and wait until evening to finish cleaning up.
- Put gas in the car on your way home from work, rather than on the way to work.
- If you are going to run errands after work, put everything that you need for the errands in your car before you go to sleep.
- If you have children, verify that they have everything that they need.
- If you use mass transportation, purchase weekly or monthly bus or subway passes. Purchase several passes at one time.

> **HINT**
> Planning helps.

Plan Each Day

You should always have a *to-do list* or *task list* that includes major as well as minor projects. Computer software can be used to create task lists, and computer calendars can be used to plan your day. Computer organization software helps list and prioritize your projects and can be used on handheld organizers or desktop computers.

Prepare a schedule of your work each day listing the projects you will work on, and set realistic timelines for each item. It is often wise to add additional time to each task as a contingency for office interruptions and unscheduled events. Review the schedule during the day, and revise it as needed. At the end of each day, prepare a work schedule for the next day.

Learn to juggle your regular job responsibilities while completing major projects. People often do not get to the major projects because they become involved in minor projects and their day disappears. If you have a major project, plan to work on a portion of it every day. Set a specific time each day for the major project and adhere to your schedule.

Efficiency

Always prioritize your work assignments. If necessary, ask your supervisor to help you prioritize your work. Review and update the list at least once a day.

If possible, arrange appointments or meetings for specific times or specific days. This method eliminates wasted time and moves people quickly from one appointment to another. For example, schedule appointments and meetings only on Tuesday and Thursday afternoons. This scheduling technique can be used when arranging appointments and meetings for your supervisor or for yourself.

When the projects are too numerous, decide if a project can be eliminated or if the project can be completed by another staff member. Do not continue to do a job just because it was always done. Question the need to do the job if it appears unnecessary. Jobs that cannot be eliminated can often be streamlined. Once you have analyzed the project and prepared an alternative, discuss the recommendation with your supervisor.

Deadlines

Keep your supervisor informed of all deadlines. Set preliminary checkpoints to measure progress. When the due date arrives, it is too late to make adjustments. If you are not going to be able to meet a deadline, inform your supervisor early, not at the last minute. This gives both you and the supervisor time to revise the deadline or add additional resources to meet the deadline.

To avoid a last-minute dilemma for yourself, ask coworkers to submit projects a couple of days before they are actually due. Then you will have time to review the projects before they are sent out of the office.

Pending Folder

Prepare a *pending folder* for all items for which you are waiting for an answer. Check your pending folder daily. If possible, decide on a specific time each day to check the folder. The best time to review the pending folder is at the end of the day when you make up the next day's to-do list.

Bring-Up Folder

Meet with your employer once a day to discuss problems and review your assignments. If possible, establish a specific time each day for the meeting and adhere to it. Go to the meeting with a prepared list of items to be discussed. Use a *bring-up folder* to store your problems and questions until the next meeting. This meeting is also a good time to compare your version of the employer's calendar with the employer's version of his or her calendar.

Carry a Memory Stick

If you telecommute and work at home, create a "carry memory stick" with the files you are currently using. Always carry two copies of the "carry memory stick" in case one is defective. These memory sticks (flash drives) always travel to the office and home with you. In addition, email files to yourself at home or work.

Business Cards

An administrative assistant and the executive should have business cards printed. The cards should be placed in a business-card holder on the top of the desk so they are easily accessible when a client visits the office. Also, each person should have a business-card carrying case that fits in a pocket or purse.

Business cards include the following:
- Company name and logo
- Person's name
- Title

Myrtle P. Silver
Communications Manager
Globe Systems
2788 Roosevelt Drive
Albany, NY 12186

Globe Systems

www.globesys.com

Fax 518-555-0769
Email MSilver@Globesys.com

Office 518-555-2276
Cell   518-555-1259

Figure 18-4   A business card with hyphens in the numbers.

- Address
- City, state, ZIP Code
- Telephone number
- Cell phone number
- Pager number
- Fax number
- Person's email address
- Business's Web address

Carry your business cards when attending meetings outside the office so the cards may be exchanged with other colleagues. People often collect business cards at meetings but later cannot remember where they met. On the back of the card, write where and when you met the person. Some people file business cards by category instead of alphabetically. Business cards can also be entered into contact management software programs that organize the information. In addition, if two people have similar Personal Information Managers (PIMs) or handheld organizers, they may be able to transfer their business cards electronically. After you have exchanged business cards, periodically contact the person to continue the relationship. The contact may be a quick email to say hello; a telephone call; or a get-together for lunch, dinner, or drinks.

If you are mailing a document to someone outside the office, clip your business card to the document. You may also write a short note on the back of the card.

HINT

Always carry your business card.

Joe R. Paddington
Director
Marino J. Enterprises
1504 Eastshore Drive
Tampa, FL 33703

Marino Enterprises

www.MJE.com

FAX 727.555.6443
Email J_Paddington@mje.com

Office 727.555.9976
Cell   727.555.4755

Figure 18-5   A business card with periods in the numbers.

Rest Breaks

Employers are becoming aware of the effects that illness, sleep deprivation, and exhaustion have on work performance. Some employers provide sofas and chairs in restrooms or company breakrooms where employees who need to rest can do so in a quiet area. Some employers may even permit employees who are ill or exhausted to take a short nap so they can improve their productivity, increase alertness, improve morale, and reduce accidents. Never nap or put your head down on your desk because it may appear that you are ignoring your duties. If you feel ill, inform you supervisor. Depending on company policy, you may be directed to go to a company health unit where you may be treated by medical staff, permitted to rest, or allowed to go home.

Security

If you must arrive early, work late, or work alone, you should be aware of your personal safety. Lock your office and car doors. Always have your keys in your hands when you walk to your car. If there are security guards, inform them of your schedule. If you must go to a dark parking lot, try to walk with someone, have a flashlight easily accessible, and always be alert to any danger. In some companies, a security officer may be available to walk you to your car.

Strains Caused by Computers

If you use a computer terminal for several hours each day, take breaks frequently. Every fifteen minutes, look away from the terminal for a few seconds. Every couple of hours, take a ten-minute break from the terminal. Periodically walk around the hallway and get a drink of water. Neck and back muscles also need a break from working at the computer terminal. If your muscles are tired or ache, loosen tight muscles by rubbing them or doing some stretching exercises.

YOUR JOB

The New Job

During the first week of any new job, you should carry a pad of paper and a pen with you at all times. Try to take notes because you will not remember everything. Write notes to yourself so you can remember names, faces, and instructions that you are given. Review your notes every night so each day you will feel more comfortable with your new job.

Be friendly with everyone, but do not form intense friendships too quickly. In a new environment, introduce yourself and be pleasant to everyone. Give yourself time to become acquainted with all the workers in your office. Quickly establishing close friendships with some coworkers may be seen as excluding others or attaching yourself to a group. Later, it may be difficult to withdraw from the group.

Employees should not gossip. Not only is gossip impolite and unprofessional, but it can be dangerous for the new employee who does not know the relationships of the people involved or the sensitivity of the information being discussed.

The new employee wants to be accepted as a credible, professional member of the staff, so demonstrate that you consider your job important. Arrive early and do not rush out the minute the workday is over. If you have nothing to do, at least look busy. Look through the files and become familiar with the company or read professional publications that are in the office. As soon as you complete one project, ask for another job. Do not wait for the supervisor to discover that you are ready for another assignment.

If you do not know how to do something, ask questions so you will be able to complete the project correctly. Always appear interested in learning all of your new duties, even if you think that they are boring and inefficient.

Changing Jobs

When seeking a new job, changing jobs, or changing fields, ask friends to introduce you to people who might be able to help you. If you want an entry-level job, do not just ask to meet the head of the organization. Ask to meet supervisors because people at this level might be better able to help you meet your job goals.

Accessing Your Personal Information

Many companies permit their employees to access their benefits program directly through the company's computer system or by using the Internet. Computer-based benefits systems allow employees to use their office or home computer to access their personal records. These computer systems often permit an employee to make changes in the number of their payroll deductions, revise their retirement withholdings, select different insurance carriers, update the record of their marital status, change their home address, and so on. Some employers use telephone-based systems that permit the employee to make the same type of changes to their personal file as the computer-based systems. Using the telephone keypad, employees can access company information about their benefits and personal file, respond to computer-based options, and make simple revisions in data. Telephone systems are often used to obtain internal job vacancy information. Companies can cut costs and reduce office personal with these self-service capabilities. They benefit employees because the systems are always available and can complete the employee's changes with little delay.

Clipping Service

Begin a clipping service for your supervisor. Read the daily newspaper, out-of-town newspapers, and professional publications. Then clip and mark articles of importance for your supervisor or company. Also, read online articles from newspapers and Web sites. Then print the important articles for your supervisor.

Dealing with the News Media

Always have approval from your supervisor prior to speaking to reporters from newspapers, broadcast stations, Web sites, or other news media.

Know Which People Have Power in Your Company

To improve your effectiveness, you should know which people in your company establish the company's goals, set the agenda, and are favored by the company's top management.

Make Your Supervisor Look Good

Always make your supervisor look good in the eyes of clients and other company personnel. If your supervisor is held in high regard, you will also be held in high esteem.

Communicate Efficiently

Office personnel are always busy. When you are asked to prepare brief explanations of projects for your supervisor, limit your comments to one page. If additional information is required, you can supply it at that time. Supervisors want brief, not lengthy, comments.

Figure 18-6   An employee responding to clients.

Chain of Command

In the business world, the term *chain of command* can have many meanings. One use of the term *chain of command* may refer to a series of people who report to each other as shown on the company's organization chart. Another chain of command may relate to a particular project, where several people may be involved in approving an action. Follow the chain of command instead of bypassing a person or bypassing required procedure. You may not understand the reasons for the procedures, and you may ignore an important step. Bypassing personnel may cause more problems for you because you have ignored or disregarded a person. People often have a long memory when they feel they are bypassed in the chain of command. To foster good relations with people who you will have to deal with in the future, always follow the chain of command.

Names

The office environment determines what you should call your supervisor. In many offices, the supervisor is addressed by first name. Depending on the environment, it may be preferable to address your supervisor with the title Ms. or Mr. while in the presence of clients. Therefore, while clients are present, you would refer to your supervisor as Ms. Gomez or Mr. Joseph. In some offices, subordinates address supervisors with a title such as Mr. Bill, Ms. Libby, Dr. Ted, and so on.

Relationships

The most important working relationship in your office is between you and your supervisor, so nurture the relationship.

Sharing Ideas

"I would like to share this information with you" is a tactful way to tell an individual something.

Expressing Understanding

Feedback is very important in a conversation. When you are being told something by a client, supervisor, or coworkers, indicate that you understand what they are saying. You can nod your head or make a noncommittal sound such as "uh huh," or change your facial expression. By indicating that you understand, you will encourage the speaker to continue the discussion. However, do not leave the speaker with the impression that you understand what he or she is saying if you do not. If you do not understand what the speaker is saying, ask him or her to clarify the comments, perhaps by giving you examples or more details.

Show Interest

If you are approached by a client, coworker, or supervisor, smile and show interest in the person. Look the person in the eye and respond verbally and with appropriate gestures. Eye contact makes people like you and makes them think that they are important. If you look at a person, he or she perceives you as being interested. Do not appear interrupted or bored.

Buddy System

Create a buddy system for your department or company. When employees have office-related problems or questions, they will have a buddy to consult. An official buddy system can be more helpful than asking a friend for help because an official system includes company-approved time for assistance.

Cross Training

Employees should be encouraged to learn as much as possible about each department and the duties of its employees. Knowledge of other jobs, whether in your department or in other departments, will help you grow professionally and may lead to a promotion. You will also be better able to answer questions for clients. It is very frustrating to both you and to clients when you must say, "I do not know the answer. Jane is the only person who knows, and she is out of town."

Making a Group Decision Stick

Before you leave a meeting, verify that everyone is satisfied with the decision. Reinforce the decision with both an oral and written summary of the meeting.

Workload

Before you volunteer for a new committee or project, evaluate your current workload. The daily and weekly routine tasks take up much of your time; therefore, you may want to assist with a new project but may not have sufficient time. Often, people are optimistic and assume that in the future, they will have more time, so they agree to work on a new project. You can stretch your day only so far—so be realistic when you plan your time.

Death in the Family

It may be your responsibility to notify the staff of the death of an employee or family member of an employee. Notification can be made by sending an email or posting a notice. It is customary to send a gift of flowers or a tray of food to the family, or to make a charitable donation in memory of the deceased. Money for these purposes may be collected from the staff or may be taken from an office fund. It is always proper to send a letter of condolence to the family. Also, it may be necessary to notify clients of the death of an employee and indicate who will assist the clients in the future.

Delegate

If possible, assign work to other employees. Do not feel that you are the only person who can do a job correctly or who should do a specific job, even if you can do the job faster than another worker. You should train other staff members so you will have time for more challenging projects.

Negotiate with Your Supervisor

Understand your supervisor's personality, and know when it is the best time to approach your supervisor to discuss an important issue. Some people are more responsive in the morning, others in the afternoon. Perhaps the best time to approach your supervisor is after he or she has had coffee or read the mail. Timing can be the key factor in receiving the response you want.

Begin a negotiation with a compliment. The compliment sets the mood for the discussion, and it is more difficult to turn down a request that is begun with a compliment. Always be honest and realistic with your compliment. For example:

"I have always enjoyed working for this company because of the help and guidance you have given me."

Be flexible, know what can be negotiated, and know what the options are. Present the benefits the company will receive by granting your request. For example:

"By allowing me to begin my day an hour later, I will be at work an hour later. Therefore, after everyone else leaves, I will still be here to help clients."

Discuss one point at a time. Do not overwhelm your supervisor by requesting too much at one time. You have a greater chance of success if you make only a single request. If you want your supervisor to agree to something you request, explain how the request will benefit the supervisor or employer.

Dealing with Problems

When you are given a project, analyze it carefully. Outline the project, list possible problems and solutions, and develop a timetable for completion. Try to anticipate problems that might occur and also allow extra time for unanticipated problems.

Do not run to your supervisor each time you have a problem; try to solve it yourself instead. If you cannot solve a problem, review your project and list possible solutions before you talk with your supervisor. This preparation will organize your thoughts and prepare you to answer your supervisor's questions.

There are some problems for which there are no easy answers. Accept the fact that you cannot solve them. If a problem does not have a deadline, try to let the problem solve itself. Put the problem in a pending file, but do not forget about it. Monitor the situation periodically.

Answering a Question

Sometimes when you answer a question, there is dead silence. No one speaks. You wonder what you said wrong. The best response is to wait and not to become unnerved. Sometimes the silence means that the other person is considering your answer and will respond to it. If the silence continues, you can ask if a further explanation is needed or if additional information is required. Sometimes the best response is to ignore the silence and move on to a new topic.

An Indecisive Supervisor

If your supervisor or coworker will not make decisions, you will have to assist in the decision-making process. When you present the person with a problem, also present a solution. If the person says, "I will get back to you later," write a note to yourself and put a reminder on your calendar. To assist the supervisor in reaching a decision, ask if you can gather any information about the subject. If have not received a decision, diplomatically jog your supervisor's memory. You may need to gently remind the person that a decision must be made for the project to continue.

Crisis Management

Some offices seem to operate by *crisis management*: management seems to respond only to a crisis and often runs from one crisis to another in a panic. While it is fine for an office to solve problems immediately, it is better to use careful planning to resolve problems before they occur. Unfortunately, not all situations can be anticipated.

Job Competition

Competition in the office between coworkers is a natural occurrence. Competition may occur for a promotion or for a special project. While everyone hopes to be selected for the promotion or to be given the favored assignment, learning to deal with disappointment is also part of professional growth. If someone received the promotion you wanted, congratulate the individual and work with the person in a professional manner.

The Unwanted Project

You may be given a project to complete that you do not want to do. You may find the project uninteresting or distasteful, or you simply may not have the time to do it. You should never flatly refuse to do a project, but the following suggestions may be helpful.

- Explain to your supervisor that you are too busy because you are involved in other projects.
- Explain that you have already had the opportunity to learn this duty, so someone else should have the same opportunity.
- Explain that it would be beneficial to have another person know how to do this job, and offer to assist the other colleague.
- Ask for help from other coworkers to complete the project.

Mistakes

Everyone is human and makes mistakes. If you make a mistake, talk with your supervisor, acknowledge the mistake, and apologize. Do not hide the mistake or try to blame someone else. In addition, tell your supervisor what action you will take to ensure that this mistake will be avoided in the future.

Responding to a Nasty Memo

At one time or another, everyone receives a memo or email that is negative in tone and that may even be rude. Do not write a nasty memo in response. It is better not to write anything. Instead, arrange a meeting so the problem can be discussed. If the memo writer is still angry at the time of the meeting, let the writer talk until the anger is released. Then attempt to solve the problem. You may not agree with the writer's position, but you should try to maintain a good working relationship with the person.

Responding to a Bad Idea

Your supervisor approaches you with an idea, and you think the idea is terrible. Before you respond in a negative manner, ask questions about the idea. Perhaps you did not understand the idea and how it could be implemented. If you still think that it is a bad idea, diplomatically make suggestions to improve the idea.

Common Business Acronyms

There are many acronyms that are often used in informal communications such as email messages and internal memos. A few of these are listed below:

ASAP	As soon as possible
BTW	By the way
CEO	Chief executive officer
CFO	Chief financial officer
CFV	Call for votes
COB	Close of business
COO	Chief operating officer
FAQ	Frequently asked question
FWIW	For what it is worth
FYI	For your information
IMHO	In my humble opinion
IT	Information technology
POS	Point of sale
Q&A	Questions and answers
TIA	Thanks in advance

> **HINT**
> Be familiar with business acronyms.

MAP READING

The ability to read a map is a valuable skill for every traveler. It can be intimidating to travel alone to a strange city, but the fear of the unknown can be eased by having a good map and being able to read it. Try, if possible, to get a map of the city or area you will be traveling to *before* you leave on your trip. Maps are available on the Internet through many sources, including MapQuest and Google Maps. In addition, many online maps provide driving directions. When using an online map, key in your starting location and ending location. The result shows step-by-step directions, miles traveled, and estimated travel time.

Although maps can be obtained after you arrive in a city, it is helpful to review a map before your trip. Look at how the city lies in relationship to major geographical features such as mountains, rivers, or the ocean. Try to locate the airport, train station, or highway you will be using. Locate the interstates, numbered routes, and major local roads, which are usually shown in thick lines.

It is always helpful to have a map of your area because you may be asked to drive to an unfamiliar location in your city or to give directions to a client.

Map sources

- Road atlases are sold in most bookstores. These atlases may have a small map of the city you will visit that displays major streets, area landmarks, and items of interest.
- Your auto club may have detailed city maps that would be helpful.

- If you have enough time, you can call the chamber of commerce of the city you will visit and request that a map be sent to you.
- Maps of many cities can be found on and printed from the Internet.
- If you rent a car, the rental agency usually has a map of the area. Be sure to ask for a map if it is not offered.
- Hotels and motels usually have maps of the immediate area—so ask for a map at the front desk when you check into the hotel or motel.
- Many communities have tourist information centers with maps and brochures of the area. These centers may be located with the chamber of commerce or at the airport. Also, information centers are usually located on interstate highways soon after the highway enters a new state.
- Gas stations frequently sell maps for a few dollars.
- The Internet has many map choices. You can print maps showing the hotel the traveler will be staying at, the meeting location, and the local area from several map programs on the Internet, as discussed in Chapter 9.

CHAPTER REVIEW

1. List ten hints that you can use in the office.

ACTIVITIES

1. Plan your school or workday for the next five days. Include your assignments, classes, meetings, future projects, employment, and personal responsibilities.
2. Write exact directions to your:
   a. School.
   b. Home.
   c. Favorite shopping center.
3. Find a partner and have each person give oral directions to a building in your area. Take notes as the oral directions are given. Can each of you now locate the building?
4. Write a description of the physical appearance of each of the three locations for which you wrote directions in Activity 2.
5. Select three friends. Prepare an information sheet on each and include the following:
   a. Name.
   b. Favorite restaurant.
   c. Birthday.
   d. Information about family—names, likes, dislikes, and so on.
6. Read your daily newspaper or a magazine. Clip articles of interest for office employees. Circulate the articles by sending them to four members of your class.
7. For the next week, select your clothes in advance. Write a description of your selections.
8. Look at your state map and write directions from your school to the state capitol.

9. Select a person who you think would be a good mentor and explain why.

10. What changes would you make in your work wardrobe and why?

11. Name four stores in your area that carry clothing appropriate for your career image.

PROJECTS

Project 35

Create the following itinerary. Add any additional information you feel is necessary.

The supervisor will be attending a meeting on Communications Changes and Updates, which will be held in the Ballroom at the Marriott at the Capitol in Austin, Texas, September 2, 3, and 4. Travel will be from Washington Dulles Airport on American Airlines flight #399, leaving at 12:36 P.M. Change planes in Dallas to flight #872, leaving at 3:44 P.M. to arrive at 4:39. The hotel confirmation number is 920342WS. The phone number for the Marriott is 512-478-1111. Return flight #1054 leaves Austin at 3:38 P.M., connecting to flight #622 in Dallas, leaving at 5:32 P.M. and arriving in Washington at 9:32 P.M.

Project 36

Set up the following information in an attractive format.

Next Year's Travel Plans

Name	Department	Destination	Month
Louis Parker	1621	Harrisburg, PA	January
Samuel Snyder	1617	Tampa, FL	February
Mike Lezcano	1620	Louisville, KY	April
Ferando Grasso	1620	Baton Rouge, LA	May
Ruth Eden	1621	Corpus Christi, TX	May
Janet Weinberg	1618	Miami, FL	July
Brian Lerner	1618	Dallas, TX	August
Laura Smyth	1621	Richmond, VA	August
Rodney Newton	1620	St. Paul, MN	September
Wanda McGee	1620	Des Moines, IA	September

HUMAN RELATIONS SKILL DEVELOPMENT

HR 18-1 Irritating Habits

Personal habits can be irritating to others. Coworkers may irritate their colleagues by drumming fingers on the desk, chewing gum and popping it, or cracking their knuckles. If a coworker's habits annoy you, the best solution is to ignore the habit, but if that has become impossible, diplomatically request that the person discontinue his or her actions. The person with the habit may not even be aware that it is irritating to others.

- What personal habits irritate you?
- Which of your personal habits could irritate your coworkers?
- What would you say to a coworker whose gum chewing is disturbing you?

HR 18-2 Supplies

The supply stockroom is open and available to all employees to use as needed. Marcy orders the supplies, and her desk is near the stockroom. You have never abused the use of the supply room. Marcy likes to make life difficult for you, but you do not know why. When you take supplies from the supply room, she continually reminds you that supplies are expensive and should not be wasted. In preparation for a seminar you are organizing for your supervisor, you take four boxes of pens to be used at the seminar. In a malicious voice, Martha told you to return any pens not used. You really do not like her attitude. The pens are for your supervisor, not you.

- How do you feel?
- How should you respond to Marcy?
- What choices do you have to solve the problem?

SITUATIONS

How would you handle each of the following situations?

- **S 18-1** You have been promoted to supervisor of your department, and you are having problems with your former coworkers who are now your subordinates. They ignore your orders and decisions.

- **S 18-2** Your supervisor informed you that next month your office will be hosting a delegation from a foreign country. How would you plan for this event?

- **S 18-3** On your business flight to Denver, you placed your briefcase in the overhead compartment. When you reached for your briefcase as you left the plane, you discovered that your briefcase was gone. A similar briefcase was found in another compartment. What suggestions do you have to avoid the problem in the future?

PUNCTUATION REVIEW

Punctuate each of the following sentences. For a review of punctuation rules, see the Appendix.

1. The local government sponsored a job fair investigated childcare facilities and developed automobile educational courses

2. The office clean up day is set for September 20 and all employees are expected to participate

3. Registration will be Friday and orientation will be Monday Tuesday and Wednesday

4. Participants gain an overview of computers graphic packages and fax machines

5. Upon successful completion of the program you will receive a certificate

6. Enclosed is a list of our clients which should be helpful to you

7. During a two month period our sales rose 25 percent but our profits fell 10 percent

8. As you may recall from my memorandum of February 12 effective March 31 our office will be implementing a Health Care Reimbursement Account Plan

9. Designed for todays mobile workforce 401(k) plans allow employees to change jobs and encourage employees to continue building on their retirement savings

10. We are happy you have joined our club but we must remind you to pay your dues

11. Under the present tax law the amount by which you may reduce your salary is limited to 14 percent of your gross income

12. West Virginia the mountain state is near Washington DC

13. Our best friend an authority on business ethics is speaking Friday September 1

14. We are constructing a new office complex at 1400 Executive Drive Omaha Nebraska

15. When I read a book I become absorbed in it

CD ASSIGNMENT

CD Assignment 18-1

Open the file **CD18-1_OA** on your Student CD and follow the instructions to complete the job.

SOFTWARE APPLICATIONS REVIEW

Word Processing Applications
Spreadsheet Applications
Database Applications

SOFTWARE APPLICATION 1

T & D ENTERPRISES

WORD PROCESSING APPLICATION

Problem 1

- Key in the document shown at the end of Problem 1.
- Change the heading to font size 18.
- Use leaders between the columns.
- Change the heading font to a font of your choice.
- Right-align the room numbers.
- Visually adjust the tab settings so the information appears to be centered.
- Save as **SA1-1**.
- Print.

Meeting Schedule

L & J Report	Room 100
Newsletter Discussion	Room 103
Future Plans	Room 105
Web Site Ideas	Room 101A
Budget Forecast	Room 107B
Satellite Communications	Room 104C
Board of Directors	Room109
Computer Security	Room 204
Legal Issues	Room 210

Problem 2

- Open the file saved in Problem 1, **SA1-1,** and revise it as follows.
- Place the following on the next line under Newsletter Discussion
  - Communications Review, Room 303
    - Use leaders between the columns.
    - Right-align the room numbers.

- Place the following on the next line under Web Site Ideas
  - L & P Report, Room 120
    - Use leaders between the columns.
    - Right-align the room numbers.
- Save as **SA1-2**.
- Print.

SOFTWARE APPLICATION 2

WILLIAMS CORPORATION
DATABASE APPLICATION

1. Create a database and name it **SA2**.

2. Create the table shown on page 411. Save it and name it **Presenter**. Let the software create the AutoNumber.

3. Create a query. Show Project, Presenter, and Number_Attending. Save as **Query 1**.

4. Create a query. Show AutoNumber, Project, Presenter, and City. Save as **Query 2**.

5. Create a query. Show Project, Presenter, and Date. Save as **Query 3**.

6. Create a query. Show Project, Presenter, and Cost_Per_Person. Save as **Query 4**.

7. Create a query. Show Project, Presenter, and City. Set criteria for Rochester. Save as **Query 5**.

8. Create a query. Show Project and Presenter. Set criteria for Joseph. Save as **Query 6**.

9. Create a query. Show Project, Presenter, and Date. Set criteria for June 20. Save as **Query 7**.

10. Create a query. Show Project, Presenter, and City. Set criteria for Annapolis. Save as **Query 8**.

11. Create a query. Show Project, Presenter, and Cost_Per_Person. Set criteria for greater than 700. Save as **Query 9**.

12. Create a form based on the Presenter Table. Include all fields. Save as **Form 1**.

13. Create a form based on the Presenter Table. Include AutoNumber, Project, and Presenter fields. Save as **Form 2**.

14. Create a form based on Query 1. Include all fields. Save as **Form 3**.

15. Create a form based on Query 2. Include all fields. Save as **Form 4**.

16. Create a form based on Query 3. Include all fields. Save as **Form 5**.

Project	Presenter	City	Date	Number_Attending	Cost_Per_Person
1001	Nguyen	Rochester	June 1	225	500
1004	Joseph	Albany	October 15	300	600
1020	Robertson	Annapolis	November 12	250	700
1004	Joseph	Jefferson City	January 15	145	600
1004	Nguyen	Miami	June 20	250	600
1020	Joseph	Rochester	November 12	300	700
1025	Robertson	Jefferson City	October 15	445	800
1001	Nguyen	Annapolis	June 20	300	500
1004	Joseph	Rochester	February 20	200	600
1020	Robertson	Jefferson City	June 20	175	700
1001	Nguyen	Annapolis	October 15	200	500

SOFTWARE APPLICATION 3

WESTERN CORPORATION

WORD PROCESSING APPLICATION

- Create an agenda similar to the example below. Create a table with the budget on a separate page.
- Save as **SA3-1**.
- Print.

Western Corporation Monthly Staff Meeting
June 1, 2011
Agenda

2:00	Call to Order
2:05	Approval of Minutes of May 1, 2011
2:15	Whitcomb Report
2:45	Committee Reports
3:15	Research Survey
4:00	Stress Management Workshop Plans
4:10	Budget
4:30	Adjournment

Attachment: Budget 2011

Budget 2011

Expenses	Quarter 1	Quarter 2	Quarter 3	Quarter 4
Salary	100,000	102,000	106,000	112,000
Benefits	22,000	22,000	24,000	24,000
Computer hardware	3,000	3,000	3,000	3,000
Computer software	1,000	1,000	1,000	1,000
Consultants	5,000	5,000	9,000	9,000
Entertainment	500	500	500	500
Honorariums	300	300	300	300
Postage	500	500	800	800
Rent	7,500	7,500	7,500	7,500
Supplies	1,500	1,500	2,500	2,500
Telephone	2,000	2,000	2,000	2,000
Travel	5,000	5,000	8,000	10,000

SOFTWARE APPLICATION 4

SNOW PROJECT

SPREADSHEET APPLICATION

- Create the following worksheet.

First Snow	Tons of Salt Used First Snow	Tons of Sand Used First Snow	Number of Hours	Cost per Hour
January 15	1,200	1,200	10	350
December 1	1,500	1,500	22	380
November 5	1,700	1,700	15	440
November 12	2,200	2,200	14	310
October 31	800	800	26	350
December 3	600	600	28	370
November 23	1,400	1,400	17	280

- Bold and center the column headings.
- Adjust the column width in each column to accommodate the longest entry.
- Add a header with your name.
- Format the dates with the style of your choice.
- Change the font color for the heading in the left column, First Snow, to blue.
- Change the font fill color for Cost per Hour to yellow.
- Calculate the total salt used.
- Calculate the average salt used.
- Calculate the total sand used.
- Calculate the average sand used.
- Create a new column at the right, titled Total Cost. Multiply the Number of Hours by the Cost per Hour. Format this column for currency.
- Where appropriate, format all values for currency.
- Set the worksheet for gridlines and landscape with fit to page.
- Save as **SA4-1**.
- Print.

SOFTWARE APPLICATION 5

BEACH RENTAL

SPREADSHEET APPLICATION

- Create the worksheet shown on page 415.
- Bold and center the headings.
- Total all columns.
- Average all columns.
- Insert a new column at the right and title it Total Chair Rentals for July per Site. Use Total Chair Rentals for June per Site and calculate a 15 percent increase. The July total should equal the June total plus the 15 percent increase.
- Insert a new column at the right and title it Chair Rental Price. Enter $10 for Piers 1–4 and $12 for Piers 5–7.
- Insert a new column at the right and title it Chair Income June. Multiply the Chair Rental Price by the Total Chair Rentals for June per Site.
- Insert a new column at the right and title it Average Number of Chairs Rented Each Day. Divide the Total Chair Rental for June per Site by the number of days in June. (*Hint:* How many days are there in June?)
- Insert a new column to the right. Title the column If Number of Umbrellas > 250 and use the If Function. If the number of Umbrellas rented in June is greater than 250, the answer is yes.
- Insert a new column to the right. Title the column If Boats in June < 20 and use the If Function. If the number of boats rented in June is less than 20, the answer is yes.
- Insert a new column to the right. Title the column If Average Number of Chairs Rented Each Day > 40 and use the If Function. If the Average Number Chairs Rented Each Day is greater than 40, the answer is yes.
- Format for currency where appropriate.
- Format the cells for color to enhance the worksheet.
- Print in landscape with fit to page.
- Save as **SA5-1**.

Location	Total Chair Rentals for June per Site	Umbrellas Rented June	Surfboards Rented June	Rafts Rented June	Boats Rented June
Pier 1	1,300	275	25	50	25
Pier 2	1,250	325	27	36	26
Pier 3	1,400	275	32	47	18
Pier 4	1,100	212	21	52	22
Pier 5	1,000	253	27	48	29
Pier 6	1,900	208	19	39	25
Pier 7	1,875	248	17	52	27

SOFTWARE APPLICATION 6

JULIE'S ICE CREAM PARLOR

SPREADSHEET APPLICATION

- Create the worksheet shown below.
- Bold all headings.
- Adjust the column width in each column to accommodate the longest entry.
- In row 12, calculate the total sales for each week.
- In A12, key in Total Sales.
- In row 13, calculate the average sales for each week.
- In A13, key in Average Sales.
- Use a yellow fill color on the Total and Average Sales calculations.
- At the right, create a new column and title it Gross Income Week 1. Then multiply the Sales Price by the No. Sales Week 1.
- At the right, create a new column and title it Gross Incomes Week 2. Then multiply the Sales Price by the No. Sales Week 2.
- Center the company name, Julie's Ice Cream Parlor, over the worksheet. Apply a light color fill to the title.
- Format the worksheet for currency where appropriate.
- Save as **SA6-1**.
- Print the worksheet in landscape with fit to one page.

Flavors	Cost per Item	Sales Price	No. Sales Week 1	No. Sales Week 2	No. Sales Week 3	No. Sales Week 4
Chocolate Chewy	1.25	2.50	500	620	540	500
Apple Spice	.99	2.00	575	785	600	475
Chocolate Fudge	1.20	2.50	496	506	522	498
Absolute Vanilla	.97	2.00	388	388	388	402
Strawberry Delight	1.04	2.25	472	472	400	489
Chocolate Nutty	1.20	2.50	605	605	627	645
Peppermint Surprise	1.00	2.25	377	378	366	399

SOFTWARE APPLICATION 7

MUSIC

DATABASE APPLICATION

- Create a database titled **SA7**.
- Create a table titled Name 1.
- Let the software create the AutoNumber.
- Input the information from the table on page 418.
- Modify the design and add a Year field.
- In the Year field, enter 1994 for Ross, Lewis, Lawson, and Stevens.
- In the Year field, enter 1996 for Wong, Kim, Nguyen, and Smithy.
- In the Year field, enter 1999 for Wallace, Gleason, Summit, and Baum.
- Query the database. Show Last_Name and City. Save as **Query 1**.
- Query the database. Show Last_Name and Music. Save as **Query 2**.
- Query the database. Show Last_Name, First_Name, and City. Save as **Query 3**.
- Query the database. Show Last_Name, Music, and Month. Save as **Query 4**.
- Query the database. Show Last_Name and Month. Save as **Query 5**.
- Query the database. Show Last_Name, First_Name, and Amount. Save as **Query 6**.
- Query the database. Show Last_Name, City, Month, and Amount. Save as **Query 7**.
- Delete Annie Lewis from the database.
- Add yourself to the database, and complete the row with the following: Music is Blues, Month is September, and Amount is 400.

First_Name	Last_Name	City	Music	Month	Amount
Clifton	Ross	Fort Wayne	Blues	June	900
Annie	Lewis	Toledo	Classical	August	500
Barbara	Lawson	Chicago	Jazz	November	700
Jane	Stevens	Houston	Rock	December	450
Amy	Wong	Chicago	Classical	August	600
Louise	Kim	Fort Wayne	Jazz	June	500
Julie	Nguyen	Chicago	Classical	December	745
Mollie	Smithy	Fort Wayne	Blues	August	800
Ted	Wallace	Toledo	Jazz	June	900
Jeff	Gleason	Fort Wayne	Blues	August	580
Roger	Summit	Toledo	Classical	June	900
Bart	Baum	Toledo	Blues	December	900

SOFTWARE APPLICATION 8

ROSEN CORPORATION YEAR-END PROJECTS
WORD PROCESSING APPLICATION

- Key in this memo to the staff. The memo is from Patrick J. Rosen, Budget Director.
- Save as **SA8-1**.
- Print the document.

As the end of the fiscal year approaches, we are completing our year-end projects. As expected, we are on a very tight schedule. Therefore, your assistance in submitting information in a timely manner is requested and greatly appreciated.

We are asking all account managers to review financial activity in preparation for year-end processing. Documentation pertaining to financial activity through the end of this month should be sent to the Business Office as soon as possible. The deadline and cutoff date for receiving forms is July 15. To ensure adequate time for processing and review of all forms by the staff for inclusion in the audited financial statements, we must meet this target date. The final financial statements are due to the Board of Directors by July 31.

If you have any questions, please contact Carmen Levy.

Thank you in advance for your cooperation in meeting our deadlines.

SOFTWARE APPLICATION 9

TOYS

DATABASE APPLICATION

- Create a database and name it **SA9**.
- Create the table shown below. Name it Toy Table. Let the software create the AutoNumber.
- Create a query. Sort on Toy. Show Toy, Recipient, and Reason. Save as **Query 1**.
- Create a query. Sort on Toy. Show Toy, Recipient, and Price. Save as **Query 2**.
- Create a query. Sort on Toy. Show Toy, Recipient, and Price. Set criteria for Price greater than $35.00. Save as **Query 3**.
- Create a query. Show Toy, Recipient, and Price. Set criteria for Price less than $25.00. Save as **Query 4**.
- Create a query. Show Toy, Recipient, and Reason. Set criteria for Birthday. Save as **Query 5**.
- Create a query. Show Toy, Recipient, and Reason. Set criteria for Valentine's Day. Save as **Query 6**.
- Create a query. Show Toy, Recipient, Purchase_Month, and Reason. Set criteria for September or New Year's Day. Save as **Query 7**.
- Create a query. Show Toy, Recipient. Set criteria for Julie. Save as **Query 8**.
- Create a query. Show Toy, Recipient. Set criteria for Penelope. Save as **Query 9**.

Toy	Recipient	Purchase_Month	Reason	Price
Doll	Julie	September	Birthday	$29.99
Stove	Hope	February	Valentine's Day	$59.99
CD	Patrick	September	New Year's Day	$17.99
Doll	Penelope	June	Birthday	$49.99
Dog	Ted	April	Spring	$25.00
Doll	Mollie	September	Birthday	$39.99
Bead Set	Penelope	February	Valentine's Day	$12.00
Giraffe	Hope	November	Thanksgiving	$24.99
Doll	Penelope	July	Birthday	$19.99
Video Game	Hope	January	New Year's Day	$17.99
Truck Set	Patrick	June	Birthday	$27.00
Video Game	Julie	January	New Year's Day	$22.99

SOFTWARE APPLICATION 10

EASTERN COLLEGE

WORD PROCESSING APPLICATION
Problem 1

Key in the exercise shown below. Save the file as **SA10-1** and print.

Fall Classes

- Computer Applications
  - Introduction to Computers
  - Word Processing
  - Spreadsheets
  - Database
- Literature
  - American Studies
  - English Literature
- History
  - Government Theory
  - United States History I
  - United States History II
- Foreign Languages
  - French
  - Spanish
  - Russian

Problem 2

Use **SA10-1.** Change the bullet style to the snowflake style. Save as **SA10-2** and print.

Problem 3

Use **SA10-2.** Change the bullet style to the numbered style. Save as **SA10-3** and print.

SOFTWARE APPLICATION 11

JENNIE'S GIFT GALLERY

SPREADSHEET APPLICATION

- Create the following worksheet.
- Bold the headings.
- Name sheet 1 January.
- Total each column.
- Average each column. Set the average for a whole number.
- Create a header with Jennie's Gift Gallery. Center the header.
- Use a blue fill color for the Total and Average calculations.
- At an appropriate location, insert a picture of a gift.
- At an appropriate location, insert the WordArt, "Gifts for All."
- Save as **SA11-1**.
- Print.

Store Number	Manager	Porcelain Figurine No. Sold	Glass Figurine No. Sold	Gift Wrap No. Sold	Collector Bears No. Sold	Photo Frames No. Sold	Tea Set No. Sold
500	Lewis	200	75	120	200	114	74
501	Wong	175	84	148	245	158	63
502	Harper	193	96	126	278	136	45
503	Garcia	224	74	145	266	147	72
504	Fulton	218	88	135	233	185	74
505	Carlton	195	73	139	224	200	93

SOFTWARE APPLICATION 12

MUSEUM PROJECT

SPREADSHEET APPLICATION

- Create the worksheet from the information shown in the table on page 424.
- Bold column headings.
- Wrap text in column headings where needed.
- Bold the Museums in Column A.
- Total the monthly attendance for each museum. (Calculate across the row.)
- Average the monthly attendance for each museum. Set for a whole number. (Calculate across the row.)
- Total attendance per month. (Calculate down the column.)
- For each museum, calculate the minimum attendance. (Calculate across the row.)
- For each museum, calculate the maximum attendance. (Calculate across the row.)
- Title a new column, July Attendance. For July, increase June's attendance as follows. Set the column for whole numbers.
  - American History, 12 percent
  - Natural Science, 8 percent
  - Space Ideas, 9 percent
  - Science and Studies, 5 percent
  - Arts and Life, 7.5 percent
  - Great Mountains, 6 percent
  - South Gallery, 6.2 percent
- Title a new column, August Attendance. For August, increase June's attendance by the number shown. Set the column for whole numbers.
  - American History, 300
  - Natural Science, 700
  - Space Ideas, 800
  - Science and Studies, 275

- Arts and Life, 300
- Great Mountains, 400
- South Gallery, 600
- Set for landscape with fit to one page.
- Save as **SA12-1**.

Museums	January Attendance	February Attendance	March Attendance	April Attendance	May Attendance	June Attendance
American History	6,602	7,415	8,802	8,772	8,802	9,815
Natural Science	8,405	7,926	9,405	9,460	9,405	10,501
Space Ideas	7,523	7,728	9,800	8,823	9,823	11,050
Science and Studies	4,908	6,025	6,754	5,688	6,008	8,040
Arts and Life	7,891	8,203	7,903	8,355	8,891	9,607
Great Mountains	3,608	3,607	2,509	3,689	4,008	6,007
South Gallery	3,502	4,663	3,892	4,533	4,792	5,007

SOFTWARE APPLICATION 13

ARNOLD CORPORATION

WORKSHEET APPLICATION

- Create a worksheet using the information shown below.
- Widen the columns as needed.
- At the right, add a new column titled Income 1. Multiply the Selling Price by the Number Units.
- At the right, add a new column titled 5% Increase. Multiply the Selling Price by 5 percent. The answer should show the original price plus the increase.
- At the right, add a new column titled 7% Increase. Multiply the Selling Price by 7 percent. The answer should show the original price plus the increase.
- At the right, add a new column titled 12% Increase. Multiply the Selling Price by 12 percent. The answer should show the original price plus the increase.
- Total the Selling Price column.
- Total the 5% Increase column.
- Total the 7% Increase column.
- Total the 12% Increase column.
- Add the header, Arnold Corporation. Left-align the header.
- Format the cells under Selling Price, Income 1, 5% Increase, 7% Increase, and 12% Increase for currency.
- Set the file for landscape.
- Make any enhancements you desire.
- Save as **SA13-2**.
- Print.

Vendor	Selling Price	Number Units
Beckman	300	120
B. W. Supplies	100	35
Sugar Limited	207	55
Cosmo Supplies	250	95
D and D Services	407	135
P & J Enterprises	250	340
Calvin's	125	150
Phu & Phu Corporation	89	135
Patrick Family Industries	95	175

SOFTWARE
APPLICATION 14

TA & U CORPORATION
WORKSHEET APPLICATION

- Create a worksheet using the information shown below.
- Widen the columns as needed.
- Calculate the total for each column.
- Calculate the average for each column. Set for a whole number.
- Calculate the maximum for each column.
- Calculate the minimum for each column.
- Calculate the total for each row.
- Insert appropriate clip art.
- Using WordArt, key in October Travel Expenses.
- Set the font color for each person's name to red.
- Insert an arrow pointing toward the Total column. Change the arrow color to blue. Change the weight of the arrow to 6 pt.
- Using each person's total, create a column chart. Place the chart on a separate sheet.
- Set the file for landscape.
- Make any enhancements you desire.
- Save as **SA14-1**.
- Print.

October Travel Expenses							
	Jung	McNeil	Davis	Garcia	Richards	Jason	Total
Hotel	700	525	675	625	950	845	
Air	585	535	475	515	685	745	
Food	325	300	345	275	355	595	
Auto Rental	275	268	395	358	512	495	
Tips	27	32	22	28	45	54	
Total							
Average							
Maximum							
Minimum							

SOFTWARE APPLICATION 15

FAREWELL PARTY FLYER
WORD PROCESSING APPLICATION

- Create a flyer inviting all employees to attend a farewell party for Julie Dennard, who has accepted a new position as Vice-President of San Diego Technology Enterprises.
- Include the following text:
  - The party will be held in the Board of Directors conference room on Friday, June 1, at 2 P.M.
  - If you would like to donate to a farewell gift, please send your contributions by May 23 to Barry Tottman.
  - Please RSVP to Lana Velasquez by May 23 at extension 9467.
- Include clip art and WordArt in your flyer.
- Add any additional information you want to the flyer.
- Save as **SA15-1**.
- Print.

SOFTWARE APPLICATION 16

R & R TECHNOLOGIESMEMO
WORD PROCESSING APPLICATION

- Send the following memorandum to the staff. The memo is from Ted Rodriguez.
- Save as **SA16-1**.
- Print.

I am delighted to announce that on October 1, Candace Sugarman will be joining our executive team as special assistant to Marcy Carlton. In this capacity, Ms. Sugarman will work closely with the Executive Department on a wide range of projects, including speech writing, community relations, internal communications, and planning.

Ms. Sugarman is a seasoned professional with more than twenty-five years of experience in management. Most recently, she served as the Assistant Director at Western Technical Research Corporation. Ms. Sugarman has worked in an executive capacity with seven well-known corporations.

I am confident that Ms. Sugarman will be a tremendous addition to our team. I hope you will join me in welcoming her to our workplace community. We are planning a reception in her honor for early next month. As soon as the reception details are finalized, you will receive an invitation to the event.

SOFTWARE APPLICATION 17

TAMPA RESEARCH CORPORATION MEMO

WORD PROCESSING APPLICATION

- Send this memo to the staff. It is from Jerry Moore.
- Save as **SA17-1**.
- Print.

A computer update is scheduled for Friday, September 1, at 10 P.M. through Saturday, September 2, at 6 P.M. As you know, periodically we must update and conduct maintenance on our computer network.

In addition to the computer maintenance, there is a planned electrical outage for Saturday, September 2, from 8 P.M. to Sunday, September 3, at 10 P.M. The purpose of this outage is to install a new automatic transfer switch and emergency generator. As we communicated to you earlier, we feel it is important to have an emergency backup plan in place.

Hopefully, this advance notice of the maintenance plan will minimize disruptions to your operations.

If you have questions, call Joe Spice at extension 6108.

SOFTWARE APPLICATION 18

C & P CORPORATION
WORKSHEET APPLICATION

- Create a worksheet using the information shown on page 431.
- Widen the columns as needed.
- Set the Item Price column for Currency.
- Add a new column titled Amount Sold October. Multiply the Item Price by the Quantity Sold October.
- Add a new column titled Amount Sold November. Multiply the Item Price by the Quantity Sold November.
- Add a new column titled Amount Sold December. Multiply the Item Price by the Quantity Sold December.
- Create a new column titled Total Income. Add Amount Sold October, Amount Sold November, Amount Sold December. (Add across the row.)
- Total all columns.
- Average all columns. Set all averages for a whole number.
- Add the header, C & P Corporation. Center-align the heading.
- Using WordArt, write Holiday Income.
- Insert an appropriate clip art.
- Set for Row and Column Headings to show.
- Set for Gridlines to show.
- Set for landscape.
- Make any enhancements you desire.
- Save as **SA18-1**.
- Print.

Store	Bakery Item	Item Price	Quantity Sold October	Quantity Sold November	Quantity Sold December
			Cookies and Cakes Project		
101	Chocolate chip cookies	$1.25	200	250	600
102	Fruit cake	$15.00	400	500	715
103	Chocolate cake	$12.50	375	475	625
104	Fudge brownies	$1.50	400	500	675
105	Snowballs	$1.10	250	315	425
106	Pecan cookies	$0.75	300	375	525

APPENDIX

REVIEW OF GRAMMAR, PUNCTUATION, AND WORD USAGE

As a member of today's technology-driven workforce, you must to use correct grammar and punctuation in all of your oral and written communications. These skills are used when you speak to clients and colleagues; answer the telephone; record telephone messages; write notes to your supervisor; write and keyboard letters, memos, and reports; proofread documents; send emails; and create Web pages.

This section of the book reviews grammar, punctuation, and spelling. A list of cities are provided so you can improve your spelling skills. Although spell-checking software is available as a component of many computer packages, the ability to spell correctly is still an important asset to your future. A list of similar-sounding words is also provided to help increase your knowledge of word usage.

GRAMMAR
Capitalization

- Capitalize the first word of every sentence.

  The final draft of the report is on my desk.

- Always capitalize the pronoun *I*.

  Matthew and I are attending the convention.

- Capitalize the days of the week, months of the year, and holidays.

  We are speaking at the meeting on Monday, May 30, which is Memorial Day.

- Capitalize proper nouns and proper adjectives.

  They video taped the Pittsburgh Business Association Conference.
  We have IBM, Xerox, Kodak, and Sharp equipment.
  The French report was translated into English, German, and Spanish.
  This year we have representatives from North Carolina, Minnesota, New Mexico, Maine, and Montreal.

Subject and Verb

- The *subject* is the name of a person, place, or thing and tells who performed the action. The *verb* is the action in the sentence, and it tells what was done.

  She pointed to the director.

she	(subject)
pointed	(verb)

  Management donated the equipment.

management	(subject)
donated	(verb)

Subject and Verb Agreement

- The verb must agree with the subject in number and person. If the subject is singular, the verb must be singular. If the subject is plural, the verb must be plural.

  Louise writes three reports a week.

Louise	(singular subject)
writes	(singular verb)

  Juan and Teki write three reports a week.

Juan and Teki	(plural subject)
write	(plural verb)

- *Helping verbs* help the main verb.

  The following are examples of singular helping verbs:

  is, am, was, has, have

  The following are examples of plural helping verbs:

  are, were, have

  The report was read by everyone in the department.

was	(singular helping verb)
read	(main verb)

  Richard and Bob were delighted with the results of the sale.

were	(plural helping verb)
delighted	(main verb)

  The following are examples of singular pronouns:

  he, she, it, you, another, anybody, anyone, each, either, everybody, everyone, neither, one, somebody, someone

  Everyone in the department was late for work because of the snow.

Everyone	(singular pronoun)
was	(singular verb)

The following are examples of plural pronouns:

they, we, you, both, few, many, others, several

Several were late for work because of the snow.

several	(plural pronoun)
were	(plural verb)

Phrase

- A *phrase* is a group of related words not containing a subject and verb.

black box	(phrase does not contain a verb)

Clause

- A *clause* is a group of words that contains a subject and a verb.
- An *independent clause* is a complete thought and can stand alone.

Julie has meetings at all three locations.

- A *dependent clause* does not make sense by itself and cannot stand alone.

If you complete the project by June, you will receive an outstanding evaluation.

If you complete the project by June	(dependent clause)

PUNCTUATION
Period

- A *period* is used at the end of a sentence that makes a statement or issues a command.

She attended every department meeting.

Question Mark

- A *question mark* is the ending punctuation for each sentence that asks a question.

When will we have the report completed?

Exclamation Mark

- An *exclamation mark* is used after words or sentences to express a strong emotion.

Our department won the contest!

Commas

- A *comma* is used to separate items in a series. A series must contain at least three items. There are two acceptable standards of punctuating a series. One puts the comma before *and*. The other omits the comma before *and*.

Ed completed the survey, evaluation, and revisions yesterday.

Yesterday I saw demonstrations of printers, scanners and network systems.

- A comma is used in apposition. An *appositive* explains the noun or pronoun that it follows.

Ms. Halley, the director, is an enthusiastic speaker.

  Ms. Halley   (noun)

  the director   (appositive)

- A comma is placed before and after nonrestrictive clauses and phrases. *Nonrestrictive clauses and phrases* are words that can be removed from the sentence while keeping the clarity of the sentence. Although words have been removed, the sentence still makes sense.

The training facility, which offers computer courses, is located at 966 Rose Tree Lane.

  which offers computer classes   (nonrestrictive clause)

- A comma is used in a direct address. *Direct address* indicates to whom you are speaking.

Jane, please finish the report by 5:00 on Friday.

  Jane   (direct address to Jane)

- A comma is used in introductory expressions. An *introductory expression* introduces the remaining part of the sentence.

When Larry returns from the Boston meeting, he will write a report summarizing the meeting.
  When Larry returns from the Boston meeting
  (introductory clause)

If I am late for the meeting, do not wait for me.
  If I am late for the meeting
  (introductory clause)

- A comma is used to separate the direct quote from the remaining portion of the sentence.

Ben said, "The guest speaker was fantastic."

- A comma is used to separate clauses in a compound sentence. A *compound sentence* contains two independent clauses and is joined by a coordinating conjunction—*and*, *but*, *for*, *or*, *nor*, and *yet*. If the clauses are very short, a comma is not used.

My office bought the latest computer software, but I do not understand it.

I like it but she doesn't.   (Clause is too short.)

Louise bought a computer, and Matthew bought a printer.

- A comma is used after *yes* and *no* when they begin the sentence.

  Yes, Richard is the reporter.

- A comma is used before and after *parenthetical expressions*. These are expressions that interrupt the sentence. The following words are examples of parenthetical expressions.

  as you know
  fortunately
  however
  I believe
  I think
  in fact
  of course
  perhaps

  Of course, she passed the test.

  Jung, as you know, is the most qualified applicant.

  Perhaps, the convention could be held January 12 in Florida.

- A comma is used to separate the day of the month from the year.

  The building is scheduled to be completed by January 27, 2010.

- A comma is used to separate two adjectives describing the same noun.

  Her office was in a large, old mansion.

  The long, difficult project was completed.

- A comma is used to separate contrasting expressions.

  The briefcase is fine leather, not vinyl.

  The meeting began at 10:00, not 9:00.

- A comma is used to separate names from titles and degrees. Numbers in names do not use commas.

  Raymond Soloman, Jr., was the guest speaker.

  We are meeting Dick Madison, Ph.D., at the airport.

  Donald Watkins III is my attorney.

- A comma is used to separate numbers of four or more digits. The comma is not used in house numbers, telephone numbers, or ZIP Codes.

  23,800 tons

Semicolon

- A semicolon is used to separate independent clauses not joined by a conjunction.

  Michelle enjoys classical music; Nancy prefers jazz.

We stayed at the convention hotel; George stayed at the hotel across the street from the convention hotel.

- A semicolon is used to separate items in a series if the series contains commas.

They spent their vacation in Portland, Maine; San Francisco, California; and Orlando, Florida.

The seminars will be held Friday, June 16; Tuesday, August 25; Thursday, September 28; and Monday, November 5.

- A semicolon may be used to separate clauses containing internal punctuation.

Marsha, my supervisor, is an effective leader; but Arleen motivates employees more quickly.

The agenda indicated that the meeting is Tuesday, October 15, XXXX; but we would like to change the meeting date to Friday, October 18, XXXX.

Colon

- The colon is used to introduce a list.

I purchased the following items: fifteen legal pads, ten computer disks, and twenty-five boxes of computer paper.

Dash

- The dash is used to indicate an abrupt change in thought.

Kathy, my mentor, is my best friend—at least I hope she is.

Parentheses

- Parentheses are used to set off words or phrases that are not essential to the sentence.

The chairperson of the committee (the woman from Tulsa) is receiving her doctorate this year.

Apostrophe

- The apostrophe is used to show omission of letters in contractions.

Walter can't attend the meeting.   (contraction of cannot)

- The apostrophe is used to show the possessive form of a noun.

Sara's office is small.

Hyphen

- The hyphen is often used with compound adjectives that precede a noun.

high-level official

- The hyphen is used when a word is broken at the end of a printed line.

scis-sors

Quotation Marks

- Quotation marks are used to enclose exactly what was said or written. Periods and commas go inside the quotation mark. Question marks are placed inside the quotation mark if only the quotation is a question. Question marks are placed outside the quotation mark if the entire sentence is a question.

  He asked, "Is the report collated?"

  (Only the quotation is a question.)

  Did he ask, "Is the report collated"?

  (The entire sentence is a question.)

  Tu said, "The report is completed."

  (Periods go inside quotes.)

SIMILAR SOUNDING WORDS
Word Usage

The following words are similar in pronunciation but have different meanings. Become familiar with the words so you can spell and use them properly.

accede	to give consent
exceed	too much; go beyond
accept	to take
except	everything but
adapt	to fit for new use
adept	proficient
adopt	to take as a member of a family; to accept (to adopt a policy)
addition	an increase
edition	form in which a literary work is published
advice	suggestion (noun)
advise	to inform; to notify (verb)
affect	to influence (verb)
effect	end result (noun)
all ready	all prepared
already	before
all together	all in one place
altogether	completely
ascent	going up
assent	agreeing to
bear	an animal
bare	without covering
by	near
buy	to purchase something

canvas	coarse fabric
canvass	to ask or solicit
capital	money; seat of government of a state or country
capitol	building where the legislature meets
carat	unit of weight
caret	a mark indicating that something is to be inserted
carrot	vegetable
cash	money
cache	place where supplies are hidden, temporary computer memory
cereal	food made of grain
serial	published in intervals
cite	to quote an authority
sight	something seen
site	location
consul	a government official living in a foreign country
council	government body
counsel	to give advice
course	method of doing something
coarse	rough
die	cease living
dye	change the color
eminent	high esteem
imminent	about to happen
envelop	surround
envelope	container for a letter
farther	distance
further	additional
flour	ingredient used in baking
flower	blossom in a garden
grate	to scrape into small pieces
great	wonderful
hangar	shelter for an airplane
hanger	device to hang garments on
hour	time
our	possessive of *we*
immoral	contrary to ethics
immortal	living forever
interstate	between different states
intrastate	within one state
new	recently received
knew	had knowledge of something; was certain
no	negative
know	to have knowledge of something; to be certain of

one	singular number
won	victorious
pair	two of the same type
pear	type of fruit
passed	met the goal; die
past	former time; ended; beyond
peace	tranquility
piece	a part of something
personal	concerning a particular person
personnel	employees in a business
precede	go before
proceed	to continue
principal	head of something; most important
principle	theory
right	correct
rite	ceremonial act
write	communication that is recorded; to inscribe
rode	past tense of *ride*
road	way for public or private passage
role	part that an actor takes in a play, movie, etc.
roll	to move by turning; list of names; food
steal	to take illegally
steel	metal
stake	support for a fence; interest in a project
steak	food
stationary	not moving
stationery	paper to write on
their	possessive noun
there	place
to	a preposition meaning direction
too	in addition
two	a number
vary	to change
very	greater degree, as in "very happy"
wait	stay in one place; inactive
weight	unit of measure
waive	to give up claim
wave	to move back and forth
ware	manufactured items
wear	to have on as a garment
where	in or at a place
weather	atmospheric conditions
whether	if that is the situation

SPELLING OF CITIES AND STATES
Cities in the United States

Akron, Ohio
Albuquerque, New Mexico
Amarillo, Texas
Anaheim, California
Anchorage, Alaska
Atlanta, Georgia
Baltimore, Maryland
Baton Rouge, Louisiana
Birmingham, Alabama
Boston, Massachusetts
Buffalo, New York
Charlotte, North Carolina
Chattanooga, Tennessee
Chicago, Illinois
Cincinnati, Ohio
Cleveland, Ohio
Columbus, Ohio
Corpus Christi, Texas
Dallas, Texas
Denver, Colorado
Detroit, Michigan
El Paso, Texas
Honolulu, Hawaii
Houston, Texas
Indianapolis, Indiana
Jacksonville, Florida
Kansas City, Missouri
Knoxville, Tennessee
Lexington, Kentucky
Los Angeles, California
Louisville, Kentucky
Madison, Wisconsin
Memphis, Tennessee
Miami, Florida
Milwaukee, Wisconsin
Minneapolis, Minnesota
Nashville, Tennessee
New Orleans, Louisiana

Newark, New Jersey
Norfolk, Virginia
Oklahoma City, Oklahoma
Omaha, Nebraska
Philadelphia, Pennsylvania
Phoenix, Arizona
Pittsburgh, Pennsylvania
Portland, Oregon
Raleigh, North Carolina
Rochester, New York
Sacramento, California
San Antonio, Texas
San Diego, California
San Jose, California
San Francisco, California
Seattle, Washington
Shreveport, Louisiana
Spokane, Washington
St. Louis, Missouri
St. Petersburg, Florida
Syracuse, New York
Tampa, Florida
Toledo, Ohio
Tucson, Arizona
Tulsa, Oklahoma
Wichita, Kansas

Cities in Canada

Calgary, Alberta
Edmonton, Alberta
Halifax, Nova Scotia
Montreal, Quebec
Toronto, Ontario
Vancouver, British Columbia
Windsor, Ontario
Winnipeg, Manitoba

ADDITIONAL COMPUTER TERMS

It is essential that you understand the following terms if you are going to work with computers.

- *Artificial intelligence* consists of technologies that try to achieve humanlike attributes of intelligence, such as reasoning.

- *Backup* is a duplicate of information or a program that is saved in case the original is damaged. A backup may be made on a hard disk drive to save the original data before making changes in a document. Backups may also be placed on diskettes, CDs, DVDs, or flash memory for storage away from the computer. Because copying all files for all employees to disks takes time and could become a storage nightmare, companies often use a tape backup system. A tape backup system is an efficient and reasonably priced method to back-up files on a large hard drive. There are three types of backups—total, modified files only, and selective files. A *total backup* backs up the entire hard drive to a tape. A *modified file* backs up only those files that have been changed since the last backup was done. A *selective backup* backs up only those files that are selected by the user. Some systems make backup copies automatically in the middle of the night, while other systems do the backup at the end of the day.

- *Bar code* is a series of spaces and lines that the computer translates into a number. Bar codes are often used for inventory control. In Chapter 5, you saw that bar codes are also used to address mail.

- *Bit* is a single binary digit. Computers store all information as the binary digits 0 or 1. Eight bits of memory are called a *byte*.

- *Boot* is to start the computer and load a program. A "cold" or "hard" boot is performed by turning the computer on. A "warm" or "soft" boot, which restarts the operating system after the computer is on, can be done in some operating systems by pressing several keys such as the Control, Alt, and Delete keys, all at the same time.

- *Byte* is eight bits of memory that are used to represent a single letter, number, or other computer character. Bytes are used as a measurement of memory storage. A *kilobyte* is 1,024 bytes; a *megabyte* is 1 million bytes; and *gigabyte* is 1 billion bytes.

- *Cache memory* consists of high-speed memory chips that hold the most frequently used data and instructions. By having this information on hand, the computer saves the time required to access the data on a hard disk.

- *Chat board* or *chat line* permits a person to use a computer to communicate with another person by keying in text and having the other person respond by keying in text.

- *Communications satellite* is a satellite that acts as a relay station by receiving data from equipment on or near the ground (*earth station*), amplifying it, and then retransmitting it to another earth station. The earth station can actually be an antenna on the top of a building, a small satellite telephone, or a device located in an airplane or on a ship. Using communications satellites, computer networks can reach locations unserved by regular phone lines or cables.

- *Cursor* is a highlighted area on the monitor or flat-panel display that marks the place where data entry will begin.

- *Documentation* is an instruction manual explaining how to operate computer hardware or software.

- *Downtime* is time when the computer is not working. It can be scheduled (for example, downtime for maintenance) or unscheduled (when the computer has a problem and is not operating).

- *Fiber-optic cable* is a transmission media that includes a glass cable that transmits data as pulses of light. A local area network (LAN) or Internet connection using a fiber-optic cable can exchange data much faster than one using phone lines or coaxial cable.

- *File server* is a computer that has enough memory and speed to store programs for quick access by many computer users.
- *Gateway* is an item of computer hardware that connects a LAN to outside computer systems.
- *Groupware* is software that helps several users to work together on projects and share information.
- *Home page* is the screen that welcomes a user to a Web site and often has text and/or graphics.
- *HTML (hypertext markup language)* is a specialized method of creating Web pages that allows a Web document to be read by any computer that has HTML software.
- *Image processing* systems use scanners to capture and electronically file an exact copy of a document. In addition to recording the document, these systems can record pertinent information about the document—for example, the date the file was created or handwritten notations attached to the document.
- *Integrated services digital network (ISDN)* is a technology that allows images, voice, and data to be transmitted simultaneously as digital signals over regular telephone lines.
- *Internet* is the worldwide group of connected networks that allows the public access to information on thousands of subjects. The user may view, print, or save the information. Business research may be conducted quickly and efficiently without leaving the office.
- *Internet relay chat (IRC)* refers to chatting or holding a live conversation on the Internet by keyboarding messages while reading responses on the screen. This service allows the user to have a real-time written conversation with several people on the Internet. Persons in different locations converse with each other by the use of an internet relay chat program.
- *Internet service provider (ISP)* is a business that provides people and businesses a connection to the Internet. Some ISPs just provide a connection to the Internet. Other ISPs also provide news, travel information, weather, and information on a multitude of topics in addition to providing a connection to the Internet. America Online (AOL) is an example of a national Internet service provider that provides information services as well as connection to the Internet.
- *Intranet* is an internal network that uses Internet and Web technologies.
- *Java* refers to a object-oriented programming language specifically designed for use on the World Wide Web.
- *License* is a contract concerning the use of computer software. When someone purchases commercial computer software, the purchaser only is authorized, or licensed, to use that software; the purchaser cannot change the software or copy the software without permission from the copyright owner. The illegal copying of software, also referred to as *software piracy*, is a concern in many offices. Most software packages provide a license for use on only one computer. Instead of purchasing an individual software program for each user, offices may purchase a site license, which allows a specified number of computers to use the same software package.
- *Local area network (LAN)* is a communications network that connects two or more computers in a limited geographic area. LANs are usually contained within a single building but can connect computers in different buildings if they are close

together. The LAN allows each computer on the network to share hardware, software, and information resources. For example, a client file may be stored on the file server, and all computers connected to the LAN may access the file. *See also* metropolitan area networks (MANs) and wide area network (WANs).

- *Mapping software* consists of computer software that uses graphics, database management, and spreadsheet features to display data geographically. Information can be presented in a map to display differences in income, education, or age levels by using mapping software.

- *Metropolitan area networks (MANs)* are exchanges located in large metropolitan areas that carry Internet communications traffic. A MAN is used to transfer data from one provider to another. *See also* LAN and WANs.

- *Mouse* is a pointing devise that allows the operator to move the cursor and input commands without using the keyboard. A small box about 2 inches by 3 inches is rolled on a tabletop to move the cursor around the computer monitor.

- *Multimedia* refers to the combination of text, graphics, sound, and video in one project.

- *Network* is a group of computers that are electronically connected so they can communicate with each other. Examples of networks include the Internet, as well as LANs, MANs, and WANs.

- *Network printer* is a printer that is connected to a network and has many users printing on it.

- *Network server* is the central computer that manages a local area network or that provides information to the Internet.

- *PC fax* is a computer that can perform as a fax machine. The computer must be turned on in order to receive a fax.

- *Plotter* is a printing device used to produce graphics using a moving pen.

- *Pop-up ads* or advertising banners may appear when you are surfing the Web or viewing email. These ads promote products or services and are designed to encourage the purchasing, downloading, or installing of software but may also cause the computer to slow down or crash. In addition, the ads may be inappropriate for children or adults. A computer code delivers the pop-up ads or advertising bars so they automatically appear on the computer screen. Proponents of adware feel it helps to recover programming development costs and minimize user costs. Some adware contains codes that track a user's personal information and share it with others without the user's knowledge or authorization. This software, called *spyware*, may be a violation of personal confidentiality and could also lead to fraud if the spyware obtains a person's or company's financial information. Pop-up blocker software is available to help diminish pop-up advertising.

- *Presentation monitor* is a computer monitor 25 to 36 inches in size that is used when making presentations to midsize groups.

- *Random access memory (RAM)* is the working memory of a computer that is used to store programs temporarily. When the computer is turned off, the information in RAM is lost.

- *Read only memory (ROM)* is internal memory that is built into the hardware and cannot be changed by the operator. When the computer is turned off, the information in ROM is not lost. ROM usually contains the program that boots (starts) the computer when it is turned on.

- *Search engines* are computer programs found on the Internet that help users search for information. After the user enters a word or phrase, a search engine reviews thousands of computer sites to find sites that may contain the type of information requested. If the user is too general when requesting information from a search engine, the results may be thousands of possible sites that might contain the requested information. Two commonly used search engines are Google and Yahoo.

- *Shareware* is a software program that is distributed at little or no charge, often by user groups. The programs can be distributed online, on diskette, or on CD. The user is frequently asked to pay for a shareware program after receiving the program. Shareware programs often mimic features of popular commercial software, but the quality of the program is usually unknown.

- *Touch screens* permit data or requests to be entered into the computer by touching the screen instead of using the keyboard. Touch screens, are often used in ATMs and information kiosks. Some personal digital assistant cell phones use touch screens to input data because they are too small to have keyboards.

- *Trackball* is a pointing device and performs the same function as a computer mouse. Because notebook computers are not used on a desktop, there is often no surface on which to place a mouse to move the cursor. A trackball is a like a large marble located near the notebook computer's keyboard. The top of the ball is rotated by a finger, which moves the cursor on the screen. A trackball can also be part of a keyboard for use with a desktop computer.

- *Voice recognition* software provides a way to enter information into a computer directly from spoken words. Through words spoken into a small microphone, the computer converts speech into digital information that can be entered into a word processing package or other office software.

- *Web addresses.* Each Web page has a special code, usually called the *uniform resource locator (URL)*, which gives the address or location of the Web site or page. Many Internet addresses begin with www and the parts of the address are separated by periods. Web addresses typically end with designators that indicate the type of organization sponsoring the computer site. Typical designators are .com for commercial organizations, .edu for educational institutions, .org for nonprofit organizations, .gov for governmental agencies, and .net for networks.

- *Wide area networks (WANS)* are communications networks that cover a large geographical area. These networks use satellites, microwaves, and telephone cables to interconnect computers across the country or around the world.

- *World Wide Web (WWW)* (often simply called the Web) is part of the Internet that uses computers, which are Web servers, to store files called Web pages. A person seeking information locates an appropriate Web page.

Business Terminology

When you work in the today's business world, you will be expected to be familiar with the following business terms. Specialized terminology used in finance, law, real estate, and accounting offices follows the general business terms.

General Business Terms

- An *annual report* is a report issued by a corporation each year that reviews the corporation's business activities and financial statements for the year and discusses its future expectations.

- *Business forecasting* provides projections of a business's future. Business forecasting is used to plan budgets, revenues, and expenses under a variety of conditions. Computers and spreadsheet programs are widely used in business forecasting.

- The *Consumer Price Index* (CPI) is an index calculated monthly by the U.S. government showing the change in the prices of a fixed group of consumer goods and services.

- *Deflation* is a general decrease in the price of goods and services and is the opposite of inflation.

- *Depreciation* is the gradual decrease in the value of an item. The value of office equipment such as computers depreciates as it ages.

- *Depression* is a very low point in a nation's economy when there is high unemployment and a decrease in the purchasing of goods and services. A depression is much worse than a recession.

- A *dot-com company* refers to one of the many companies that have been created specifically to provide services via the Internet. The term "dot com" comes from Internet addresses for commercial organizations which end in ".com". Some of these companies actually have ".com" as part of their name.

- A *fiscal year* is a 12-month calendar period used for budgeting and planning purposes. For the federal government, a fiscal year begins on October 1 and ends the next September 30. State and local governments usually run on a July 1 to June 30 fiscal year or on an October 1 to September 30 fiscal year. A private business can begin its fiscal year with any month, although most begin with January, April, July, or October. A fiscal year usually is referred to by the year that the cycle ends. For example, the U.S. government's fiscal year 2011 (FY '11) begins October 1, 2010 and ends September 30, 2011. Businesses report their earnings and file their tax returns based on their fiscal year.

- The *Gross National Product* (GNP) is the total value of all goods and services produced by a country in one year. GNP is an index used to compare the size of a country's economy over a period of years or to compare one country's total output with another country's total output.

- *Inflation* is a general increase in the price of goods and services. An example of inflation is a house that cost $50,000 twenty years ago, now sells for $150,000. The house may be the same house, but it now takes many more dollars to purchase it. If wages have risen at the same inflation rate as houses, then houses remain affordable even if the price is three times what it was twenty years ago.

- *Liquidating* means converting securities (stocks or bonds) to cash.

- A *monopoly* is a situation where there is only one supplier of a good or service or where one supplier is so large that it controls the market. In the United States, monopolies are permitted only where government policy determines that a single provider is in the public interest. Many industries which were formerly monopolies such as telephone or electric services have been deregulated by the government and the consumer now has many choices in purchasing these services.

- The *Producer Price Index* (PPI) is an index calculated monthly by the U.S. government showing the change in prices of farm products, processed foods, and industrial products.

- A *quarter* is one of four parts of the business fiscal year. Most businesses review their financial status at the end of each quarter of their fiscal year. Each of the four quarters of the business year contains three months. The first quarter is the first three months of the fiscal year, while the fourth (or last) quarter is the final three months of the fiscal year. Financial activity often increases near the end of a quarter as businesses try to complete transactions for inclusion in their financial reports. At the end of the quarter, corporations may issue quarterly reports to their shareholders that report the activities during the period.
- A *recession* is a slowdown in economic activity, which is often accompanied by a reduction in sales, profits, and employment.
- *Retained earnings* is the money remaining after paying taxes and dividends.

Terms Used in Financial Institutions

- A *bear market* is a time period during which the prices of stocks decline.
- The *Big Board* is an informal term used to refer to the New York Stock Exchange.
- *Blue chip* is an informal term for the common stock of a company that is known for long-term, high-quality financial performance. Blue-chip stocks are generally thought of as investments with low risk.
- A *broker* is a person (agent) who handles the sale or purchase of securities, including stocks, bonds, mutual funds, insurance, or annuities.
- A *bull market* is a time period during which the prices of stocks rise.
- A *call provision* is a clause in a bond agreement which allows the bond's issuer to redeem (call) the bond prior to the maturity date by purchasing the bond from its owner.
- A *certificate of deposit* (CD) relates to a specific type of account in a bank or other financial institution. A CD is an investment for a fixed term and pays a higher rate of interest than a regular interest account. Usually the interest is guaranteed during the term of the CD.
- A *commission* is a broker's fee for buying or selling a security for a client. The commission can be a fixed fee or a percentage of the security's purchase or selling price.
- The *Dow Jones Industrial Average* is the most common benchmark used for comparing the price level of common stocks on the New York Stock Exchange. The Dow Jones Company, publisher of *The Wall Street Journal*, calculates the value of a stock portfolio of 30 large companies. Changes in the stocks are compared on a daily basis. The Dow Jones Industrial Average, often referred to as the Dow Jones Average (or the Dow), is only one of many averages used to track the advances and declines of the stock market. Other averages exist for specific areas, such as banking stocks or transportation stocks. There are also averages calculated for many other types of securities, such as international stocks, bonds, and many other financial securities.
- *Electronic Trading* or *Online Trading* permits a person to establish an account with a broker and then buy and sell stocks, bonds, and other securities using a computer.
- An *Individual Retirement Account* (IRA) is a special account permitted by the Federal government to encourage people to save money for retirement. There are two types of IRA accounts, and both types allow people to earn

income on their investments in the IRA account without paying taxes each year. Money invested in *a traditional IRA* can be deducted from a person's gross income for income tax purposes and payment of taxes on income earned in the IRA account is delayed until the person withdraws the money, usually at retirement. In a *Roth IRA*, taxes are paid on the funds that are placed in the Roth IRA, but no taxes are paid on the earnings while they are in the IRA account or when they are withdrawn. An IRA must be established with an approved financial institution, and can be invested in a variety of securities including CDs, stocks, bonds, and mutual funds.

- *Initial public offering* (IPO) refers to a new stock issue. People buy stock in start-up companies in hopes of making great profit. Investing in an IPO is very risky, however, as many new companies fail and investors can lose all of their money.

- *Junk bonds* are bonds that pay a high rate of interest because of a low credit rating that reflects a higher risk of default.

- The *margin* is the amount of money a customer puts down toward the purchase price when buying a security on credit. The broker loans the remainder of the purchase price.

- A *market order* is an order to buy or sell a security (stock or bond) at the best price available when the order reaches the Stock Exchange floor.

- The *market price* is the last price at which a security (stock or bond) was bought or sold.

- The *maturity date* (or redemption date) is the date that the bond issuer will pay the *principal* (face value) of the bond.

- *Mutual funds* are investments where a financial firm purchases stocks or bonds from many organizations, places the stocks or bonds in a fund, and then sells shares in the fund to the public. The goal of a mutual fund is to diversify investment and, therefore, reduce client risk. Mutual funds often specialize in the types of securities they purchase or in their investment objectives.

- *NASDAQ* is an electronic stock market with over 4,500 companies listed. Many of the companies listed are leaders in the technology or financial service fields.

- An *odd lot* is an order for the purchase of stock in quantities other than 100-share units.

- A *portfolio* is a group of securities owned by a person or a company.

- The *price-earnings ratio* (PE) is the ratio between the market price of stock and its earnings per share. A stock that sells for $50 per share and earns $2 per share each year has a PE of 25.

- A *prospectus* is a brochure describing securities offered for sale. The Securities and Exchange Commission requires that a purchaser be supplied with a prospectus before a security is purchased.

- A *round lot* is a stock bought or sold in 100-share units.

- The *Securities and Exchange Commission* (SEC) is an agency of the U.S. government that regulates the sale of stocks and bonds. It is the Securities and Exchange Commission's responsibility to ensure that the public is provided truthful information about securities.

- A *speculator* is a person who assumes a large risk in anticipation of receiving a high profit.

- A *stock exchange* is a place where stocks and bonds are traded. Examples of stock exchanges include the New York, American, Philadelphia, Pacific, Tokyo, and Toronto Stock Exchanges. Brokerage firms that are members of a stock exchange are referred to as having a seat on a stock exchange.
- In a *stock split*, a company issues additional shares of stock to its stockholders. For example, a company may double the number of shares (a two-for-one split). Each stockholder will then own twice as many shares as before the split. Each share, however, will sell for approximately half the previous value. Companies may split the stock in the hope that a stock selling at a lower price will be attractive to more investors. In a reverse split, a company may reduce the number of shares of a stock owned by all stockholders by issuing new stock for each two or three shares previously issued. In a one-for-two reverse split, the new share would be worth approximately twice the value of the old share.
- A *stop order* is an order to buy or sell a stock when the price reaches a predetermined level.
- The *yield* is a return on an investment. The yield is usually referred to as a percentage of the purchase price.

Legal Terms

- *Affidavit*: a statement in writing made under oath, usually given before a notary or a judicial officer authorized to administer oaths.
- *Appellate court*: a higher court that reviews a lower court's decision.
- *Contributory negligence*: failure to do what was wise and reasonable.
- *Decree*: an order of the court.
- *Defendant*: person against whom a suit or complaint is brought.
- *Felony*: a grave crime punishable by heavy penalties.
- *Habeas corpus*: a writ (written order) requiring that a person be brought before a judge before being held.
- *Injunction*: an order issued by a court requiring someone to do or refrain from doing a particular act.
- *Misdemeanor*: a crime less severe than a felony.
- *Perjury*: swearing that something is true while knowing it is false.
- *Plaintiff*: person who brings a suit or complaint.
- *Tort*: a legal wrong that prompts a civil lawsuit.

Real Estate Terms

- *Appraisal*: an estimate of the value of an item, building, or property.
- *Assessment*: a charge by the government against real estate to cover improvements such as a sewer. The assessment is usually a percentage of the appraised value of the property.
- *Deed*: a written form that transfers property from one owner to a new owner.
- *Domicile*: the place where a person has a permanent residence.
- *Easement*: one person's right to use or pass through another person's property.
- *Encroachment*: property that trespasses on another person's property.

- *Escrow*: a deed or money given to a third party to hold until an obligation is fulfilled. An example of escrow is giving the homeowner's insurance payment or real estate taxes to the mortgage company to hold until the payment is due.
- *Foreclosure*: the removal of the right to continue paying the mortgage and owning the property.
- *Mortgage*: a contract, usually on a house or real estate, specifying that a sum of money will be paid periodically for the repayment of a loan.

Accounting Terms

- *Account*: a form that separates business transactions into similar groups.
- *Asset*: anything that a business owns. Examples of assets include buildings, cash, furniture, and equipment.
- *Audit*: a verification of accounting records. An individual not affiliated with the company being audited usually performs an audit.
- *Capital*: what the business is worth. Capital is found by subtracting the liabilities from assets.
- *Credit*: an entry on the right side of an account ledger.
- *Debit*: an entry on the left side of an account ledger.
- *Ledger*: a group of accounts.
- *Liability*: anything that a business owes. Examples of liabilities include mortgages, credit card charges, and auto loans.
- *Petty Cash*: an office cash fund for small expenses.
- *Trial Balance*: shows that the debits and credits in the ledger are equal.

INDEX